Research in Social Work

An Introduction

Second Edition

Margaret Williams
Leslie M. Tutty
Richard M. Grinnell, Jr.

Faculty of Social Work
The University of Calgary

 F.E. Peacock Publishers, Inc., Itasca, Illinois

Contents in Brief

Contents in Detail

Preface

THIS BOOK is the second edition of *Research in Social Work: A Primer*. With the help and encouragement of a new coauthor, the revisions became so extensive that we decided to retitle the book in order to more accurately reflect its contents. Nevertheless, the intended audience remains the same as in the first edition—the generalist BSW student taking a one-semester (or quarter) beginning social work research methods course.

GOAL AND OBJECTIVES

Our goal has been to write a "user-friendly," straightforward introduction to social work research methods couched within the positivistic research tradition—the approach most commonly used to generate relevant social work knowledge.

To accomplish our goal, we strived to meet three simple objectives. Our first objective was to include only the core material that is realistically needed in order for the BSW student to appreciate and understand the role of research in social work. Our guiding philosophy was to only include research material that a BSW student needs to know to function adequately at an entry-level social work position; information overload was avoided at all costs. Our second objective was to prepare BSW students to become beginning critical consumers of the professional research literature. Finally, our third objective was to provide the BSW student with a solid foundation for more advanced social work research courses and texts.

What This Book Does Not Do

With the above goal and objectives in mind, we have eliminated research material that an undergraduate student in social work does not need to know. First, we do not prepare the BSW student with the necessary knowledge and skills to actually conceptualize, operationalize, and carry out a research study—no introductory research methods text can accomplish this. We believe this task is best left to graduate-level social workers who have obtained those skills from intermediate or advanced research methods books that were geared toward the graduate level.

In introductory social work research methods texts that are on the market today, authors state that their books can be used at both the undergraduate and graduate levels. However, we are of the opinion that a single book that can be utilized at both levels is doing our students and our profession a disservice. We firmly believe that there should be two levels of research methods books: those such as this one, that provide an introduction to research methods written for BSW students, and those that provide more substance and intermediate (or advanced) theoretical discussions of research methodology that were written for MSW and PhD students.

Second, we neither attempt to present an "original" integration of the various ways of knowing nor attempt to "blend" quantitative and qualitative research approaches to form a "unique research continuum" of some kind or another. There are other books on the market that to do this. More importantly, we are of the belief that the breath and depth of these tasks extend far beyond what a BSW student needs to know, to appreciate, to understand, as well as to become a beginning critical consumer of the research literature—the objectives of our book.

In addition, some of the other "postpositivistic" approaches to social work research, such as the heuristic approach, *have not yet* generated practice-relevant findings that are of any practical use to social work practitioners. We feel that a BSW student needs to thoroughly understand and appreciate one tried and proven research approach (the positivistic approach) before he or she can begin to understand how other nonpositivistic research approaches can be useful in the generation of practice-relevant social work knowledge. We are of the opinion that increasing the students' capacity for critical thought via the positivistic research approach will improve their readiness to take additional research courses and to read more advanced research methods books.

THEME AND ORGANIZATION

Like the original, this edition is organized to reflect the four phases of the problem-solving method. The major theme is that knowledge of the problem-solving process enhances the effectiveness of professional social work practice. The material presented in this book is explained in terms of social work examples that BSW students will appreciate. Many of the examples center around women and minorities, in recognition of the need for social workers to be knowledgeable of their special needs and problems. We have given special consideration to the application of research methods to the study of questions concerning these groups.

In this spirit, we begin where every researcher begins—that is, with finding a meaningful problem area to study within a social work context (Chapters 1-3) and developing middle-range theories and initial hypotheses (Chapters 4 & 5). We proceed from measuring variables (Chapters 6 & 7), constructing research designs (Chapters 8-12), and collecting (Chapters 13 & 14) and analyzing data (Chapter 15) through proposal and report writing (Chapter 16).

LEARNING FEATURES

We have incorporated a number of learning features in our book:

- Each chapter contains ten study questions that can be used to assess the readers' mastery of the material.
- Each chapter contains extensive up-to-date advanced readings that can be helpful in obtaining more information about a chapter's content.
- Boxes are inserted in each chapter to complement and expand the text; these present interesting research examples, provide additional aids to learning, and offer historical, social, and political contexts of social work research.
- A glossary of all key terms contained in the chapters is provided at the end of the book.

ACKNOWLEDGMENTS

We have been teaching social work research methods for quite some time. We thank the countless number of BSW students whom we have had the privilege of teaching (and learning from) as they have directly contributed to the conceptual development of this book.

We would like to thank our dean, Ray J. Thomlison, Faculty of Social Work at The University of Calgary. Without Ray's support and encouragement, this book would have never seen the light of day. We are proud to be among the few authors who have the privilege of working with, and for, a competent dean. Our thanks to Ray for providing us with an academic atmosphere in which to work and for establishing one of the finest social work faculties that we have seen.

Our thanks go to Terry Teskey for copy editing the initial drafts of the manuscript and to John Beasley for copy editing the final draft. We would be remiss not to mention that the people at F.E. Peacock Publishers have been more than supportive in our second adventure, and it is once again a privilege to publish under the Peacock banner.

Copyright Acknowledgments

We thank the following publishing houses for providing permission to reprint their material:

Figure 1.1: Adapted and modified from Wayne D. Duehn, "Practice and Research," in Richard M. Grinnell, Jr. (Ed.). *Social Work Research and Evaluation* (2nd ed.). Copyright © 1985 by F.E. Peacock Publishers. Used with permission.

Boxes 1.1, 3.1, 3.2, 4.2, 5.1, & 5.2: From *Approaches to Social Research*, Second Edition, by Royce A. Singleton, Jr., Bruce C. Straits, and Margaret Miller Straits. Copyright © 1988, 1993 by Oxford University Press, Inc. Reprinted by permission.

Figure 1.2: Adapted and modified from Richard M. Grinnell, Jr. and Deborah H. Siegel, "The Place of Research in Social Work," in Richard M. Grinnell, Jr. (Ed.). *Social Work Research and Evaluation* (3rd ed.). Copyright © 1988 by F.E. Peacock Publishers. Used with permission.

Boxes 2.1, 2.2, 2.3, 3.3, 4.1 (by Patricia Fisher), & 12.2: From *Research Methods for Social Work*, 2nd Edition, by Allen Rubin and Earl Babbie. Copyright © 1993 by Brooks/Cole Publishing Co. Reprinted by permission.

Figure 2.2: Source: *Code of Ethics of the National Association of Social Workers*, part 1, sect. E (Silver Spring, MD: National Association of Social Workers, Inc.), p. 4. Used with permission.

Figure 5.1: Adapted and modified from Norman J. Smith, "Formulating Research Goals and Problems," in Richard M. Grinnell, Jr. (Ed.). *Social Work Research and Evaluation* (3rd ed.). Copyright © 1988 by F.E. Peacock Publishers. Used with permission.

Figure 5.2: Source: Eva Ferguson, *Calgary Herald*, Calgary, Alberta, Canada, September 6, 1991, Sect. A, p. 1. Used with permission.

Figure 5.3: Source: *Calgary Herald*, Calgary, Alberta, Canada, September 6, 1991, Sect. B, p. 6. Used with permission.

Figure 5.4: Adapted and modified from Michael Rothery, "Problems, Questions, and Hypotheses," in Richard M. Grinnell, Jr. (Ed.). *Social Work Research and Evaluation* (4th ed.). Copyright © 1993 by F.E. Peacock Publishers. Used with permission.

Figure 6.1: General Contentment Scale. Copyright 1992, Walter W. Hudson. Used with permission.

Figure 6.2: From Gerald J. Bostwick, Jr. and Nancy S. Kyte, "Measurement," in Richard M. Grinnell, Jr. (Ed.). *Social Work Research and Evaluation.* Copyright © 1981 by F.E. Peacock Publishers. Used with permission.

Figure 7.1: Adapted and modified from Deborah H. Siegel, "Integrating Data-Gathering Techniques and Practice Activities," in Richard M. Grinnell, Jr. (Ed.). *Social Work Research and Evaluation* (3rd ed.). Copyright © 1988 by F.E. Peacock Publishers. Used with permission.

Figure 7.2: Adapted and modified from Michael J. Austin and Jill Crowell, "Survey Research," in Richard M. Grinnell, Jr. (Ed.). *Social Work Research and Evaluation* (2nd ed.). Copyright © 1985 by F.E. Peacock Publishers. Used with permission.

Figure 7.3: Adapted and modified from Charles H. Mindel, "Instrument Design," in Richard M. Grinnell, Jr. (Ed.). *Social Work Research and Evaluation* (4th ed.). Copyright © 1993 by F.E. Peacock Publishers. Used with permission.

Pages 116, 118-119, 120, 121-125: Adapted and modified from Cathleen Jordan, Cynthia Franklin and Kevin Corcoran, "Standardized Measuring Instruments," in Richard M. Grinnell, Jr. (Ed.). *Social Work Research and Evaluation* (4th ed.). Copyright © 1993 by F.E. Peacock Publishers. Used with permission.

Chapters 8, 9, & 11: Adapted and modified from Richard M. Grinnell, Jr., "Group Research Designs," in Richard M. Grinnell, Jr. (Ed.). *Social Work Research and Evaluation* (4th ed.). Copyright © 1993 by F.E. Peacock Publishers. Used with permission.

Figure 11.7: Adult/Adolescent Parenting Inventory (AAPI) by Stephen J. Bavoleck. Copyright © 1984. Family Development Resources, Inc. Used with permission

Tables 12.1, 12.2, & 12.3: Adapted and modified from, Peter A. Gabor, "Sampling," in Richard M. Grinnell, Jr. (Ed.). *Social Work Research and Evaluation* (4th ed.). Copyright © 1993 by F.E. Peacock Publishers. Used with permission.

Figures 12.1 & 12.2: Adapted and modified from, Peter A. Gabor, "Sampling," in Richard M. Grinnell, Jr. (Ed.). *Social Work Research and Evaluation* (4th ed.). Copyright © 1993 by F.E. Peacock Publishers. Used with permission.

Box 12.1: From *Interviewer's Manual* (Revised Edition). Copyright © 1976 by the Survey Research Center, Institute of Social Research, University of Michigan. Used with permission.

Figure 13.1: Adapted and modified from Charles H. Mindel and Lynn McDonald, "Survey Research," in Richard M. Grinnell, Jr. (Ed.). *Social Work Research and Evaluation* (3rd ed.). Copyright © 1988 by F.E. Peacock Publishers. Used with permission.

Figure 13.2: Adapted and modified from Michael J. Austin and Jill Crowell, "Survey Research," in Richard M. Grinnell, Jr. (Ed.). *Social Work Research and Evaluation* (2nd ed.). Copyright © 1985 by F.E. Peacock Publishers. Used with permission.

Figures 13.3, 13.4, & 13.5: Adapted and modified from Don A. Dillman, *Mail and Telephone Surveys: The Total Design Method.* Copyright © 1978 by John Wiley & Sons, Inc. Reprinted by permission of John Wiley & Sons, Inc.

Figures 13.6 & 13.7: Source: W.V. Clemens, "Test Administration," in R.L. Thorndike (Ed.), *Educational Measurement* (2nd ed.). Copyright © 1971 by the American Council on Education. Used with permission.

Figure 13.8: Source: Shirley Jenkins and Elaine Norman, *Filial Deprivation and Foster Care.* Copyright © 1972. Reprinted by permission of the publisher, Columbia University Press.

Figure 13.9: Adapted and modified from Steven L. McMurtry, "Survey Research," in Richard M. Grinnell, Jr. (Ed.). *Social Work Research and Evaluation* (4th ed.). Copyright © 1993 by F.E. Peacock Publishers. Used with permission.

Figure 14.1: From Richard M. Grinnell, Jr., and Margaret Williams, *Research in Social Work: A Primer.* Copyright © 1990 by F.E. Peacock Publishers. Used with permission.

Pages 270-272: Adapted and modified from Craig Winston LeCroy and Gary Solomon, "Content Analysis," in Richard M. Grinnell, Jr. (Ed.). *Social Work Research and Evaluation* (4th ed.). Copyright © 1993 by F.E. Peacock Publishers. Used with permission.

Figure 15.5: Source: Donald W. Beless, "Univariate Analyses," in Richard M. Grinnell, Jr. (Ed.). *Social Work Research and Evaluation.* Copyright © 1981 by F.E. Peacock Publishers. Used with permission.

Pages 311-312, 319-320, 323, 324, 325-326: Adapted and modified from Joel Fischer, "Evaluating Positivistic Research Reports," in Richard M. Grinnell, Jr. (Ed.). *Social Work Research and Evaluation* (4th ed.). Copyright © 1993 by F.E. Peacock Publishers. Used with permission.

Glossary: Adapted and modified from Irene Hoffart and Judy Krysik, "Glossary," in Richard M. Grinnell, Jr. (Ed.). *Social Work Research and Evaluation* (4th ed.). Copyright © 1993 by F.E. Peacock Publishers. Used with permission.

A LOOK TOWARD THE FUTURE

Research courses in undergraduate social work education are continuing to grow and develop, and we believe this edition will contribute to that growth. A third edition is anticipated, and suggestions for it are more than welcome. Please send your suggestions directly to Richard M. Grinnell, Jr., Faculty of Social Work, University of Calgary, Calgary, Alberta, Canada T2N 1N4, or call (403) 220-6154 or FAX (403) 282-7269.

MARGARET WILLIAMS
LESLIE M. TUTTY
RICHARD M. GRINNELL, JR.

Part I

Foundations

THE TWO CHAPTERS OF PART I introduce readers to the place of research in social work. More specifically, Chapter 1 presents the basic ways of obtaining knowledge and describes the characteristics of how social work research studies are done using the problem-solving model. It also discusses the various research roles that social workers can undertake in contemporary practice. Chapter 2 elaborates on Chapter 1 by presenting an in-depth discussion of the various factors that affect social work research studies. In overview, Chapter 1 presents how research is relevant to social work while Chapter 2 discusses the personal, ethical, political, and social considerations that shape how it is performed.

Chapter 1

Introduction

W HEN GALILEO LOOKED through his telescope in the year 1610, he saw four satellites circling the planet Jupiter. His discovery presented a problem, as it was believed that there were seven heavenly bodies: the sun, the moon, and five planets. Seven was a sacred number, but the addition of Jupiter's satellites brought the number to eleven, and there was nothing mystic about the number eleven. It was partly for this reason that professors of philosophy denounced the telescope and refused to believe in the existence of Jupiter's satellites.

In the twentieth century, we may find it incredible that educated people would behave in this way. After all, the doubting professors in Galileo's time had only to look through the telescope in order to see Jupiter's satellites for themselves. However, today's "see for yourself" philosophy is based on the belief that "true" knowledge can best be gained through scientific enquiry, which begins with objective observations of the real world. In the seventeenth century, obtaining knowledge by direct observations was considered a less valid source of knowledge development than tradition, authority, and experience (hereafter referred to as practice wisdom). Hence, the professors may not have accepted the "objective observations" of their eyes as "truth" if this new truth conflicted with traditional beliefs and the established authority of the state or church.

WAYS OF OBTAINING KNOWLEDGE

Each of us already has a great deal of knowledge about various things. Some of the things we know stem from tradition because they are commonly thought of as "true" by everyone in our culture. For example, we now "know" that the earth is round; although, if we had been born a few centuries earlier, we would have "known" that it was flat. Some things we know because someone in authority told us about them: We may have been told that smoking causes cancer, or that when one spouse batters the other it results in a helpless response rather than flight. Other things we know because we have personally experienced them: We found out that knives are sharp the first time we came into contact with one.

The previous three ways of obtaining knowledge—tradition, authority, and practice wisdom—combined with the problem-solving method form four ways of developing knowledge in social work. These four ways are interactive; however, for the sake of simplicity, each one will be discussed separately.

Tradition

Most people tend to accept traditional cultural beliefs without much question. They may doubt some of them and test others for themselves, but, for the most part, they behave and believe as tradition demands. Such conformity has its uses. Society could not function if each custom and belief were reexamined by each individual in every generation. On the other hand, unquestioning acceptance of traditional dictates can lead to stagnation and to the perpetuation of wrongs. It would be unfortunate if women had never been allowed to vote because "women had never traditionally voted," or if racial segregation were perpetuated because that was the "way things were done."

Authority

As indicated, we also obtain knowledge from authority figures. The same dilemma exists with authority as with tradition—the question of the accuracy of the information obtained. Students have a right to expect that information given to them by their teachers is current and accurate. They will not learn very much if they decide it is essential to verify everything the teacher says. In the same way, the general public trusts that statements made by experts will be true. This trust is necessary, since lay people usually have neither the time nor the energy to conduct or evaluate the specialized research studies leading to scientific discoveries.

Advertisers both use and misuse this necessary reliance on authority figures. Cat foods are promoted by veterinarians, since veterinarians are assumed to be experts on the nutritional needs of cats and it is expected that cat owners will heed their pronouncements. On the other hand, all kinds of products are promoted by movie stars, rock stars, and athletes, whose authority lies not in their specialized knowledge but only in their personal charisma and status in the public eye.

As you might expect, it is advisable to place most trust in experts speaking within their field of expertise and less trust in those who lack expert knowledge. However, even experts can be wrong, and the consequences can sometimes be disastrous. A good example is a social work treatment intervention that was developed several decades ago. The intervention focused on families in which one member suffered from schizophrenia, and the intervention tried to change the family system as its primary treatment modality. At the time, authority figures in psychoanalysis and family therapy believed that schizophrenia was caused by faulty parenting, so emphasis was placed on such factors as parental discord, excessive familial interdependency, and mothers whose overprotective and domineering behaviors did not allow the child to develop an individual identity.

Following this theory, some social workers assumed that all families with a schizophrenic member must be dysfunctional. Because they focused their interventions on changing the family system, they often inadvertently instilled guilt into the parents and increased tensions rather than helping the parents to cope with their child who had been diagnosed as schizophrenic.

Recently, research studies have shown that schizophrenia is caused largely by genetic and other biological factors, not by bad parenting. Furthermore, one of the most effective interventions is to support the family in providing a nonstressful environment. It is not surprising that, previously, social workers acted on the beliefs of experts in schizophrenia without personally evaluating the research studies that had led to those beliefs. Had they investigated for themselves, and had they been trained in research techniques, they may have found that there was little real evidence to support the bad-parenting theory. Consequently, they may have been more supportive of parents and thus more effective helpers.

While you are in school, your learning is largely structured for you. However, it is likely that you will spend far more time as a practicing social worker than you will in school; and there is an old saying that learning does not really begin until formal education has ended. Out in the field, you will still be required to attend workshops, conferences, and staff training sessions, but most of your learning will come from what you read and from what people tell you. Your reading material is likely to consist mostly of books and journal articles related to your specific field of practice—whether it be senior citizens, children who have been abused, adolescent offenders, or some other special group. Most of the articles that you read will deal with research studies; many of the books you come across will interpret, synthesize, and comment upon research studies. None of them will explain how research studies ought to be conducted, because it is assumed you learned that in school.

Practice Wisdom

The third way of obtaining knowledge is through practice wisdom. What people tell you will come, in turn, from what they read and what people tell *them*: an accumulation of procedures, traditions, and approaches which, when practiced together, constitute "practice wisdom."

When you first enter a social work agency, as either a practicum student or a graduate social worker, your supervisor and colleagues will start to show you how the agency runs. You may be given a manual detailing agency policies and procedures: everything from staff holidays, to locking up client files at night, to standard techniques for interviewing children who have been physically and emotionally abused. Informally, you will be told other things: how much it costs to join the coffee club, whom to ask when you want a favor, whom to phone for certain kinds of information, and what form to complete to be put on the waiting list for a parking space.

In addition to this practical information, you may also receive advice about how to help your clients. Colleagues may offer opinions about the most effective treatment intervention strategies. For example, if you work in a child sexual abuse treatment agency, it may be suggested to you that the nonoffending mother of a child who has been sexually abused does not need to address her own history of abuse in therapy in order to empathize with and protect her daughter. Such a view would support the belief that the best interventive approach is a behavioral/learning one, perhaps helping the mother learn better communication skills in her relationship with her daughter. Conversely, the suggestion may be that the mother's personal exploration is essential and that, therefore, the intervention should be of a psychodynamic nature.

Whatever the suggestion, it is likely that you, as a beginning social worker, will accept it, along with the information about the coffee club and the parking space. You will want to fit in, to be a member of the team. If this is the first client for whom you have really been responsible, you may also be privately relieved that the intervention decision has been made for you. You may rightfully believe that your colleagues, after all, have more experience than you and they should surely know best.

Perhaps they do know best. At the same time, it is important to remember that they were once beginning social workers like yourself and they formed their opinions in the same way as you are presently forming yours. They too once trusted in their supervisors' knowledge bases and the experiences of their colleagues. In other words, much of what you will initially be told is based upon tradition and authority. Like all knowledge derived from these two sources, the "practice wisdom" offered by your colleagues allows you to learn from the achievements and mistakes of those who have tried to do your job before you. You do not have to "reinvent the wheel." You are being given a head start.

On the other hand, knowledge derived from tradition and authority has the disadvantage that it can become too comfortable. You know that the traditional approaches to client problems practiced in your agency are effective because everyone says they are; you know that certain intervention strategies work because they have worked for years. And armed with this comfortable and certain knowledge, you may not look for better ways of helping your clients.

In addition, you may not wish to test the intervention methods presently employed to see if they work as well as your colleagues say. You may even be inclined to reject out-of-hand evidence that your present interventions are ineffective or that there is a better way. And if you do happen to seek and find new interventions, you may discover that your colleagues are unreceptive or even hostile. Tradition dies hard. Authority is not so easily relinquished. Practice wisdom is very satisfying, even if it turns out later to be wrong.

The Problem-Solving Method

As mentioned in the previous sections, tradition, authority, and practice wisdom are three ways of obtaining knowledge, and the scientific method, commonly referred to as the problem-solving method, is the fourth. We will highlight this method, as it is today's primary method of obtaining knowledge in contemporary social work research. However, we emphasize that the other three forms of knowledge development are of equal importance in the knowledge-building enterprise.

Essentially, discovery through the problem-solving method involves four steps:

1. Observing a person, an object, or an event
2. Making an assumption on the basis of the observation
3. Testing the assumption to see to what extent it is true
4. Revising the assumption on the basis of the test

For example, suppose we observe that the hairy males of our acquaintance seem more intelligent than males endowed with a lesser amount of body hair. It has, in fact, been suggested—though by no means proven—that body hair is related to intelligence, since the skin and brain develop from the same embryonic tissues. Therefore, we might make the assumption that, if males in general are placed on a continuum from the most hairy to the least hairy, those on the hairy end will be significantly more intelligent than those on the other end.

We might test this assumption by randomly selecting a large number of males, measuring their intelligence, and devising a means of measuring their body hair that is both accurate and socially acceptable. If we find that pronounced hairiness is positively associated with high intelligence in a significant number of cases, we can be reasonably certain that our original assumption was correct. If we find no such association, our assumption was probably wrong.

Whatever we find, our conclusions will be suspect until someone else has undertaken a similar study and confirmed our results. Science is a *public method of knowing*. It relies not on private avenues to knowledge—such as inspiration or visions—but rather on a careful sequence of activities that can be duplicated by other people. We will be more certain of the relationship between hairiness and intelligence if someone else has found the same relationship. The more people who find it, the more certain we will become.

Even then, there will be some doubt. The problem-solving method of knowing holds that, in most cases, something exists if we can see it. To guard against things that are seen although they do not exist, such as cool pools of water observed by people dying of thirst in deserts, science has taken the premise one step further. A thing exists if we can *measure* it. The cool pools of water would probably not give a reading on a depth gauge or thermometer.

Nevertheless, we cannot be *certain* that a thing exists, no matter how many people have measured it. We cannot be certain that there is a relationship between two or more things no matter how many people have found one. Nothing is certain: nothing is absolute. It is a matter of slowly acquiring knowledge by making objective observations, deriving theories from those observations, and testing the theories by making further observations. Even the best-tested theory is held to be true only until something comes along to disprove it. Nothing is forever.

Beside the comfortable certainty of tradition and authority, science is a prickly bedfellow. But, of all the possible ways of knowing, we have discovered that the problem-solving method has brought us farthest in terms of food, clothing, shelter, and freedom from diseases. Mystic numbers have not successfully predicted the end of the world; authoritative statements have often proved inaccurate; and ill-conceptualized efforts at helpfulness, no matter how well intended, may not provide assistance to some of our clients. Social workers must know *how* to help—for our own sakes, and for the sake of our profession and the clients we serve.

However, the development of knowledge through the use of theories and problem-solving methods is not always as rational as one may predict as is illustrated in Box 1.1. Let us now turn to a detailed look at the problem-solving method as it is used in contemporary social work practice and research.

THE PROBLEM-SOLVING METHOD

Social work research as presented in this book is based on the problem-solving method, with specific, identifiable phases that have been applied in the twentieth century to a wide range of situations, from organizational decisions to classroom exercises. A problem is identified, defined, and specified. Then an intervention to address the problem is selected; the intervention is implemented; and the result is evaluated. A social work "practitioner" employs the same methods and modes of thought in approaching a practice problem as a social work "researcher" does in undertaking a research study.

This generic type of problem-solving method is applicable to both social work research and practice. These phases are not separate entities but rather interconnected parts of a complete whole. The problem-

---

Box 1.1

The Serendipity Pattern in Science

Scientific inquiry, for the most part, works within the framework of a theory. Hypotheses are derived, research studies are planned, and observations are made and interpreted in order to test and elaborate theories. Occasionally, however, unanticipated findings occur that cannot be interpreted meaningfully in terms of prevailing theories as the *serendipity pattern*. In the history of science, there are many cases of scientific discoveries in which chance, or serendipity, played a part. One of these is Pasteur's discovery of immunization.

> Pasteur's researches on fowl cholera were interrupted by his vacation, and when he resumed he encountered an unexpected obstacle. Nearly all the cultures had become sterile. He attempted to revive them by sub-inoculation into broth and injection into fowls. Most of the sub-cultures failed to grow and the birds were not affected, so he was about to discard everything and start afresh when he had the inspiration of re-inoculating the same fowls with a fresh culture. His colleague Duclaux relates: "To the surprise of all, and perhaps even of Pasteur, who was not expecting such success, nearly all these fowls withstood the inoculation, although fresh fowls succumbed after the usual incubation period." This resulted in the recognition of the principle of immunization with attenuated pathogens. (Beveridge, 1957:27)

Social science has had its share of serendipitous findings also. The well-known "Hawthorne effect," which refers to the effect that a worker's awareness of being under study has on his or her performance, was an unanticipated finding of a series of studies carried out between 1927 and 1932 at the Western Electric Hawthorne plant in Chicago (Roethlisberger & Dickson, 1939). In one of the studies six women with the task of assembling telephone relays were placed in a special test room for observation. The idea of the study was to determine the effects of various changes in working conditions (e.g., method of payment, number and length of rest pauses, length of working day) on productivity, as measured by the number of relays completed. Over an extended period of time, numerous changes, each lasting several weeks, were introduced while the women's output was recorded. To the researchers' surprise, however, the changes were not related systematically to output. Instead, the women's output rate rose slowly and steadily throughout the study, even when working conditions introduced early in the study were reintroduced later. As the women were questioned it became evident that their increased productivity was a response to the special attention given to them as participants in what was considered an important experiment. The fun of the test room and the interest of management simply had made it easier to produce at a higher rate. This was an important finding in the history of social research, for it indicated that subjects' awareness of being under study could affect the very actions that an investigator wishes to observe. Experiments, in particular, must take into account such effects, as prescribed in Chapter 8.

solving method is a rational, orderly, systematic series of steps directed toward a goal. It consists of the four basic phases identified in Figure 1.1:

1. Problem identification, definition, and specification
2. Generation of alternatives and selection of strategies for problem solution
3. Implementation
4. Evaluation and dissemination of findings

In reality, problem solving does not always proceed in the orderly sequence outlined in Figure 1.1. Nevertheless, the various phases must always be kept in mind. In general, one phase must be satisfactorily completed before the next can be addressed. For example, if the problem is defined inadequately, it is unlikely that any of the suggested solutions will address the real difficulty, and no attempted solution could possibly work. Those who fail to follow the rational procedures of problem solving may act uncritically or impulsively, or reach inappropriate conclusions. If errors and biases are allowed to multiply and become compounded, problem solvers can easily be misled into searching for solutions to the wrong problems. Ultimately, this limits their ability to solve or mitigate the problems they are addressing.

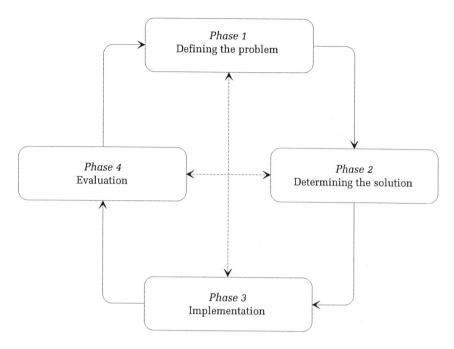

FIGURE 1.1   The Problem-Solving Method

The problem-solving method serves as a map or cognitive framework to help social workers stay focused and goal-directed, instead of getting lost in the details of a situation or being sidetracked by tangential issues. In all these respects, research and practice are identical processes. Figure 1.2 lists the parallels between social work research and practice and shows how the generic problem-solving method undergirds both. In order to plan how to measure a possible problem to be worked on with a client—either for assessment or to monitor change—it is necessary to examine how that problem is selected, how it can be specified, the type and direction of change desired, and the interventions used.

All social work activities, both practice and research, are organized around this central assumption: There is a preferred order of thinking and action which, when rigorously and consciously followed, will increase the likelihood of achieving the overall goal. This way of looking at social work practice and research activities is not new. Social work practitioners and researchers base their conclusions on careful observation, experimental trial, and intelligent analysis. Both observe, reflect, conclude, try, monitor results, and continuously reapply the same process until the problem in hand is either solved or abandoned.

PHASE 1: DEFINING THE PROBLEM
    General Problem Solving:
        Recognizing that a problem exists
    Social Work Research:
        Identifying the research problem
    Social Work Practice:
        Diagnosis and assessment

PHASE 2: DETERMINING THE SOLUTION
    General Problem Solving:
        Suggesting possible solutions to the problem
    Social Work Research:
        Formulating the research question, hypothesis, and design
    Social Work Practice:
        Selecting and planning an intervention

PHASE 3: IMPLEMENTATION
    General Problem Solving:
        Carrying out the selected solution
    Social Work Research:
        Collecting data and carrying out the research design
    Social Work Practice:
        Implementation of the selected intervention

PHASE 4: EVALUATION
    General Problem Solving:
        Evaluating the outcome of the selected solution
    Social Work Research:
        Analyzing, interpreting, and reporting findings
    Social Work Practice:
        Evaluating the client's progress and terminating

FIGURE 1.2   Parallels Among General Problem Solving and Social
Work Research and Practice

CHARACTERISTICS OF THE PROBLEM-SOLVING METHOD

The problem-solving method of gaining knowledge differs in a number of important ways from the methods of tradition, authority, and practice wisdom. These differences stem from the five essential characteristics of science that are embraced in the problem-solving method: empiricism, objectivity, reducing uncertainty, duplication, and standardized procedures.

Striving Toward Empiricism

The problem-solving method tries to be as *empirical* as possible. That is, knowledge gained through this method is based on objective observations and measurements of the real world, not on someone's opinions, beliefs, or past experiences. Conversely, knowledge gained through tradition or authority *depends* on people's opinions and beliefs. Entities that cannot be measured, or even seen, such as id, ego, or superego, are not amenable to scientific study but rather rely on tradition and authority. In short, the phenomena we believe to exist must be measurable. However, at this point in our discussion, it is useful for you to remember that practically everything in life is measurable—whether observable or not. We will elaborate on this concept later.

Striving Toward Objectivity

The problem-solving method strives to be as *objective* as possible. The direct measurements of the real world that comprise *empirical data* must not be affected in any way by the person doing the observing. Physical scientists have observed inanimate matter for centuries, confident in the belief that objects do not change as a result of being observed. However, in the subworld of the atom, physicists are beginning to learn what social researchers have always known. Things *do* change when they are observed. People, especially, think, feel, and behave very differently as a result of being observed. Not only do they change, they change in different ways depending on who is doing the observing. A quick review of the last section of Box 1.1 provides a clear example of how people change their behaviors when they are being watched.

There is yet another problem. Observed behavior is open to interpretation by the observer. To illustrate this point, let us take a simple example of a client you are seeing, named Ron, who is severely withdrawn. He may behave in one way in your office in individual therapy sessions, and in quite another way when his mother joins the interview. You may think that Ron is unduly silent, while his mother remarks on how much he is talking. If his mother *wants* him to talk, perhaps as a sign that he is emerging from his withdrawal, she may perceive him to be talking more than he really is.

Researchers go to great lengths to ensure that their own hopes, fears, beliefs, and biases do not affect their research results, and that the biases of others do not affect them either. Nevertheless, as discussed in later chapters, complete objectivity is rarely possible in social work despite the many strategies we have developed in our efforts to achieve it. For example, suppose that a social worker is trying to help a mother interact more positively with her child. The social worker, together with a colleague, may first observe the child and mother in a playroom setting, recording how many times the mother makes eye contact with the child, hugs the child, criticizes the child, makes encouraging comments, and so forth. The social worker may perceive a remark that the mother has made to the child as "neutral," while the colleague thinks it was "encouraging."

In such a situation, it is impossible to resolve the disagreement. However, if there were six objective observers, five opting for "neutral" and only one for "encouraging," the one observer is more likely to be wrong than the five, and it is very likely that the mother's remark was neutral. As more people agree on what they have observed, the less likely it becomes that the observation was distorted by bias; and the more likely it is that the agreement reached is objectively true.

Objectivity is, therefore, very largely a matter of agreement. There are some things—usually physical phenomena—about which most people agree. For example, most people agree that objects fall when dropped, water turns to steam at a certain temperature, sea water contains salt, and so forth. There are other things—mostly to do with values, attitudes, and feelings—about which agreement is more rare. For example, an argument about whether Beethoven is a better composer than Bach cannot be objectively resolved. Neither can a dispute about the rightness of euthanasia or abortion. It is not surprising, therefore, that physical researchers, who work with physical phenomena, are able to be more objective than social researchers, who work with human beings. In an effort to describe how physical and social researchers differ in regard to observation and measurement, it may be useful at this point to skip ahead and read Box 5.1 in Chapter 5.

Striving Toward Reducing Uncertainty

The problem-solving method tries to rule out uncertainty. Since all observations in both the physical and social sciences are made by human beings, personal bias cannot be entirely eliminated, and there is always the possibility that an observation is in error, no matter how many people agree about what they saw. There is also the possibility that the conclusions drawn from even an accurate observation will be wrong. A number of people may agree that an object in the sky is a UFO when in fact it is a meteor. Even if they agree that it is a meteor, they may come to the conclusion—probably erroneously—that the meteor is a warning from an angry extraterrestrial person.

In the twentieth century, most people do not believe that natural phenomena have anything to do with extraterrestrial people. They prefer the explanations that modern researchers have proposed. Nevertheless, no researcher would say—or at least be quoted as saying—that meteors and extraterrestrial beings are not related for certain. In science, nothing is certain. Even the best-tested theory is only tentative, accepted as true until newly discovered evidence shows it to be untrue or only partly true. All knowledge gained through the problem-solving method is thus provisional. Everything presently accepted as true is true only with varying degrees of probability.

Let us say that you have lived all of your life all alone in a log cabin in the middle of a large forest. You have never ventured as much as a hundred yards from your cabin and have had no access to the outside world. You have observed for your entire life that all of the ducks that flew over your land were white. You have never seen a different–colored duck. Thus, you theorize, and rightfully so, that all ducks are white. You would only have to see one nonwhite duck fly over your land to disprove your theory: Nothing is certain no matter how long you "objectively observed" it.

Striving Toward Duplication

The problem-solving method tries to do research studies in such a way that they can be duplicated. If they cannot be duplicated, they are not really scientific endeavors. As we have said, science is a public method of knowing. Evidence for the relationship between hairiness and intelligence in males must be open to public inspection if it is to be believed. Furthermore, belief is more likely if a second researcher, and preferably a third, can produce the same evidence.

In scientific laboratories, the word "replication" refers to the same experiment conducted more than once in the same way, at approximately the same time, by the same person. For example, a person testing a city's water supply for pollutants will take several samples of the water and test them simultaneously under identical conditions, expecting to obtain close to identical results. If the water needs to be retested for some reason, further samples will be taken and the same procedures followed, but now another person may do the work and the test conditions may be very slightly different: A recent downpour of rain may have flushed some of the pollutants out of the reservoir, for example. The second set of tests are then said to be *duplicates* of the first.

Social work researchers are not able to replicate research studies, because no person, situation, or event is identical to any other. Therefore, despite the fact that most social work texts use the word "replicate" in reference to repeating studies, we will use the word "duplicate" instead. It is possible to duplicate studies by repeating the procedure used in the first study to see if the same results will be produced. For example, suppose that you are running a 12-week intervention program to help fathers who have abused their children to manage their anger without resorting to physical violence. You have put a great deal of effort into designing this program, and you believe that your intervention (the program) is more effective than other interventions currently used in other anger-management programs. You develop a method of measuring the degree to which the fathers in your group have learned to dissipate their anger in nondamaging ways; and you find that, indeed, the group shows marked improvement.

Improvement shown by one group of fathers is not convincing evidence for the effectiveness of your program. Perhaps your measurements were in error and the improvement was not as marked as you thought. Perhaps the improvement was a coincidence, and the fathers changed because they had joined a health club and each had vented his fury on a punching bag. In order to be more certain, you repeat your program and measuring procedures with a second group of fathers: In other words, you duplicate your study.

After you have used the same procedures with a number of groups and obtained similar results each time, you might expect that other social workers will eagerly adopt your methods. However, tradition dies hard, as you have learned already. Other social workers have a vested interest in *their* interventions, and they may suggest that you found the results you did only because you *wanted* to find them.

In order to counter any suggestion of bias, you ask another, independent social worker to use the same anger-management program and measuring methods with other groups of fathers. If the results are the same as before, your colleagues in the field of anger management may choose to adopt your intervention method (the program). However, tradition does not merely die hard—it dies with enormous difficulty—and you should not be surprised if your colleagues choose, instead, to continue using the familiar interventions they have always used.

Whatever your colleagues decide, you are excited about your newfound program. You wonder if your methods would work as well with women as they do with men, with adolescents as well as with adults, with Native Indians, Asians, or African Americans as well as with Caucasians, with mixed groups, larger groups, or groups in different settings. In fact, you have found yourself a lifetime project, since you will have to repeatedly apply your program and measuring procedures to all these different groups.

Striving Toward the Use of Standardized Procedures

The problem-solving method tries to use well-accepted standardized procedures. For research studies to be creditable, they must use standardized procedures. Before others can accept your results, they must be satisfied that your study was conducted according to accepted scientific standardized procedures. The allegation that your work lacks objectivity is only one of the criticisms they might bring. In addition, they might suggest that the group of fathers you worked with was not typical of abusive fathers in general, and that your results are not therefore applicable to other groups of fathers. It might be alleged that you did not make proper measurements, or you measured the wrong thing, or you did not take enough measurements, or you did not analyze your data correctly, and so on.

In order to negate these kinds of criticisms, social work researchers have agreed on a set of standard procedures and techniques that are thought most likely to produce true and unbiased knowledge. Certain tasks must be performed in a certain order. Foreseeable errors must be guarded against. Ethical behavior to research participants and colleagues must be maintained. These procedures must be followed if a study is both to generate usable results and to be accepted as useful by other social workers.

DEFINITIONS OF RESEARCH

So far, we have discussed the four ways of obtaining knowledge and looked at the characteristics of the problem-solving method. Armed with this knowledge, we now need a definition of *research*, which is composed of two syllables, *re* and *search*. Dictionaries define the former syllable as a prefix meaning again, anew, or over again, and the latter as a verb meaning to examine closely and carefully, to test and try, or to probe. Together, these syllables form a noun describing a careful and systematic study in some field of knowledge, undertaken to establish facts or principles. Research therefore can be defined as follows:

> Research is a structured inquiry that utilizes acceptable scientific methodology to solve problems and creates new knowledge that is generally applicable.

In social work, the research or structured inquiry is applied to social work problems. Thus:

> Social work research is a scientific inquiry about a social work problem that provides an answer contributing to an increase in the body of generalizable knowledge about social work concerns.

While social workers obtain much of their knowledge base from the findings derived from research studies, all research studies have built-in biases and limitations that create errors and keep researchers from being absolutely certain about the outcome. This text will help social workers understand these limitations and take them into account in their interpretation of research findings, and it will help social work researchers avoid making errors or obtaining wrong answers. One of the principal products of a research study is obtaining information—via the problem-solving method—about reality as it is, unbiased and error-free.

THE SOCIAL WORKER'S ROLES IN RESEARCH

Now that we know what social work research is, let us explore how social workers can perform three research-related roles: (1) the research consumer, (2) the creator and disseminator of knowledge, and (3) the contributing partner.

The Research Consumer

As we have said, social workers deal with people's lives. They have a responsibility to evaluate the effectiveness of their interventions before they use them with clients; and they must also ensure that the interventions they select are the best possible ones, given the limits of social work knowledge. In other words, social workers must keep up with advances in their field, as doctors and other professionals do. They must acquaint themselves with the findings from the latest research studies and decide for themselves which findings are important, which might possibly be useful, and which are best ignored.

Sometimes, social workers want to conduct their own studies, particularly when they have read about findings that come into the "possibly useful" category. Nevertheless, every new intervention must be tried once for the first time, and a social worker who wants to build a repertoire of interventions will experience a number of "first times." It is particularly important to understand how others have implemented the intervention—if others have—and to monitor the client's progress carefully, using the scientific problem-solving method.

Social workers contemplating larger research studies will obviously need to be well acquainted with previous studies. However, it is a mistake to believe that only those who "do research" read research studies. The purpose of a research study is to collect information, which is combined with other information to generate knowledge. The purpose of generating knowledge, in social work, is to pass the knowledge to social workers, who will accomplish the primary purpose of the profession—helping clients to help themselves. Consuming research findings—reading with understanding in order to utilize the findings—is the most important research role a social worker can play.

Knowledge Creator and Disseminator

Social workers who conduct their own research studies are helping to create knowledge, provided that they inform others about their findings. Many social workers try something new from time to time. Comparatively few social workers use the problem-solving method of testing their new interventions in an effort to gather objective evidence about how well these interventions work with different clients in various situations. Even fewer share their findings—or even their interventions—with their colleagues; and fewer still disseminate the information to the profession as a whole by writing manuscripts to submit to professional journals for possible publication.

The consequence, as previously mentioned, is that most of the best work accomplished by social work professionals is never recorded and never used by anyone but its creator. Clients who could be helped derive no benefit, because a social worker in Chicago does not know that the problem has already been solved by a colleague in Boston.

Contributing Partner

The third research role that social workers undertake is that of contributing partner. We have said that researchers conducting a large study are often dependent on agency staff for help and advice, and many studies can succeed only if staff and researchers form a team. Different staff members can contribute their own various talents to the team effort. One member may be particularly acute and accurate when it comes to observing client behavior; another may have practical and innovative ideas about how to solve a problem; a third may act as a liaison between researcher and client, or between one agency and another. All may be asked to help in testing and designing measuring instruments and gathering or providing data.

It is a rare social worker who is not involved in one research study or another. Some social workers are cooperative, some less so, depending on their attitudes toward research. The ones who know most about research methods tend to be the most cooperative, and also the most useful. Hence, the greater the number of social workers who understand research principles, the more likely it is that relevant studies will be successfully completed and social work knowledge will be increased.

Integrating the Three Research Roles

The three research roles are not independent of one another. They must be integrated if research is to accomplish its goals of increasing the knowledge base of the profession and improving the effectiveness of interventions with clients.

The issue is not whether social workers should consume research findings, produce and disseminate research results, or become contributing partners in research studies. Rather it is whether they can engage the full spectrum of available knowledge and skills in the continual improvement of their practices. Social workers who adopt only one or two research roles are shortchanging themselves and their clients. As William J. Reid and Audrey D. Smith (1989) note:

... If research is to be used to full advantage to advance the goals of social work, the profession needs to develop a climate in which both doing and consuming research are normal professional activities. By this we do not mean that all social workers should necessarily do research or that all practice should be based on the results of research, but rather that an ability to carry out studies at some level and the facility in using scientifically based knowledge should be an integral part of the skills that social workers have and use. (p. ix)

SUMMARY

Knowledge is essential to human survival. Over the course of history, there have been many ways of knowing, from divine revelation to tradition and the authority of elders. By the beginning of the seventeenth century, people began to rely on a different way of knowing—the scientific method, more commonly referred to as the problem-solving method. Knowledge derived from science is knowledge derived through our senses. We believe in what we observe, provided that the same thing is observed by a sufficient number of people, and provided that it is observed a sufficient number of times.

The more people who agree about an observation, the more certain we become that the agreed-on truth is the real truth. But nothing in science is ever absolutely certain; there are only probabilities. Theories built from observations exist only until further observations prove them wrong.

Social workers derive their knowledge from the tradition and authority comprising practice wisdom, as well as from research studies conducted with problem-solving methods. The problem-solving method of knowing differs in important ways from the other three methods of tradition, authority, and practice wisdom. These differences stem from the five essential characteristics of science: empiricism, increasing objectivity, reducing uncertainty, duplication, and standardized procedures.

Social workers engage in three research roles. They can consume research findings by using the findings of others in their day-to-day practices, they can produce and disseminate research results for others to use, and they can participate in research studies in a variety of ways.

Now that we have explored the place of research in social work, in the following chapter we will turn to the contexts in which it takes place.

STUDY QUESTIONS

1. List and describe in detail the four ways of obtaining knowledge in social work. Provide an example of each that you believe was used to produce a certain piece of "today's" social work knowledge. Describe in detail how each way of obtaining knowledge can be useful for social workers.

2. List and discuss in detail the five characteristics of the problem-solving method. Why are these five characteristics necessary in order to produce scientific knowledge for the profession? What other characteristics do you feel could be added to the list? Why?

3. In your own words, define social work research. How is your definition different from that in this chapter?

4. List and discuss in detail the three research roles that social workers play in developing knowledge for our profession. Provide an example of each for a social worker in an agency designed to help people immigrating into the local community.

5. Go to the library and identify a social work research article. Discuss in detail how this study could have used each one of the four methods of obtaining knowledge to arrive at its conclusions. What would be the advantages and disadvantages to each knowledge-generation method? Do you feel that the four methods could have been combined within the study? Why, or why not?

6. In the library, choose another social work research article. Do you feel that the definition of social work research we have presented applies to the study? Why, or why not? How would you revise the book's definition of social work research given the methodology that was utilized in the study?

7. Go to the library and identify a social work research article that focuses on a particular client population. Describe in detail the three research roles that a social worker could use when working with the clients in the research article. Provide clear examples of how each one of the three roles would benefit the individual social worker, the client, and the profession.

8. Review Figure 1.2. Do you see any other parallels among general problem solving and social work research and practice? Why, or why not? Describe in detail how a social worker goes through the four phases of the problem-solving model when working with a client. Now describe how you think a researcher goes through the four phases when doing a research study. Do you see any differences between what the practitioner does when compared to the researcher?

9. Review Box 1.1. What other possible serendipitous research findings do you feel have contributed to social work's knowledge base? Discuss in detail.

10. In the library, find a research article that utilized the problem-solving method to obtain some research finding. Did the article go through all four phases of the problem-solving method as identified in this chapter? Why, or why not? What would you have done differently in the study? Why?

REFERENCES AND FURTHER READINGS

Adams, G.R., & Schvaneveldt, J.D. (1991). *Understanding research methods* (2nd ed., pp. 7-24). White Plains, NY: Longman.
Anastas, J.W., & MacDonald, M.L. (1994). *Research design for social work and the human services* (pp. 3-32). New York: Lexington Books.

Babbie, E.R. (1992). *The practice of social research* (6th ed., pp. 14-65, 484-487). Pacific Grove, CA: Wadsworth.

Bailey, K.D. (1994). *Methods of social research* (4th ed., pp. 3-20, 474-486). New York: Free Press.

Beveridge, W.I.B. (1957). *The art of scientific investigation* (3rd ed.). London: Heinemann.

Balassone, M.L. (1994). Does emphasizing accountability and evidence dilute service delivery and the helping role? No! In W.W. Hudson, & P.S. Nurius (Eds.). *Controversial issues in social work research* (pp. 15-19). Needham Heights, MA: Allyn & Bacon.

Bronson, D.E. (1994). Is a scientist-practitioner model appropriate for direct social work practice? No! In W.W. Hudson, & P.S. Nurius (Eds.). *Controversial issues in social work research* (pp. 81-86). Needham Heights, MA: Allyn & Bacon.

Chandler, S.M. (1994). Is there an ethical responsibility to use practice methods with the best empirical evidence of effectiveness? No! In W.W. Hudson, & P.S. Nurius (Eds.). *Controversial issues in social work research* (pp. 106-111). Needham Heights, MA: Allyn & Bacon.

Cheetham, J. (1992). Evaluating social work effectiveness. *Research on Social Work Practice, 2,* 265-287.

Compton, B.R., & Galaway, B. (Eds.). (1995). *Social work processes* (5th ed.). Pacific Grove, CA: Brooks/Cole.

Dangel, R.F. (1994). Is a scientist-practitioner model appropriate for direct social work practice? Yes! In W.W. Hudson, & P.S. Nurius (Eds.). *Controversial issues in social work research* (pp. 75-79). Needham Heights, MA: Allyn & Bacon.

DePoy, E., & Gitlin, L.N. (1994). *Introduction to research: Multiple strategies for health and human services* (pp. 1-27). St. Louis, MO: Mosby.

Duehn, W.D. (1981). The process of social work practice and research. In R.M. Grinnell, Jr. (Ed.), *Social work research and evaluation* (pp. 11-34). Itasca, IL: F.E. Peacock.

Duehn, W.D. (1985). Practice and research. In R.M. Grinnell, Jr. (Ed.), *Social work research and evaluation* (2nd ed., pp. 19-48). Itasca, IL: F.E. Peacock.

Frankfort-Nachmias, C., & Nachmias, D. (1992). *Research methods in the social sciences* (4th ed, pp. 3-50). New York: St. Martin's Press.

Gabor, P.A., & Grinnell, R.M., Jr. (1994). *Evaluation and quality improvement in the human services* (pp. 3-17). Needham Heights, MA: Allyn & Bacon.

Garvin, C.D. (1981). Research-related roles for social workers. In R.M. Grinnell, Jr. (Ed.), *Social work research and evaluation* (pp. 547-552). Itasca, IL: F.E. Peacock.

Grinnell, R.M., Jr. (1981). Becoming a knowledge-based social worker. In R.M. Grinnell, Jr. (Ed.), *Social work research and evaluation* (pp. 1-8). Itasca, IL: F.E. Peacock.

Grinnell, R.M., Jr. (1985). Becoming a practitioner/researcher. In R.M. Grinnell, Jr. (Ed.), *Social work research and evaluation* (2nd ed., pp. 1-15). Itasca, IL: F.E. Peacock.

Grinnell, R.M., Jr., Rothery, M., & Thomlison, R.J. (1993). Research in social work. In R.M. Grinnell, Jr. (Ed.), *Social work research and evaluation* (4th ed., pp. 2-16). Itasca, IL: F.E. Peacock.

Grinnell, R.M., Jr., & Siegel, D.H. (1988). The place of research in social work. In

R.M. Grinnell, Jr. (Ed.), *Social work research and evaluation* (3rd ed., pp. 9-24). Itasca, IL: F.E. Peacock.

Grinnell, R.M., Jr., & Williams, M. (1990). *Research in social work: A primer* (pp. 28-57). Itasca, IL: F.E. Peacock.

Judd, C.M., Smith E.R., & Kidder, I.H. (1991). *Research methods in social relations* (6th ed., pp. 3-27). Fort Worth, TX: Harcourt Brace.

Leedy, P.D. (1993). *Practical research: Planning and design* (3rd ed., pp. 7-24, 109-114). New York: Macmillan.

Marlow, C. (1993). *Research methods for generalist social work practice* (pp. 3-21, 277-293). Pacific Grove, CA: Wadsworth.

Monette, D.R., Sullivan, T.J., & DeJong, C.R. (1994). *Applied social research* (3rd ed., pp. 1-30). Fort Worth, TX: Harcourt Brace.

Neuman, W.L. (1994). *Social research methods* (2nd ed., pp. 1-16). Needham Heights, MA: Allyn & Bacon.

Reid, W.J., & Smith, A.D. (1989). *Research in social work* (2nd ed.). New York: Columbia University Press.

Roethlisberger, F.J., & Dickson, W.J. (1939). *Management and the worker: An account of a research program conducted by the Western Electric Co. Hawthorne Works, Chicago.* Cambridge, MA: Harvard University Press.

Royse, D.D. (1991). *Research methods in social work* (pp. 1-17, 37-52). Chicago: Nelson-Hall.

Rubin, A., & Babbie, E. (1993). *Research methods for social work* (2nd ed., pp. 2-55, 91-93). Pacific Grove, CA: Wadsworth.

Ruckdeschel, R. (1994). Does emphasizing accountability and evidence dilute service delivery and the helping role? Yes! In W.W. Hudson, & P.S. Nurius (Eds.). *Controversial issues in social work research* (pp. 9-14). Needham Heights, MA: Allyn & Bacon.

Sherman, E., & Reid, W.J. (Eds.). (1994). *Qualitative research in social work.* New York: Columbia University Press.

Tripodi, T. (1994). Is a scientist-practitioner model appropriate for social work administrative practice? Yes! In W.W. Hudson, & P.S. Nurius (Eds.). *Controversial issues in social work research* (pp. 128-133). Needham Heights, MA: Allyn & Bacon.

Weinbach, R.W., & Grinnell, R.M., Jr. (1995). *Applying research knowledge: A workbook for social work students* (pp. 1-8). Needham Heights, MA: Allyn & Bacon.

Yegidis, B.L., & Weinbach, R.W. (1991). *Research methods for social workers* (pp. 3-17). White Plains, NY: Longman.

Chapter 2

Research Contexts

I N THE PREVIOUS CHAPTER we presented the place of research in social work and four ways of obtaining knowledge. We highlighted the problem-solving method as the most useful approach to knowledge development within our profession, as this approach has the capability of producing objective, unbiased data through the means of research studies. This chapter will continue our discussion by presenting the contexts in which these research studies must take place. No social work research study is conducted in a vacuum. People engaged in studies work with colleagues and research participants (who are often clients), frequently in a social work agency whose operation is affected by social and political factors. In addition, and most importantly, researchers must follow strict ethical procedures when carrying out their studies.

FACTORS AFFECTING RESEARCH STUDIES

Essentially, there are six factors that have a major impact on the way a research study is conducted. For the sake of clarity, they will be presented separately although in reality they always act in combination. These factors are: (1) the social work profession, (2) the social work agency, (3) the researcher, (4) the social work practitioner, (5) professional ethics, and (6) political and social considerations.

The Social Work Profession

Doing a research study in a social work practice setting is enormously different from doing one in a scientific laboratory or in an artificial setting. Research participants (who many times are clients) have special needs that must be taken into consideration, beyond the ethical concerns that will be discussed later in this chapter. If we are to remain involved in the well-being of our clients, we must become more active in assessing the effectiveness and efficiency of social work programs.

Identifying a body of social work knowledge, as distinct from sociological or psychological knowledge, is often a difficult task. Social work has always been something of a poor relation among the social sciences, borrowing bits from psychology, anthropology, and sociology, pieces from political science and economics, and never finding much that can be classed as distinctly and uniquely social work. However, social workers are hardly in a position to complain about this. The knowledge garnered from psychology is obtained largely from research studies undertaken by psychologists. Similarly, the knowledge borrowed from anthropology, sociology, political science, and economics is gathered by people in these fields. It seems only reasonable that social work knowledge should be obtained by social workers conducting their own research studies in their particular areas of expertise.

There are other reasons for the growing importance of research studies in social work. One has to do with economic restraint as well as a simultaneous loss of faith in the idea that throwing money at social problems will solve them in the end. For example, the problem of domestic violence will not be solved by indiscriminate funding of emergency shelters for women who have been battered, treatment for men who have been abusive toward their partners, services for children who have been victimized, or education for all and sundry. Careful research studies are needed both to determine the most effective ways of helping people and to evaluate the usefulness of the programs currently being funded.

Evaluation of existing programs is no longer the rather lackadaisical affair that it once was. As recently as the 1970s, it would have been enough for a program director to convince a funding body that the program it was funding was meeting its goal, keeping within its budget and generally providing a useful service to the community, without having to produce detailed documentation to that effect. Today, funders want objective data that goals are being met at the least possible cost. They want the results of evaluative studies, performed according to the problem-solving method and reported in the accepted manner, accompanied by charts, graphs, and tables. They want objective scientific proof.

The demand for evaluation is so pervasive that if social work staff do not evaluate their own agency, the evaluation will often be conducted for them by a professional evaluator, hired by the funding body. Until recently, all evaluations of social work programs were carried out by non-social workers who were skilled in such techniques as planning, programing, and budget systems (PPBS) but who knew very little about social work values and practices. However, few social work programs are cost efficient in the way that businesses must be in order to survive. The purpose of a business is to make a profit; the purpose of a social work program is to salvage human lives. As such, social work administrators objected to the use of business cost efficiency criteria to measure the worth of human services. They questioned the meaning of the word "efficient" in the human context: Did it mean efficient in terms of time, money, labor, suffering, human rights, or something else?

Eventually, social workers began to conduct evaluative studies and tried to reach a compromise between PPBS efficiency and client needs. The prestige of the social work profession has benefitted from the fact that social workers are now empowered to evaluate their own agencies in light of their own value systems. Clients have also benefitted, since their needs are not now sacrificed arbitrarily to costs. However, these gains are lost if agency staff ignore evaluation until it is imposed upon them from outside the agency.

In sum, it would be to the benefit of both social workers and their clients if social work professionals were to take more responsibility for conducting research studies on their own programs. This should provide us with the authority to advocate for clients, to be heard by other professionals with regard to clients, to maintain control over programs serving clients, and to bring about needed change. In this present age of accountability, there is no doubt that a profession that strives for status must be accountable. To some degree it is a question of "the more accountability the more status," because accountability *is* status. It symbolizes power. It is apparent, therefore, that if the social work profession wishes to make its way up the status ladder, its driving force must be accountability—accountability through well-designed objective research studies.

We must never forget that accountability is not all a facade. The problem-solving method as a way of knowing is not just a path to authority and status. It allows us to determine how best to serve our clients, how effective the services are, and how the services can be further improved.

The Social Work Agency

The second factor affecting research studies is the social work agency. Most social workers are employed by a social work program housed within an agency. For example, a child protection agency may run an investigation program whose purpose is to investigate alleged cases of child abuse and neglect. The same agency may provide in-home support services to families who have abused or neglected their children—a second program. The agency may run a survivor-witness program for children and nonoffending parents who have to appear in court—a third program.

Research studies are usually conducted within the confines of a program. The word "confines" is used advisedly since no study can be undertaken without the support, or at least the toleration, of the program's director. Some program directors are supportive of research studies, while others shiver at the merest mention, but there are some things that all of them have in common. The first of these is that they all worry about money.

Program directors of social work agencies have very little money. They worry that in the coming year they may have even less money: that their funding will be cut or even terminated, clients will suffer, and staff will be unemployed. They worry that all these disasters will follow in the wake of an evaluative research study. People doing social work research studies often have access to client files and to clients. They sometimes talk to staff and examine agency procedures. They are in an excellent position to embarrass everyone by breaching client confidentiality, making inappropriate statements at the wrong times to the wrong people, and writing reports that comment on the program's weaknesses but disregard its strengths.

All programs, like all people, have flaws. Few are efficient in the business sense and most are open to doubt concerning their effectiveness. Program directors know this. They work to improve programs, serving their clients as best they can with limited resources and knowledge that is patchy at best—because the knowledge has not been gained and the research studies necessary to gain it have not been undertaken.

It is not surprising, then, that program directors find themselves torn with regard to the place of research in the social work profession. They understand that increased knowledge is necessary in order to serve clients better but sometimes they wish that the knowledge could be gathered somewhere else: not through their program, not with their client files, not using their resources, and not taking up the time of their staff. They argue that resources given to research studies are resources taken away from client service. They may think, privately, that research reports are useful only to those engaged in the study.

However, there is an upside to all this gloom. It is possible that the research report might reflect the program in a good light, delighting its funders and improving its standing in the public eye. In addition, the study might reveal a genuinely practical way in which the program could improve its services to clients or do what it does more efficiently. Many program directors will therefore give permission for research studies to be conducted, provided that the person(s) doing the study is of good standing in the social work community, the proposed study meets with approval, and agreements are entered into concerning confidentiality and the use of staff and financial resources. Larger agencies often have a special committee to evaluate research requests.

However, few, if any, social work programs are designed with the notion that someday the program will be engaged in the research process. In some programs, client files have become more ordered with the advent of the computer, but frequently data are difficult both to find and to interpret. The entries in client files may be made by different workers at different times, in writing ranging from copperplate to scrawl, with different viewpoints on the people and events involved, and sometimes with vital data missing. Policies and procedures manuals, long outdated, may bear little relationship to the policies presently in place and the procedures actually undertaken. When this occurs, we must often become dependent upon the goodwill of staff to provide guidance and explanations, even when the original plan was just a quiet session with client files. A researcher's positive relationships with program staff cannot be overemphasized.

The Researcher

The third factor affecting social work research is the person doing the study—the researcher. At every stage in the research process, there are decisions to be made based on the knowledge and value systems of the person conducting the research study. For example, if you are investigating poverty and you believe that poverty results from character flaws in the poor, you might study treatment interventions designed to overcome those flaws. If you believe that ghettos are a factor, you might prefer to focus on environmental causes. The research questions you select are determined by your own value systems as well as by the social and political realities of the hour.

Another factor in your study of poverty would be your own definition of poor. What annual income should a person earn in order to be categorized as poor? You may decide that "poor," in the context of your study, means an annual income of less than $5,000, and that you do not need to talk to anyone who earns more than that. If you decide that the upper limit should be $20,000, you are automatically including many more people as potential participants for your study. Thus, the information you collect about "the poor" will depend largely on whom you define as poor.

Your final report on the study of poverty will probably include recommendations for change based on the study's findings. These recommendations, too, will depend on your personal value systems, modified by social, political, and economic realities. It may be your private opinion that welfare recipients should be given only the absolute minimum of resources necessary to sustain life in order to motivate them to find work. On the other hand, you may believe that a decent standard of living is every human being's birthright. Whatever your opinion, it is likely that you will clothe it in suitable phraseology and incorporate it somehow into your recommendations.

Personal value systems are particularly evident in program evaluation. Social work programs are often labeled as ineffective, not as a result of poor goal achievement, but because there is disagreement about the goal itself. Is a drug prevention program "successful" if it *reduces* drug use among its clients, or must clients *abstain* altogether before success can be claimed? Then there is the question of how much success constitutes "success." Is a job placement program worth funding if it finds jobs *only* for 50 percent of its clients? Should an in-home support program be continued if the child is removed from the home in 30 percent of the cases? Next, there is the matter of what types of clients are the most deserving. Should limited resources be used to counsel people dying of cancer, or would the money be better spent on those who are newly diagnosed? Is it worthwhile to provide long-term treatment for one family whose potential for change is small, while other families with more potential linger on the waiting list?

The Social Work Practitioner

The fourth factor affecting social work research is the practitioner. Social workers' beliefs and attitudes also affect the place of research in agency settings. For example, some social workers refuse to have an observer present at an interview with a client on the grounds that the client will be unable to speak freely and the social worker-client relationship will be disrupted. This difficulty can be resolved in facilities with one-way mirrors; but, if no such mirror exists, a person wishing to evaluate a treatment intervention may not be able to watch the intervention in a practical, clinical setting.

An alternative to the physical presence of the person doing the study is a video recorder. However, some social workers—whose belief in disruption leads them to be disrupted—also object to video recorders, although experience has shown that most clients ignore video recorders after the first few curious glances. Indeed, some social workers seem to believe that there is a sort of an aura surrounding practice relationships that is shattered by such devices.

To the extent that video recorders, paper-and-pencil questionnaires, and computer question-and-answer programs are shunned out of hand, the effectiveness of the intervention can never be objectively established. To a degree, it is true that the act of measuring alters what it measures, but often the change is neither great nor long-lasting. The opinions, beliefs, and attitudes of social workers in regard to research practices thus play a vital part in the outcome of the study. It is not just the researcher's attitude that makes a difference; it is the attitudes of *everyone* involved in the study.

Ethical Considerations

The fifth important factor affecting social work research directly is ethics. Physical scientists are by no means exempt from ethical considerations. Consider Robert Oppenheimer and other atomic scientists, who learned too late that their scientific findings about splitting the atom were used to create an atomic bomb, a purpose the scientists themselves opposed. However, a physical scientist who wishes to run tests on water samples does not have to consider the feelings of the water samples or worry about harming them. No large dilemma is presented if one of the water samples must be sacrificed to the cause of knowledge building.

For people engaged in social work research studies, the ethical issues are far more pervasive and complex. A fundamental principle of social work research is that increased knowledge, while much to be desired, must never be obtained at the expense of human beings. Since much of social work research revolves directly around human beings, safeguards must be put in place to ensure that research participants are never harmed, either physically or psychologically.

An American committee known as the National Commission for the Protection of Human Subjects of Biomedical and Behavioral Research is only one of several professional organizations and lay groups that focus on protecting the rights of research participants. (Most research participants have never heard of any of them.) Clients participating in studies do not put their trust in committees; they trust the individual practitioners who involve them in the studies. It is therefore incumbent upon all social workers to be familiar with ethical principles so that the client's trust will never be betrayed.

Essentially, there are three precautionary ethical measures that must be taken before beginning any research study. These are: (1) obtaining the participant's informed consent, (2) designing the study in an ethical manner, and (3) ensuring that others will be properly told about the study's findings.

Obtaining Informed Consent. The first and most important consideration in any research study is to obtain the participants' *informed* consent. The word "informed" means that each participant fully understands what is going to happen in the course of the study, why it is going to happen, and what its effect will be on him or her. If the participant is psychiatrically challenged, mentally delayed, or in any other way incapable of full understanding, the study must be explained to someone else—perhaps a parent, guardian, social worker, or spouse, or someone to whom the participant's welfare is important.

It is clear that no research participant may be bribed, threatened, deceived, or in any way coerced into participating. Questions must be encouraged, both initially and throughout the course of the study. People who believe they understand may have misinterpreted our explanation or understood it only in part. They may say they understand, when they do not, in an effort to avoid appearing foolish. They may even sign documents they do not understand to confirm their supposed understanding, and it is our responsibility to ensure that their understanding is real and complete.

It is particularly important for participants to know that they are not signing away their rights when they sign a consent form. They can decide at any time to withdraw from the study *without penalty*, without so much as a reproachful glance. The results of the study will be made available to them as soon as the study has been completed. No promise will be made to them that cannot be fulfilled. Figure 2.1 contains an example of a simple consent form that was used by a research department within a child welfare agency. The purpose of the study was to obtain the line-level practitioners' views on burnout.

A promise that is of particular concern to many research participants is that of anonymity. A drug offender, for example, may be very afraid of being identified; a person on welfare may be concerned whether anyone else might learn that he or she was on welfare. Also, there is often some confusion between the terms "anonymity" and "confidentiality." Some studies are designed so that no one, not even the person doing the study, knows which research participant gave what response. An example is a mailed survey form, bearing no identifying mark and asking the respondent not to give a name. In a study like this, the respondent is *anonymous*. However, it is more often the case that we do know how a particular participant responded and have agreed not to divulge the information to anyone else. In such cases, the information is *confidential*. Part of our explanation to a potential research participant must include a clear statement of what information will be shared with whom.

All this seems reasonable in theory, but ethical obligations are often difficult to fulfill in practice. For example, there are times when it is very difficult to remove coercive influences because these influences are inherent in the situation. A woman awaiting an abortion may agree to provide private information about herself and her partner because she believes that, if she does not, she will be denied the abortion. It is of no use to tell her that this is not true: She feels she is not in a position to take any chances.

There are captive populations of people in prisons, schools, or institutions who may agree out of sheer boredom to take part in a research study. Or, they may participate in return for certain privileges, or because they fear some penalty or reprisal. There may be people who agree because they are pressured into it by family members, or they want

[Agency Letterhead]

Ms. Blackburn, MSW
Intake Worker II
City Social Services
Dallas, Texas 75712

Dear Ms. Blackburn:

As discussed on the phone, burnout among child protection workers is an issue of concern not only to child protection workers like yourself but to management alike. Research Services is asking you to voluntarily participate in our study. We will need this signed informed consent form before our interview can begin. We are deeply appreciative of your willingness to voluntarily participate in the department's research project.

Our interview will be held in your office and should last no more than one hour. Our objective is to elicit your views on the nature of the stresses (if any) that you face on a day-to-day basis. We may be discussing politically sensitive issues from time to time, and you have our assurance that we will maintain absolute confidentiality with respect to views expressed by you.

We will be asking you to complete a standardized measuring instrument that assesses a worker's degree of burnout before our interview begins. This task should take no more than ten minutes. All research materials will be kept in a locked file, and the identity of all workers interviewed for this study will be safeguarded by assigning each a number, so that names do not appear on any written materials.

With respect to any research or academic publications resulting from this study, specific views and/or opinions will not be ascribed either to you or to your organization without your prior written consent.

Your signature below indicates that you have understood to your satisfaction the information regarding your participation in our research project. Should you decide not to participate for whatever reason, or should you wish to withdraw at a later date, this will in no way affect your position in the agency. If you have any further questions about our study, please contact Research Services and we will address them as quickly as possible.

Sincerely,

Beulah Wright, MSW
Director, Research Services

YES: I AM WILLING TO PARTICIPATE IN THE RESEARCH PROJECT

Signature_____ Today's Date:_____

FIGURE 2.1   Example of a Simple Consent Form

to please the social worker, or they need some service or payment that they believe depends on their cooperation. Often, situations like this cannot be changed, but at least we can be aware of them and try to deal with them in an ethical manner.

A written consent form should be only part of the process of informing research participants of their roles in the study and their rights as volunteers. It should give participants a basic description of the purpose of the study, the study's procedures, and their rights as voluntary participants. All information should be provided in plain and simple language, without jargon.

A consent form should be no longer than two pages of single-spaced typing. All participants should be given a copy of the consent form. Questionnaires may have an introductory letter containing the required information, with the written statement that the completion of the questionnaire is the person's agreement to participate. In telephone surveys, the information below will need to be given verbally and must be standardized across all calls.

A written consent form should contain the following items, recognizing that the relevancy of this information and the amount required will vary with each research project:

1. A brief description of the purpose of the research study, as well as the value of the study to the general/scientific social work community (probability and nature of direct and indirect benefits) and to the participants and/or others.
2. An explanation as to how and/or why participants were selected and a statement that participation is completely voluntary.
3. A description of experimental conditions and/or procedures. Some points that should be covered are:
   a. The frequency with which the participants will be contacted.
   b. The time commitment required by the participants.
   c. The physical effort required and/or protection from overexertion.
   d. Emotionally sensitive issues that might be exposed and/or follow-up resources that are available if required.
   e. Location of participation (e.g., need for travel/commuting).
   f. Information that will be recorded and how it will be recorded (e.g., on paper, by photographs, videotape, audiotape).
4. Description of the likelihood of any discomforts and inconveniences associated with participation, and of known or suspected short- and long-term risks.
5. Explanation of who will have access to information collected and to the identity of the participants (i.e., level of anonymity or confidentiality of each person's participation and information) and how long the data will be stored.
6. Description of how the data will be made public (e.g., scholarly

presentation, printed publication). An additional consent is required for publication of photographs, audiotapes, and/or videotapes.

7. Description of other research projects or other people who may use the data.
8. Explanation of the participants' rights:
   a. That they may terminate or withdraw from the study at any point.
   b. That they may ask for clarification or more information throughout the study.
   c. That they may contact the appropriate administrative body if they have any questions about the conduct of the people doing the study or the study's procedures.

Designing an Ethical Study. A second necessary precaution before beginning a research study is to ensure that the study is designed in an ethical manner. One of the more useful research designs, presented in Chapter 11, involves separating participants into control and experimental groups, and providing a treatment to the experimental group but not to the control group. The essential dilemma here is whether or not it is ethical to withhold a treatment, assumed to be beneficial, from participants in the control group. Even if control group participants are on a waiting list and will receive the treatment at a later date, is it right to delay service in order to conduct the study?

Proponents of this research design argue that people on a waiting list will not receive treatment any faster whether they are involved in the research study or not. Furthermore, it is only *assumed* that the treatment is beneficial; if its effects were known for sure, there would be no need to do the study. Surely, social workers have an ethical responsibility to test such assumptions through research studies before they continue with treatments that may be ineffective or even harmful.

The same kind of controversy arises around a research design in which clients are randomly assigned to two different groups whereby each group receives a different treatment intervention. Proponents of this research design argue that no one is sure which treatment is better—that is what the research study is trying to discover—and so it is absurd to assert that a client in one group is being harmed by being denied the treatment offered to the other group. Social workers, however, tend to have their own ideas about which treatment is better. Ms. Gomez's worker may believe that she will derive more benefit from behavioral than from existential therapy, and that it will be harmful to her if random assignment happens to put her in the existential group.

Controversy also exists around the ethics of deception when the study's results will not be valid without the deception. For example, we may wish to study the prevalence of abuse and neglect of adolescents who are psychiatrically challenged and live in residential institutions. Staff in institutions are unlikely to abuse or neglect residents while being directly watched, but a person who poses as a new staff member may be able to document mistreatment (if any). Some social workers may consider that such a deception is justified in order to protect the adolescents. Others may argue that it is unethical to spy on people, no matter how noble the cause. Consider the ethical implications of Stanley Milgram's 1963 study, presented in Box 2.1.

Box 2.1

Observing Human Obedience

One of the more unsettling cliches to come out of World War II was the German soldier's common excuse for atrocities: "I was only following orders." From the point of view that gave rise to this comment, any behavior—no matter how reprehensible—could be justified if someone else could be assigned responsibility for it. If a superior officer ordered a soldier to kill a baby, the fact of the *order* was said to exempt the soldier from personal responsibility for the action.

Although the military tribunals that tried the war crime cases did not accept the excuse, social scientists and others have recognized the extent to which this point of view pervades social life. Very often people seem willing to do things they know would be considered wrong by others, *if* they can cite some higher authority as ordering them to do it. Such was the pattern of justification in the My Lai tragedy of Vietnam, and it appears less dramatically in day-to-day civilian life. Few would disagree that this reliance on authority exists, yet Stanley Milgram's study (1963, 1974) of the topic provoked considerable controversy.

To observe people's willingness to harm others when following orders, Milgram brought 40 adult men—from many different walks of life—into a laboratory setting designed to create the phenomenon under study. If you had been a subject in the experiment, you would have had something like the following experience.

You would have been informed that you and another subject were about to participate in a learning experiment. Through a draw of lots, you would have been assigned the job of "teacher" and your fellow subject the job of "pupil." He would have then been led into another room, strapped into a chair, and had an electrode attached to his wrist. As the teacher, you would have been seated in front of an impressive electrical control panel covered with dials, gauges, and switches. You would have noticed that each switch had a label giving a different number of volts, ranging from 15 to 315. The switches would have had other labels, too, some with the ominous phrases "Extreme-Intensity Shock," "Danger—Severe Shock," and "XXX."

The experiment would run like this. You would read a list of word pairs to the learner and then test his ability to match them up. Since you couldn't see him, a light on your control panel would indicate his answer. Whenever the learner made a mistake, you would be instructed by the experimenter to throw one of the switches—beginning with the mildest—and administer a shock to your pupil. Through an open door between the two rooms, you'd hear your pupil's response to the shock. Then you'd read another list of word pairs and test him again.

As the experiment progressed, you'd be administering ever more intense shocks, until your pupil was screaming for mercy and begging for the experiment to end. You'd be instructed to administer the next shock anyway. After a while, your pupil would begin kicking the wall between the two rooms and screaming. You'd be told to give the next shock. Finally, you'd read a list and ask for the pupil's answer—and there would be no reply whatever, only silence from the other room. The experimenter would inform you that no answer was considered an error and instruct you to administer the next higher shock. This would continue up to the "XXX" shock at the end of the series.

What do you suppose you would have done when the pupil first began screaming? Or when he became totally silent and gave no indication of life? You'd refuse to continue giving shocks, right? Of the first 40 adult men Milgram tested, nobody refused to administer the shocks until the pupil began kicking the wall between the two rooms. Of the 40, 5 did so then. Two-thirds of the subjects, 26 of the 40, continued doing as they were told through the entire series—up to and including the administration of the highest shock.

As you've probably guessed the shocks were phoney, and the "pupil" was another experimenter. Only the "teacher" was a real subject in the experiment. You wouldn't have been hurting another person, even though you would have been led to think you were. The experiment was designed to test your *willingness* to follow orders, to the point of presumably killing someone.

Milgram's experiments have been criticized both methodologically and ethically. On the ethical side, critics particularly cited the effects of the experiment on the subjects. Many seem to have personally experienced about as much pain as they thought they were administering to someone else. They pleaded with the experimenter to let them stop giving the shocks. They became extremely upset and nervous. Some had uncontrollable seizures.

How do you feel about this research study? Do you think the topic was important enough to justify such measures? Can you think of other ways in which the researcher might have examined obedience?

The study cited in Box 2.1 may be judged to be unethical for a number of reasons, but Milgram did not consider it unethical or he would not have performed it. Ethics, like politics, hinges on points of view, values, ideologies, cultural beliefs, and perspectives. People disagree about the political aspects of research studies just as they do about ethics.

Informing Others About Findings. A third important ethical consideration in a research study is the manner in which the findings are reported. It may be tempting, for example, to give great weight to positive findings while playing down or ignoring altogether negative or disappointing findings. There is no doubt that positive findings tend to be more enthusiastically received, often by journal editors who should know better; but it is obviously just as important to know that two things are not related as to know that they are. Consider the ethical implications of William Epstein's study contained in Box 2.2.

Box 2.2

Social Worker Submits Bogus Article to Test Journal Bias

This illustration of an ethical controversy is the first well-publicized ethical controversy involving a social worker's research. Several articles reported it in national news media, including two stories on it in the *New York Times* (September 27, 1988, pp. 21, 25 and April 4, 1989, p. 21) and one in the *Chronicle of Higher Education* (November 2, 1988, p. A7). The information for this illustration was drawn primarily from those three news articles.

The social worker, William Epstein, hypothesized that journal editors were biased in favor of publishing research articles whose findings confirmed the effectiveness of evaluated social work interventions and biased against publishing research articles whose findings failed to support the effectiveness of tested interventions. To test his hypothesis, Epstein fabricated a fictitious study that pretended to evaluate the effectiveness of a social work intervention designed to alleviate the symptoms of asthmatic children. (Asthma is often thought to be a psychosomatic illness.)

Epstein concocted two versions of the bogus study. In one version, he fabricated findings that supported the effectiveness of the intervention; in the other version, he fabricated data that found the intervention to be ineffective.

Epstein submitted the fictitious article to 146 journals, including 33 social work journals and 113 journals in allied fields. Half of the journals received the version supporting the effectiveness of the intervention, and half received the other version. Epstein did not enter his own name as author of his fabricated article; instead, he used a pair of fictitious names.

In his real study, Epstein interpreted his findings as providing some support for his hypothesis that journal editors were biased in favor of publishing the version of the bogus article with positive findings and against publishing the version with negative findings. Among the social work journals, for example, 8 accepted the positive version and only 4 accepted the negative version. Nine journals rejected the positive version, and 12 rejected the negative version. Among the journals in allied fields, 53 percent accepted the positive version, compared to only 14 percent that accepted the negative version. A statistical analysis indicated that the degree of support these data provided for Epstein's hypothesis was "tentative" and not statistically significant.

After being notified of the acceptance or rejection of his fictitious article, Epstein informed each journal of the real nature of his study. Later, he submitted a true article, under his own name, reporting his real study, to the *Social Service Review*, a prestigious social work journal. That journal rejected publication of his real study, and its editor, John Schuerman, led a small group of editors who filed a formal complaint against Epstein with the National Association of Social Workers. The complaint charged Epstein with unethical conduct on two counts: (1) deceiving the journal editors who reviewed the bogus article, and (2) failing to obtain their informed consent to participate voluntarily in the study. Schuerman, a social work professor at the University of Chicago and an author of some highly regarded research articles, recognized that sometimes the benefits of a study may warrant deceiving subjects and not obtaining their informed consent to participate. But he argued that in Epstein's (real) study, the benefits did not outweigh the time and money costs associated with many editors and reviewers who had to read and critique the bogus article and staff members who had to process it.

When an article is submitted for publication in a professional social work journal, it is usually assigned to several volunteer reviewers, usually social work faculty members who are not reimbursed for their review work. The reviewers do not know who the author is, so that the review will be fair and unbiased. Each reviewer is expected to read each article carefully, perhaps two or three times, recommend to the journal editor whether the article should be published, and develop specific suggestions to the author for improving the article. The journal editor, too, is usually a faculty member volunteering his or her own time as part of one's professional duties as an academician. Schuerman noted that in addition to the time and money costs mentioned, there is an emotional cost: "the chagrin and embarrassment of those editors who accepted the [bogus] article" (*New York Times*, September 27, 1988, p. 25).

Epstein countered that journal editors are not the ones to judge whether the benefits of his (real) study justified its costs. In his view, the editors are predisposed to value their own costs very dearly and unlikely to judge any study that would deceive them as being worth those costs. Epstein argued that the journals are public entities with public responsibilities, and that testing whether they are biased in deciding what to publish warrants both the deception and lack of informed consent to participate that were necessary to test for that bias.

One might argue that if journal editors and reviewers are biased against publishing studies that fail to confirm the effectiveness of tested interventions, then the field may not learn that certain worthless interventions in vogue are not helping clients. Moreover, if several studies disagree about the effectiveness of an intervention, and only those confirming its effectiveness get published, then an imbalanced and selective set of replications conceivably might be disseminated to the field, misleading the field into believing that an intervention is yielding consistently favorable outcomes when in fact it is not. This could hinder the efforts of social workers to provide the most effective services to their clients, and therefore ultimately reduce the degree to which we enhance the well-being of clients.

One could argue that Epstein's study could have been done ethically if he had forewarned editors that they might be receiving a bogus paper within a year and obtained their consent to participate in the study without knowing the specifics of the paper. An opposing viewpoint is that such a warning might affect the phenomenon being studied, tipping off the reviewers in a manner that predisposes them to be on guard not to reveal a real bias that actually does influence their publication decisions.

Some scholars who have expressed views somewhat in sympathy with those of Epstein have argued that journal editors and reviewers exert great influence on our scientific and professional knowledge base and therefore their policies and procedures should be investigated. Schuerman, who filed the charges against Epstein, agreed with this view, but argued that Epstein's study was not an ethical way to conduct such an investigation.

In an editorial in the March 1989 issue of the *Social Service Review*, Schuerman elaborated his position. He noted that journals have low budgets and small staffs and depend heavily on volunteer reviewers "who see their efforts as a professional responsibility" and receive few personal or professional benefits for their work (p. 3). He also portrayed Epstein's research as "badly conducted," citing several design flaws that he deemed to be so serious that they render the anticipated benefits of the Epstein study as minimal, and not worth its aforementioned costs. Schuerman also cited Epstein as admitting to serious statistical limitations in his study and to characterizing his research as only exploratory. "It is at this point that issues of research design and research ethics come together," Schuerman argued (p. 3). In other words, Schuerman's point is that the methodological quality of a study's research design can bear on its justification for violating ethical principles. If the study is so poorly designed that its findings have little value, then it becomes more difficult to justify the ethical violations of the study on the grounds that its findings are so beneficial.

The initial ruling of the ethics board of the National Association of Social workers was that Epstein had indeed violated research rules associated with deception and failure to get informed consent. It could have invoked serious sanctions against Epstein, including permanent revocation of his membership in the professional association and referral of the case to a state licensing board for additional sanctions. But Epstein was permitted to appeal the decision before any disciplinary action was taken. His appeal was upheld by the executive committee of the Association, which concluded that his research did not violate its ethical rules. The committee exonerated Epstein, ruling that the case was a "disagreement about proper research methodology," not a breach of ethics. It did not publicize additional details of its rationale for upholding Epstein's appeal and reversing the initial ruling. Epstein speculated that the reversal may have been influenced by the publicity the case received in the press.

If Epstein's speculation is valid, one might wonder whether the reversal was prompted by the executive committee's sincere judgment that the research really did not violate ethical rules or by expedience considerations, perhaps connected to concerns regarding potential future publicity or other costs. What do *you* think? What ideas do you have about the two rulings and about the ethical justification for Epstein's study? Which ruling do you agree with? Do you agree with Schuerman's contention that methodological flaws in the research design can bear on research ethics? Is it possible to agree with Schuerman on that issue and still agree with the executive committee that this case was a disagreement about methodology and not a breach of ethics? If, just for the sake of discussion, you assume that Epstein's study had very serious design flaws that prevented the possibility of obtaining conclusive findings, how would that assumption affect your position on the ethical justification for Epstein's study?

All studies have limitations, because practical considerations make it difficult to use the costly and complex designs that yield the most certain results. Since studies with more limitations yield less trustworthy findings, it is important for us to be honest about a study's limitations and for other social workers to be able to understand what the limitations imply.

Finally, there are issues around giving proper credit to colleagues and ensuring that results are shared in an appropriate manner. With the exception of single-system designs, presented in Chapter 10, where one social worker may do all the work, research studies are normally conducted by teams. The principal person, whose name is usually listed first on the report, must be sure that all team members are given recognition and all research participants are apprised of the results.

Sometimes, the sharing of results will be a delicate matter. Staff may be reluctant to hear that the program is less effective than they thought. It will also be difficult, and often inadvisable, for us to share with research participants results that show them in an unfavorable light. For example, it may be honest to tell Mr. Yen that he scored high on the anxiety scale, but it may also be extremely damaging to him. Social workers wrestle every day with the problems of whom to tell, as well as how, when, and how much. The same difficulties arise in social work research.

To summarize, the National Association of Social Workers (1980) has published a code of ethics in which scholarship and research are addressed in six ethical guidelines. These guidelines are presented in Figure 2.2 below.

Political and Social Considerations

The last factor that affects social work research is political and social considerations. Ethics and politics are closely interrelated, but a useful distinction exists in that ethics has mostly to do with the methods employed in the research study, whereas politics is concerned with the practical costs and uses of the study's findings.

Consider, for example, the area of race relations. Most social researchers in the 1960s supported the cause of African American equality in America. In 1969, Arthur Jensen, a Harvard psychologist, examined data on racial differences in IQ test results and concluded that genetic differences between African Americans and Caucasians accounted for the lower IQ scores of African Americans. Jensen was labeled a racist,

---

Guidelines for Social Work Research

E. **Scholarship and Research.** The social worker engaged in study and research should be guided by the conventions of scholarly inquiry.

1. The social worker engaged in research should consider carefully its possible consequences for human beings.
2. The social worker engaged in research should ascertain that the consent of participants is voluntary and informed, without any implied deprivation or penalty for refusal to participate, and with due regard for participants' privacy and dignity.
3. The social worker engaged in research should protect participants from unwarranted physical or mental discomfort, distress, harm, danger, or deprivation.
4. The social worker who engages in the evaluation of services or cases should discuss them only for professional purposes and only with persons directly and professionally concerned with them.
5. Information obtained about participants in research should be treated as confidential.
6. The social worker should take credit only for work actually done in connection with scholarly and research endeavors and should credit contributions made by others.

FIGURE 2.2 Scholarship and Research Guidelines for Social Work Researchers

and such was the furor surrounding his study, that other people were reluctant to pursue any line of inquiry involving comparisons between Caucasians and African Americans.

Consequently, a needed investigation into the higher rate of mortality seen in African American women with breast cancer as compared to similarly afflicted Caucasian women was not conducted. The study may have revealed racial differences in genetic predispositions to breast tumors, and the National Cancer Institute, at that time, was understandably reluctant to use the word "genetic" in connection with African Americans. It is not infrequently the case that sensitivity about vulnerable populations leads to avoidance of research studies that might benefit those groups. Consider Box 2.3 that presents a useful discussion on bias and insensitivity regarding gender and culture.

Politics plays an important role not only in what research studies are

---

Box 2.3

Bias and Insensitivity Regarding Gender and Culture

In several chapters of this book you will encounter examples of how gender and cultural bias and insensitivity can hinder the methodological quality of a study and therefore the validity of its findings. Much has been written about these problems in recent years, and some have suggested that when researchers conduct studies in a sexist manner or in a culturally insensitive manner, they are not committing just methodological errors, but they are also going awry ethically.

The question of ethics arises because some studies are perceived to perpetuate harm to women and minorities. Feminist and minority scholars have suggested a number of ways that such harm can be done. Interviewers who are culturally insensitive can offend minority respondents. If they conduct their studies in culturally insensitive ways, their findings may yield implications for action that ignore the needs and realities of minorities, may incorrectly (and perhaps stereotypically) portray minorities, or may inappropriately generalize in an unhelpful way. By the same token, studies with gender bias or insensitivity may be seen as perpetuating a male-dominated world or failing to consider the potentially different implications for men and women in one's research.

Various authors have recommended ways to try to avoid cultural and gender bias and insensitivity in one's research. We will cover some of these recommendations in greater depth in later chapters on methodology, but we'll mention them here as well, in light of their potential ethical relevance. Among the more commonly recommended guidelines regarding research on minorities are the following:

- Spend some time immersing yourself directly in the culture of the minority group(s) that will be included in your study (for example, using participant observation methods described in Chapter 14) before finalizing your research design.
- Engage minority scholars and community representatives in the formulation of the research problem and in all the stages of the research to ensure that the research is responsive to the needs and perspectives of minorities.
- Involve representatives of minority groups who will be studied in the development of the research design and measurement instruments.
- Do not automatically assume that instruments successfully used in prior studies of whites can yield valid information when applied to minorities.
- Use culturally sensitive language in your measures, perhaps including a non-English translation.
- Use in-depth pretesting of your measures to correct problematic language and flaws in translation.
- Use bilingual interviewers when necessary.
- Be attuned to the potential need to use minority interviewers instead of non-minorities to interview minority respondents.
- In analyzing your data, look for ways in which the findings may differ among different categories of ethnicity.
- Avoid an unwarranted focus exclusively on the deficits of minorities; perhaps focus primarily on their strengths.

In her book, *Nonsexist Research Methods*, Margrit Eichler recommends the following feminist guidelines to avoid gender bias and insensitivity in one's research:

- If a study is done on only one sex, make that clear in the title and the narrative and don't generalize the finding to the other sex.
- Don't use sexist language or concepts (i.e., males referred to as head of household, while females referred to as spouses).
- Don't use a double standard in framing the research question (such as looking at the work-parenthood conflict for mothers but not for fathers).
- Don't overemphasize male-dominated activities in research instruments (such as by assessing social functioning primarily in terms of career activities and neglecting activities in homemaking and child rearing).
- In analyzing your data, look for ways in which the findings may differ for men and women.
- Don't assume that measurement instruments that have been used successfully with males are automatically valid for women.
- Be sure to report the proportion of males and females in your study sample.

funded or conducted but in what findings are published. Contrary opinions or unpopular opinions are no longer punished, as they were in Galileo's day, by the Inquisitional Tribunal or the rack, but they are still punished. Punishment may be delivered in the form of articles and books that are never published, invitations to present research papers that are never offered, academic appointments that are never given—and research proposals that are never funded.

A research study can be an extremely expensive endeavor. If a funding body cannot be found to support the research proposal, the study may never be conducted. Funding bodies tend either to be governments or to be influenced by government policies; and a person doing a social work research study is as interested as anyone else in money, recognition, and professional advancement. It is therefore often the case that funded studies follow directions consistent with the prevailing political climate. For example, studies under one government may inquire into ways of improving social services and better designs for public housing. Under another government, attention may shift to the efficiency of existing programs, as measured through program evaluation.

It is important to remember, though, that not all research studies are expensive and many can be conducted without the aid of government money. No extra funding is needed to integrate evaluation into the normal routine of clinical practice. Program evaluations do not cost large amounts of money when conducted by program staff themselves.

In sum, social work research projects are affected not only by the personal biases of the person conducting the study, but also by prevailing beliefs on such sensitive issues as race, gender, poverty, disability, sexual orientation, violence, and so forth. Government positions both shape and are shaped by these beliefs, leading to support of some research directions but not of others. Legitimate inquiry is sometimes restricted by fear that data uncovered on one of these sensitive issues will be misinterpreted or misused, thereby bringing harm to vulnerable client groups.

SUMMARY

Essentially, in this text we deal with the standardized procedures used to conduct a social work research study. Underlying these procedures, however, are the research contexts in which the studies must take place. Some of these factors are the profession, the social work agency, the researcher, the practitioners, professional ethics, and political and social factors.

Before beginning any study, there are three precautionary ethical measures that must be taken: obtaining the participant's informed written consent, designing the study in an ethical manner, and ensuring that others will be properly told about the findings.

In this chapter we have presented the basic contexts that underlie social work research studies and the social and political contexts in which they are conducted. Now that we know the six factors that shape all research studies, we will turn our attention to how we go about selecting *what* to study—the topic of Chapter 3.

STUDY QUESTIONS

1. List and describe in your own words the six factors that affect social work research studies. Provide a social work example of each.

2. Out of the six factors you listed in Question 1, which one do you feel affects social work research studies the most? Why? The least? Why?

3. How would you go about trying to account for each one of the six factors that affect social work research studies when doing a study on abortion?

4. A simple consent form is presented in Figure 2.1. Does it contain all the necessary information that it should, taking into consideration the contents of this chapter? Why, or why not? Justify your answer.

5. Write a hypothetical informed consent form for each one of the studies in Boxes 2.1 and 2.2. Do you feel that an informed consent form would have biased the studies contained in the two boxes? Why, or why not? Justify your responses. How could the studies contained in the two boxes have been conducted differently so that they might have been more ethical?

6. Review Box 2.1. Answer the questions that were raised at the end of the box.

7. Review Box 2.2. Answer the questions that were raised at the end of the box.

8. At the library, choose a social work research article. Discuss how each of the six factors that affect social work research could have affected the study. Discuss in detail.

9. At the library, choose a social work research article. Write a hypothetical informed consent form that the researcher could have used in his or her study, given the contents of this chapter.

10. Go to the library and identify a social work research article. Discuss the political and social considerations that you think drove the researcher to do the study.

REFERENCES AND FURTHER READINGS

Adams, G.R., & Schvaneveldt, J.D. (1991). *Understanding research methods* (2nd ed., pp. 25-35, 261-263). White Plains, NY: Longman.

American Psychological Association. (1973). *Ethical principles in the conduct of research with human participants.* Washington, DC: Author.

Anastas, J.W., & MacDonald, M.L. (1994). *Research design for social work and the human services* (pp. 233-257). New York: Lexington Books.

Babbie, E.R. (1992). *The practice of social research* (6th ed., pp. 462-482). Pacific Grove, CA: Wadsworth.

Bailey, K.D. (1994). *Methods of social research* (4th ed., pp. 453-472). New York: Free Press.

Bisno, H., & Borowski, A. (1985). The social and psychological contexts of research. In R.M. Grinnell, Jr. (Ed.). *Social work research and evaluation* (2nd ed., pp. 83-100). Itasca, IL: F.E. Peacock.

Borowski, A. (1988). Social dimensions of research. In R.M. Grinnell, Jr. (Ed.),

Social work research and evaluation (3rd ed., pp. 42-64). Itasca, IL: F.E. Peacock.

Chronicle of Higher Education: "Scholar who submitted bogus article to journals may be disciplined," November 2, 1988, pp. A1, A7.

Eichler, M. (1988). *Nonsexist research methods.* Boston: Allen & Unwin.

Frankfort-Nachmias, C., & Nachmias, D. (1992). *Research methods in the social sciences* (4th ed., pp. 73-94). New York: St. Martin's Press.

Gabor, P.A., & Grinnell, R.M., Jr. (1994). *Evaluation and quality improvement in the human services* (pp. 301-316). Needham Heights, MA: Allyn & Bacon.

Gilchrist, L.D., & Schinke, S.P. (1988). Research ethics. In R.M. Grinnell, Jr. (Ed.), *Social work research and evaluation* (3rd ed., pp. 65-79). Itasca, IL: F.E. Peacock.

Grinnell, R.M., Jr., & Williams, M. (1990). *Research in social work: A primer* (pp. 2-26). Itasca, IL: F.E. Peacock.

Judd, C.M., Smith E.R., & Kidder, I.H. (1991). *Research methods in social relations* (6th ed., pp. 477-528). Fort Worth, TX: Harcourt Brace.

Leedy, P.D. (1993). *Practical research: Planning and design* (3rd ed., pp. 128-131). New York: Macmillan.

Marlow, C. (1993). *Research methods for generalist social work practice* (pp. 13-14, 40, 58-59, 94-95, 117-120). Pacific Grove, CA: Wadsworth.

Milgram, S. (1963). Behavioral study of obedience. *Journal of Abnormal and Applied Social Psychology, 67,* 371-378.

Milgram, S. (1974). *Obedience to authority: An experimental view.* New York: Harper & Row.

Monette, D.R., Sullivan, T.J., & DeJong, C.R. (1994). *Applied social research* (3rd ed., pp. 44-67). Fort Worth, TX: Harcourt Brace.

National Association of Social Workers. (1980). *National association of social workers code of ethics.* Silver Spring, MD: Author.

Neuman, W.L. (1994). *Social research methods* (2nd ed., pp. 427-459). Needham Heights, MA: Allyn & Bacon.

New York Times: "Test of journals is criticized as unethical," September 27, 1988, pp. 21, 25.

New York Times: "Charges dropped on bogus work," April 4, 1989, p. 21.

Royse, D.D. (1991). *Research methods in social work* (pp. 233-252). Chicago: Nelson-Hall.

Rubin, A., & Babbie, E. (1993). *Research methods for social work* (2nd ed., pp. 56-87). Pacific Grove, CA: Wadsworth.

Schinke, S.P. (1981). Ethics. In R.M. Grinnell, Jr. (Ed.), *Social work research and evaluation* (pp. 57-70). Itasca, IL: F.E. Peacock.

Schinke, S.P. (1985). Ethics. In R.M. Grinnell, Jr. (Ed.), *Social work research and evaluation* (2nd ed., pp. 101-114). Itasca, IL: F.E. Peacock.

Schuerman, J. (1989). Editorial. *Social Service Review, 63,* 1,3.

Weinbach, R.W. (1985). The agency and professional contexts of research. In R.M. Grinnell, Jr. (Ed.), *Social work research and evaluation* (2nd ed., pp. 66-82). Itasca, IL: F.E. Peacock.

Weinbach, R. W. (1988). Agency and professional contexts of research. In R.M. Grinnell, Jr. (Ed.), *Social work research and evaluation* (3rd ed., pp. 25-41). Itasca, IL: F.E. Peacock.

Yegidis, B.L., & Weinbach, R.W. (1991). *Research methods for social workers* (pp. 18-32). White Plains, NY: Longman.

Part II

Problem Formulation

PART II CONTAINS FIVE CHAPTERS that introduce readers to the problem formulation and measurement processes in social work research. More specifically, Chapter 3 provides a discussion on how research problems, or ideas, are developed. Chapter 4 describes how research questions are derived from these problem areas, while Chapter 5 discusses how to derive and formulate research hypotheses from research questions. Chapter 6 introduces the concepts of validity and reliability, and Chapter 7 presents some of the more common measuring instruments that can be used in social work research.

Chapter 3

Research Problems

T HE LAST CHAPTER presented the various "research" contexts that we must take into consideration when doing a research study. In this chapter we discuss the factors that influence how research ideas, more commonly referred to as research problems, are selected. Throughout the remainder of the book, we shall continue to explore the problem-solving process, beginning in this chapter with a closer look at the factors that affect the first phase in the process: selecting research problems to study.

FACTORS INFLUENCING PROBLEM SELECTION

In social work practice, the client's problem, or at least the general problem area, is determined largely by the client (with the help of the worker). Researchers, however, have the freedom to select research problems at their leisure, and this freedom, in itself, may sometimes be a problem. It is a little like walking through a shopping mall, looking for a gift to give a friend, surrounded by tantalizing possibilities, and wondering what to buy. In general, the selection of the gift will be influenced by four main factors. It will be something that the giver likes and can afford, something the recipient will like, something that is socially acceptable—perhaps not a book on social work research—and, very probably, something that just happens to catch the giver's eye.

The selection of a social work research problem is influenced by the same four factors that were faced by the gift-giver above. First, the problem must attract the researcher and must not be too difficult to solve, given the researcher's own capabilities and resources. Second, the problem must be important to those who will receive, consume, or facilitate the research study such as agency staff, administrators, and the professional community. Third, the problem should take into account the current social and cultural values. And, fourth, there will probably be an element of opportunity or luck.

The Researcher

Personal interest on the part of the researcher is usually the main motivating factor in the selection of a research problem. A research study may continue for a lengthy period, sometimes years; it may involve dull and seemingly endless stretches in which the work is mechanical and boring. Therefore, it is important for the initial interest to be deep and abiding, not just a passing fancy.

The interest will often arise from personal or work experience. The person doing a study may be interested in bereavement counseling because of a personal loss, or in parent-support groups because of family problems with a child. Perhaps a past client's experience in court provoked an interest in the justice system, or an interest in single mothers stemmed from work with high school adolescents who were pregnant.

Interest on the part of the researcher forms the foundation of a successful study. However, interest can also prejudice the study's results since people tend to hold the firmest opinions on subjects they feel most strongly about. A research study must therefore be designed in such a way that the biases of the researcher have the least possible chance of influencing the study's results.

The selection of the research problem will be influenced not only by personal interest but also by the researcher's particular abilities. A researcher who has a great deal of skill and experience in interviewing children may choose a problem area in which data must be collected through interviews with children. For example, the problem selected may be to discover if there is a relationship between the success of foster care placements and foster children's attitudes toward their biological parents. Some of the data on both "success" and "attitudes" will need to be collected through interviews with children.

The selection of the problem will also depend on the researcher's personal resources. If there is no money for travel, for example, the problem cannot be one that involves interviewing children across the country. Money for travel might be acquired through a research grant, but then the researcher has to have the skills and contacts necessary to acquire the grant. Similarly, the researcher will need to have the professional status required to gain permission to interview the children. It is not only the desire to solve a problem that is important: Personal skills, professional status, and access to resources also play a part.

Professional and Agency Considerations

Sometimes, a researcher's own interest is directed or shaped by outside sources. Career aspirations may necessitate some research experience, even for people whose talents and interests lie in other areas. A student in a graduate program may be offered a position as a research assistant that involves various research tasks. Similarly, staff members working in an agency may be asked to take on a research study for their organization. Perhaps the board of directors may decide that a program evaluation should be undertaken and a senior staff member will be asked to oversee the task. Or a problem may arise within the agency that a particular departmental supervisor is expected to resolve.

For example, there may be a concern that child protection staff are spending too much time investigating child abuse allegations that turn out to be unfounded. The director may want to know if this is so and, if it is so, why. Perhaps there really has been an increase in the number of unfounded child abuse complaints, possibly due to increased pressure on local teachers to report the slightest suspicion of child abuse. Perhaps less experienced staff are failing to verify actual abuse, or new regulations have led to confusion about how "unfounded" is defined.

Research studies related to agencies are frequently required of senior staff, even those who have little interest in research and only rudimentary skills in research methods. Often line-level workers will be involved, sometimes gathering data as directed and sometimes participating more fully in the development of problem-solving strategies. Occasionally, line-level workers will themselves identify problems and initiate smaller studies, either alone or together with other staff. It is, therefore, very important that all social workers know at least enough about research methods to be able to competently tackle problems arising within the normal course of day-to-day agency operations.

Research endeavors are not only useful in terms of solving problems: They can improve the agency's image in the eyes of its funders and community groups. The image-building aspect is particularly important if the agency serves a client group that has caught the public's attention. For example, public attention may focus on the mentally delayed following a decision to integrate these children into the "regular" school system. Concern about the decision will more readily be averted if research results can show that integration is beneficial to these children, has no adverse effect upon the "regular" school population, and serves, in addition, to increase public acceptance of these children in general.

The danger here is that the decision to integrate may precede the research studies necessary to determine the advantages and limitations of the integration. If this is the case, there will inevitably be pressure upon researchers, first to select integration as a topic for study and, second, to produce the "right" results: That is, results that support a decision already made. Even the least biased researcher using the best possible research design will find it difficult to maintain total objectivity under such conditions.

Nevertheless, it is not uncommon for policy decisions to be made without the support of objective evidence, often because the relevant data are not available when the decision has to be made. Instead, decisions may be based upon such factors as political expediency, personal beliefs, and the social and cultural values accepted at the time.

Applied and Pure Research Studies. There is no doubt that research results can be immediately useful to agencies in terms of satisfying funding bodies, promoting good public relations, or improving the agency's own service delivery. Research that is useful in this way is known as *applied research*. Often, the problem selected by the applied researcher is concerned with evaluating the effectiveness or efficiency of agency practice. How well is the agency serving its clients? How well is it meeting the needs of the local community? Does it wastefully duplicate services provided by some other local social service agency? These kinds of applied research questions are the province of *program evaluation*.

Applied research techniques can also be used by individual social workers to evaluate the effectiveness of their personal practice with clients. How effective is a particular intervention with a particular type of client or client system? Is one intervention more effective than another in solving a particular problem? Questions like these are addressed through *single-system designs*, which are discussed in Chapter 10.

Applied research studies involve problems that need to be solved in order to aid decision making at line levels, managerial levels, or policy levels. Such studies are designed to directly benefit a specific client system, whether it be a national organization, a single agency, or an individual worker helping a client. However, some research studies are not intended to be immediately and practically useful. Instead, their purpose is to increase theoretical knowledge in the belief that such knowledge will provide indirect benefit to all agencies and clients later on. These studies are known as *pure research studies* and involve problems that are unrelated to the immediate needs of the agencies in which the studies are conducted.

For example, a pure research problem might concern the relationship between divorce and loneliness, or between family cohesion and delinquency. A study of delinquent youths in less and more cohesive families will require cooperation from one or several agencies in order to locate the families and collect the data. Since the study will not directly benefit the agency, the staff will inevitably have to give time to the project, and some reluctance on the part of the agency is to be expected.

Cooperation will likely be given only if the research study is designed to use the least possible amount of the agency's resources, and to intrude only minimally on the agency's normal operations and its current or former clients. The research problem will have to be selected with these limitations in mind, and perhaps its scope will have to be reduced to meet the agency's requirements.

In sum, applied research embraces two complementary aspects: program evaluation, whose purpose is to evaluate the effectiveness or efficiency of the whole or part of a social program; and single-system designs, whose purpose is to evaluate the effectiveness of interventions with a single-client system. Applied research directly benefits agencies, administrators, social workers, and clients in that it facilitates immediate decision making. Conversely, the purpose of pure research is to increase knowledge for the indirect benefit of social workers and clients at a later time.

Personal, Social, and Cultural Values

The previous chapter indicated the importance of how current value systems shape research studies. Values also shape how research problems are selected. Research studies in sensitive areas may not be undertaken and, even if they are undertaken, their results may not be used. For example, as president of the United States, Richard Nixon appointed a national commission to inquire into the consequences of pornography. One of the results of the commission was that no connection could be found between exposure to pornography and an increased likelihood of committing sex crimes. Since this finding ran contrary to the prevalent belief that viewing pornography leads to sex crimes, the research results were disregarded.

The probability that results will be used is usually taken into account when selecting a research problem. It will not be useful to explore the possible effectiveness of sex education in the local school, for example, if members of the school board believe that sex education is sinful. On the other hand, the researcher may not be interested in the reactions of the board. He or she may prefer to adopt a pure research perspective, aiming to increase knowledge about the consequences of sex education in general, without reference to the needs of any particular school.

Social value systems are inextricably linked to the issue of social change. Few social work scholars would be comfortable investigating poverty without some hope that the results of their studies would be used to alleviate the conditions of the poor. Similarly, most researchers into women's issues would like their studies to contribute to the improved status of women. The danger here is that the search for truth may be compromised by the desire to effect political reform.

A researcher with a feminist orientation may not wish to publish a finding suggesting that some women invite sexual harassment, because such a finding may hinder political action or offend feminist colleagues. The result of attention to social-change issues may thus be that unpalatable results are deliberately not found, or are not published if they are found: in other words, that truth is compromised.

From the opposite perspective, of course, the result of attention to truth may be that legitimate social-change goals remain unmet. It is a matter for the individual researcher to decide whether a particular research study should be *about* the problem or *for* the problem: *about* poverty or *for* the poor, *about* women or *for* women. The nature of the research problem selected will be greatly influenced by this decision.

Opportunity or Luck

Very often, the final decision about which research problem will be studied depends on chance. The researcher may encounter an old acquaintance who suggests cooperating in a certain study; an agency serving a particular client group may offer facilities; data about a particular problem may be found to be available; a research proposal made long ago may suddenly be accepted; or funding may be offered for a research study into a specific problem area. None of these eventualities alone will determine the problem to be studied, but there is no doubt that the balance is often tipped by an unforeseen opportunity, an element of luck. Consider the origins of research ideas presented in Boxes 3.1 and 3.2.

Box 3.1

On the Origins of Research Ideas

In this chapter, we outline some of the sources of ideas for social work research. As discussed, some research studies are derived from existing theory. This is especially true of the hypothesis-testing research that characterizes experiments to be discussed in Chapter 8. More often than not, however, we get our research ideas from everyday observations and experiences.

According to John Darley, his and Bibb Latane's research study on bystander interventions stemmed from a widely publicized incident in New York City. A young woman named Kitty Genovese was brutally murdered while thirty-eight of her neighbors watched from their windows without so much as calling the police until her assailant had departed. Shocked by this incident, Darley and Latane:

met over dinner and began to analyze the bystanders' reactions. Because we were social psychologists, we thought not about how people are different nor about the personality flaws of the "apathetic" individuals who failed to act that night, but rather about how people are the same and how anyone in that situation might react as did these people. By the time we finished our dinner, we formulated several factors that together could lead to the surprising result: no one helping. Then we set about conducting experiments that isolated each factor and demonstrated its importance in an emergency situation. (Reported in Myers, 1983:394)

Box 3.2

More on the Origins of Research Ideas

Robert Cialdini (1980:27-28), whose research study involves social influence processes, tells how a personal experience led him to investigate a highly effective fund-raising tactic.

I answered the door early one evening to find a young woman who was canvassing my neighborhood for the United Way. She identified herself and asked if I would give a monetary donation. It so happened that my home university has an active United Way organization and I had given in-house a few days earlier. It was also the end of the month and my finances were low. Besides, if I gave to all the solicitors for charity who came to my door, I would quickly require such service for myself. As she spoke, I had already decided against a donation and was preparing my reply to incorporate the above reasons. Then it happened. After asking for a contribution, she added five magic words. I know they were *the* magic words because my negative reply to the donation request itself literally caught in my throat when I heard them. "Even a penny will help," she said. And with that, she demolished my anticipated response. All the excuses I had prepared for failing to comply were based on financial considerations. They stated that I could not afford to give to her now or to her, too. But she said, "Even a penny will help" and rendered each of them impotent. How could I claim an inability to help when she claimed that "even a penny" was a legitimate form of aid? I had been neatly finessed into compliance. And there was another interesting feature of our exchange as well. When I stopped coughing (I really had choked on my attempted rejection), I gave her *not* the penny she mentioned but the amount I usually allot to charity solicitors. At that, she thanked me, smiled innocently, and moved on.

Together with his then-graduate student Dave Schroeder, Cialdini analyzed the situation and concluded that two sources of social influence had been activated by the addendum "Even a penny will help." First, it removed any excuses for not offering at least some aid. Second, it made it more difficult to maintain one's altruistic self-image without contributing. Cialdini and Schroeder then went out to find a naturalistic fund-raising context for testing their ideas.

CRITERIA FOR RESEARCH PROBLEMS

No final decision can be made about the problem to be studied until we have determined that the prospective problem meets four criteria. These criteria are that the research problem must be (1) relevant, (2) researchable, (3) feasible, and (4) ethically acceptable.

Relevancy

Every conceivable research problem is relevant to someone in some context. Relevancy here will therefore be taken to mean relevant to social workers in a social work context. Since the person undertaking the study will be a social worker, the first questions to be asked with regard to relevancy are: Would persons in other disciplines be more qualified than social workers to study the problem? and, Will they study it if social workers do not?

For example, consider a study to explore the relationship between family stress and children dropping out of school. Such a study would be of interest to educational psychologists and sociologists as well as to social workers, and might properly be undertaken by people within any of these three disciplines. However, one of the purposes of the study may be to assess whether hiring a social worker to combat family stress would assist a certain school board in its efforts to reduce its student dropout rate. If this is the case, it could be argued that the problem is particularly a social work problem since it is specifically relevant to social workers.

Naturally, of most importance is that the study is conducted, no matter by whom. Disciplines in the social sciences—social work, sociology, psychology, anthropology, political science, education, economics—overlap to such a degree that it is often difficult to distinguish *social work* research from *social* research. A general rule of thumb is that the problem must be relevant to some aspect of social welfare: It must be important to social workers whether or not it is important to others as well.

A second question to be asked with regard to relevancy has to do with priorities. In an ideal world, any problem of concern to people or society would be worthy of study, but in the real word of limited resources, the relative importance of the problem has to be addressed. Some problems have already been studied to such an extent that, while not everything is known, further studies would be difficult to justify. For example, the effects of poverty on social functioning are widely understood, and additional data may only confirm what is already known.

"Known" of course, is a relative word in itself since nothing in science is known for certain, and all confirmatory studies are useful in that they increase the likelihood of the known being true. Nevertheless, research efforts are best focused on gaps in knowledge: what do we *not* know and, most important, how badly do we want to know it?

The relative importance of various areas of study is a sensitive topic since the majority of social work practitioners and researchers would argue that their own field of endeavor is at least as important as any other, and more important than most. Probably the best way to ascertain what gaps in knowledge most need to be filled is to turn to the professional literature. Journal articles and books often indicate that more work needs to be done in such and such a specific area. When several authors agree that a knowledge gap exists, the reader can be fairly sure that it does exist and that others are interested in seeing it filled.

If there are several knowledge gaps, all of potential interest to the researcher, an additional criterion might be the practical use to which the results of the study can be put. Some pure research problems are highly abstract and, while they are of interest, have little foreseeable practical application. Other problems, of more immediate practical concern, might have a higher priority in these times of budget restraint.

Researchability

When a problem has been tentatively selected for study, the next question to ask is: Is it researchable? As previously mentioned, some problems by their very nature do not lend themselves to scientific study. The difficulty that so absorbed medieval theologians concerning how many angels could sit on the head of a pin is one such problem. Problems relating to ethical controversies, phrased in terms of "should" or "ought," are another example.

It is not possible to use the problem-solving method to determine whether abortion is "right" and should be legalized. Neither is it possible to solve the problem of whether fathers ought to have the same rights as mothers to decide to abort an unborn child. These are issues of ethics, and opinion, and research studies cannot determine a "correct" answer to either question.

Feasibility

If the problem can be solved using the problem-solving method, the next question is: How readily can it be solved? or How feasible is it? This is a question that relates both to available resources and to ethical concerns. Some problems, for example, are just too large to be tackled without an army of researchers and a multimillion-dollar budget. Sexism in the workplace is a problem falling into this category, whereas the smaller problem of discriminatory hiring by employers in a particular profession might be a feasible project for study.

All research studies involve the collection of data. Sometimes data are collected from clients or people involved with clients, sometimes from client files or other agency records. Data are often very hard to obtain. Records may be incomplete; clients may disappear or refuse to be interviewed; court records may be sealed; permission may not be granted by agencies to access various files.

Sometimes, the difficulty of obtaining the necessary data can be resolved without abandoning or altering the problem. For example, a problem concerning the effect of community action on street gangs requires information about street gangs. It may not be possible or safe to interview street gang members, but data collected through interviews with police and probation officers and community leaders may be sufficient, depending on the precise nature of the research question.

Sometimes, the difficulty of obtaining data cannot be satisfactorily resolved. If the problem concerns the attitudes of the terminally ill toward social work counseling, for example, and permission is not granted by a hospital to interview its patients who are terminally ill, the study cannot be conducted. A different problem will have to be formulated: perhaps the attitudes of relatives of the terminally ill toward social work counseling. Be that as it may, possible difficulties associated with collecting the data must always be considered before a researcher decides to explore a particular problem.

It is not only data collection that is sometimes difficult: The data must also be analyzed. The researcher's own skills, previously mentioned as an important factor, play a large part here. If the researcher does not have the expertise to perform the required data analysis and cannot afford to hire a consultant, the solution of the problem is not feasible for that particular researcher.

Issues of time and cost may also mean that a study is not feasible for a particular researcher. Costs can be easily underestimated. There may be travel costs to collect data, long-distance telephone charges, printing and copying expenses, costs for data processing and analysis, postage costs for mailing out questionnaires, and perhaps remuneration if research assistants are to be hired for interviewing or data entry. Non-response to questionnaires may mean multiple mailings; cancelled interviews may involve additional travel costs.

In sum, a problem is researchable if it lends itself to solution by the problem-solving method. The solution of the problem is feasible if all the necessary data can be collected and analyzed by the particular researcher, given his or her own resources and situation.

Ethical Acceptability

Ethical acceptability is a primary issue in any research study. Most universities have ethics committees to which proposed studies by faculty or students must be submitted for approval before the study commences. Many social service agencies have similar committees, whose responsibility it is to see that ethical standards are not violated by any research study conducted within the agency.

Usually, the ethical standards in question have to do with service to clients. Client confidentiality is always a concern since many researchers request access to clients and/or client files. A second concern is that service to clients may be interrupted or compromised by research requirements. Social work practitioners may be understandably reluctant to have clients who are in crises bothered by researchers whose primary interest lies with the research study and not with the client. The completion of questionnaires takes time: time that the worker may well feel could be better spent in direct work with clients.

In addition, there is the ever-controversial matter of random selection of clients. The ethical dilemmas associated with randomly assigning clients to control and experimental groups were discussed in Chapter 2, as were dilemmas to do with deceiving research participants. It is sufficient here to stress again the fundamental principle of social work research: Increased knowledge must never be obtained at the expense of human beings. Consider the ethical implications presented in Box 3.3.

SUMMARY

The selection of a research problem is influenced by four main factors: the researcher's personal history, professional and agency considerations, social and cultural values, and opportunity (or luck). A particular problem area is considered to be appropriate for a social work research study only if it meets four criteria: relevancy, researchability, feasibility, and ethical acceptability.

In the next chapter, we will discuss how general research problems as just presented are refined into more specific research questions.

Box 3.3

Welfare Study Withholds Benefits from 800 Texans

The preceding front page headline greeted readers of the Sunday, February 11, 1990 edition of the *Dallas Morning News*. On the next line they read:

> Thousands of poor people in Texas and several other states are unwitting subjects in a federal experiment that denies some government help to a portion of them to see how well they live without it.

This was pretty strong stuff, and soon the story was covered on one of the national TV networks. Let's examine it further to assess its ethical acceptability.

The Texas Department of Human Services received federal money to test the effectiveness of a pilot program designed to wean people from the welfare rolls. The program was targeted to welfare recipients who found jobs or job training. *Before* the new program was implemented, these recipients received four months of free medical care and some child care after they left the welfare rolls. The new program extended these benefits to one year of Medicaid coverage and subsidized child care. The theory was that extending the duration of the benefits would encourage recipients to accept and keep entry-level jobs that were unlikely to offer immediate medical insurance or child care.

The federal agency granting the money attached an important condition. States receiving grants were required to conduct a scientifically rigorous experiment to measure the program's effectiveness in attaining its goal of weaning people from welfare. Some federal officials insisted that this requirement entailed randomly assigning some people to a control group that would be denied the new (extended) program and instead kept on the old program of only four months of benefits. The point of this was to maximize the likelihood that the recipient group (the experimental group) and the nonrecipient (control) group were equivalent in all relevant ways except for the receipt of the new program. If they were, and if the recipient group was weaned from welfare to a greater extent that the nonrecipient group, then it could be safely inferred that the new program, and not something else, caused the successful outcome. (We will examine this logic further in Chapter 11.)

If you have read many journal articles reporting on experimental studies, you are probably aware that many of them randomly assign about one-half of their subjects to the experimental group and the other half to the control group. Thus, this routine procedure denies the experimental condition to about one-half of the subjects. The Texas experiment was designed to include all eligible welfare recipients statewide, assigning 90 percent of them to the experimental group and 10 percent to the control group. Thus, only 10 percent of the subjects, which in this study amounted to 800 people, would be denied the new benefits if they found jobs. Although this seems more humane than denying benefits to 50 percent of the subjects, the newspaper account characterized the 800 people in the control group as "unlucky Texans" who seemed to be unfairly left out of a program that was extending benefits to everyone else who was eligible statewide, who numbered in the many thousands. Moreover, the newspaper report noted that the 800 control subjects would be denied the new program for two years in order to provide ample time to compare outcomes between the two groups. To boot, these 800 "unlucky Texans" were not to be informed of the new program or of the experiment. They were to be told of only the normal four-month coverage.

Advocates of the experiment defended this design, arguing that the control group would not be denied benefits. They would receive routine benefits, and the new benefits would not have been available for anyone in the first place unless a small group was randomly assigned to the routine policy. In other words, the whole point of the new benefits was to test a new welfare policy, not merely to implement one.

They further argued that the design was justified by the need to test for unintended negative effects of the new program, such as the possibility that some businesses might drop their child care or insurance coverage for employees, knowing that the new program was extending these benefits. That, in turn, they argued, could impel low-paid employees in those businesses to quit their jobs and go on welfare. By going on welfare and then getting new jobs, they would become eligible for the government's extended benefits, and this would make the welfare program more expensive.

Critics of the study, on the other hand, argued that it violated federal ethics standards such as voluntary participation and informed consent. Anyone in the study must be informed about it and all its consequences and must have the option to refuse to participate. One national think tank expert on ethics likened the experiment to the Tuskegee syphilis study, saying, "It's really not that different." He further asserted, "People ought not to be treated like things, even if what you get is good information."

In the aftermath of such criticism, Texas state officials decided to try to convince the federal government to rescind the control group requirement so that they could extend the new benefits to the 800 people in the control group. Instead of using a control group design, they wanted to extend benefits to everyone and find statistical procedures that would help ferret out program defects (a design that might have value, but which would be less conclusive as to what really causes what, as we will see in later chapters). They also decided to send a letter to the control group members explaining their special status.

Two days after the *Dallas Morning News* broke this story, it published a follow-up article reporting that the secretary of the U.S. Department of Health and Human Services, in response to the first news accounts, instructed his staff to cooperate with Texas welfare officials so that the project design would no longer deny the new program to the 800 control group members. Do you agree with his decision? Did the potential benefits of this experiment justify its controversial ethical practices?

It probably would not have been possible to form a control group had recipients been given the right to refuse to participate. Who would want to be denied extended free medical and child care benefits? Assuming it were possible, however, would that influence your opinion of the justification for denying them the new program? Do you agree with the expert who claimed that this study, in its original design, was not that different from the Tuskegee syphilis study? What if, instead of assigning 90 percent of the subjects to the experimental group, the study assigned only 10 percent to it? That way, the 800 assigned to the experimental group may have been deemed "lucky Texans," and the rest might not have been perceived as a small group of unlucky souls being discriminated against. In other words, perhaps there would have been fewer objections if the state had merely a small amount of funds to test out a new program on a lucky few. Do you think that would have changed the reaction? Would that influence your perception of the ethical justification for the experiment?

STUDY QUESTIONS

1. List and describe in your own words the four factors that influence the selection of research problems. Provide a social work example of each.

2. The previous chapter presented the various contexts that must be considered when doing a social work research study. This chapter presented the various factors that influence the selection of research problems. Integrate the contents of both chapters by writing an essay on how the contexts of research (Chapter 2) and the factors that influence problem selection (this chapter) are highly related to one another by providing an example of a research study that focuses on abortion issues for young adolescents.

3. List and discuss in your own words the four criteria that must be met for the selection of a final research problem. Provide an extended social work example throughout your discussion that specifically addresses the four criteria for problem selection.

4. Discuss how the four factors that influence problem selection are related to one another by providing one social work example that highlights each factor.

5. Go to the library and choose a social work research article. Discuss how each one of the four factors that influence problem selection could have affected the researcher doing the study. What additional factors do you feel influenced the researcher? Why?

6. Go to the library and identify a social work research article. Discuss how each of the four criteria for problem selection could have affected the researcher doing the study. What additional criteria do you feel could be added to the list? Why?

7. Go to the library and identify a social work research article. What agency and professional considerations do you feel the researcher had to consider when doing the study?

8. Discuss how the four factors that influence a problem area are relevant to a research study that focuses on abortion.

9. Discuss how the four criteria for research problems would be addressed in a study that focuses on political correctness or date rape.

10. Out of the four factors that influence problem selection, which one do you feel has the largest weight? The least weight? Why?

REFERENCES AND FURTHER READINGS

Adams, G.R., & Schvaneveldt, J.D. (1991). *Understanding research methods* (2nd ed., pp. 18-24). White Plains, NY: Longman.

Anastas, J.W., & MacDonald, M.L. (1994). *Research design for social work and the human services* (pp. 33-56). New York: Lexington Books.

Babbie, E.R. (1992). *The practice of social research* (6th ed., pp. 110, 40-44). Pacific Grove, CA: Wadsworth.

Bailey, K.D. (1994). *Methods of social research* (4th ed., pp. 21-38). New York:

Free Press.

Cialdini, R.B. (1980). Full-cycle social psychology. In L. Bickman (Ed.), *Applied social psychology annual* (vol 1, pp. 21-47). Beverly Hills, CA: Sage.

Dallas Morning News: "Welfare study withholds benefits from 800 Texans," February 11, 1990, p. 1.

Darley, J.M., & Latane, B. (1968). Bystander intervention in emergencies: Diffusion of responsibility. *Journal of Personality and Social Psychology, 8,* 377-383.

Frankfort-Nachmias, C., & Nachmias, D. (1992). *Research methods in the social sciences* (4th ed., pp. 51-54). New York: St. Martin's Press.

Grinnell, R.M., Jr., & Williams, M. (1990). *Research in social work: A primer* (pp. 58-85). Itasca, IL: F.E. Peacock.

Judd, C.M., Smith E.R., & Kidder, I.H. (1991). *Research methods in social relations* (6th ed., pp. 20-27). Fort Worth, TX: Harcourt Brace.

Leedy, P.D. (1993). *Practical research: Planning and design* (3rd ed., pp. 59-86). New York: Macmillan.

Marlow, C. (1993). *Research methods for generalist social work practice* (pp. 23-45). Pacific Grove, CA: Wadsworth.

Monette, D.R., Sullivan, T.J., & DeJong, C.R. (1994). *Applied social research* (3rd ed., pp. 68-76). Fort Worth, TX: Harcourt Brace.

Myers, D.G. (1983). *Social psychology.* New York: McGraw-Hill.

Neuman, W.L. (1994). *Social research methods* (2nd ed., pp. 55-78, 108-112). Needham Heights, MA: Allyn & Bacon.

Polansky, N.A. (1975). Theory construction and the scientific method. In N.A. Polansky (Ed.), *Social work research: Methods for the helping professions* (rev. ed., pp. 18-37). Chicago: University of Chicago Press.

Rothery, M. (1993). Problems, questions, and hypotheses. In R.M. Grinnell, Jr. (Ed.), *Social work research and evaluation* (4th ed., pp. 17-37). Itasca, IL: F.E. Peacock.

Royse, D.D. (1991). *Research methods in social work* (pp. 38-39). Chicago: Nelson-Hall.

Rubin, A., & Babbie, E. (1993). *Research methods for social work* (2nd ed., pp. 88-104). Pacific Grove, CA: Wadsworth.

Smith, N.J. (1985). Research goals and problems. In R.M. Grinnell, Jr. (Ed.), *Social work research and evaluation* (2nd ed., pp. 49-65). Itasca, IL: F.E. Peacock.

Smith, N.J. (1988). Formulating research goals and problems. In R.M. Grinnell, Jr. (Ed.), *Social work research and evaluation* (3rd ed., pp. 89-110). Itasca, IL: F.E. Peacock.

Yegidis, B.L., & Weinbach, R.W. (1991). *Research methods for social workers* (pp. 35-46). White Plains, NY: Longman.

Chapter 4

Research Questions

THE RESEARCH PROBLEMS considered in Chapter 3 have covered a wide area and were intentionally vague: for example, the attitudes of people toward counseling the terminally ill, or the relationship between family stress and high school dropout rates. These general and vague problem areas cannot be studied until they have been defined more precisely. What exactly do we want to know about the terminally ill and social work counseling? Why is the information needed? What precisely is the problem? What is the question, or more precisely, what is the specific *research* question that is contained within the general problem area?

TYPES OF RESEARCH QUESTIONS

All research ideas, or research problems, as presented in the last chapter must be further developed and refined into specific research questions. In general, research questions fall into three broad categories: exploration, description, and explanation. If little is known about the general problem area and we want to simply explore and gather facts, an *exploratory* study will be in order. Neither will such a study provide information that can be relied upon with any certainty nor can its results be generalized to other individuals with similar experiences who were not included in the study. The purpose of exploratory studies is largely to prepare the ground for later, more intensive work.

When some knowledge has been obtained through exploratory studies, the next task may be to describe a specific aspect of the problem area in greater detail, in either words or numbers. This will entail a *descriptive* study.

After descriptive studies have provided a substantial knowledge base in the problem area, we will be in a position to ask very specific and complex questions that hopefully will explain the facts that were previously gathered. These *explanatory* studies are needed in order to confirm or reject the possible explanations that were proposed in the descriptive study.

As shown in Figure 4.1, the three types of studies—exploratory, descriptive, and explanatory—lie on a knowledge continuum. Exploratory studies, at the left end of the continuum, begin with very little knowledge in the problem area and produce knowledge at only a low level of certainty. Descriptive studies, at the center of the continuum, begin with more knowledge and produce knowledge at a higher level of certainty. Explanatory studies, at the right end of the continuum, begin with quite a lot of knowledge and produce the most certain results.

It should be stressed that the knowledge-building continuum is just that—it is a *continuum*. Neither the level of knowledge possessed prior to the study nor the level of knowledge attained by the study can be assigned to discrete sections labeled exploratory, descriptive, and explanatory. Such a distinction is totally arbitrary.

Despite the arbitrary nature of the labels, exploratory, descriptive, and explanatory studies do differ considerably with respect to the way a research study is designed and the nature of the research question asked.

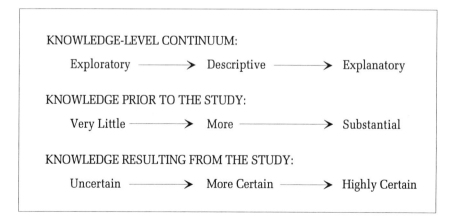

KNOWLEDGE-LEVEL CONTINUUM:

  Exploratory ———▶ Descriptive ———▶ Explanatory

KNOWLEDGE PRIOR TO THE STUDY:

  Very Little ———▶ More ———————▶ Substantial

KNOWLEDGE RESULTING FROM THE STUDY:

  Uncertain ———▶ More Certain ———▶ Highly Certain

FIGURE 4.1 The Knowledge-Generation Enterprise

Exploratory Research Questions

Exploratory studies are most useful when the problem area is relatively new. For example, in the United States during the 1970s, the development of new drugs to control the symptoms of mental illness together with new federal funding for small community-based mental health centers resulted in a massive discharge of people from large state-based mental health institutions.

Some social workers applauded this move as restoring the civil liberties of these people; others were concerned that inadequate community facilities would result in harm to them and community members alike. Social workers active in the 1970s were anxious to explore the results of the new movement, some with an eye to influencing local, state, and federal social policy. Others were interested in developing social programs to serve these people and their families.

The general problem area here is very broad: What are the consequences of a massive discharge of people who were psychiatrically challenged and who were once institutionalized? Many widely different research questions pertaining to this situation can be asked. Where are these recently discharged people living? Alone? In halfway houses? With their families? On the streets? Are they receiving proper medication and nutrition? What are their financial situations? What stresses are they imposing on family members and the communities in which they now reside? Do neighbors ridicule or help them? How do they spend their time? What work and leisure activities are appropriate for them? How do local authorities respond to them?

These kinds of questions are exploratory and attempt to gather facts in a hitherto unmapped general problem area. No single research study can answer all of them. We must decide what specific aspect of the general research problem the study will address, always in light of the use that will be made of the information derived from the study. For example, we may consider setting up community support groups for the families of these discharged people. In this case, a relevant question might be: What types of community support (if any) would most benefit families trying to care for them? Alternatively, we may try to determine their needs in order to develop various sorts of community-based social support facilities such as halfway houses. Relevant questions here might be: What type of previously institutionalized person would benefit the most from a halfway house?

These two different, but related, questions will involve attention to different factors. In the first case, the study would focus on the needs of the families with respect to the provision of community services. In the second case, the focus would be on the discharged people in relation to the services provided by halfway houses.

In each situation, the underlying purpose of the study would be to explore the problem of a massive discharge of people who were psychiatrically challenged and were once institutionalized, by asking more specific questions related to the problem area. The broad, vague, general problem area is gradually being refined until it is small enough and specific enough to be the subject of a feasible research study.

So, for example, at an exploratory level, we might interview these previously institutionalized people in an attempt to identify meaningful themes or issues that these people may have. These themes may raise further, more specific questions about the initial broad problem area. In response to the current question of what happens to these people after discharge, interviews with them may reveal a central theme, or issue: Because of difficulty finding housing, many return home to live with their parents. This situation then leads to emotional turmoil for some, but support for others. Having identified this trend to move home, we might then decide to pursue further inquiry focused on a descriptive question such as, "How many families are supportive to them and how many are not?"

The process of sifting a feasible research question from the broad mass of a problem area is like putting the problem through a series of successively finer sieves. Much of the larger problem will be temporarily set aside as topics for other studies. Only the small, definitive question surviving the final sieve will be addressed in the present study.

Descriptive Research Questions

The same sifting process applies to all three types of research studies—exploratory, descriptive, or explanatory. A descriptive study can describe one factor within a problem area, or it may describe the ways in which one factor is related to a second factor. Taking the previous example, we may decide to investigate not only how many of these previously institutionalized people return home to live with their families, but also how many of the families are supportive and how many are not. We could hypothesize that those families who are not supportive tend to have negative views about their offspring and to communicate these nonverbally, through exasperated sighs and angry confrontations.

Such negative reactions in response to family members diagnosed with a mental illness have been labeled "expressed emotion." We may decide to administer a standardized measuring instrument, which measures expressed emotion, to families who do not appear supportive to see whether, in fact, they show high levels of expressed emotion. The purpose of doing a descriptive research study is to gather facts. No attempts are be made to explain *why* some families are more supportive than others, or *why* some families have high expressed emotion while others do not. The *why* belongs to an explanatory study. A descriptive study only determines the *what*.

Explanatory Research Questions

Suppose a descriptive study has determined that the families who are perceived as supportive to their previously institutionalized children show low levels of expressed emotion, while those perceived as nonsupportive show high levels. An explanatory study may be undertaken to determine why this is so, or to identify appropriate interventions that might lower their expressed emotions.

If we hypothesize that high levels of expressed emotion are found when families do not know how to communicate clearly, we may wonder whether a psychoeducational group treatment intervention aimed at improving communication in families would resolve the amount of support perceived by their children. We may also look at the problem from many different angles. We might want to know whether involving these previously institutionalized people in a supportive network of peers could improve their self-independence so that they have less need of support from their parents. Again, these different questions will involve attention to different factors. One study may be concerned with family interaction and another with peer support. The research question finally selected determines the basic concepts around which the study will be designed.

CONCEPTS

Concepts are nothing more than ideas. The research questions mentioned previously all involve *concepts*. Take a female university professor, for example. She is a woman, and also a teacher. If she is married, she is a wife. If she has children, she is a mother. She may be a home owner, a committee member, an Asian, or a Catholic. She may be demanding or compassionate. All these characteristics of the university professor are concepts: They are ideas that are shared among members of a society to a greater or lesser degree.

Some ideas are perceived by all members of the same society in much the same way, while other ideas give rise to disagreement. For example, the concept of being a mother involves the concept of children and, specifically, the concept of having given birth to a child. Today, few people would deny that giving birth to a child is the only way of defining a mother. However, the idea of motherhood in Western society involves more than that.

Also involved are the concepts of loving, of caring for the child's physical needs, of offering the child emotional support, of advocating for the child with others, of accepting legal and financial responsibility for the child, and of being there for the child in all circumstances and at all times. Some would argue that a woman who does all these things is a mother, whether she has given birth or not. Further, however we feel about it, others would say that the biological mother is the only real mother even if she abandoned the child at birth.

Abstract Definitions Within Concepts

Abstract definitions are just that—they are abstract and mean many different things to many different people. They tend to give rise to controversy even when the concept being abstractly defined is a basic idea, like motherhood. Generally, the more abstract the concept, the greater is the potential for disagreement. Consider compassion, for example. A single individual may know what he or she means when describing another person as compassionate. However, it is unlikely that others will totally agree with his or her definition. The dictionary may not agree with anyone and may define compassion as "pity for suffering, with desire to help or to spare." Additionally, everyone may agree that this is, indeed, what is meant by compassion.

However, difficulties still arise because the quality of compassion, no matter how well defined, cannot be directly observed. "Pity for suffering" must be inferred from words or actions, and so must "desire to help." In other words, compassion can only be recognized by means of *indicators*. An indicator is something that is directly measurable that may or may not be directly observable within the concept. For the sake of simplicity and for all practical purposes, we will call indicators variables.

Often, it is not the concept about which people disagree; it is the variables that we believe make up the concept. Such disagreements about what variables make up concepts have profound implications for research studies. It will not be possible, for example, to undertake a study to find out whether women are more compassionate than men if no agreement can be reached about what words, feelings, or behaviors (variables) indicate compassion.

To summarize, a concept is nothing more than an idea. Specific, simple concepts such as gender directly reflect the real world. Male and female exist, can be observed, and can be "measured" in the sense that the observation can be recorded by placing a check mark in the appropriate box on a questionnaire or form. Similarly, age is a specific concept that can be observed and measured in various ways, from the passage of years to the degree of wear on organs in the body.

The more complex a concept becomes, the more theoretical and abstract it becomes, and the more difficult it is to observe directly. Concepts that cannot be observed directly are inferred through use of indicators: Depression, for example, may be inferred through body language and/or a score on a standardized measuring instrument that assesses the level of depression. Body language and the standardized measuring instrument are two (of the many) ways depression can be measured.

CONCEPTUALIZATION

The process of selecting the concepts to include in a research study is known as *conceptualization*. It is also the process whereby fuzzy and imprecise concepts are made more specific and precise by selecting variables that will be used to describe the concept under investigation. Like many other qualities of interest to social workers, compassion is a highly complex, abstract concept with many possible dimensions. Intelligence is another such complex concept, as are alienation, morale, conformity, cohesion, motivation, delinquency, prejudice, social status, and a host of others.

None of the above concepts exist in the sense that they can be touched, seen, heard, or in any way directly observed. They do not exist at all, in fact, except as abstractions in the human mind. Let us return to our example and ask the research question: Where do people who were once psychiatrically challenged and institutionalized live after they are discharged? There are two related concepts here, "previously institutionalized people who were psychiatrically challenged" and "discharged." Both concepts must be further clarified. Should these individuals be conceptualized as a people who have previously received treatment for a mental disorder but are not presently receiving treatment? If this definition is accepted, what about some of those who suffer frequent relapses and are "in treatment" and "not in treatment" alternately over long periods?

Similarly, a discharged person could be conceptualized as a person who was once institutionalized and no longer is. But what about individuals who were released from an institution on the understanding that they continue to receive treatment on an out-patient basis. Can they be said to have been "discharged" for the purposes of the study?

We could conceptualize a "discharged person" as a person who was "psychiatrically challenged and received institutional care but is not receiving it at the time of the study, whether or not he or she is still receiving out-patient care, and whether or not he or she is expected to need institutional care in the future."

We could also conceptualize a discharged person simply as a person who is no longer obliged to live in an institution. So far, the "discharged people," no matter how well defined, still includes all similar individuals everywhere, even those who were discharged a very long time ago. If our study is to be feasible, we need to define "previously institutionalized people who were psychiatrically challenged" in such a way that a research study can feasibly take place.

If the study is being conducted in the Oak Lawn community, for example we may decide that only those previously institutionalized people who were psychiatrically challenged in Oak Lawn will be included; or, if Oak Lawn happens to be a large community with several institutions that once served people with psychiatric diagnoses, only those from one of the institutions may be included. If the purpose of the study is to explore a recent massive discharge, only those recently discharged—say, within the last six months—may be of interest.

OPERATIONALIZATION

After the concepts have been identified in any given research study, the next step is to operationalize the variables within them. Operationalization goes one step beyond conceptualization in that it is the process of developing operational definitions of the variables contained within the concepts included in the study.

Operational Definitions

Operational definitions are the concrete and specific ways the variables are going to be measured. The unambiguous clarity of variables will never be sufficient to permit the measurement of them. Having made these decisions, we are now in a position to define, operationally, "previously institutionalized people who were psychiatrically challenged," as:

> A person who received residential care for a minimum of one year at Pine Brook Homes but is not receiving it at the time of the study, whether or not he or she is still receiving out-patient care, and whether or not he or she is expected to need institutional care in the future.

The above operational definition is sufficiently narrow and precise to enable us to list all the people who fit the definition, and to ask them where they are presently living and where they have lived since discharge.

In sum, operational definitions are precise definitions that help us to measure all the variables involved in a research study. Others may not agree with our operational definitions (or variables for that matter), but at least they will be in no doubt as to what our definitions are. Another person, who believes that a different result would be obtained if, for example, "previously institutionalized people who were psychiatrically challenged" were operationally defined differently, may choose to repeat the study, using another operational definition and making whatever measurements the definition demands. A concept usually contains a number of potential variables that can be used to measure it. Box 4.1 presents an interesting discussion of how the operationalization process is related to the naming of variables.

Let us review what we have said so far by using an example that is close to home—a good social worker. The concept is "good social work-

Box 4.1

The Importance of Variable Names

Operationalization is one of those things that's easier said than done. It is quite simple to explain to someone the purpose and importance of operational definitions for variables, and even to describe how operationalization typically takes place. However, until you've tried to operationalize a rather complex variable, you may not appreciate some of the subtle difficulties involved. Of considerable importance to the operationalization effort is the particular name that you have chosen for a variable. Let's consider an example from the field of Urban Planning.

A variable of interest to planners is citizen participation. Planners are convinced that participation in the planning process by citizens is important to the success of plan implementation. Citizen participation is an aid to planners' understanding of the real and perceived needs of a community, and such involvement by citizens tends to enhance their cooperation with and support for planning efforts. Although many different conceptual definitions might be offered by different planners, there would be little misunderstanding over what is *meant* by citizen participation. The name of the variable seems adequate.

However, if we asked different planners to provide very simple operational measures for citizen participation, we are likely to find a variety among their responses that does generate confusion. One planner might keep a tally of attendance by private citizens at city commission and other local government meetings; another might maintain a record of the different topics addressed by private citizens at similar meetings; while a third might record the number of local government meeting attendees, letters and phone calls received by the mayor and other pubic officials, and during a particular time period. As skilled researchers, we can readily see that each planner would be measuring (in a very simplistic fashion) a different *dimension* of citizen participation: extent of citizen participation, issues prompting citizen participation, and form of citizen participation. Therefore, the original *naming* of our variable, citizen participation, which was quite satisfactory from a conceptual point of view, proved inadequate for purposes of operationalization.

The precise and exact naming of variables is important in research. It is both essential to and a result of good operationalization. Variable names quite often evolve from an iterative process of forming a conceptual definition, then an operational definition, then renaming the concept to better match what can or will be measured. This looping process continues (our example above illustrates only one iteration), resulting in a gradual refinement of the variable name and its measurement until a reasonable fit is obtained. Sometimes the concept of the variable that you end up with is a bit different from the original one that you started with, but at least you are measuring what you are talking about, if only because you are talking about what you are measuring!

er." What is a good social worker? There are probably hundreds of indicators that can be used to determine "a good social worker" from "a bad social worker"—everything from client success (at one end of the continuum) to obtaining good grades in school (on the other end of the continuum). Let us take the easy one, grades, which can also be broken down into specific indicators such as grades in research, social policy, human behavior, practicum, and methods. The point is that concepts must be broken down into indicators, or variables, that are meaningful to the concept from which they were drawn. A student's grade in a research course (one variable) may not be a good indication of his or her overall grade point average (second variable), which in turn may not be relevant to being a good social worker (the concept). However, assuming that everything else is equal, it is logical to assume that a social work student who has a high G.P.A. will be a better social worker than one who has a low G.P.A.—the operative words are "everything else being equal."

VARIABLES

A variable must be capable of varying from one value to another. Suppose we have posed the question: Do job training programs help participants find jobs? This study is concerned with two variables—job training programs, and whether or not the participants who attended the programs found jobs—and these will be the two variables under investigation. From the way the question is presently phrased, the first variable, job training programs, refers to *all* job training programs everywhere. Similarly, the second variable, jobs found by program participants, involves all jobs found by all participants in every job training program the world over.

Unless the person doing a research study has unlimited money and time, such a study will not be feasible, and the research question needs to be more narrowly phrased. It may be more sensible to ask: Does a job training program, Program *X*, help participants find jobs? Now, the first variable refers only to a single job training program—Program *X*—and the second variable involves only jobs found by participants in Program *X*.

If the program has been running for a long time, all the jobs found by all the participants may still add up to a larger number than we wish to handle. Perhaps the research question should be rephrased yet again, as: Did Program *X* help participants to find jobs within six months after leaving the program? The point here is that the two variables that are going to be studied are directly derived from the research question, which is derived from the general problem area (unemployment). If they do not seem sensible, or if they cannot be measured, it is time to go back and look again at the research question.

Let us take another example. Suppose that a study is being conducted to determine whether the establishment of a small community mental health center, a form of a social work intervention, increases the social adjustment of previously institutionalized people who were psychiatrically challenged in the Oak Lawn community. At first glance, it may appear that there are four variables involved in this study: the community health center (the intervention), social adjustment, previously institutionalized people who were psychiatrically challenged, and the Oak Lawn community.

However, it is not just social adjustment that the study will explore. It is the social adjustment of previously institutionalized people who were psychiatrically challenged. Similarly, the study is not concerned with *all* previously institutionalized people who were psychiatrically challenged—only those in the Oak Lawn community. On closer examination, therefore, it becomes apparent that there are really only two variables: the community mental health center, and the social adjustment of previously institutionalized people who were psychiatrically challenged in the Oak Lawn community. These two variables can be classified into two types: independent variables and dependent variables.

Independent and Dependent Variables

Many research studies, such as the one concerning the community mental health center, focus on the relationship between two variables, called a *bivariate relationship*, from the prefix *bi-*, meaning *two*. It asks, in general terms: Does Variable X affect Variable Y? Or, *How* does Variable X affect Variable Y? If one variable affects the other, the variable that does the affecting is known as the *independent variable*, symbolized by X; and the variable that is affected is known as the *dependent variable*, symbolized by Y. If enough is known about the topic, and we have a good idea of what the effect will be, the question may be phrased: If X occurs, will Y result? If Variable X affects Variable Y, whatever happens to Y will depend on X.

In both of the examples given above, the purpose of the study was to determine whether one variable affected another. In the first example, the study sought to determine whether a job training program affected the jobs found by participants within six months after they finished the program. The job training program is not dependent on anything; at least, it is not dependent on anything made evident in the research question, and it is certainly not dependent on the jobs found by its graduates.

So, the number of jobs found by participants is the dependent variable and will hopefully be affected by the job training program, which is the independent variable. In the second example, the purpose is to discover whether the community mental center affects the social adjustment of previously institutionalized people who were psychiatrically challenged. Similarly, the social adjustment of these people is the dependent variable, while the independent variable is the community mental health center.

Some studies toward the exploratory end of the knowledge continuum are not concerned with the effect that one variable might have on another. Perhaps it is not yet known whether the variables are even associated, and it is far too soon to postulate what the relationship between them might be. For example, a descriptive study might ask: Is there a relationship between the attitudes of social workers toward transracial adoptions and the proportion of successful transracial adoptions in the Bowness community? Here, there are two variables, the attitudes of social workers toward transracial adoptions in the Bowness community and the proportion of successful transracial adoptions in the community. However, there is no suggestion that one affects the other. There is no independent variable; neither is there a dependent variable. They are just two variables.

Extraneous Variables

We are rarely in a position to control all the factors that might influence the results of a particular research study. Thus, we must identify (if at all possible) other important variables that we need to control for. Suppose, for example, a study is conducted to determine the effectiveness of a particular treatment intervention in reducing drug use among adolescents. The research question could be: To what degree does a social work intervention, say a small community-based educational prevention program, reduce drug use in adolescents who attend the program? As we know by now, the independent variable is the prevention program, and the dependent variable is adolescent drug use.

In theory, the question may be answered by measuring the adolescents' drug use before and after they attend the program and calculate the difference. However, all sorts of factors may contribute to reduced drug use, quite apart from the prevention program. Perhaps a new drug abuse awareness program was offered in all the high schools in the community and made an impression on a number of the adolescents who attended the community-based program. Suppose one of the adolescents who had dropped out of the community-based program died of an overdose—an upsetting experience for everyone. If we were unaware of all these other influences we could well conclude that the program was responsible for the observed reduction in drug use. However, in fact, the other factors, the high school awareness programs and the death of the friend, were really responsible for the decrease in drug use among the adolescents. In visual terms, Figure 4.2 explains what may have actually happened.

In other words, a number of other extraneous (or other independent) variables may have been introduced into the study without our knowl-

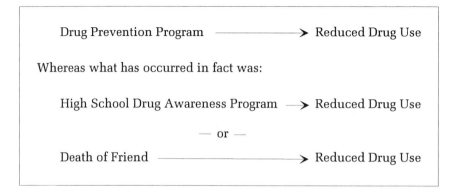

Drug Prevention Program ——————→ Reduced Drug Use

Whereas what has occurred in fact was:

High School Drug Awareness Program —→ Reduced Drug Use

— or —

Death of Friend ————————→ Reduced Drug Use

FIGURE 4.2   Possible Relationship Between and Among Variables

edge. Extraneous variables such as these can invalidate the relationship between the independent and dependent variables that we imagine has been found.

Let us take another example. Suppose a previous research study has determined that the proportion of reported AIDS cases is higher in one ethnic group than in another. Erroneous conclusions may easily be drawn from such results: that one ethnic group is genetically more susceptible to AIDS than the other; or that homosexuality or drug use is more prevalent in one group than in the other. In fact, a variety of socioeconomic factors may be at work. Perhaps the group with a higher proportion of AIDS cases is also the group with higher rates of poverty, school dropout, substance abuse, and related social problems. Perhaps the higher AIDS rate has more to do with greater intravenous drug use and less awareness of AIDS prevention than it does with genetic susceptibility or homosexuality. Box 4.2 presents an interesting example, involving the incidence of heart attacks, of how variables can be potentially related to one another.

CONSTANTS

As mentioned, most research studies involve concepts that vary and thus are called variables. Concepts that do not vary are called *constants*. For example, as before, we might want to compare the social adjustment of previously institutionalized people who were psychiatrically challenged to the social adjustment of people in the general population. In this situation, whether the person is, or is not, a previously institutionalized person who was psychiatrically challenged will fluctuate and, so, is a variable. If, however, it is not feasible to include a group of "normal" individuals in the study, then the research participants will all be previously institutionalized people who were psychiatrically challenged. In

Box 4.2

Problems in Causal Interpretation:
The Case of Exercise and Heart Attacks

Of the three criteria needed to establish a causal relationship, the most difficult to assess is nonspuriousness. One can never be sure that a causal connection exists between correlated variables. Indeed, mistaken impressions of causality may remain undetected for years. An interesting example of this problem in social science research is related by psychologists Schuyler Huck and Howard Sandler (1979:151, 152, 227).

In recent years there has been much interest in the relative benefits of regular exercise. One controversial claim is that exercise can reduce the risk of heart attacks. An early study by Dr. J.N. Morris of London shows, however, just how difficult this is to establish. Examining drivers and conductors of London's double-decker buses, Morris found that the drivers were far more likely to suffer from heart disease and to die from coronaries than the conductors. Since the drivers sat in their seats all day while the conductors ran up and down stairs to collect fares, he concluded that it was the differential amount of exercise inherent in the two jobs that brought about the observed differences in health. Before reading further, you might try to think of variables other than exercise that could have produced the difference in heart problems between the drivers and conductors. Morris uncovered one variable in a follow-up study, and Huck and Sandler mention two others.

Some time after the publication of the above results, Morris examined the records maintained on the uniforms issued to drivers and conductors and discovered that drivers tended to be given larger uniforms than conductors. Therefore, he concluded, differences in weight rather than exercise might be the causal factor. That is, heavier men, who were more coronary-prone to begin with, may have chosen the sedentary job of driver, whereas thinner men chose the more physically active job of conductor.

Another explanation is related to the amount of tension associated with the two jobs. As Huck and Sandler (1979:227) point out.

> The conductors probably experienced very little tension as they went up and down the bus collecting fares from the passengers; the worst thing that they probably had to deal with in their jobs was a passenger who attempted to ride free by sneaking around from one seat to another. Normally, however, we suspect that the conductors actually enjoyed their interaction with other people while on the job.
>
> But on the other hand, each driver had the safety of everyone on the bus as his responsibility. And as anyone who lives in or visits a city knows, driving in rush-hour traffic is anything but restful. Having to dodge pedestrians, being cut off by other vehicles, watching for signal changes—these activities can bring about temporary outbursts of anger and chronic nervousness. Imagine how it would affect your heart to be in the driver's seat of a bus for eight hours each working day!

Finally, a third variable that could account for the different rate of heart problems is age. If mobility or seniority or some other function of age were related to job assignment, then employees assigned to the driver jobs may have been older and those assigned to the conductor jobs younger. And since we would expect more heart attacks among older persons, age rather than the nature of the job could be the causal variable.

In this example it is difficult if not impossible to tell which cause– exercise, weight, job stress, or age–may have produced the observed differences in health between drivers and conductors. Since both weight and age are antecedent to job type and heart disease, either of these uncontrolled extraneous variables could have created a spurious relationship. However, if exercise or job stress were the correct interpretation, then the original relationship would not be spurious, since exercise and job stress specify intervening variables through which the job itself can make a person more or less susceptible to heart problems. The diagram below shows the difference in those two outcomes.

Age $\nearrow$ Job type

$\searrow$ Heart disease

Job type $\longrightarrow$ Exercise $\longrightarrow$ Heart disease

Of course, it is possible that two or more of these variables are operating jointly to produce the health differential between the two groups. The only safe conclusion is that we really do not know which interpretation is correct.

In general, correlation does not imply causation. All correlations must be interpreted; like any fact, they do not speak for themselves. To infer a causal relationship from a correlation, an investigator must detect and control for extraneous variables that are possible and plausible causes of the variable to be explained. The fatal flaw in Morris's study is that relevant extraneous variables were not controlled; without directly assessing the effects of such "hidden" causes, we cannot tell which interpretation is valid.

that research design, these people would be a constant. It is important to note that, depending on how a study is conceptualized, a concept can be a constant in one study and a variable in another.

SUMMARY

Reading and discussion around the general problem area will enable the researcher to continually narrow the focus of interest until specific research questions related to the problem can be developed. The researcher will usually ask different kinds of questions, depending on the purpose for which the answers are required. The possible reasons for conducting a research study can be categorized broadly as exploration, description, and explanation. These three categories fall on a knowledge continuum. At one end of the continuum, exploratory studies yield only uncertain knowledge and are conducted when there is little prior knowledge in the problem area. Further along the continuum, when some knowledge has been obtained, descriptive studies are undertaken to yield additional descriptive information. At the far end of the continuum, when substantial knowledge is available, explanatory studies attempt to explain the facts already gathered.

A research question is considered appropriate for a social work study when it meets the same four criteria as the research problem (see Chapter 3), plus one additional criterion: specificity. The research question should be written so that the reader is in no doubt as to the meaning of the concepts and the types of relationships being considered.

The process of selecting the variables for study is known as conceptualization. The process of defining the variable in such a way that it can measured is called operationalization.

In Chapter 5, we discuss how research questions can be further refined into research hypotheses.

STUDY QUESTIONS

1. Discuss the differences among exploratory, descriptive, and explanatory research questions. Which type do you feel is most important for our profession? Why? Which is the least? Why?

2. Discuss how concepts are related to abstract definitions. Provide a social work example in your discussion.

3. What is the difference between conceptualization and operationalization? Provide a social work example in your discussion.

4. What are operational definitions? How are they useful in social work research? Social work practice? Provide a social work example in your discussion.

5. What is the difference between variables and constants? Provide a social work example in your discussion.

6. What is the difference between independent, dependent, and extraneous variables? Provide a social work example in your discussion.

7. Formulate the general problem area of homelessness (Chapter 3) into five research questions. Conceptualize and operationalize each research question whereby each contains one independent variable and one dependent variable. Also indicate other extraneous variables that might affect the dependent variable.

8. Go to the library and identify a social work research article. What is the general problem area of the study? What is the research question?

9. Go to the library and choose a social work research article. What is the independent variable in this study? What is the dependent variable?

10. Go to the library and identify a social work research article. With the same general problem, what other research questions do you feel could have been addressed in the study? Why?

REFERENCES AND FURTHER READINGS

Babbie, E.R. (1992). *The practice of social research* (6th ed., pp. 110, 40-44). Pacific Grove, CA: Wadsworth.

Bailey, K.D. (1994). *Methods of social research* (4th ed., pp. 21-38). New York: Free Press.

Frankfort-Nachmias, C., & Nachmias, D. (1992). *Research methods in the social sciences* (4th ed., pp. 51-54). New York: St. Martin's Press.

Grinnell, R.M., Jr., & Williams, M. (1990). *Research in social work: A primer* (pp. 58-85). Itasca, IL: F.E. Peacock.

Huck, S.W., & Sandler, H.M. (1979). *Rival hypotheses: Alternative interpretations of data-based conclusions.* New York: Harper & Row.

Judd, C.M., Smith E.R., & Kidder, I.H. (1991). *Research methods in social relations* (6th ed., pp. 20-27). Fort Worth, TX: Harcourt Brace.

Leedy, P.D. (1993). *Practical research: Planning and design* (3rd ed., pp. 59-86). New York: Macmillan.

Marlow, C. (1993). *Research methods for generalist social work practice* (pp. 23-45). Pacific Grove, CA: Wadsworth.

Monette, D.R., Sullivan, T.J., & DeJong, C.R. (1994). *Applied social research* (3rd ed., pp. 68-76). Fort Worth, TX: Harcourt Brace.

Myers, D.G. (1983). *Social psychology.* New York: McGraw-Hill.

Neuman, W.L. (1994). *Social research methods* (2nd ed., pp. 55-78, 108-112). Needham Heights, MA: Allyn & Bacon.

Polansky, N.A. (1975). Theory construction and the scientific method. In N.A. Polansky (Ed.), *Social work research: Methods for the helping professions* (rev. ed., pp. 18-37). Chicago: University of Chicago Press.

Rothery, M. (1993). Problems, questions, and hypotheses. In R.M. Grinnell, Jr. (Ed.), *Social work research and evaluation* (4th ed., pp. 17-37). Itasca, IL: F.E. Peacock.

Royse, D.D. (1991). *Research methods in social work* (pp. 38-39). Chicago: Nelson-Hall.

Rubin, A., & Babbie, E. (1993). *Research methods for social work* (2nd ed., pp. 88-104). Pacific Grove, CA: Wadsworth.

Smith, N.J. (1985). Research goals and problems. In R.M. Grinnell, Jr. (Ed.), *Social work research and evaluation* (2nd ed., pp. 49-65). Itasca, IL: F.E. Peacock.

Smith, N.J. (1988). Formulating research goals and problems. In R.M. Grinnell, Jr. (Ed.), *Social work research and evaluation* (3rd ed., pp. 89-110). Itasca, IL: F.E. Peacock.

Yegidis, B.L., & Weinbach, R.W. (1991). *Research methods for social workers* (pp. 35-46). White Plains, NY: Longman.

Chapter 5

Research Hypotheses

A DESCRIPTIVE RESEARCH STUDY may begin with the idea that X, the independent variable, may be related to Y, the dependent variable. Perhaps in an explanatory study, we can go so far as to speculate that if X occurs, then Y will result. Our speculation can be written in the form of an explanatory statement—"X affects Y." The explanatory statement form is known as a *hypothesis*. In short, a hypothesis is an answer to a specific research question before a research study has been conducted to test whether the answer is true or not.

A hypothesis is not just any statement: It is a statement that can be proved or disproved by comparison with observed facts. "Twenty four angels can sit on the head of a pin" is not a hypothesis because it is not possible to count the number of angels who may (or may not) be sitting on a pin. "Moral values are declining" is not a good hypothesis because it is difficult to define "moral values" precisely in order to determine whether they are declining or not. Besides, the word "declining" begs the question, declining from what?

However, as we know from the previous chapter, it *is* possible to define and measure the concept "moral values" via its indicators, or variables that it contains. Moral values might be conceptualized in terms of such variables as divorce rates, worship attendances, rights for homosexuals, or a host of other variables depending on the personal values of the researcher. "Declining" can also be conceptualized as the difference in moral values now as opposed to 50 years ago. "Moral values are declining" is not an impossible statement to be used as a hypothesis, but it is certainly not a sensible one. If we want to test the speculation that one variable of "moral values" is the proportion of people attending religious services, then why not write a statement to this effect? In any case, a debate about what does and does not constitute a hypothesis is probably less fruitful than establishing criteria for a good one.

CRITERIA FOR GOOD HYPOTHESES

A hypothesis is derived from the research question (Chapter 4), which is derived from the research problem area (Chapter 3). There are four criteria that can used to differentiate a good, useful hypothesis from one that is not so good or useful. They are: (1) relevance, (2) completeness, (3) specificity, and (4) potential for testing.

Relevance

It is hardly necessary to stress that a useful hypothesis is one that contributes to knowledge in the problem area. Nevertheless, some social work problem areas are enormously complex, and it is common for people to get so sidetracked in reading the professional literature that they develop very interesting hypotheses totally unrelated to the original problem area they wanted to investigate in the first place. The relevancy criterion is a reminder that, to repeat, the research hypothesis must be directly related to the research question, which in turn must be directly related to the general research problem area.

Completeness

A hypothesis should be a complete statement that expresses our intended meaning in its entirety. The reader should not be left with the impression that some word or phrase is missing. "Moral values are declining" is one example of an incomplete hypothesis. Other examples include a whole range of comparative statements without a reference point. For example, the statement, "Males are more aggressive," may be assumed to mean "Men are more aggressive than women," but someone investigating the social life of animals may have meant, "Male humans are more aggressive than male gorillas."

Specificity

A hypothesis must be unambiguous. The reader should be able to understand what each variable contained in the hypothesis means and what relationship, if any, is hypothesized to exist between them. For example, consider the hypothesis, "Badly timed family therapy affects success." Badly timed family therapy may refer to therapy offered too soon or too late for the family to benefit; or to the social worker or family being late for therapy sessions; or to sessions that are too long or too short to be effective. Similarly, "success" may mean resolution of the family's problems as determined by objective measurement, or it may mean the family's—or the social worker's—degree of satisfaction with therapy, or any combination of these.

With regard to the relationship between the two variables, the reader may assume that we are hypothesizing a negative correlation: That is, the more badly timed the therapy, the less success will be achieved. On the other hand, perhaps we are only hypothesizing an association: Bad timing will invariably co-exist with lack of success.

Be that as it may, the reader should not be left to guess at what we mean by a hypothesis. If we are trying to be both complete and specific, we may hypothesize, for example:

> Family therapy that is undertaken *after* the male perpetrator has accepted responsibility for the sexual abuse of his child is more likely to succeed in reuniting the family than family therapy undertaken *before* the male perpetrator has accepted responsibility for the sexual abuse.

The above hypothesis is complete and specific. It leaves the reader in no doubt as to what we mean, but it is also somewhat wordy and clumsy. One of the difficulties in writing a good hypothesis is that complete, specific statements tend to need more words than incomplete, ambiguous statements.

Potential for Testing

The last criterion for judging whether a hypothesis is good and useful is the ease with which the truth of the hypothesis can be verified. Some statements cannot be verified at all with presently available measurement techniques. "Telepathic communication exists between identical twins," is one such statement. Much of Emile Durkheim's work on suicide was formulated in such a way that it was not testable by the data-gathering techniques available in the 1960s.

A hypothesis of sufficient importance will often generate new data-gathering techniques, which will enable it to be eventually tested. Nevertheless, as a general rule, it is best to limit hypotheses to statements that can be tested immediately by available measurement methods in current use.

TYPES OF HYPOTHESES

In light of the preceding four criteria, a research hypothesis may be defined as a complete, specific, testable statement which, when verified, will generate knowledge relevant to the problem area being investigated. Arriving at such a statement is often a difficult and time-consuming task that involves a detailed review of the professional literature, extensive dialogue with colleagues, repeated revisions of the research question, and several unsuccessful attempts at formulating the actual hypothesis.

For research purposes, there are two major types of hypotheses—research hypotheses and rival hypotheses.

Research Hypotheses

Suppose, for example, that we are interested in why some social workers seem to develop negative attitudes toward our profession and others do not. As a result of reading, conversation, and personal experience, we may come to believe that social workers' attitudes toward our profession are influenced mainly by their own value systems. Accordingly, a research hypothesis may be developed, stating:

Research Hypothesis:
Social workers who value a social institutional change model of practice will evidence more negative attitudes toward the social work profession than social workers who value an individual client change model.

The above hypothesis is a research hypothesis. A *research* hypothesis is a statement that we propose to test and hope to verify by undertaking the research study. It is the entire focus of the study. It guides the study's research design, the data-collection methods and instruments used, the selection of the research participants studied, and the type of data analysis used.

There are two types of research hypotheses—one-tailed research hypotheses and two-tailed research hypotheses.

One-Tailed Research Hypotheses. A one-tailed research hypothesis simply predicts a specific relationship between the independent variable and the dependent variable. For example, the following hypothesis is one-tailed: The more positive support statements that social workers provide clients during individual therapy sessions, the better the chances of positive client outcomes. This statement is predicting a direct and specific relationship between an independent variable (number of positive support statements) and a dependent variable (client outcome). One-tailed research hypotheses are used mainly in explanatory research studies where there is a large amount of previous literature available.

Two-Tailed Research Hypotheses. Unlike the one-tailed research hypothesis, which predicts a specific relationship between two variables, the two-tailed hypothesis does not. The following hypothesis is an example of a two-tailed research hypothesis: There is a relationship between the gender of social workers and their effectiveness with their clients. This statement does not say whether male social workers will be more effective with their clients than will female workers, or vice versa. All it says is that it predicts a relationship between the two variables—gender of workers and their effectiveness with their clients. These types of hypotheses are used primarily in descriptive research studies.

Rival Hypotheses

A hypothesis that competes with one- and two-tailed research hypotheses is known as a *rival hypothesis*. Rival hypotheses use other extraneous independent variables that may affect the dependent variable. In some cases, the best way to show that a research hypothesis is true is to show that other, or rival hypotheses, are *not* true. For example, if it can be shown that social workers' attitudes toward our profession (dependent variable) are *not* affected by their socioeconomic background (independent variable) it becomes more likely that their attitudes toward our profession are determined solely by whether they value a social institutional change model or individual client change model of practice.

If we wished to verify the above research hypothesis, we could hypothesize that the social workers' socioeconomic backgrounds were also related to their attitudes in the hope that this rival hypothesis would be untrue.

In order to test the initial research hypothesis, we need to: (1) select a sample of social workers, (2) measure their attitudes toward the social work profession, (3) determine which model of practice each values most, and (4) perform a statistical analysis to discover whether the workers who value a social institutional change model have more negative attitudes toward our profession than social workers who value an individual client change model. The possibility that socioeconomic background might be an extraneous variable can be controlled by making it an independent variable in the following rival hypothesis:

Rival Hypothesis:
Social workers who have high socioeconomic backgrounds (a second potential independent variable) will evidence more negative attitudes toward the

social work profession (the same dependent variable) than social workers who have low socioeconomic backgrounds.

Obviously there are other extraneous variables that could invalidate the results, such as gender, age, personality, type of job, educational level, parents' occupations, or length of work experience. We could formulate further rival hypotheses to deal with these, a potentially confusing procedure. An alternative is to declare that these extraneous variables might have affected the study's results but were not addressed in the current study. Others interested in the area may choose to address these extraneous variables in future studies.

STEPS IN FORMULATING HYPOTHESES

It may be helpful at this point to summarize the process by which a general research problem becomes a specific research question and finally a testable hypothesis. Essentially, there are five interrelated steps: (1) identifying the general problem area as presented in Chapter 3, (2) gathering information and categorizing ideas as presented in Chapter 3, (3) formulating the research question as presented in Chapter 4, (4) conceptualizing and operationalizing the variables as presented in Chapter 4, and (5) formulating the hypothesis, given the four criteria identified at the beginning of this chapter.

The final steps, of course, will be, first, to test the hypothesis by implementing the research design and, second, to disseminate the results in the form of journal papers or reports so that knowledge in the problem area is increased. Let us now turn to the first step in hypothesis formulation.

Step 1: Identifying the Problem Area

As previously discussed, we need to select a general problem area based on our own interests and value systems, as well as on the professional and agency considerations presented in Chapter 2. It is a good idea right from the beginning of any research study to keep a research logbook, which is like a diary in where ideas, comments, actions, and decisions can be chronologically recorded. When it is time to write the final research report, perhaps one or two years after the study was initially started, the logbook will be an invaluable aid to our memory of both what was done, when, how, and why, and what difficulties were encountered and what progress resulted.

Step 2: Gathering Information and Categorizing Ideas

Throughout the study, we will spend long hours reviewing the literature on the problem area and discussing ideas with colleagues who are particularly knowledgeable about one aspect or the other. During the process of reading and discussion, vague ideas about the problem area will gradually coalesce, and we will become more certain about what aspects need to be explored and how the knowledge gained might be of use.

For example, suppose we are interested in the professional career patterns of social workers, and particularly in why some social workers continue to enjoy their work while others become increasingly frustrated and finally resign. Knowledge in this area might be useful to those responsible for selecting social work students, educating them, and initiating them into the workplace.

We might want to explore not only the social work literature but also the literature of other allied disciplines, particularly sociology and psychology. Ideas and questions will emerge. The literature may have identified two time periods as being of particular importance in the molding of social workers' attitudes toward our profession: the educational period itself; and the first experience in the workplace, often termed reality shock. But suppose students enter social work education already inclined to one of two opposing beliefs: either that the environment is largely to blame for clients' problems (social institutional change model); or that the fault lies with the clients themselves (individual client change model).

For the sake of simplicity, let us suppose that social work students fall into only one of these two camps, depending on such factors as their age, gender, ethnic origin, socioeconomic background, and previous life experience. Suppose that some of them believe they can change the client or the client's environment or both, and they grow frustrated when they find that people and organizations are not so easily changed. Suppose that older students, or minority or female students, have discovered this already and are better able to cope with reality shock. Suppose that reality shock is softened or reinforced depending on the career choice the graduating student makes.

As a result of all this supposing, we will emerge with a large number of concepts that may be related to each other in numerous and different ways. Concepts so far include social workers, the characteristics of social work students, social work education, work experience, career choices, reality shock, the coping capacities of social workers, the two different professional models preferred by social workers, and the degree of frustration felt by social workers at various points in their careers.

Our next task is to examine all the possible relationships between these concepts, perhaps by writing each concept on a plain card and moving the cards around to show diagrammatically the different relationships. Some of the possible relationships will seem more interesting or important than others, and it is from these relationships that research questions and hypotheses will emerge.

Step 3: Formulating the Research Question

Perhaps we have decided that the most interesting relationship is the one between the social workers' preferred professional model and their attitudes toward our profession. There may be evidence to suggest that the individual client change model is still the paramount ideology in social work. We may wish to explore the possibility that social workers, whose personal value systems conflict with this paramount ideology, will develop negative attitudes toward our profession; and, conversely, we may speculate that social workers who concur with the ideology will show positive attitudes toward our profession. Research questions follow quite logically from this: For example, "Do social workers who value a social institutional change model of practice exhibit more negative attitudes toward our profession than social workers who value an individual client change model of practice?"

Once tentatively formulated, the adequacy of the research question must be judged according to the same criteria used to assess the research problem presented in Chapter 3—relevancy, researchability, feasibility, and ethical acceptability. In addition, the research question must be specific. The reader must be able to understand precisely what we are asking, without needing to speculate about the meanings of words or the nature of the relationships proposed.

Step 4: Conceptualizing and Operationalizing Variables

When the research question has been tentatively formulated, we now need to conceptualize and operationalize the variables contained within the study's concepts (Step 3). For example, what is meant by a social worker in the context of this study? Perhaps we could conceptually and operationally define social workers as:

> All people who hold an MSW degree from an accredited graduate school of social work and who have been employed on a full-time basis for the last 24 months within Agency A.

A person who defines social workers in this way must have sensible reasons for excluding people with other qualifications, as well as people who work part-time, or in other agencies, or have worked for less than 24 months.

In a similar manner, we need to conceptualize and operationally define attitudes toward the social work profession. There will have to be

Box 5.1

Operationalization Across the Sciences

One aspect of the stereotype of science shared by many educated persons is that it invariably involves precise measurements with instruments that are accurate to several decimal places. Indeed, this is seen as a crucial difference between the so-called hard sciences, such as chemistry and physics (more accurately called the natural or physical sciences), and the soft sciences, such as psychology, sociology, and anthropology (most of which are social sciences).

Of course, the hard–soft distinction is not meant to be flattering to that which is considered soft; and many natural scientists, who misunderstand the nature of social measurement, believe that the social sciences do not constitute science at all. According to biologist Jared Diamond (1987), however, this criticism misses two crucial points. First, all scientists, natural or social, face the task of operationalizing concepts. As Diamond says, "To compare evidence with theory requires that you measure the ingredients of your theory." Second, the "task of operationalizing is inevitably more difficult and less exact in the [social] sciences, because there are so many uncontrolled variables."

Diamond illustrates operationalization with examples drawn from both the natural and social sciences. Learning how various scientists go about this should help your understanding and appreciation of the measurement process.The first example comes from mathematics. As Diamond says,

> I'd guess that mathematics arose long ago when two cave women couldn't operationalize their intuitive concept of "many." One cave woman said, "Let's pick this tree over here, because it has many bananas." The other cave woman argued, "No, let's pick that tree over there, because it has more bananas." Without a number system to operationalize the concept of "many," the two cave women could never prove to each other which tree offered better pickings. (p. 38)

Diamond's second example comes from another "hard" science, analytical chemistry, which generally seeks to measure the properties of substances.

> When my colleagues and I were studying the physiology of hummingbirds, we knew that the little guys liked to drink sweet nectar, but we would have argued indefinitely about how sweet it was if we hadn't operationalized the concept by measuring sugar concentrations. The method we used was to treat a glucose solution with an enzyme that liberates hydrogen peroxide, which reacts (with the help of another enzyme) with another substance called dianisidine to make it turn brown, whereupon we measured the brown color's intensity with an instrument called a spectrophotometer. A pointer's deflection on the spectrophotometer dial let us read off a number that provided an operational definition of sweet. (p. 38)

One of Diamond's "soft" science examples is taken from the field of clinical psychology, specifically his wife Marie Cohen's work with cancer patients and their families. Marie was interested in how doctors reveal the diagnosis of cancer. What determines how frank they are and how much information they withhold? She guessed that this

> might be related to differences in doctors' attitudes toward things like death, cancer, and medical treatment. But how on earth was she to operationalize and measure such attitudes . . . ? . . . Part of Marie's solution was to use a questionnaire that other scientists had developed by extracting statements from sources like tape-recorded doctors' meetings and then asking other doctors to express their degree of agreement with each statement. It turned out that each doctor's responses tended to cluster in several groups, in such a way that his [or her] responses to one statement in a cluster were correlated with his [or her] responses to other statements in the same cluster.
>
> One cluster proved to consist of expressions of attitudes toward death, a second cluster consisted of expressions of attitudes toward treatment and diagnosis, and a third cluster consisted of statements about patients' ability to cope with cancer. The responses were then employed to define attitude scales, which were further validated in other ways, like testing the scales on doctors at different stages in their careers (hence likely to have different attitudes). By thus operationalizing doctors' attitudes, Marie discovered (among other things) that doctors most convinced about the value of early diagnosis and aggressive treatment of cancer are the ones most likely to be frank with their patients. (p. 39)

Notice how the problem (finding and creating ways of operationalizing one's intuitive concepts) is the same in each case. Notice also how operationalization can be very indirect, as in both the chemistry and clinical psychology examples, irrespective of the accuracy of the measurement. Finally, these examples might suggest, as Diamond (p. 39) concludes, that the "ingrained labels 'soft science' and 'hard science' could be replaced by hard (i.e., difficult) science and easy science, respectively" For the social sciences "are much more difficult and [to some] intellectually challenging than mathematics and chemistry."

some way of measuring social workers' attitudes. This could be done by looking at some observable indicator(s) such as frequent absenteeism, a larger-than-average number of cancelled appointments with clients, lateness, client dissatisfaction as recorded on client evaluation forms, refusal to work with certain types of clients, habitual silence at staff meetings, or, probably most appropriately, the use of some standardized measuring instrument that measures attitudes toward the social work profession (or some similar helping profession).

Whatever indicators, or variables are chosen to conceptualize the concept of "attitudes," there must be sensible reasons for selecting these rather than others—some evidence that lateness, for example, does indicate a negative attitude and not just an unfortunate bus connection. In addition, we must be sure that the attitudes expressed are attitudes toward the social work profession as a whole, not just dissatisfaction with Agency A.

While considering the subject of measurement, we need to ensure that all the needed data will be available. If one variable is to be client satisfaction, for example, will Agency A permit access to client evaluation forms? Does Agency A even have client evaluation forms? In the absence of evaluation forms, will we be able to interview clients? What proportion of clients have terminated with the agency and can no longer be traced?

If we find that some variables included in the research question cannot be feasibly measured, it will be necessary to revise it or, in an extreme case, to go back to the beginning and formulate another question. Once the question has been decided, a specific hypothesis or set of hypotheses can be derived. Box 5.1 presents an interesting discussion of how the operationalization of variables differs between the "hard" and "soft" sciences.

Step 5: Formulating the Final Hypothesis

The last step before undertaking an explanatory study is to construct the hypothesis. For example, let us take the following hypothesis:

> Social workers who value an individual client change model of practice will exhibit more negative attitudes toward the social work profession than will social workers who value a social institutional change model of practice.

The above is the research hypothesis, or the statement that we hope to verify by undertaking the study. An important part of hypothesis construction is to identify extraneous variables—that is, extraneous factors that may affect the dependent variable (their attitudes) and so invalidate the study's results. There are numerous extraneous variables in this particular example. Social workers may have negative attitudes toward the profession for many reasons quite apart from the model of practice they value. As previously mentioned, one way to control for these extraneous variables is to construct a rival hypothesis around each one and design the study so that the rival hypotheses can be tested as well.

The best research hypothesis fits with an existing theory. Preferably, it should be derived from a gap in the body of knowledge, and the answer should contribute to an extension or revision of what was known before. We should be able to explain why the hypothesis is important and in what ways the answer might be used. However, consider the contents in Box 5.2 in relation to using existing theory to form hypotheses.

Box 5.2

The Hypothetico-Deductive Method:
An Example from the History of Medicine

Carl Hempel (1966), noted philosopher of science, provides an excellent example of the application of the hypothetico-deductive method in his story of Ignaz Semmelweis's work on a fatal illness known as puerperal fever, or childbed fever. The physician Semmelweis worked from 1844 to 1848 at the Vienna General Hospital. As a medical staff member of the First Maternity Division, he was distressed by the division's high incidence of childbed fever, especially compared with the incidence in the Second Maternity Division of the same hospital.

According to Hempel's account, Semmelweis entertained numerous explanations. "Some of these he rejected out of hand as incompatible with well-established facts; others he subjected to specific tests." For example, one view held that overcrowding was the cause; however, Semmelweis noted that overcrowding was in fact heavier in the Second Division than in the First. Two other conjectures were similarly rejected "by noting that there were no differences between the two Divisions in regard to diet or general care of the patients." Among several other ideas suggested to Semmelweis was the position of the women during delivery: in the First Division, women delivered lying on their backs, while in the Second, they delivered on their sides. But when the lateral position was introduced in the First Division, mortality remained unchanged.

In a similar fashion, Semmelweis rejected idea after idea until finally, in 1847, an accident gave him the critical clue for solving the puzzle. While performing an autopsy, a colleague of his, Kolletschka, received a puncture wound from a scalpel and "died after an agonizing illness during which he displayed the same symptoms that Semmelweis had observed in the victims of childbed fever." Semmelweis reasoned that "cadaveric matter" introduced into Kolletschka's bloodstream from the scalpel "had caused his colleague's fatal illness."

> And the similarities between the course of Kolletschka's disease and that of the women in his clinic led Semmelweis to the conclusion that his patients had died of the same kind of blood poisoning; he, his colleagues, and the medical students had been the carriers of the infectious material, for he and his associates used to come to the wards directly from performing dissections in the autopsy room, and examine the women in labor after only superficially washing their hands, which often retained a characteristic foul order. (p. 5)

Semmelweis tested this idea by having all medical personnel who attended the women carefully disinfect their hands before making an examination. The mortality from childbed fever promptly decreased.

In seeking to explain childbed fever, Semmelweis repeatedly applied the hypothetico-deductive method. First, he formulated a hypothesis: that the illness was due to overcrowding, delivery position, or blood poisoning from cadaveric matter. Second, he deduced testable consequences from this hypothesis. That is, he reasoned that if his hypothesis were true, then certain facts or observations should follow: overcrowdedness will be greater in the First Division than the Second; adoption of the lateral position in the First Division will reduce the mortality; or having attendants disinfect their hands will reduce fatalities. Third, Semmelweis checked the observable consequences of the hypothesis against reality. In the case of the delivery position and blood poisoning hypotheses, this meant first establishing certain conditions for making his observations—changing the delivery procedure or requiring disinfection. Finally, having found the observable consequences to be true or false, Semmelweis drew conclusions about his hypotheses. When the consequences were disconfirmed (e.g., when it was shown that the lateral position did *not* decrease fatalities), he rejected the hypothesis. When the consequences were confirmed (e.g., when disinfection lowered fatalities), he tentatively accepted the hypothesis as true.

The process of hypothesis construction within the context of the previous four chapters is presented in Figure 5.1 below.

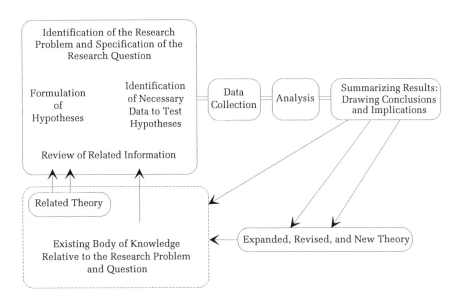

FIGURE 5.1   Hypothesis Construction and the Research Process

Another Kidnap Bid Has Parents Nervous

INNISFAIL—Anxious parents are uniting to protect their kids after the fifth child abduction incident since June in this normally peaceful town.

And teachers are on red alert for strangers.

The drastic precautions have been forced on them by the latest kidnap bid—the attempted abduction last Friday of a seven-year-old girl inside the town's only elementary school.

As John Wilson Elementary School ended its day Tuesday, the parking lot was jammed with parents, big brothers, big sisters, friends and neighbours.

"Now, everybody's coming to the school to pick up their kids—or other people's kids. Even parents that never used to come and get their kids are walking them to school every day now," said Jeanette Clark, waiting for her daughter.

"We have to make sure every child gets home safely now.

"This last abduction was really serious because the guy went right into the school," she said.

The culprit, described as a 50-year-old white male with brown hair and a moustache, walked into the school, grabbed the girl, who was just coming out of the bathroom, and demanded: "Come with me."

But the girl bit his arm and ran for help.

Laurie Moore, mother of a Grade 3 girl, said she and her friends with children are emphasizing "stay away from strangers" warnings.

"I tell my daughter not to talk to anyone, and if anyone comes near her she has to scream and run. It really is sad that we all have to go through this," she said.

School Principal Bill Hoppins has created a volunteer program where parents can help each other by supervising kids on the playground during the morning.

Tim Belbin, whose daughter attends Grade 2, said he's willing to offer his time to watch his and other children.

"I find this all really disturbing . . . really scary."

The abduction attempt has also prompted teachers to supervise all the students in their classes as they leave the school grounds and make sure they can identify all adults in the area.

"If we don't know them, we have to go up and ask them, even if they don't like it," said Hoppins.

And Hoppins said that when students are absent without a parental warning, their homes are called immediately. "There have been a number of precautions taken here since the last abduction attempt. And we are working together with the parents."

FIGURE 5.2   Newspaper Article on Child Molester

FROM PROBLEMS TO QUESTIONS TO HYPOTHESES

Two contemporary examples will be used to illustrate how a researcher goes from a general problem area (Chapter 3) to formulating research questions from the problem area (Chapter 4) to formulating hypotheses (this chapter). Figures 5.2 and 5.3 are two newspaper articles that have appeared in Canada. However, as can be easily seen, they could have appeared anywhere in the world. Figure 5.2 focuses upon a child molester in an elementary school and Figure 5.3 focuses on racism.

Show Ignores Native Stereotype

GIBSONS, B.C. (CP)–Native actress Marianne Jones had to fight to keep from laughing when a script once called for her to utter the line: "Him shot six times."

"It was really a difficult thing to say," recalls Jones, who now plays Laurel on CBC's Beachcombers.

That, she says, is typical of the way natives are portrayed on TV and films.

And that, she says, is what's different about Beachcombers.

"It's one of the only shows that portray native people on a day-to-day basis," says Jones.

"No other series has that sort of exposure. When you think of how many native people there are in the country, it's amazing that there isn't more."

Television's portrayal of natives touches a nerve in Jones.

The striking actress with shoulder-length raven hair cherishes her Haida heritage. She identifies her birthplace as "Haida Gwaii–that's the Queen Charlotte Islands, the real name."

The four natives in Beachcombers are depicted as people rather than stereotypes.

"I've done a lot of other shows and they sort of want to put you in a slot: You're a noble savage, you know, the Hollywood stereotypes that have been perpetuated forever."

She admits that natives are struggling with their identity these days–wrestling with tradition and the attractions of the 20th century.

"We're all weighing the traditional life, the spirituality, against being human . . . . We're living today.

"Everybody has a fridge, so to speak," she adds with a raspy laugh.

Jones is doing her part by venturing into video production, starting with a documentary on a Haida artist.

"For a long time, native people have not been allowed or able to define their own images.

"We need to take control to get rid of those Hollywood stereotypes, and to change native people on television to real people."

FIGURE 5.3 Newspaper Article on Racism

Figure 5.4 below clearly illustrates how the two general problem areas depicted in the two articles (Figure 5.2 on child molestation and Figure 5.3 on racism) have been refined to research questions and hypotheses. It must be kept in mind that there are many other research questions and hypotheses that could have been formulated from the same two general problem areas.

1. EXAMPLES OF GENERAL PROBLEM AREAS

   (*a*) Threats of abduction and sexual abuse of schoolchildren.
   (*b*) Racism and its effects on the cultural identities of Native Americans.

2. EXAMPLES OF PROBLEMS AFTER BEGINNING SPECIFICATION

   (*a*) Families react in different ways to threats like the danger facing the children at the school in Innisfail. How might other possible familial reactions affect the emotional responses of the children to this threat?
   (*b*) Can we identify different stereotypes presented to Native American children that are particularly important in their effect on cultural identity?

3. EXAMPLES OF RESEARCH QUESTIONS DERIVED FROM PROBLEMS

   (*a*) What do different families say when their children are threatened with abuse by a stranger? How are the children affected by these reactions with respect to their anxiety levels?
   (*b*) How does the portrayal of Native Americans in standard school textbooks affect the cultural identity of students?

4. EXAMPLES OF RESEARCH QUESTIONS AFTER SPECIFICATION (OPERATIONALIZATION) OF CONCEPTS

   (*a*) How do children at John Wilson Elementary School from egalitarian families differ from children from patriarchal families in the amount of anxiety they experience respecting the threat posed by the abductor?
   (*b*) Who do latency-age (6-11) Native American boys choose as heroes to identify with, and how does this relate to their expressed pride in their native culture?

5. EXAMPLES OF RESEARCH HYPOTHESES

   (*a*) Girls from patriarchal families will be more anxious than girls from egalitarian families when confronted with the threat of adult male violence.
   (*b*) Latency-age (6-11 years old) Native American children who name nonnatives as their heroes will have lower self-esteem than those who name natives as their heroes.

FIGURE 5.4   Examples of Problems, Questions, and Hypotheses

SUMMARY

When a research question has been adequately formulated, a research hypothesis can be directly derived. A hypothesis is a statement that we propose to test and hope to verify by undertaking the study. A good hypothesis can be differentiated from one that is not so good on the basis of four criteria: relevance, completeness, specificity, and potential for testing. The hypothesis cannot be adequately tested unless the study has been appropriately conceptualized and operationalized. In Chapter 6 we discuss how to assess the validity and reliability of the measures used to operationalize variables that have been selected to represent the concepts under investigation.

STUDY QUESTIONS

1. Discuss the criteria that are used in formulating good hypotheses. How are these criteria different from the ones used in formulating research questions? Provide a social work example in your discussion.

2. Discuss the differences between a research hypothesis and a rival hypothesis. Provide a social work example in your discussion.

3. Discuss the role that extraneous variables play when testing research hypotheses. Provide a social work example in your discussion.

4. Review Figure 5.1. Describe the figure in your own words, using a general problem area of your choice throughout your discussion.

5. Take the following hypothesis, "females make better social workers than males." Rewrite the hypothesis so that it meets the four criteria for good hypothesis construction.

6. Discuss how the above hypothesis, as written, would be unethical to test.

7. How would you conceptualize "better social workers" in the hypothesis stated in Question 5? Why?

8. How would you operationalize the gender of the social workers?

9. Go to the library and select a social work research article. Given the general problem area, construct various additional research questions that could have been explored. Justify your response.

10. At the library, identify a social work research article. Given the general problem area, construct various additional research questions and hypotheses that could have been explored. Justify your response.

REFERENCES AND FURTHER READINGS

Adams, G.R., & Schvaneveldt, J.D. (1991). *Understanding research methods* (2nd ed., pp. 18-24). White Plains, NY: Longman.
Babbie, E.R. (1992). *The practice of social research* (6th ed., pp. 110, 40-44).

Pacific Grove, CA: Wadsworth.

Bailey, K.D. (1994). *Methods of social research* (4th ed., pp. 21-38). New York: Free Press.

Calgary Herald: "Another kidnap bid has parents nervous," September 6, 1991, p. 1.

Calgary Herald: "Show ignores Native stereotype," September 6, 1991, Section B, p. 6.

Diamond, J. (1987). Soft sciences are harder than hard sciences. *Discover, 8* (August), 34-39.

Frankfort-Nachmias, C., & Nachmias, D. (1992). *Research methods in the social sciences* (4th ed., pp. 51-54). New York: St. Martin's Press.

Grinnell, R.M., Jr., & Williams, M. (1990). *Research in social work: A primer* (pp. 58-85). Itasca, IL: F.E. Peacock.

Hemple, C.G. (1966). *Philosophy of natural science*. Englewood Cliffs, NJ: Prentice-Hall.

Judd, C.M., Smith E.R., & Kidder, I.H. (1991). *Research methods in social relations* (6th ed., pp. 20-27). Fort Worth, TX: Harcourt Brace.

Leedy, P.D. (1993). *Practical research: Planning and design* (3rd ed., pp. 59-86). New York: Macmillan.

Marlow, C. (1993). *Research methods for generalist social work practice* (pp. 23-45). Pacific Grove, CA: Wadsworth.

Monette, D.R., Sullivan, T.J., & DeJong, C.R. (1994). *Applied social research* (3rd ed., pp. 68-76). Fort Worth, TX: Harcourt Brace.

Myers, D.G. (1983). *Social psychology*. New York: McGraw-Hill.

Neuman, W.L. (1994). *Social research methods* (2nd ed., pp. 55-78, 108-112). Needham Heights, MA: Allyn & Bacon.

Polansky, N.A. (1975). Theory construction and the scientific method. In N.A. Polansky (Ed.), *Social work research: Methods for the helping professions* (rev. ed., pp. 18-37). Chicago: University of Chicago Press.

Rothery, M. (1993). Problems, questions, and hypotheses. In R.M. Grinnell, Jr. (Ed.), *Social work research and evaluation* (4th ed., pp. 17-37). Itasca, IL: F.E. Peacock.

Royse, D.D. (1991). *Research methods in social work* (pp. 38-39). Chicago, IL: Nelson-Hall.

Rubin, A., & Babbie, E. (1993). *Research methods for social work* (2nd ed., pp. 88-104). Pacific Grove, CA: Wadsworth.

Smith, N.J. (1985). Research goals and problems. In R.M. Grinnell, Jr. (Ed.), *Social work research and evaluation* (2nd ed., pp. 49-65). Itasca, IL: F.E. Peacock.

Smith, N.J. (1988). Formulating research goals and problems. In R.M. Grinnell, Jr. (Ed.), *Social work research and evaluation* (3rd ed., pp. 89-110). Itasca, IL: F.E. Peacock.

Yegidis, B.L., & Weinbach, R.W. (1991). *Research methods for social workers* (pp. 35-46). White Plains, NY: Longman.

Chapter 6

Measurement

I N THE PREVIOUS THREE CHAPTERS, we have discussed how to: select general research problem areas (Chapter 3), specify research questions from these problems (Chapter 4), and formulate specific hypotheses from the research questions (Chapter 5). The next step in the research process is to operationalize, or measure, the variables contained within research questions or hypotheses.

Let us say we want to do a research study to find out the ratio of males to females employed at managerial levels in social work agencies. At a descriptive level, we might be interested in whether proportionately more males than females are managers, or vice versa. Having discovered that there are more males than females at these levels, we might be interested, at an explanatory level, in why this is the case. Is it entirely a matter of sexual discrimination or are there other contributing, or extraneous, factors? Could it be that females are generally older than males when they enter the profession and thus have less time to ascend the promotional ladder? Do more females than males work part-time, rendering themselves ineligible for management positions? Do females tend to value high career status less than males, with the result that they are less likely to achieve it?

As discussed in the last two chapters, the variables that are finally measured in a research study naturally emerge from the final research question or hypothesis. If we decide to explore the possibility that proportionally fewer women achieve managerial status because they value it less, the variables of interest will be gender, managerial status, and the value systems of social workers pertaining to career status. We now need to operationally define these variables: that is, define them in a way that will allow them to become measurable. In this chapter, we will present how to measure variables in a valid and reliable way—commonly referred to as measurement validity and measurement reliability.

MEASUREMENT VALIDITY

The measurement of a variable is valid if it measures what it is supposed to measure. Suppose, for example, that we want to do a research study that involves the measurement of the depression levels of AIDS patients in a local hospital. The variable, depression, is operationalized by Walter W. Hudson's, *General Contentment Scale* (*GCS*), as illustrated in Figure 6.1. Each research participant completes the *GCS* by placing numbers to the left of each statement, or item, indicating the degree to which it is true for him or her.

The *GCS* provides an overall measure (via the final score of its 25 items) of the person's depression level from 0 (no depression) to 100 (severe depression). A novice researcher who is not familiar with the *GCS* may wonder if it really measures depression, rather than some other similar variable such as self-esteem, self-concept, anxiety, or hostility. In short, "Is the *GCS* valid? Is it really measuring depression?" But there is more to validity than that. In order to be valid, not only must the *GCS* measure depression, it must measure depression accurately.

One of the main things to remember is that we must think not in terms of validity but in terms of *validities*. A measuring instrument, such as the *GCS* illustrated in Figure 6.1, is valid only if it fulfills the purpose for which it was designed, and an instrument may have several purposes. There are many kinds of validity, of which we will briefly discuss four: (1) content, (2) face, (3) concurrent, and (4) predictive.

Content Validity

In the context of content validity, we ask whether a measuring instrument is really measuring the variable it was designed to measure. If the *GCS* is supposed to measure depression, for example, is it really measuring depression, or is it measuring something else, like self-esteem, or is it just producing a meaningless score? In order to decide whether an instrument is really measuring, say, depression, we first have to be able to conceptualize what depression is. That is, we have to be able to define depression in terms of feelings and/or behaviors that can

Name: _____ Today's Date:_____

This questionnaire is designed to measure the way you feel about your life and surroundings. It is not a test, so there are no right or wrong answers. Answer each item as carefully and as accurately as you can by placing a number beside each one as follows.

1 None of the time
2 Very rarely
3 A little of the time
4 Some of the time
5 A good part of the time
6 Most of the time
7 All of the time

Please begin.

1. _____ I feel powerless to do anything about my life.
2. _____ I feel blue.
3. _____ I think about ending my life.
4. _____ I have crying spells.
5. _____ It is easy for me to enjoy myself.
6. _____ I have a hard time getting started on things that I need to do.
7. _____ I get very depressed.
8. _____ I feel there is always someone I can depend on when things get tough.
9. _____ I feel that the future looks bright for me.
10. _____ I feel downhearted.
11. _____ I feel that I am needed.
12. _____ I feel that I am appreciated by others.
13. _____ I enjoy being active and busy.
14. _____ I feel that others would be better off without me.
15. _____ I enjoy being with other people.
16. _____ I feel that it is easy for me to make decisions.
17. _____ I feel downtrodden.
18. _____ I feel terribly lonely.
19. _____ I get upset easily.
20. _____ I feel that nobody really cares about me.
21. _____ I have a full life.
22. _____ I feel that people really care about me.
23. _____ I have a great deal of fun.
24. _____ I feel great in the morning.
25. _____ I feel that my situation is hopeless.

FIGURE 6.1 General Contentment Scale

be measured.

For example, what is it that makes people think they are depressed? Is it whether they think they are in hopeless situations (Item 25), whether they get upset easily (Item 19), or whether they feel lonely (Item 18)? Probably, it is all of these and a great many more. In order to have a valid measure of depression, the *GCS* should include at least one item for each of the feelings and behaviors that go to make up depression— that is, all of them. The trouble with including all of the factors that go to make up a variable like depression is that we have to *know* all of them. Since the people who develop measuring instruments are human, they often disagree as to what precisely constitutes "all of the factors" and whether they have all been included in the instrument. An instrument may be content valid to one expert, therefore, and not to another.

This is strictly a matter of personal judgment. In fact, no measuring instrument of a practical length can possibly contain all the factors that go to make up a complex concept such as depression, even if all these factors can be known. No instrument, therefore, can be perfectly content valid. But it can be more content valid (or less) depending on what items are selected for inclusion by the person who constructs it. Thus, as the name suggests, *content validity* has to do with the contents of a measuring instrument, or the nature of the items that comprise it.

Let us take another example of content validity. Suppose that we want to measure students' "general social work knowledge" and that we use an exam as the measuring instrument. If all the exam's questions, or items, are on social work research, the exam might provide a very adequate measure of the students' knowledge of social work research. But what about social welfare policy, human behavior, ethnicity and cultural sensitivity issues, racism, AIDS, group work, and community organization? If, on all these other topics, items are added, the exam will provide a more adequate measure of a student's general social work knowledge than it did before. But the exam still does not contain items on social work administration or interviewing skills.

The exam will not be content valid for the purpose of measuring "general social work knowledge" unless it includes items on every possible aspect of "general social work knowledge." In order to construct a content valid exam, therefore, the examiners must first define the variable, *general social work knowledge,* in terms of all the topics it might include. More often than not, disagreements will arise. One examiner might consider that "general social work knowledge" should include an understanding of the process of learning, including behaviorist approaches and social learning theory, while a second examiner believes that theories of learning more properly belong to psychology.

Even topics that are an accepted part of "general social work knowledge," such as group work, may present difficulties if all aspects of the topics are not included in the exam. A specialist in group work may point out to the examiners that the exam does not include items dealing with group cohesion and is therefore not a content valid assessment of knowledge with respect to group work.

Even if the exam includes items on every possible aspect of every possible topic comprising "general social work knowledge," the distribution of the items within the instrument itself may be biased. Perhaps the examiner who favored including learning theory was so persuasive that numerous items on the exam are now devoted to learning theory, leaving all the other topics with a single item each. This exam will not be content valid since a content valid instrument for measuring "general social work knowledge" must reflect not only all the topics pertinent to "general social work knowledge" but the relative importance of each.

Relative importance is obviously a matter of opinion, as is the decision about what topics (and items related to the topics), ought to be included. Even if agreement could be reached, an entirely content valid exam designed to measure a broad variable like "general social work knowledge" would be of a completely impractical length. Since similar difficulties arise with respect to measuring complex concepts such as prejudice, alienation, or ego strength, no instrument to measure them will be completely content valid. Instead, the instrument will be *more or less* content valid, depending on the skill and judgment of the people involved in its construction. In short, content validity of an instrument is determined by the researcher who develops it, and it must appear to measure what the researcher wants it to measure.

Face Validity

As we have seen, content validity is for the researcher. Face validity is for the individual who completes the measuring instrument—the research participant. It has to do with the face value of the instrument: that is, whether it *appears* valid to the person who is completing it. For example, graduate-level social work management students, being tested on basic management theory, could be presented with an exam designed for graduate business students. The exam may be content valid inasmuch as it contains numerous items on basic management theory, which is taught to both social work and business students alike. However, because the exam is couched in business terms and draws on examples from business situations, it may not appear to have much to do with the profession of social work.

Social work students would probably do less well on this exam than they would on one designed especially for them, not just because the terminology is unfamiliar but because they do not consider the content to be relevant to social work. The fact that they do less well means that the business exam has not succeeded in measuring their knowledge of basic management theory as accurately as a social work exam would have done. "Less accurate" means "less valid"—hence, a measuring instrument that may be theoretically content valid becomes less content valid in reality, merely because it does not *appear* to be relevant to the people who complete it.

A measuring instrument designed to measure the degree of racism in Caucasian, middle-class adolescents may be less content valid when applied to African American, working-class adolescents, not only because the words used within the instrument may be unfamiliar but because the examples and the underlying cultural concepts may be perceived to be irrelevant. Face validity is thus not the same thing as content validity—an instrument can be content valid without being face valid, or vice versa—but an instrument that the research participant does not perceive to be relevant is very unlikely to provide an accurate measurement of the variable that is being measured.

Concurrent Validity

Concurrent validity deals with the present. A measuring instrument has concurrent validity if it gives an accurate measure of an individual's *current* status. For example, the *GCS*, designed to measure depression, is concurrently valid if it accurately measures a research participant's present degree of depression—not how depressed the research participant was before some traumatic event, or how depressed the research participant would like to be, or how depressed he or she has the potential to be, but how depressed the research participant *is*.

Predictive Validity

Predictive validity deals with the future. As the name might suggest, a measuring instrument has predictive validity if it has the ability to predict an individual's future performance or status from present performance or status. For example, we may develop an instrument to predict which children will need remedial reading services in six months' time based on their present performance. The only way to validate the predictive validity of the instrument is to wait six months to see if its predictions were right. If a school social worker agrees that those children identified six month ago, and only those children, are now in need of services, we can be reasonably confident that the instrument had predictive validity.

Similarly, we might develop a measuring instrument to differentiate between offenders who will reoffend and offenders who will not. The predictive validity of the instrument is the degree to which the instrument's predictions turn out to be right.

MEASUREMENT RELIABILITY

A useful measuring instrument must not only be valid: it must also be reliable. That is, it must be capable of measuring the same variable over and over again and giving the same, or almost the same, result each time. Of course, there is no guarantee that the result it so reliably gives will be the right result. If our instrument is not valid, we might reliably measure a research participant's depression for quite a long time before we discover that what we have actually been measuring is self-esteem. In other words, it is perfectly possible to have reliability without validity.

However, it is not possible to have validity without reliability. An instrument is valid if it measures the right thing and measures it accurately. If we get a different result each time we measure a variable, we can hardly say that we have measured the variable accurately. There are many types of reliability, of which we will briefly discuss four: (1) the test-retest method, (2) the alternate-forms method, (3) the split-half method, and (4) the coefficient alpha method.

Test-Retest Method

As the name suggests, the test-retest method involves administering the instrument to the same individual or group of individuals on two or more separate occasions. If the instrument is reliable, we can expect to get the same result, or close to the same result, each time. The test-retest method of establishing reliability measures the instrument's temporal stability—that is, it determines how stable the instrument is from one administration to the next.

However, when we say that "we expect to get the same result each time," we are assuming that everything about the measurement situation is the same each time. If we are measuring a research participant's self-esteem, for example, we are assuming that the self-esteem itself is at the same level as it was the last time, and that all the various factors that might affect its measurement are also the same. The more temporally stable an instrument is, the less susceptible it is to random changes in the person's mood or the physical conditions surrounding the measurement environment.

However, to a certain extent, a change in the research participant's mood is what the instrument is supposed to measure. If the second measurement is different from the first, how can we know whether the person's self-esteem has really changed or whether the instrument is unreliable? In order to answer this question, we must first consider the possibility that the first measure affected the second. Perhaps the research participants remembered what they wrote the last time and are writing something different this time merely to enliven the proceedings;

or perhaps they are bored with the same measuring instrument and are answering items at random without bothering to read them.

There is also the possibility that the act of completing the instrument the first time has actually affected the variable being measured. Measuring instruments designed to assess the kinds of variables of interest to social workers often contain items that encourage introspective thought. Let us take the example of Roberto, who is one of our research participants who has just placed a 1 on Item 21 on the *GCS* (Figure 6.1). He thinks about "a full life" in a way that he had never thought about "a full life" before. If it is true that he feels he does not have a full life—and presumably this is correct or he would not have said so—perhaps trying to produce "a full life" would be a good idea.

Perhaps, after completing the measuring instrument for the first time, Roberto may make huge efforts to make his life more full, and reports, quite truthfully, a 5 on Item 21 the next time he completes the *GCS*. The *GCS* will now give a different result, not because it is unreliable but because there has been a change in the variable being measured (for only one item, that is); and it was the act of completing the instrument for the first time that caused the change to occur.

We thus have two possibilities that can confuse our efforts to test the temporal stability of a measuring instrument. First, there is the possibility that Roberto answered the instrument's items differently the second time because it *is* the second time, and he is bored with the instrument, or he is making an effort to be different, or familiarity has led to carelessness. Second, there is the possibility that his depression has actually changed as a result of completing the instrument. Both of these possibilities are time dependent.

If a long time has elapsed between the first administration of the instrument and the second, the research participant's boredom or familiarity with the instrument is less likely to affect the results than if only a short time has elapsed. In this respect, therefore, we should allow as long a time as possible to elapse between administrations when the purpose is to test the temporal stability of the instrument. However, the longer the time that elapses, the more likely it is that the variable being measured will have changed.

Timing, therefore, is a matter of balance. We have to wait long enough between administrations for the effects of the first administration to wear off, but not long enough for any real change to occur in the variable being measured. On a general level, for most instruments a two- to four-week interval is generally suitable, and the interval should rarely exceed six months.

In sum, the test-retest method of assessing reliability allows a measuring instrument to be compared directly with itself, and it reveals the continuity or stability of the instrument over time. The major limitation is that, however hard we strive to achieve a balanced interval between administrations, errors due to recall, practice, and repetition may still occur. The second method of establishing reliability, the alternate-forms method, overcomes this limitation.

Alternate-Forms Method

An alternate form of a measuring instrument, as the name suggests, is a second instrument that is as similar as possible to the first except that the actual items contained within it have been changed. Reliability can be established by presenting to the same individual or group the original instrument on the first occasion and an alternate form on the second. Because the actual items are different, it is less likely that recall will affect the results obtained from the alternate form.

For example, suppose we are going to conduct a four-week educational program in a certain community to improve attitudes toward racial minorities. One way to find out whether the program has the desired effect is to administer an instrument to measure the community's racial attitudes both before and after the program is implemented. We will obtain an initial measure of the community's attitudes toward racial tolerance, which we can designate O_1. When the program has been implemented and completed, we obtain a second measure of the community's attitudes, O_2, and the difference between O_2 and O_1 provides a crude measure of the effectiveness of the program. As will be discussed in Chapter 11, this research design is called the one-group pretest-posttest design and is written as:

$$O_1 \quad X \quad O_2$$

Where:

O_1 = First measurement of the community's attitudes, the dependent variable

X = Introduction of the educational program, the independent variable

O_2 = Second measurement of the community's attitudes, the dependent variable

If the educational program lasts four weeks, there will be four weeks between the first administration of the measuring instrument and the second. This is perhaps a short enough time for recall or boredom to affect the scores on the second administration if the same form of the instrument is used on both occasions. We can solve this problem by administering the original form of the instrument the first time and the alternate form the second: recall will not now affect the scores since the second instrument's items are different from the first one.

Using an alternative form of the original instrument will work only if we are quite sure that the two forms are equivalent. We may talk about two different forms, but what we have in fact is two different instruments. They may be the same in that there are the same number of items, expressed in the same kind of language and hopefully equivalent in content; but, nevertheless, the actual items are different and we must be sure that they are not so different as to affect the participant's scores.

Split-Half Method

If we have assessed the temporal stability of our instrument using the test-retest method, we have established that the instrument is stable: that is, it is neither influenced by incidental hazards such as research participants' sleepless nights nor is it unduly affected by the passage of time. If we have assessed reliability using the alternate-forms method, we also know that our instrument has equivalence. However, we do not know that it is homogeneous—that is, the same all the way through, or internally consistent.

In some cases, it may be particularly important that the items at the end are not more difficult, or do not take longer to complete, or are not of a different kind than the items at the beginning. One way to test for an instrument's homogeneity is to use the split-half method, in which the instrument is split in half and the two halves are administered in succession. If the first half yields the same, or almost the same, result as the second half, we can be fairly sure that the instrument is homogeneous, or internally consistent. We might obtain the halves by counting the total number of items and dividing by two; the first 15 items of a 30-item instrument would be administered first and the next 15 immediately after, for example.

Or, we could split the instrument into two halves by assigning all the odd-numbered items to one half and all the even-numbered items to the other half. We can then test for internal consistency by seeing if the odd-numbered items yield approximately the same score as the even-numbered items. If our instrument has internally consistency as well as stability and equivalency, we will know that it is reliable.

Coefficient Alpha Method

The coefficient alpha method is closely related to the split-half method in that it also determines an instrument's internal consistency. Coefficient alpha looks at how well, or how consistently, the items included within an instrument fit with each other. As we have seen, an instrument must be content valid—that is, it must include all the items that measure a particular variable such as self-esteem or racism. Not only must it contain relevant items, it must contain items that are related to each other.

Coefficient alpha (a statistical test), provides an estimate of the interrelatedness of the items. High coefficients, such as .80 and above, demonstrate that the items are highly related to each other and that the instrument is internally consistent. Lower coefficients, for example those below .60, suggest that the instrument is not as reliable for use in measuring a particular variable.

One note of caution, however: Longer instruments, those that are over 30 items, tend to have higher internal consistencies, whereas shorter ones will have lower internal consistencies. Therefore, the strength of coefficient alpha should be viewed keeping in mind the length of the instrument. A 10-item instrument with a coefficient alpha of .75, might be considered to be about as reliable as a 30-item instrument with a coefficient alpha of .90, given the relative lengths.

THE VALIDITY-RELIABILITY RELATIONSHIP

We have seen that a valid instrument is one that measures the variable it was designed to measure—and accurately. A reliable instrument is one that yields the same score, or almost the same score, every time it is administered, provided that the variable being measured has not changed. As we have also seen, an instrument can be reliable without being valid: It can consistently deliver the wrong results just as a watch can be consistently half an hour slow and a person can be consistently half an hour late. However, no instrument can be valid without being reliable, since we cannot say that our measure is accurate if it is different every time.

The relationship between validity and reliability can best be illustrated by using a simple analogy. Suppose we fire five rounds from a rifle at a target as shown in Figure 6.2. A valid aim would hit the bulls-eye: a reliable aim would place all the bullet-holes in the same spot, or close to the same spot. In Figure 6.2a, the aim is neither reliable nor valid since the bullet holes are scattered.

After we adjust the rifle, the shots are all in essentially the same place, as shown in Figure 6.2b, but that place is not the bulls-eye. The aim now is reliable but not valid. After a further adjustment, the shots are all in the bulls-eye, as in Figure 6.2c, and the aim is both reliable and valid.

MEASUREMENT ERROR

A measurement error is a variation in the result obtained from an instrument when there has been no variation in the variable being

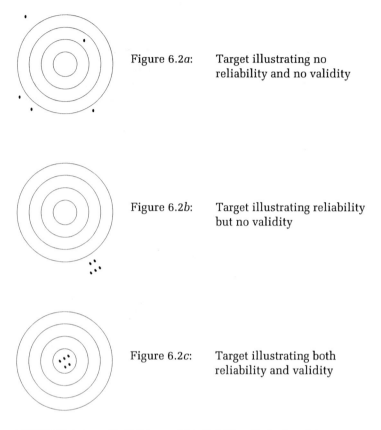

Figure 6.2*a*:   Target illustrating no reliability and no validity

Figure 6.2*b*:   Target illustrating reliability but no validity

Figure 6.2*c*:   Target illustrating both reliability and validity

FIGURE 6.2   Validity and Reliability Relationship

measured. The greater the variation or error, the less reliable, and thus less valid, the instrument becomes. Sources of error come in many forms, but they can generally be categorized as either constant errors or random errors.

Constant Errors

Constant errors are errors that remain with us throughout a study. They remain with us because they come from an unvarying source, such as the intelligence, education, socioeconomic status, race, culture, or religion of our research participants. Suppose, for example, that we have a number of students waiting to be assigned to different research courses and, in order to assign them, we want to measure their knowledge of research. We give them all the same research test, but it turns out that they are of various nationalities and some of them have a poor understanding of English. In this situation, we would be measuring not just their knowledge of research but also their ability to read and write English. It would not be possible to tell whether they failed to answer a question because they did not know the research content or because they did not understand the question. The varying standard of the English fluency of research participants constitutes a constant error.

Constant errors can also be due to the personal style of the research participants. These errors include acquiescence (a tendency to agree with anything, regardless of what it is); social desirability (a tendency to give answers that make one look good); and deviation (a tendency to give unusual responses). It is not only research participants who can introduce error into the measurement process; observers can as well. These are the people who complete instruments about other individuals' behavior; for example, parents counting a child's nightmares, or the staff in a nursing home counting how many hours each resident spends alone. Observers can commit various errors in a constant fashion, for example:

1. *Contrast Error*—to rate others as opposite to oneself with respect to a particular characteristic.
2. *Halo Effect*—to think that someone is altogether wonderful or terrible because he or she has one good or bad trait. Or to think that the trait being observed must be good or bad because the person is altogether wonderful or terrible.
3. *Error of Leniency*—always to give a good report.
4. *Error of Severity*—always to give a bad report.
5. *Error of Central Tendency*—to stay comfortably in the middle and avoid both ends.

Since these five errors are constant (i.e., they are present throughout the study), we often notice them and are able to do something about them. We might use another observer for example, or make allowances for one particular research participant's tendency to be different. Errors that are not constant—that is, random errors—are harder to find and to make allowances for.

Random Errors

Random errors are all those unknown factors that affect the variable being measured and the process of measurement in an inconsistent fashion. It has been suggested that eventually they cancel each other out and, ultimately, they probably do cancel each other. There are three types of random errors: transient qualities of the individual, situational factors, and administrative factors.

Transient qualities of the individual include things such as a research participant's bad night, boredom, fatigue, or anything temporary that might affect the way the measuring instrument is completed.

Situational factors include the unexpected noise outside the interview office window, the weather, the news, or anything that might affect the way a research participant fills out the measuring instrument.

Administrative factors include anything relating to the way in which the measuring instrument is administered. For example, interviewers who are supposed to ask people questions and fill in the answers on a sheet can affect a research participant's answers by the way they look, talk, and dress when asking the questions.

SUMMARY

Whenever we make a measurement, the instrument we use must be valid and reliable. A valid instrument is one that measures the variable it is supposed to measure and measures it accurately. In this chapter, we briefly presented four types of validity: content validity, face validity, concurrent validity, and predictive validity.

An instrument can be valid only if it is also reliable: that is, if it gives the same result consistently over repeated administrations, provided that the variable being measured has not changed. Reliability can be assessed in four ways, using: the test-retest method to establish temporal stability, the alternate-forms method to establish equivalency, and the split-half and coefficient alpha methods to establish homogeneity or internal consistency. An instrument that is reliable is not necessarily valid, since it is quite possible for a measuring instrument, like a watch, to be reliably wrong.

A measurement error is a variation in the result obtained from an instrument when there has been no variation in the variable being measured. Measurement errors can be categorized as either constant errors or random errors. Constant errors most often have to do with the way the study is designed and with the nature of the research participants and interviewers or observers. Random errors are errors that do not occur consistently or in any particular direction. There are three main types of random error: transient qualities of the individual, situational factors, and administrative factors.

In this chapter we have considered validity and reliability of measuring instruments. In Chapter 7 we discuss some of the common measuring instruments that can be used in social work research situations.

STUDY QUESTIONS

1. What is measurement validity? Provide an example of measurement validity via a social work example.

2. Discuss how a measuring instrument is assessed for its content validity. How can you tell if an instrument is content valid? Go to the library and select a social work research article. Is the measuring instrument content valid? Why or why not? Provide a rationale for your opinion.

3. What is face validity? What is the difference between content validity and face validity? Provide a social work example throughout your discussion. Go to the library and choose a social work research article. Is the measuring instrument face valid? Why or why not? Provide a rationale for your opinion.

4. What is the difference between concurrent validity and predictive validity? Describe a situation in which you would use an instrument that has concurrent validity. Describe a situation in which you would use an instrument that has predictive validity. Go to the library and select a relevant social work research article. Does the measuring instrument have concurrent validity or predictive validity? Provide a rationale for your opinion.

5. What is measurement reliability? Provide an example of measurement reliability via a social work example.

6. What does the test-retest method of reliability determine? Provide a social work example of how it could be used.

7. What is the alternate-forms method of reliability? Discuss how it could be determined in a social work situation.

8. What is the split-half method of reliability? Discuss how it could be determined in a social work situation.

9. Discuss the relationship between measurement validity and measurement reliability as presented in this chapter. Provide a social work example throughout your discussion.

10. What is measurement error? Discuss the two types and provide a social work example of each.

REFERENCES AND FURTHER READINGS

Adams, G.R., & Schvaneveldt, J.D. (1991). *Understanding research methods* (2nd ed., pp. 75-98, 149-158). White Plains, NY: Longman.

Babbie, E.R. (1992). *The practice of social research* (6th ed., pp. 115-144). Pacific Grove, CA: Wadsworth.

Bailey, K.D. (1994). *Methods of social research* (4th ed., pp. 61-104). New York: Free Press.

Bostwick, G.J., Jr., & Kyte, N.S. (1981). Measurement. In R.M. Grinnell, Jr. (Ed.), *Social work research and evaluation* (pp. 93-129). Itasca, IL: F.E. Peacock.

Bostwick, G.J., Jr., & Kyte, N.S. (1985). Measurement. In R.M. Grinnell, Jr. (Ed.), *Social work research and evaluation* (2nd ed., pp. 149-160). Itasca, IL: F.E. Peacock.

Bostwick, G.J., Jr., & Kyte, N.S. (1985). Validity and reliability. In R.M. Grinnell, Jr. (Ed.), *Social work research and evaluation* (2nd ed., pp. 161-184). Itasca, IL: F.E. Peacock.

Bostwick, G.J., Jr., & Kyte, N.S. (1988). Validity and reliability. In R.M. Grinnell, Jr. (Ed.), *Social work research and evaluation* (3rd ed., pp. 111-136). Itasca, IL: F.E. Peacock.

Bostwick, G.J., Jr., & Kyte, N.S. (1993). Measurement in research. In R.M. Grinnell, Jr. (Ed.), *Social work research and evaluation* (4th ed., pp. 174-197). Itasca, IL: F.E. Peacock.

Frankfort-Nachmias, C., & Nachmias, D. (1992). *Research methods in the social sciences* (4th ed., pp. 30-34, 147-168). New York: St. Martin's Press.

Gabor, P.A., & Grinnell, R.M., Jr. (1994). *Evaluation and quality improvement in the human services* (pp. 98-120). Needham Heights, MA: Allyn & Bacon.

Grinnell, R.M., Jr., & Williams, M. (1990). *Research in social work: A primer* (pp. 86-114). Itasca, IL: F.E. Peacock.

Hudson, W.W. (1981). Development and use of indexes and scales. In R.M. Grinnell, Jr. (Ed.), *Social work research and evaluation* (pp. 130-155). Itasca, IL: F.E. Peacock.

Hudson, W.W. (1982). *The clinical measurement package: A field manual.* Pacific Grove, CA: Wadsworth.

Jordan, C., Franklin, C., & Corcoran, K.J. (1993). Standardized measuring instruments. In R.M. Grinnell, Jr. (Ed.), *Social work research and evaluation* (4th ed., pp. 198-220). Itasca, IL: F.E. Peacock.

Judd, C.M., Smith E.R., & Kidder, I.H. (1991). *Research methods in social relations* (6th ed., pp. 41-67). Fort Worth, TX: Harcourt Brace.

Leedy, P.D. (1993). *Practical research: Planning and design* (3rd ed., pp. 31-42, 213-215). New York: Macmillan.

Marlow, C. (1993). *Research methods for generalist social work practice* (pp. 47-63). Pacific Grove, CA: Wadsworth.

Monette, D.R., Sullivan, T.J., & DeJong, C.R. (1994). *Applied social research* (3rd ed., pp. 93-118). Fort Worth, TX: Harcourt Brace.

Neuman, W.L. (1994). *Social research methods* (2nd ed., pp. 120-144). Needham Heights, MA: Allyn & Bacon.

Nunnally, J.C. (1978). *Psychometric theory* (2nd ed.). New York: McGraw-Hill.

Nurius, P.S., & Hudson, W.W. (1993). *Human services: Practice, evaluation, and computers.* Pacific Grove, CA: Brooks/Cole.

Royse, D.D. (1991). *Research methods in social work* (pp. 15-16, 20-21, 24-29, 181-185). Chicago: Nelson-Hall.

Rubin, A., & Babbie, E. (1993). *Research methods for social work* (2nd ed., pp. 119-181). Pacific Grove, CA: Wadsworth.

Weinbach, R.W., & Grinnell, R.M., Jr. (1995). *Statistics for social workers* (3rd ed.). White Plains, NY: Longman.

Yegidis, B.L., & Weinbach, R.W. (1991). *Research methods for social workers* (pp. 160-174). White Plains, NY: Longman.

Chapter 7

Measuring Instruments

I N THE PREVIOUS CHAPTER we presented a brief introduction to measurement validity and reliability. Here we will apply these two concepts to standardized and nonstandardized measuring instruments that can be used to collect data to answer research questions and test hypotheses.

STANDARDIZED MEASURING INSTRUMENTS

The most reliable and valid way to measure a variable is through the use of one or more standardized measuring instruments. Four considerations should be kept in mind when using a standardized measuring instrument.

First, the instrument should measure the variable as directly as possible. That is, it should measure the behavior or feeling itself rather than measuring something else—an image in a Rorschach inkblot, for example—that symbolizes the behavior or feeling. Like much else in social work, directness in measurement comprises a continuum from *completely direct* (e.g., counting the number of cigarettes a client smokes daily as a measure of smoking behavior) to *completely indirect* (e.g., the Rorschach inkblot). Most standardized instruments fall somewhere between the two extremes. For example, measuring aggression indirectly by means of a self-administered questionnaire is less direct than observing aggressive behavior, but more direct than deducing aggressive tendencies from a person's artwork. Wherever practically possible, the most direct measurement method of the variable should be chosen.

Second, the instrument should provide a valid and reliable measure of the variable being measured, as discussed in the previous chapter.

Third, the instrument must be sensitive to any small changes that have actually occurred in the variable being measured. If we are measuring depression, for example, we want to select an instrument that accurately measures depression and nothing else, and which is stable over time, does not reflect transient changes in the person's mood, and yet is sensitive to small changes in the person's actual depression level.

Fourth, and finally, the instrument must be practical: of a reasonable length, easy to administer and score, and acceptable to the research participant's own particular situation.

Cathleen Jordan, Cynthia Franklin, and Kevin Corcoran (1993) delineate six questions that need to be answered when selecting a standardized measuring instrument:

1. Why will the measurement occur?
   a. Research
   b. Assessment/diagnosis
   c. Evaluation
2. What will be measured?
   Specify_____
3. Who is appropriate for making the most direct observations?
   a. Research participant/client
   b. Practitioner or researcher
   c. Relevant other
4. Which type of format is acceptable?
   a. Inventories and surveys
   b. Indexes
   c. Scales
   d. Checklists and rating systems
5. Where will the measurement occur?
   a. General setting
   b. Situation-specific environment
6. When will the measurement occur?
   a. Random
   b. Posttest only
   c. Repeated over time

Advantages

There are two main characteristics that differentiate a standardized instrument from a nonstandardized instrument (to be discussed later in this chapter). First, standardized instruments have uniform items, administration procedures, and scoring systems, where nonstandardized instruments do not. Second, there is information available about a standardized instrument that enables the user to make a judgment about the instrument's suitability in a particular measurement situation. No such information is available about a nonstandardized instrument.

One very useful characteristic of a standardized instrument is that it has been developed by professionals. Someone else has decided what questions, or items, the instrument will contain, in what kind of format, how the respondent's answers will be scored, and how the instrument should be administered to the respondent in order to produce the most valid and reliable results.

Uniformity. Standardized measuring instruments have uniformity in the items they contain, in their administration procedures, and in their scoring procedures.

Uniform Items. A standardized measuring instrument is one that contains a series of standardized items designed to elicit information from a research participant or client. In other words, other people have done the work of deciding what items would constitute a content valid instrument (e.g., Figure 6.1).

Uniform Administration. Second, a standardized instrument has uniform procedures for its administration. Instruments to be completed by the respondent will usually begin with clear instructions such as those contained in the *GCS* (Figure 6.1).

Instructions at the beginning of the instrument ensure that everyone who completes it receives the same instructions and that people who complete it more than once receive the same instructions each time. There will be less likelihood of measurement errors as a result of the instrument being presented to a person differently this week than it was two weeks ago, or because one respondent understands clearly what to do while another has received only garbled instructions.

Similarly, if instructions are to be read out—to a child, for example—the administrator will have a written copy of what is to be read, and if the administrator is to complete the instrument personally after receiving oral responses from the client, these instructions, too, will be written down. In short, the administrator is required to adhere to a uniform administrative procedure and thus has limited opportunity to bias the respondent's answers or to make other administrative errors.

Uniform Scoring. Third, a standardized instrument has uniform scoring procedures. Sometimes, scoring is simply a matter of adding the numbers selected by the respondent for each of the items on the instrument. Several items in an instrument may need to be reverse scored (such as those listed on the bottom of the *GCS* presented in Figure 6.1), but standardized instruments have the advantage that the accompanying instructions tell us which these items are and how to do the scoring. Similarly, some instruments may use a true/false or yes/no scoring system, or be scored on a +3 to −3 scale or on a 10-point scale. Whatever scoring system is used, it is a *system*: it is the same every time the instrument is used, no matter who does the responding, administering, or scoring. Furthermore, the final score obtained is a single number so that no judgment is required on the part of scorer—only care in adding the figures. A uniform scoring system with no judgmental element means that measurement error due to scoring is minimal when a standardized instrument is used.

Many standardized measurements can be found in books such as the ones listed below (Jordan, Franklin, & Corcoran, 1993):

Bloom, M., Fischer, J., & Orme, J. (1994). *Evaluating practice: Guidelines for the accountable professional* (2nd ed.). Englewood Cliffs, NJ: Prentice-Hall.

Fischer, J., & Corcoran, K. (1994). *Measures for clinical practice: A sourcebook* (2nd ed., 2 vols.). New York: Free Press.

Keyser, D.J., & Sweetland, R.C. (Eds.) (1984-85). *Test critiques* (3 vols.). Kansas City, MO: Test Corporation of America.

Keyser, D.J., & Sweetland, R.C. (Eds.) (1987). *Test critiques compendium: Reviews of major tests from the test critiques series.* Kansas City, MO: Test Corporation of America.

Krysik, J., Hoffart, I., & Grinnell, R.M., Jr. (1993). *Student study guide for the fourth edition of social work research and evaluation.* Itasca, IL: F.E. Peacock.

Mitchell, J.V., Jr. (Ed.). (1974 to date). *Tests in print: An index to tests, test reviews and the literature on specific tests.* Lincoln, NE: Buros Institute of Mental Measurements, University of Nebraska-Lincoln.

Mitchell, J.V., Jr. (Ed.). (1983 to date). *Mental measurements yearbook.* Lincoln, NE: Buros Institute of Mental Measurements, University of Nebraska-Lincoln.

Nurius, P.S., & Hudson, W.W. (1993). *Human services: Practice, evaluation, and computers.* Pacific Grove, CA: Brooks/Cole.

Sweetland, R.C., & Keyser, D.J. (Eds.). (1986). *Tests: A comprehensive reference for assessments in psychology, education, and business.* Kansas City, MO: Test Corporation of America.

Tests in microfiche: *Annotated index.* (1975 to date). Princeton, NJ: Educational Testing Service.

In addition to books, standardized instruments can also be purchased from professional publishing companies such as the ones listed below (Jordan, Franklin, & Corcoran, 1993):

Academic Therapy Publications, 20 Commercial Boulevard, Novato, CA,

94947; (415) 883-3314.

Behavior Science Press, P.O. Box BV, University, AL, 35486; (205) 759-2089.

Biometrics Research, Research Assessment and Training Unit, New York State Psychiatric Institute, 722 West 168th Street, Room 341, New York, NY, 10032; (212) 960-5534.

Bureau of Educational Measurements, Emporia State University, Emporia, KS, 66801; (316) 343-1200.

Centre for Epidemiologic Studies, Department of Health and Human Services, 5600 Fishers Lane, Rockville, MD, 20857; (301) 443-4513.

Consulting Psychologists Press, Inc., 577 College Avenue, P.O. Box 11636, Palo Alto, CA, 94306; (415) 857-1444.

Educational and Industrial Testing Service (EDITS), P.O. Box 7234, San Diego, CA, 92107; (619) 222-1666.

Family Development Resources, Inc., 3160 Pinebrook Road, Park City, UT; (800) 649-5822.

Family Life Publications, Inc., Box 427, Saluda, NC, 28773; (704) 749-4971.

Institute for Personality and Ability Testing, Inc. (IPAT), P.O. Box 188, 1062 Coronado Drive, Champaign, IL, 61820; (217) 652-2922.

Merrill Publishing Company, 1300 Alum Creek Drive, Box 508, Columbus, OH, 43216; (614) 258-8441.

Personnel Research Institute (PRI), Psychological Research Services, Case Western Reserve University, 11220 Bellflower Road, Cleveland, OH, 44106; (216) 368-3546.

Professional Assessment Services Division, National Computer Systems, P.O. Box 1416, Minneapolis, MN, 55440; (800) 328-6759.

Psychological Assessment Resources, Inc., P.O. Box 98, Odessa, FL, 33556; (813) 920-6357.

Psychological Services, Inc., Suite 1200, 3450 Wilshire Boulevard, Los Angeles, CA, 90010; (213) 738-1132.

Research Concepts, A Division of Test Maker, Inc., 1368 East Airport Road, Muskegon, MI, 49444; (616) 739-7401.

Research Press, Box 317760, Champaign, IL, 61820; (217) 352-3273.

Science Research Associates, Inc. (SRA), 155 North Wacker Drive, Chicago, IL, 60606; (800) 621-0664, in Illinois (312) 984-2000.

Scott, Foresman, & Company, Test Division, 1900 East Lake Avenue, Glenview, IL, 60025; (708) 729-3000.

University Associates, Inc., Learning Resources Corporation, 8517 Production Avenue, P.O. Box 26240, San Diego, CA, 92126; (714) 578-5900.

United States Department of Defense, Testing Directorate, Head-Quarters, Military Enlistment Processing Command, Attention: MEPCT, Fort Sheridan, IL, 60037; (708) 926-4111.

WALMYR Publishing Company, P.O. Box 24779, Tempe, AZ, 85285; (602) 897-8168.

Western Psychological Services, 12031 Wilshire Boulevard, Los Angeles, CA, 90025; (213) 478-2061.

Information Available. The second characteristic that differentiates a standardized instrument from a nonstandardized one is that information is usually available about the former. This information will normally include a description of the instrument, a statement of its purpose, and sections on reliability, validity, scoring, administration, and norms. Since we have already discussed scoring and administration, we will focus here on reliability, validity, and norms.

Reliability and Validity. Chapter 6 presented the various methods for determining an instrument's reliability. Many standardized instruments report reliability data. For example, the information accompanying the instrument may say that its temporal stability and internal consistency are high.

Further, the information may say that the instrument has good predictive validity because it was able to predict respondent's solutions to specific assertive dilemmas. Given this information, the user will know to what degree a particular instrument can be trusted to measure what it is supposed to measure and measure it accurately.

Normative Data. The information accompanying a standardized instrument will often include normative data. Norms, as the name suggests, refer to a particular person's score on an instrument as compared with scores obtained by similar people who have completed the same instrument. In other words, norms are concerned with the interpretation of individual scores.

Cathleen Jordan, Cynthia Franklin, and Kevin Corcoran (1993) have listed some factors to consider when evaluating a standardized measuring instrument:

1. The Sample from which Data were Drawn:
   a. Are the samples representative of pertinent populations?
   b. Are the sample sizes sufficiently large?
   c. Are the samples homogeneous?
   d. Are the subsamples pertinent to respondents' demographics?
   e. Are the data obtained from the samples up to date?
2. The Validity of the Instrument:
   a. Is the content domain clearly and specifically defined?
   b. Was there a logical procedure for including the items?
   c. Is the criterion measure relevant to the instrument?
   d. Was the criterion measure reliable and valid?
   e. Is the theoretical construct clearly and correctly stated?
   f. Do the scores converge with other relevant measures?
   g. Do the scores discriminate from irrelevant variables?
   h. Are there cross-validation studies that conform to the above concerns?
3. The Reliability of the Instrument:
   a. Is there sufficient evidence of internal consistency?
   b. Is there equivalence between various forms?
   c. Is there stability over a relevant time interval?

4. The Practicality of Application:
   a. Is the instrument an appropriate length?
   b. Is the content socially acceptable to respondents?
   c. Is the instrument feasible to complete?
   d. Is the instrument relatively direct?
   e. Does the instrument have utility?
   f. Is the instrument relatively nonreactive?
   g. Is the instrument sensitive to measuring change?
   h. Is the instrument feasible to score?

FORMATS OF STANDARDIZED INSTRUMENTS

Cathleen Jordan, Cynthia Franklin, and Kevin Corcoran (1993) have provided one of the clearest discussions on the formats of standardized instruments to date. Thus, most of this section is taken from their work (Jordan, Franklin, & Corcoran, 1993). There are three basic types of measurement instruments: rating scales, questionnaire-type scales, and modified scales. All three formats of standardized measures aim to measure variables; the difference lies in the scaling techniques they use. Rating scales use judgments by self or others to assign an individual a single score (or value) in relation to the variable being measured. Questionnaire-type scales combine the responses of all the questions within an instrument to form a single overall score for the variable being measured. Modified scales are variants of rating scales and questionnaire-type scales, and do not fit into the above two classifications.

Rating Scales

The common feature in the various types of rating scales is the rating of individuals on various traits or characteristics at a point on a continuum or a position in an ordered set of response categories. In order to rate the individual, numerical values are assigned to each category.

Rating scales may be completed by the person being evaluated (self-rating) or by some significant other, such as a parent, supervisor, spouse, or social worker. Sometimes a client and a significant other are asked to complete the same rating scale in order to provide the social worker with two different views. For example, a wife and her husband might each rate the latter's openness to communication and other characteristics. Some people consider self-ratings superior to ratings by others, because individuals can evaluate their own thoughts, feelings, and behaviors most accurately, provided they are self-aware and willing to be truthful.

There are four types of rating scales: (1) graphic, (2) itemized, (3) comparative, and (4) self-anchored.

Graphic Rating Scales. In graphic rating scales, a variable is described on a continuum from one extreme to the other, such as "low to high" or "most to least." The points of the continuum are ordered in equal intervals and are assigned numbers. Most points have descriptions to help respondents locate their correct positions on the scale. The example below is a "feeling thermometer," which asks children to rate their level of anxiety from "very anxious" to "very calm" (Judd, Smith, & Kidder, 1991):

```
Check below how anxious you are.
100 ____  Very anxious
 90 ____
 80 ____
 70 ____
 60 ____
 50 ____  Neither anxious nor calm
 40 ____
 30 ____
 20 ____
 10 ____
  0 ____  Very calm
```

A second example of a graphic rating scale asks clients to rate their individual therapy sessions, from "not productive" to "very productive":

Please circle the number that comes closest to describing your feelings about the session you just completed.

1	2	3	4	5
Not productive		Moderately productive		Very productive

The major advantage of graphic rating scales is that they are easy to use, though care should be taken in the development of appropriate descriptive statements. For example, end statements that are so seemingly radical that it is unlikely anyone would choose them, such as "extremely hot" or "extremely cold," should not be used.

Itemized Rating Scales. Itemized rating scales offer a series of statements designed to rank different positions on the variable being measured. Respondents may be asked to check all the statements with which they agree, or only the one statement that is closest to their own position. For example, the itemized rating scale below asks clients to prioritize questions related to self-image.

If someone asked you to describe yourself, and you could tell only one thing about yourself, which of the following answers would you be most likely to give? (Put a check mark in the space next to that question.)

___ I come from (home state).
___ I work for (employer).
___ I am a (my occupation or type of work).
___ I am a (my church membership or preference).
___ I am a graduate of (my school).

Itemized rating scales vary according to the number of statements given and the specificity of the descriptions. Higher reliability is associated with clear definitions of categories. However, even the use of precise categories cannot obviate the fact that people respond differentially, due to their individual frames of reference. The less homogeneous the group of respondents, the less suitable is an itemized rating scale.

Comparative Rating Scales. In comparative rating scales, respondents are asked to compare an individual (or object) being rated with others. An often cited example is the ratings that professors are asked to give for students applying to enter graduate schools. Professors are often asked to compare a student with other students they have known and then to place the rated student in the top 10 percent, 20 percent, and so on of the total group.

A variation of the comparative rating scale is the rank-order scale, in which the rater is asked to rank individuals (or objects) in relation to one another on some characteristic. Below is an example of a rank-order scale that asks a social work supervisor to rank-order all the workers in the department who have been recommended for promotion:

Below are the four individuals whom your department has recommended for promotion. Please rank order these individuals from highest to lowest.

___ Mary Wong
___ Mike Shapiro
___ Bernice Liddie
___ Raymond Sanchez

The assumption underlying comparative rating scales is that there is some knowledge of the comparison groups—that is, a small, select group is being ranked. The scale would have little usefulness in other settings or with other groups.

Self-Anchored Rating Scales. Self-anchored rating scales are similar to others in that respondents are asked to rate themselves on a continuum, usually a seven- or nine-point scale from low to high. However, the specific referents for each point on the continuum are defined by the respondent. This type of scale is often used to measure such attributes as intensity of feeling or pain.

For example, clients who have difficulty in being honest in group therapy sessions could complete the following question, which is intended to measure their own perceptions of their honesty. The advantage is that they do not have to attempt to compare themselves with any external group.

Extent to which you feel you can be honest in the group.

1	2	3	4	5	6	7	8	9
Can never be honest			Can sometimes be honest				Can always be completely honest	

Questionnaire-Type Scales

Whereas rating scales require judgments on the part of a respondent who is asked to make a single judgment about the topic of interest, questionnaire-type scales include multiple items to which the individual is asked to respond. Then a total composite score of all the questions is obtained to indicate the respondent's position on the variable of interest. There are many different types of questionnaire-type scales. However, the most useful questionnaire-type scale for social work research is the summated scale.

Summated Scales. Summated scales are widely used in assessing individual or family problems, for needs assessment, and for other types of program evaluations. In the summated scale, respondents indicate the degree of their agreement or disagreement with each item. Response categories, may include "strongly agree," "agree," "neutral," "disagree," or "strongly disagree." An excellent example of a summated scale is Walter W. Hudson's *GCS*, presented in Figure 6.1.

Modified Scales

The third format of standardized measures is the modified scale, such as the semantic differential scale and the Goal Attainment Scale. They are modifications of rating scales and questionnaire-type scales.

Semantic Differential Scales. The semantic differential scale rates the individual's perception of three dimensions of the concept under study: evaluation (bad-good), potency (weak-strong), and activity (slow-fast). Each dimension includes several questions scored on a 7- or 11-point continuum on which only the extreme positions are identified. Below are a few questions taken from a scale designed to measure patients' feelings toward the nursing home in which they live (Atherton & Klemmack, 1982):

> Below are 29 pairs of words that can be used to describe nursing homes in general. For each pair of words, we would like you to circle the number that comes closest to your feelings about nursing homes. For example, if you feel that nursing homes are more good than bad, circle a number closer to good. The closer the number you circle is to good, the more good and less bad you feel nursing homes, in general, to be. Continue with each pair.

Good	1	2	3	4	5	6	7	Bad
Beautiful	1	2	3	4	5	6	7	Ugly
Rigid	1	2	3	4	5	6	7	Flexible
Dirty	1	2	3	4	5	6	7	Clean
Happy	1	2	3	4	5	6	7	Sad

The semantic differential scale correlates well with and appears more direct than some other scales. However, the scale is not completely comparable across variables. Much depends on the variable being measured and whether or not the three dimensions—evaluation, potency, and activity—are the best ways to measure a particular variable.

Goal Attainment Scales. Goal Attainment Scaling (GAS) is used widely to evaluate human services, primarily client or program outcomes. Specific areas of change are described and the range of possible outcomes, which usually consists of "most unfavorable" to "best anticipated" or "most favorable" outcomes, is identified. These scales can be completed by clients, judges, social workers, or other interested persons. Figure 7.1 is an example of a GAS for a nine-year-old boy with three problem areas: being overweight, spending too much time alone, and problems in school.

NONSTANDARDIZED MEASURING INSTRUMENTS

Wherever possible, a researcher should select a standardized measuring instrument, not only because it has been developed and tested by someone else—which saves us an inestimable amount of time and trouble—but also because of the advantages it has with regard to uniformity of content, administration, and scoring. However, there will be occasions when no standardized instrument seems to be right for the researcher's particular purpose. Some standardized instruments are excessively long, complicated, and difficult to score and interpret: That is, they do not meet the criteria for practicality previously mentioned.

Let us take an example from a practice perspective on how to use nonstandardized instruments. No standardized instrument may enable

Outcomes	Scale 1 Overweight	Scale 2 Spending Time Alone	Scale 3 Behavior Problems in School
Most unfavorable outcome thought likely (Score –2)	Gain of 3 lbs.	Spends 12 hours or more in own room	School contract indicates fighting and time in isolation
Less favorable outcome (Score –1)	Loss of 1 lb.	Spends 10 hours in own room	School contract indicates fighting
Expected outcome (Score 0)	Loss of 5 lbs.	Goes to activity room on staff suggestion	School contract shows point loss for behavior modification
More favorable outcome (Score +1)	Loss of 7 lbs.	Spends time in activity room on own initiative	School contract shows no point loss
Most favorable outcome thought likely (Score +2)	Loss of 10 lbs.	Participates in some activities	School contract gives points for cooperation

FIGURE 7.1   Example of a Goal Attainment Scale

us to discover how Ms. Yen feels about her daughter's marriage. The only way to get this information is to ask Ms. Yen; and if we want to keep on asking Ms. Yen—if the object of our intervention, say, is to help her accept her daughter's marriage—it will be best to ask the questions in the same way every time, so that we can compare the answers and assess her progress with some degree of certainty.

In other words, we will have to develop our own measuring instrument. Perhaps we might begin by asking Ms. Yen to list the things that bother her about her daughter's marriage; that is, we might ask her to develop an inventory. Or, if we do not think Ms. Yen is up to making a list, we might develop our own checklist of possibly relevant factors and ask her to check off all that apply.

Once we know what the factors are, we might be interested in knowing to what degree each one bothers Ms. Yen. Perhaps her daughter's marriage will involve moving to a distant town with her new husband, and it is this that is most important to Ms. Yen. Or perhaps her daughter's prospective husband has characteristics that Ms. Yen perceives as undesirable: He may be non-Asian, while Ms. Yen is Asian, or he may hold unacceptable religious or political views, or come from the "wrong" social or occupational class, and so on.

With Ms. Yen's help, we might develop a simple scale, running from "very bothersome" to "not at all bothersome." Perhaps, we might settle on something like the following:

> Here are a number of statements about your daughter's marriage. Please show how bothersome you find each statement to be by writing the appropriate number in the space to the left of each statement.
>
> 1 = Not at all bothersome
> 2 = A little bothersome
> 3 = Quite bothersome
> 4 = Very bothersome
>
> _____ 1. My daughter will move away after her marriage.
> _____ 2. My daughter's husband is non-Asian.
> _____ 3. My daughter's husband has been married before.
> _____ 4. I don't like my daughter's husband's family.
> _____ 5. My daughter's husband is unemployed.
> _____ 6. ...

We might decide to assess Ms. Yen's total botherment by adding up her scores on the individual items.

Sometimes a researcher will stumble across an existing instrument that has not been standardized. Figure 7.2 presents a checklist of some questions to ask when trying to determine if a specific nonstandardized instrument should be used.

Advantages

The major advantage of a nonstandardized instrument is that it is customized: That is, it is totally pertinent and appropriate to a particular client because it was designed with the client in view; possibly it was even designed *by* the client or at least with the client's help. We are not worried, as we would be with a standardized instrument, that the instrument was developed with a population different from the client's, or that the sample used for development and testing was not representative of the population from which it was drawn.

This advantage is more likely to apply if we have developed our own instrument than if we have borrowed one from a colleague who happened to have a similar client in a similar situation. Our colleague's client is not our client, and so we do not really know how appropriate the instrument will be. Neither can we be sure that we are administering

	YES	NO
1. Will the responses to the questionnaire provide the data needed to answer the research question?	___	___
2. Does the questionnaire address the same types of variables that are to be studied (i.e., value, attitude, personality trait, behavior, knowledge, skill, perception, judgment)?	___	___
3. Is the level of measurement appropriate for the intended statistical analyses?	___	___
4. Is the format of the items appropriate to the level of inquiry?	___	___
5. Does the questionnaire have known reliability? Are the circumstances in which reliability was established known?	___	___
6. Does the questionnaire have known validity?	___	___
7. Have there been other applications of the instrument? Or has the instrument been reviewed by other professionals in journals, books, or other publications?	___	___
8. Is the language of the questionnaire appropriate for the intended sample or population?	___	___
9. Are the instructions clear and easy to follow?	___	___
10. Do the items meet standards for item construction (i.e., clear, precise, not double-barreled, or biased)?	___	___
11. Is the flow of the questionnaire logical and easy to follow?	___	___
12. Is the questionnaire the appropriate length for the time available for data collection, the attention span of intended respondents, and other circumstances related to the design?	___	___

FIGURE 7.2 Checklist for Assessing Existing Nonstandardized Measuring Instruments

or scoring the instrument in the same way as did our colleague, since the administration and scoring instructions are unlikely to be written down.

If we develop our own instrument, it will probably be simple to administer and score because we knew when we designed it that we would personally have to administer and score it. Most of the previous questions about an instrument's practicality will have been answered in the affirmative. We know that the instrument provides useful information, and that it is relatively direct, of an appropriate length, feasible to complete, and acceptable to the client. We do not know, however, whether it is sensitive to real, small changes and to what degree it is nonreactive.

The main advantage, then, of using nonstandardized measures is that they can be constructed for an individual measurement purpose. For example, a researcher could use an instrument like the one displayed in Figure 7.3 below. Here, the researcher is interested in ascertaining the perceptions of people who live in a specific community—Northside.

This part of the survey is to learn more about your perceptions of these problems in the community. Listed below are a number of problems some residents of Northside have reported having. Please circle the number which represents how much of a problem they have been to you within the last year:

1. No problem (or not applicable to you)
2. Moderate problem
3. Severe problem

Questions	No Problem	Moderate Problem	Severe Problem	
1. Finding the product I need	1	2	3	_____
2. Impolite salespeople	1	2	3	_____
3. Finding clean stores	1	2	3	_____
4. Prices that are too high	1	2	3	_____
5. Not enough Spanish-speaking salespeople	1	2	3	_____
6. Public transportation	1	3	3	_____
7. Getting credit	1	2	3	_____
8. Lack of certain types of stores in Northside	1	2	3	_____
9. Lack of an employment assistance program	1	2	3	_____
10. Finding a city park that is secure	1	2	3	_____
11. Finding a good house	1	2	3	_____

FIGURE 7.3   Example of a Nonstandardized Survey Measuring Instrument

Disadvantages

Because the instrument is nonstandardized, we do not know to what degree it is valid and reliable. With respect to reliability, we do not know whether a difference in score from one administration to the next means that Ms. Yen's attitudes toward her daughter's marriage have really changed, or whether the difference is due to the instrument's instability over time or measurement error. With respect to validity, we do not know to what degree the instrument is content valid: that is, to what degree the items on our instrument include every aspect of Ms. Yen's feelings about the marriage. Perhaps what is really bothering her is that she believes her daughter suffers from an emotional disorder and is in no fit state to marry anyone. She has not mentioned this, there is no item on the instrument that would reveal it, and so we will never be able to discuss the matter with her.

In other words, we are not sure to what degree our instrument is providing a reliable and valid measure of Ms. Yen's attitudes toward her daughter's marriage. Perhaps the instrument focuses too much on the prospective husband, and it is really Ms. Yen's attitudes toward the husband that we are measuring, not her attitudes toward the marriage.

However, unless we have a real interest in the development of measuring instruments, we are unlikely to run validity and reliability checks on instruments we have developed ourselves. Our nonstandardized instruments may therefore be somewhat lacking with respect to validity and reliability. We will not be able to use them to evaluate our own practice, nor to compare our client's scores with the scores of other similar people in similar situations. However, we will be able to use them both to help determine the problem and to assess the client's progress in solving the problem. And a nonstandardized instrument is sometimes better than no instrument at all.

SUMMARY

All measuring instruments essentially fall into two categories: standardized and nonstandardized instruments. When we select a measuring instrument, we are looking for four characteristics. First, we want the instrument to measure the variable or problem as directly as possible. Second, we want it to provide a valid and reliable measure of the variable. Third, we want it to be sensitive to any small change that has actually occurred in the variable being measured; and, finally, we want it to be practical. While not perfect in all four respects, standardized instruments do have two advantages: uniformity regarding content, administration, and scoring; and availability of information.

Standardized instruments come in many different formats. Which particular standardized instrument we select will depend on our measurement need. The particular variable we wish to measure and the depth to which we want to study it will therefore determine, to some extent, which instrument we use. Whenever possible, the instrument will be used where and when the problem occurs, and environmental conditions such as distractions or limited time for completion must also be taken into account. In addition, the instrument must be geared to the person who is to use it. If the data are to be collected by clients or family members, the instrument's design must be appropriate for them.

STUDY QUESTIONS

1. Discuss the role that standardized measuring instruments play in the social work research process. Provide a social work example throughout your discussion.

2. List and discuss in detail the six questions that must be asked when selecting a standardized measuring instrument. Provide a social work example throughout your discussion.

3. List and discuss in detail the advantages of using standardized measuring instruments. Provide a social work example throughout your discussion.

4. List and describe the various formats that standardized measuring instruments can take. Provide a social work example of each format.

5. What are the differences between rating scales and questionnaire-type scales? Discuss the advantages and disadvantages of each. Provide a social work example throughout your discussion.

6. List and discuss the four different kinds of rating scales. Discuss the advantages and disadvantages of each. Provide a social work example throughout your discussion.

7. List and discuss the two different kinds of modified scales. Discuss the advantages and disadvantages of each. Provide a social work example throughout your discussion.

8. What are nonstandardized measuring instruments? Compare these instruments with standardized ones. Provide a social work example throughout your discussion.

9. List and discuss in detail the advantages and disadvantages of using nonstandardized measuring instruments. Provide a social work example throughout your discussion.

10. Do you feel the *GAS* as presented in Figure 6.1 has all the criteria to be classified as a standardized measuring instrument? Explain your answer in detail.

REFERENCES AND FURTHER READINGS

Adams, G.R., & Schvaneveldt, J.D. (1991). *Understanding research methods* (2nd ed., pp. 158-167, 200-201). White Plains, NY: Longman.

Atherton, C., & Klemmack, D. (1982). *Research methods in social work.* Lexington, MA: Heath.

Austin, M.J., & Crowell, J. (1985). Survey research. In R.M. Grinnell, Jr. (Ed.), *Social work research and evaluation* (2nd ed., pp. 275-305). Itasca, IL: F.E. Peacock.

Babbie, E.R. (1992). *The practice of social research* (6th ed., pp., 144-189). Pacific Grove, CA: Wadsworth.

Bailey, K.D. (1994). *Methods of social research* (4th ed., pp. 105-146, 349-376). New York: Free Press.

Bloom, M., Fischer, J., & Orme, J. (1994). *Evaluating practice: Guidelines for the accountable professional* (2nd ed.). Englewood Cliffs, NJ: Prentice-Hall.

Blythe, B.J., & Tripodi, T. (1989). *Measurement in direct practice.* Newbury Park, CA: Sage.

Fischer, J., & Corcoran, K. (1994). *Measures for clinical practice: A sourcebook* (2nd ed., 2 vols.). New York: Free Press.

Frankfort-Nachmias, C., & Nachmias, D. (1992). *Research methods in the social sciences* (4th ed., pp., 239-269, 427-446). New York: St. Martin's Press.

Grinnell, R.M., Jr., & Williams, M. (1990). *Research in social work: A primer* (pp. 86-114). Itasca, IL: F.E. Peacock.

Hudson, W.W. (1981). Development and use of indexes and scales. In R.M. Grinnell, Jr. (Ed.), *Social work research and evaluation* (pp. 130-155). Itasca, IL: F.E. Peacock.

Hudson, W.W., & Thyer, B.A. (1987). Research measures and indices in direct practice. In A. Minahan (Ed.). *Encyclopedia of social work* (pp. 487-498). Washington, DC: National Association of Social Workers.

Jordan, C., Franklin, C., & Corcoran, K.J. (1993). Standardized measuring instruments. In R.M. Grinnell, Jr. (Ed.), *Social work research and evaluation* (4th ed., pp. 198-220). Itasca, IL: F.E. Peacock.

Judd, C.M., Smith E.R., & Kidder, I.H. (1991). *Research methods in social relations* (6th ed., pp. 145-170, 228-253). Fort Worth, TX: Harcourt Brace.

Leedy, P.D. (1993). *Practical research: Planning and design* (3rd ed., pp. 187-199). New York: Macmillan.

Marlow, C. (1993). *Research methods for generalist social work practice* (pp. 75, 83-87). Pacific Grove, CA: Wadsworth.

Mindel, C. (1985). Instrument design. In R.M. Grinnell, Jr. (Ed.), *Social work research and evaluation* (2nd ed., pp. 206-230). Itasca, IL: F.E. Peacock.

Monette, D.R., Sullivan, T.J., & DeJong, C.R. (1994). *Applied social research* (3rd ed., pp. 153-172, 340-363). Fort Worth, TX: Harcourt Brace.

Neuman, W.L. (1994). *Social research methods* (2nd ed., pp. 145-168, 232-234). Needham Heights, MA: Allyn & Bacon.

Nurius, P.S., & Hudson, W.W. (1993). *Human services: Practice, evaluation, and computers.* Pacific Grove, CA: Brooks/Cole.

Royse, D.D. (1991). *Research methods in social work* (pp. 22-24, 129-147). Chicago: Nelson-Hall.

Rubin, A., & Babbie, E. (1993). *Research methods for social work* (2nd ed., pp. 182-216). Pacific Grove, CA: Wadsworth.

Yegidis, B.L., & Weinbach, R.W. (1991). *Research methods for social workers* (pp. 175-192). White Plains, NY: Longman.

Part III

Research Designs

IN THE FIRST FIVE CHAPTERS of Part III we introduce readers to the logic of research designs and the sampling procedures they can utilize. Chapter 8 provides a brief discussion of what constitutes an "ideal" experiment, while Chapter 9 addresses internal and external validity issues. Chapters 10 and 11 discuss single-system designs and group research designs, respectively, while Chapter 12 presents basic sampling procedures that can be utilized in social work research studies.

Chapter 8

The "Ideal" Experiment

ACH OF THE RESEARCH DESIGNS presented in Chapters 10 and 11 is typically evaluated on how much it resembles an "ideal" experiment. However, not all research designs that are used in social work research are intended to mimic an "ideal" experiment. In reality, most social work research studies do not even attempt to come close to one for a variety of reasons.

Although "ideal" experiments are seldom carried out by social workers because of difficulties in meeting the explicit criteria, they can be seen as a model against which all other designs can be compared. It is helpful to first establish the characteristics that differentiate an "ideal" experiment, which leads to explanatory knowledge, from other descriptive and exploratory designs as presented in Figure 4.1. What then are the characteristics of "ideal" experiments?

CHARACTERISTICS OF "IDEAL" EXPERIMENTS

An "ideal" experiment is one in which a research study most closely approaches certainty about the relationship between the independent and dependent variables. The purpose of doing an "ideal" experiment is to ascertain whether it can be concluded from the study's findings that the independent variable is, or is not, the only cause of change in the dependent variable. As pointed out in previous chapters, some social work research studies have no independent variable—for example, those studies that just want to find out how many people in a certain community wish to establish a community-based halfway house for people who are addicted to drugs.

The concept of an "ideal" experiment is introduced with the word "ideal" in quotes because such an experiment is rarely achieved in social work research situations. On a general level, in order to achieve this high degree of certainty and qualify as an "ideal" experiment, an explanatory research design must meet the following six conditions:

1. The time order of the independent variable must be established.
2. The independent variable must be manipulated.
3. The relationship between the independent and dependent variables must be established.
4. The research design must control for rival hypotheses.
5. At least one control group should be used.
6. Random sampling and random assignment procedures must be employed in choosing the sample for the study.

Time Order of Variables

In an "ideal" experiment, the independent variable must precede the dependent variable in time. Time order is crucial if the research study is to show that one variable causes another, because something that occurs later cannot be the cause of something that occurred earlier.

Suppose we want to study the relationship between adolescent substance abuse and gang-related behavior. The following hypothesis is formulated after some thought:

Adolescent substance abuse causes gang-related behavior.

In the above hypothesis, the independent variable is adolescent drug use, and the dependent variable is gang-related behavior. The substance abuse must come *before* gang-related behavior because the hypothesis states that adolescent drug use causes gang-related behavior.

However, we could also come up with the following hypothesis:

Adolescent gang-related behavior causes substance abuse.

In this hypothesis, adolescent gang-related behavior is the independent variable, and substance abuse is the dependent variable. According to this hypothesis, gang-related behavior must come *before* the substance abuse.

Manipulation of the Independent Variable

Manipulation of the independent variable means that we must do something with the independent variable in terms of at least one of the research participants in the study. In the general form of the hypothesis, if X occurs then Y will result, the independent variable (X) must be manipulated in order to effect a variation in the dependent variable (Y). There are essentially three ways in which independent variables can be manipulated:

1. *X present versus X absent.* If the effectiveness of a specific treatment intervention is being evaluated, an experimental group and a control group could be used. The experimental group would be given the intervention, the control group would not (see Box 3.3).
2. *A small amount of X versus a larger amount of X.* If the effect of treatment time on client's outcomes is being studied, two experimental groups could be used, one of which would be treated for a longer period of time.
3. *X versus something else.* If the effectiveness of two different treatment interventions is being studied, Intervention X_1 could be used with Experimental Group 1 and Intervention X_2 with Experimental Group 2.

There are certain variables, such as the gender or race of study participants, that obviously cannot be manipulated because they are fixed. They do not vary, so they are called constants, not variables, as was pointed out in Chapter 4. Other constants, such as socioeconomic status or IQ, may vary for participants over their life spans, but they are fixed quantities at the beginning of the study, probably will not change during the study, and are not subject to alteration by the one doing the study.

Any variable that is subject to alteration by the researcher (e.g., treatment time) can be considered an independent variable. At least one independent variable must be manipulated in a research study if it is to be considered an "ideal" experiment.

Relationships Between Variables

The relationship between the independent and dependent variables must be established in order to infer a cause-effect relationship at the explanatory knowledge level. If the independent variable is considered to be the cause of the dependent variable, there must be some pattern in the relationship between these two variables. An example is the hypothesis: The more time clients spend in treatment (independent variable), the better their progress (dependent variable). See Box 4.1 for an interesting example of how hard it is to establish relationships between and among variables.

Control of Rival Hypotheses

Rival hypotheses, or alternative hypotheses as described in Chapter 5, must be identified and eliminated in an "ideal" experiment. The logic of this requirement is extremely important, because this is what makes a cause-effect statement possible.

The prime question to ask when trying to identify a rival hypothesis is, "What other extraneous variables might affect the dependent variable?" (What else might affect the client's outcome besides treatment time?) At the risk of sounding redundant, "What else besides X might affect Y?" Perhaps the client's motivation for treatment, in addition to the time spent in treatment, might affect the client's outcome. If so, motivation for treatment is an extraneous variable that could be used as the independent variable in the rival hypothesis, "The higher the clients' motivation for treatment, the better their progress."

Perhaps the social worker's attitude toward the client might have an effect on the client's outcome, or the client might win the state lottery and ascend abruptly from depression to ecstasy. These extraneous variables could potentially be independent variables in other rival hypotheses. They must all be considered and eliminated before it can be said with reasonable certainty that a client's outcome resulted from the length of treatment time and not from any other extraneous variables.

Control over rival hypotheses refers to efforts on the researcher's part to identify and, if at all possible, to eliminate the extraneous variables in these alternative hypotheses. Of the many ways to deal with rival hypotheses, three of the most frequently used are to keep the extraneous variables constant, use correlated variation, or use analysis of co-variance.

Keeping Extraneous Variables Constant. The most direct way to deal with rival hypotheses is to keep constant the critical extraneous variables that might affect the dependent variable. As we know, a constant cannot affect or be affected by any other variable. If an extraneous variable can be made into a constant, then it cannot affect either the study's real independent variable or the dependent variable.

Let us take an example to illustrate the above point. Suppose, for example, that a social worker who is providing counseling to anxious clients wants to relate client outcome to length of treatment time, but most of the clients are also being treated by a consulting psychiatrist with antidepressant medication. Because medication may also affect the clients' outcomes, it is a potential independent variable that could be used in a rival hypothesis. However, if the study included only clients who have been taking medication for some time before the treatment intervention began, and who continue to take the same medicine in the same way throughout treatment, then medication can be considered a constant (in this study anyway).

Any change in the clients' anxiety levels after the intervention will, therefore, be due to the intervention with the help of the medication. The extraneous variable of medication, which might form a rival hypothesis, has been eliminated by holding it constant. In short, this study started out with one independent variable, the intervention, then added the variable of medication to it so the final independent variable is the intervention plus the medication.

This is all very well in theory. In reality, however, a client's drug regime is usually controlled by the psychiatrist and may well be altered at any time. Even if the regime is not altered, the effects of the drugs might not become apparent until the study is under way. In addition, the client's level of anxiety might be affected by a host of other extraneous variables over which the social worker has no control at all: for example, living arrangements, relationships with other people, the condition of the stock market, or an unexpected visit from an IRS agent. These kinds of pragmatic difficulties tend to occur frequently in social work practice and research. It is often impossible to identify all rival hypotheses, let alone eliminate them by keeping them constant.

Correlated Variation. Rival hypotheses can also be controlled with correlated variation of the independent variables. Suppose, for example, that we are concerned that income has an effect on a client's compulsive behavior. The client's income, which in this case is subject to variation due to seasonal employment, is identified as an independent variable. The client's living conditions in a hotel room rented by the week is then identified as the second independent variable that might well affect the client's level of compulsive behavior. These two variables, however, are correlated since living conditions are highly dependent on income.

Correlated variation exists if one potential independent variable can be correlated with another. Then only one of them has to be dealt with in the research study.

Analysis of Covariance. In conducting an "ideal" experiment, we must always aim to use two or more groups that are as equivalent as possible on all important variables. However, sometimes this goal is not feasible. Perhaps we are obliged to use existing groups that are not as equivalent as we would like. Or, perhaps during the course of the study we discover inequivalencies between the groups that were not apparent at the beginning.

A statistical method called *analysis of covariance* can be used to compensate for these differences. The mathematics of the method is far beyond the scope of this text, but an explanation can be found in many advanced statistics texts.

Use of a Control Group

An "ideal" experiment should use at least one control group in addition to the experimental group. The experimental group may receive an intervention that is withheld from the control group, or equivalent groups may receive different interventions or no interventions at all.

A social worker who initiates a treatment intervention is often interested in knowing what would have happened if the intervention had not been used or had some different intervention been substituted. Would members of a support group for alcoholics have recovered anyway without the social worker's efforts? Would they have recovered faster or more completely had family counseling been used instead of the support group approach?

The answer to these questions will never be known if only the support group is studied. But, what if another group of alcoholics is included in the research design? In a typical design with a control group, two equivalent groups, 1 and 2, would be formed, and both would be administered the same pretest to determine the initial level of the dependent variable (e.g., degree of alcoholism). Then an intervention would be initiated with Group 1 but not with Group 2. The group treated—Group 1 or the experimental group—would receive the independent variable (the intervention). The group not treated—Group 2 or the control group—would not receive it. At the conclusion of the intervention, both groups would be given a posttest (the same measure as the pretest). The pretest and posttest consist of the use of some sort of data-gathering procedure, such as a survey or self-report measure, to measure the dependent variable before and after the introduction of the independent variable.

Group designs can be written in symbols as follows:

$$\text{Experimental Group:} \quad R \quad O_1 \quad X \quad O_2$$
$$\text{Control Group:} \quad R \quad O_1 \quad\quad O_2$$

Where:

R = Random assignment to group
O_1 = First measurement of the dependent variable
X = Independent variable
O_2 = Second measurement of the dependent variable

The two Rs in this design indicate that the research participants are to be randomly assigned to each group. The symbol X, which, as usual,

TABLE 8.1   Client Outcomes by Group

Group	Pretest (O_1)	Posttest (O_2)	Difference $(O_1 - O_2)$
Experimental	24	68	– 44
Control	26	27	– 1

stands for the independent variable, indicates that an intervention is to be given to the experimental group after the pretest (O_1) and before the posttest (O_2). The absence of X for the control group indicates that the intervention is not to be given to the control group.

The design presented on the preceding page is called the classical experimental design because it comes closest to having all the characteristics necessary for an "ideal" experiment. It will be described in more detail in Chapter 11.

Table 8.1 displays results from a research study of this type. If the experimental group is equivalent to the control group, the pretest results should be approximately the same for both groups. Within an acceptable margin of error, 24 is approximately the same as 26. Since the control group has not received the intervention, the posttest results for this group would not be expected to differ appreciably from the pretest results. In fact, the posttest score, 27, differs little from the pretest score, 26, for the control group.

— Because the experimental and control groups may be considered equivalent, any rival hypotheses that affected the experimental group would have affected the control group in the same way. No rival hypothesis affected the control group, as indicated by the fact that without the intervention, the pretest and posttest scores did not differ. Therefore, it can be assumed that no rival hypothesis affected the experimental group, either, and the difference (-44) between pretest and posttest scores for the experimental group was probably due to the intervention and not to any other factor.

Random Sampling and Random Assignment

Random sampling and assignment procedures are essential to assure that the results of research studies apply not only to the people who actually took part in them but to a much larger population. This makes it possible to generalize a study's findings to other settings or to other people with similar characteristics, provided that we are able to establish that the sample—those who are chosen to take part in a study—is representative of the population to whom the findings are to be generalized. A sample may also consist of cases or elements chosen from a set or population of objects or events, but most social work studies deal with people, individually or in groups.

Random sampling is the procedure used to select a sample from a population in such a way that the chosen individuals (or objects or events) accurately represent the population from which they were drawn. Once a sample has been randomly selected, the individuals in it are randomly assigned to either an experimental or a control group in such a way that the two groups are equivalent. This procedure is known as random assignment or randomization. In random assignment, the word *equivalent* means equal in terms of the variables that are important to the study, such as the clients' motivation for treatment, or problem severity.

If the effect of treatment time on clients' outcomes is being studied, for example, the research design might use one experimental group that is treated for a comparatively longer time, a second experimental group that is treated for a shorter time, and a control group that is not treated at all. If we are concerned that the clients' motivation for treatment might also affect their outcomes, the research participants can be assigned so that all the groups are equivalent (on the average) in terms of their motivation for treatment.

The process of random sampling from a population followed by random assignment of the sample to groups is illustrated in Figure 8.1. Let us say that the research design calls for a sample size of one-tenth of the population. From a population of 10,000, therefore, a random sampling procedure is used to select a sample of 1,000 individuals. Then random assignment procedures are used to place the sample of 1,000 into two equivalent groups of 500 individuals each. In theory, Group A will be equivalent to Group B, which will be equivalent to the random sample, which will be equivalent to the population in respect to all important variables studied. Various sampling strategies will be discussed in detail in Chapter 12.

Matched Pairs. Besides randomization, another, more deliberate method of assigning people or other units to groups involves matching. The matched pairs method is suitable when the composition of each

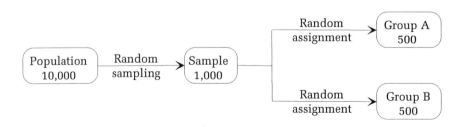

FIGURE 8.1   Random Sampling and Random Assignment Procedures

group consists of variables with a range of characteristics. One of the disadvantages of matching is that some individuals cannot be matched and so cannot participate in the study. When available research participants are few, this can be a serious drawback.

Suppose a new training program for teaching parenting skills to foster mothers is being evaluated, and it is important that the experimental and control groups have an equal number of highly skilled and less skilled foster parents before the training program is introduced. The women chosen for the sample would be matched in pairs according to their skill level; the two most skilled foster mothers are matched, then the next two, and so on. One person in each pair of approximately equally skilled foster parents is then randomly assigned to the experimental group and the other is placed in the control group.

Let us suppose that in order to compare the foster mothers exposed to the new training program with women who were not, a standardized measuring instrument that measures parenting skill level (the dependent variable) is administered to a sample of ten women. The scores can range from 100 (excellent parenting skills) to zero (poor parenting skills). Then their scores are rank ordered from the highest to the lowest, and out of the foster mothers with the two highest scores, one is selected to be assigned to either the experimental group or the control group. It does not make any difference which group the first participant is randomly assigned to, as long as there is an equal chance that the participant will go to either the control group or the experimental group. In this example the first person is randomly chosen to go to the experimental group, as illustrated below:

Rank Order of Parenting Skills Scores (in parentheses)

> *First Pair:*
> (99) Randomly assigned to the experimental group
> (98) Assigned to the control group
>
> *Second Pair:*
> (97) Assigned to the control group
> (96) Assigned to the experimental group
>
> *Third Pair:*
> (95) Assigned to the experimental group
> (94) Assigned to the control group
>
> *Fourth Pair:*
> (93) Assigned to the control group
> (92) Assigned to the experimental group
>
> *Fifth Pair:*
> (91) Assigned to the experimental group
> (90) Assigned to the control group

The foster parent with the highest score (99) is randomly assigned to the experimental group, and this person's "match," with a score of 98, is assigned to the control group. This process is reversed with the next matched pair, where the first person is assigned to the control group and the match is assigned to the experimental group. If the assignment of research participants according to scores is not reversed for every other pair, one group will be higher than the other on the variable being matched.

To illustrate this point, suppose the first participant (highest score) in each match is always assigned to the experimental group. The experimental group's average score would be 95 (99 + 97 + 95 + 93 + 91 = 475/5 = 95), and the control group's average score would be 94 (98 + 96 + 94 + 92 + 90 = 470/5 = 94). If every other matched pair is reversed, however, as in the example, the average scores of the two groups are closer together; 94.6 for the experimental group (99 + 96 + 95 + 92 + 91 = 473/5 = 94.6) and 94.4 for the control group (98 + 97 + 94 + 93 + 90 = 472/5 = 94.4). In short, 94.6 and 94.4 (difference of 0.2) are closer together than 95 and 94 (difference of 1).

SUMMARY

In this chapter we have presented the characteristics that are necessary for an "ideal" experiment. In an "ideal" experiment the following six characteristics will all be present: the independent variable must come before the dependent variable, the independent variable must be manipulated, a relationship must be established between the independent and dependent variable, rival hypotheses must be controlled, at least one control group must be used, and random sampling and random assignment procedures must be utilized.

At this point, it should be relatively clear that the necessity of including each of these characteristics makes it an unusual event for social workers to utilize an "ideal" experimental design. Because social work research is usually conducted in the natural environment rather than in laboratory settings, we rarely have the ability to control for or influence our research study to the degree necessary for an "ideal" experiment. Nevertheless, having the classical experimental design as a standard for excellence reminds us of what we might aspire to in designing research studies at the explanatory level.

STUDY QUESTIONS

1. Discuss why very few social work research studies ever come close to "ideal" experiments. What are some of the reasons why it would be unethical to do "ideal" experiments with clients?

2. Discuss in detail each one of the six characteristics that are necessary to approach an "ideal" experiment in social work research. Provide a social work example in your discussion.

3. Design an "ideal" experiment with the general problem area of child sexual abuse.

4. Construct an "ideal" explanatory-level experiment with the research problem of suicide. What ethical problems did you run into?

5. Construct an "ideal" explanatory-level experiment with the research problem of abortion. What ethical problems did you run into?

6. Go to the library and identify a research article that comes closest to an "ideal" experiment. What were the characteristics that were missing in the study that prevented it from becoming an "ideal" experiment?

7. With the article you selected for Question 6, hypothetically redesign the study using the six characteristics for an "ideal" experiment.

8. In your own words, discuss why it is important for you to know the six characteristics of an "ideal" experiment when you design any given research study.

9. Why is it necessary to use at least one control group (or comparison group) when trying to design an "ideal" experiment?

10. Write an explanatory-level research hypothesis in which Variable A (some variable of your choice) is the independent variable and Variable B (some variable of your choice) is the dependent variable. Now rewrite the same hypothesis with the two variables reversed. Which hypothesis do you think is correct? Why? How would you go about testing the two hypotheses? Include in your discussion how you would address all six of the characteristics of an experiment.

REFERENCES AND FURTHER READINGS

Adams, G.R., & Schvaneveldt, J.D. (1991). *Understanding research methods* (2nd ed., pp. 101-118, 228-251). White Plains, NY: Longman.

Babbie, E.R. (1992). *The practice of social research* (6th ed., pp. 86-112). Pacific Grove, CA: Wadsworth.

Bailey, K.D. (1994). *Methods of social research* (4th ed., pp. 36-41, 275-292). New York: Free Press.

Campbell, D.T., & Stanley, J.C. (1963). *Experimental and quasi-experimental designs for research*. Skokie, IL: Rand McNally.

Frankfort-Nachmias, C., & Nachmias, D. (1992). *Research methods in the social sciences* (4th ed., pp. 97-99, 271-290). New York: St. Martin's Press.

Grinnell, R.M., Jr. (1993). Group research designs. In R.M. Grinnell, Jr. (Ed.), *Social work research and evaluation* (4th ed., pp. 118-153). Itasca, IL: F.E. Peacock.

Grinnell, R.M., Jr., & Stothers, M. (1988). Research designs. In R.M. Grinnell, Jr. (Ed.), *Social work research and evaluation* (3rd ed., pp. 199-239). Itasca, IL: F.E. Peacock.

Grinnell, R.M., Jr., & Williams, M. (1990). *Research in social work: A primer* (pp. 138-176). Itasca, IL: F.E. Peacock.

Judd, C.M., Smith E.R., & Kidder, I.H. (1991). *Research methods in social relations* (6th ed., pp. 27-36, 298-320). Fort Worth, TX: Harcourt Brace.

Leedy, P.D. (1993). *Practical research: Planning and design* (3rd ed., pp. 113-128, 137-147). New York: Macmillan.

Marlow, C. (1993). *Research methods for generalist social work practice* (pp. 66-68, 95-96, 137-138). Pacific Grove, CA: Wadsworth.

Monette, D.R., Sullivan, T.J., & DeJong, C.R. (1994). *Applied social research* (3rd ed., pp. 82-92). Fort Worth, TX: Harcourt Brace.

Neuman, W.L. (1994). *Social research methods* (2nd ed., pp. 55-78). Needham Heights, MA: Allyn & Bacon.

Royse, D.D. (1991). *Research methods in social work* (pp. 43-44, 79-81, 120-121, 217-232). Chicago: Nelson-Hall.

Rubin, A., & Babbie, E. (1993). *Research methods for social work* (2nd ed., pp. 29-30, 106-112, 357-365). Pacific Grove, CA: Wadsworth.

Toseland, R.W. (1985). Research methods. In R.M. Grinnell, Jr. (Ed.), *Social work research and evaluation* (2nd ed., pp. 115-130). Itasca, IL: F.E. Peacock.

Tripodi, T. (1974). *Uses and abuses of social research in social work.* New York: Columbia University Press.

Tripodi, T. (1981). The logic of research design. In R.M. Grinnell, Jr. (Ed.), *Social work research and evaluation* (pp. 198-225). Itasca, IL: F.E. Peacock.

Tripodi, T. (1985). Research designs. In R. M. Grinnell, Jr. (Ed.), *Social work research and evaluation* (2nd ed., pp. 231-259). Itasca, IL: F.E. Peacock.

Yegidis, B.L., & Weinbach, R.W. (1991). *Research methods for social workers* (pp. 73-90). White Plains, NY: Longman.

Chapter 9

Internal and External Validity

W E MUST REMEMBER that the research design finally selected for a research study should always be evaluated on how close it comes to an "ideal" experiment in reference to the six characteristics presented in the previous chapter. As stressed throughout this book, most research designs used in social work do not closely resemble an "ideal" experiment. However, the research design selected needs to be evaluated on how well it meets its primary objective—to adequately answer a research question or to test a hypothesis. In short, a research design will be evaluated on how well it controls for internal and external validity factors.

Internal validity has to do with the ways in which the research design ensures that the introduction of the independent variable (if any) can be identified as the sole cause of change in the dependent variable. In contrast, external validity has to do with the extent to which the research design allows for generalization of the findings of the study to other groups and other situations.

Both internal and external validity are achieved in a research design by taking into account various threats that are inherent in all research efforts. A design for a study with both types of validity will recognize and attempt to control for potential factors that could affect the study's outcome or findings. An "ideal" experiment tries to control as many threats to internal and external validity as possible.

THREATS TO INTERNAL VALIDITY

In any explanatory research study, we should be able to conclude from the study's findings that the independent variable is, or is not, the only cause of change in the dependent variable. If a study does not have internal validity, such a conclusion is not possible, and the study's findings can be misleading.

Internal validity is concerned with one of the requirements for an "ideal" experiment—the control of rival hypotheses, or alternative explanations for what might bring about a change in the dependent variable. The higher the internal validity of a research study, the greater the extent to which rival hypotheses can be controlled; the lower the internal validity, the less they can be controlled. Thus, we must be prepared to rule out the effects of factors other than the independent variable that could influence the dependent variable.

History

The first threat to internal validity, history, refers to any outside event—either public or private—that may affect the dependent variable and was not taken into account in the research design. Many times, it refers to events occurring between the first and second measurement of the dependent variable (the pretest and the posttest). If events occur that have the potential to alter the second measurement, there would be no way of knowing how much (if any) of the observed change in the dependent variable is a function of the independent variable and how much is attributable to these events.

Suppose, for example, that a study is being conducted to investigate the effect of an educational program on racial tolerance. We may decide to measure the dependent variable, racial tolerance in the community, before introducing the independent variable, the educational program.

The educational program is then implemented. Since it is the independent variable, it is represented by X. Finally, racial tolerance is measured again, after the program has run its course. This final measurement yields a posttest score, represented by O_2. The entire one-group pretest-posttest study design can be written as:

$$O_1 \quad X \quad O_2$$

Where:

O_1 = First measurement, or pretest score, of racial tolerance (dependent variable)

X = Educational program (independent variable)

O_2 = Second measurement, or posttest score, of racial tolerance (dependent variable)

The difference between the values O_2 and O_1 represent the difference in racial tolerance in the community before and after the educational program. If the study is internally valid, $O_2 - O_1$ will be a crude measure of the effect of the educational program on racial tolerance; and this is what we were trying to discover. However, suppose that, before the posttest could be administered, an outbreak of racial violence occurred in the community such as the type that occurred in Los Angeles in the summer of 1992. Violence can be expected to have a negative effect on racial tolerance, and the posttest scores may, therefore, show a lower level of tolerance than they would have done if the violence had not occurred. The effect, $O_2 - O_1$, will now be the combined effects of the educational program *and* the violence, not the effect of the program alone, as we intended.

Racial violence is an extraneous variable that we could not have anticipated and did not control for when designing the study. Other examples might include an earthquake, an election, illness, divorce, or marriage—any event, public or private that could affect the dependent variable. Any such variable that is unanticipated and uncontrolled for is an example of history.

Maturation

Maturation, the second threat to internal validity, refers to changes, both physical and psychological, that take place in a study's participants over time and can affect the dependent variable. Suppose that we are evaluating an interventive strategy designed to improve the behavior of adolescents who engage in delinquent behavior. Since the behavior of adolescents changes naturally as they mature, the observed changed behavior may have been due as much to their natural development as it was to the intervention strategy. However, maturation refers not only to physical or mental growth. Over time, people grow older, more or less anxious, more or less bored, and more or less motivated to take part in a research study. All these factors and many more can affect the way in which people respond when the dependent variable is measured a second or third time.

Testing

The third threat to internal validity, testing, is sometimes referred to as the initial measurement effect. Thus, the pretests that are the starting point for many research designs are another potential threat to internal validity. One of the most utilized research designs involves three steps: measuring some dependent variable, such as learning behavior in school or attitudes toward work; initiating a program to change that variable (the independent variable); then measuring the dependent variable again at the conclusion of the program. This simple one-group pretest-posttest design can be written in symbols as follows:

$$O_1 \quad X \quad O_2$$

Where:

O_1 = First measurement of the dependent variable, or pretest score
X = Independent variable
O_2 = Second measurement of the dependent variable, or posttest score

The testing effect is the effect that taking a pretest might have on posttest scores. Suppose that Roberto, a research participant, takes a pretest to measure his initial level of racial tolerance before being exposed to a racial tolerance educational program. He might remember some of the items on the pretest, think about them later, and change his views on racial issues before taking part in the educational program. After the program, his posttest score will reveal his changed opinions, and we may incorrectly assume that the program was responsible, whereas the true cause was his experience with the pretest.

Sometimes, a pretest induces anxiety in a participant, so that Roberto receives a worse score on the posttest than he should have; or boredom with the same questions repeated again may be a factor. In order to avoid the testing effect, we may wish to use a design that does not require a pretest. If a pretest is essential, we then must consider the length of time that elapses between the pretest and posttest measurements. A pretest is far more likely to affect the posttest when the time between the two is short. The nature of the pretest is another factor. Questions dealing with factual matters, such as knowledge levels, may have a larger testing effect because they tend to be more easily recalled.

Instrumentation Error

The fourth threat to internal validity is instrumentation error, which refers to all the troubles that can afflict the measurement process. The instrument may be unreliable or invalid, as presented in Chapter 6. It may be a mechanical instrument, such as an electroencephalogram (EEG), that has malfunctioned. Occasionally, the term *instrumentation error* is used to refer to an observer whose observations are inconsistent; or to measuring instruments, such as the ones presented in Chapter 7, that are reliable in themselves, but not administered properly.

"Administration," with respect to a measuring instrument, means the circumstances under which the measurement is made: where, when, how, and by whom. For example, a mother being asked about her attitudes toward her children may respond in one way in the social worker's office and in a different way at home when her children are screaming around her feet. A client's verbal response may differ from her written response; or she may respond differently in the morning than she would in the evening, or differently alone than she would in a group. These different situational responses do not indicate a true change in the feelings, attitudes, or behaviors being measured, but are only examples of instrumentation error. Most standardized measures include specific directions so that each individual is introduced to the instrument in the same way. Such considerations control for the threat of instrumentation.

Statistical Regression

The fifth threat to internal validity, statistical regression, refers to the tendency of extremely low and high scores to regress, or move toward the average score. Suppose that a student, named Maryanna, has to take a multiple-choice exam on a subject she knows nothing about. There are many questions, and each question has five possible answers. Since, for each question, Maryanna has a 20 percent (one in five) chance of guessing correctly, she might expect to score 20 percent on the exam just by guessing. If she guesses badly, she will score a lot lower; if well, a lot higher. The other members of the class take the same exam and, since they are all equally confused, the average score for the class is 20 percent.

Now suppose that the instructor separates the low scorers from the high scorers and tries to even out the level of the class by giving the low scorers special instruction. In order to determine if the special instruction has been effective, the entire class then takes another multiple-choice exam. The result of the exam is that the low scorers do better than they did the first time, and the high scorers worse. The instructor believes that this has occurred because the low scorers received special instruction and the high scorers did not.

However, according to the logic of statistical regression, both the low scorers and the high scorers would move toward the total group's average score. Even without any special instruction and still in their state of ignorance, the low scorers would be expected to score higher than they did before; that is, by moving toward the total group's average, their scores would increase. The high scorers would be expected to score lower than they did before.

It would be easy for the research instructor to assume that the low scores had increased because of the special instruction and the high scores had decreased because of the lack of it. Not necessarily so, however; the instruction may have had nothing to do with it. It may all be due to statistical regression.

Differential Selection of Study Participants

The sixth threat to internal validity is differential selection of study participants. To some extent, the participants selected for a research study are different from one another to begin with. "Ideal" experiments, however, require random sampling and random assignment to conditions, as presented in the previous chapter. This assures that the results of a study will be generalizable to a larger population, thus addressing threats to external validity. In respect to differential selection as a threat to internal validity, "ideal" experiments control for this since equivalency among the groups at pretest is assumed through the randomization process.

This threat is, however, present when we are working with preformed groups or groups that already exist, such as classes of students, self-help groups, or community groups. In terms of the external validity of such designs, because there is no way of knowing whether the preformed groups are representative of any larger population, it is not possible to generalize the study's results beyond the people (or objects or events) that were actually studied. The use of preformed groups also affects the internal validity of a study, though. It is quite probable that different preformed groups will not be equivalent with respect to relevant variables, and that these initial differences will invalidate the results of the posttest.

For example, a child abuse prevention educational program for children in schools might be evaluated by comparing the prevention skills of one group of children who have experienced the educational program with the skills of a second group who have not. In order to make a valid comparison, the two groups must be as similar as possible, with respect to age, gender, intelligence, socioeconomic status, and anything else that might affect the acquisition of child abuse prevention skills. We would have to make every effort to form or select equivalent groups, but the groups are sometimes not as equivalent as might be hoped, especially if we are obliged to work with preformed groups, such as classes of students or community groups. If the two groups are different before the intervention was introduced, there is not much point in comparing them at the end.

Accordingly, preformed groups should be avoided whenever possible. If it is not feasible to do this, rigorous pretesting must be done to determine in what ways the groups are (or are not) equivalent, and differences must be compensated for with the use of statistical methods.

Mortality

The seventh threat to internal validity is mortality, which simply means that individual participants may drop out of the various groups before the end of the study. Their absence will probably have a significant effect on the study's findings because people who drop out are likely to be different in some ways from the other participants who stay in the study. For example, people who drop out may be less motivated to participate in the intervention than people who stay in.

Since dropouts often have such characteristics in common, it cannot be assumed that the attrition occurred in a random manner. If considerably more people drop out of one group than out of the other, the result will be two groups that are no longer equivalent and cannot be usefully compared. We cannot know at the beginning of the study how many people will drop out, but we can watch to see how many do. Generally speaking, mortality will not be problematic if dropout rates are five percent or less *and* if the dropout rates are similar for the various groups.

Reactive Effects of Study Participants

The eighth threat to internal validity is reactive effects. Changes in the behaviors or feelings of research participants may be caused by their reaction to the novelty of the situation or the knowledge that they are participating in a research study. For example, a mother practicing communication skills with her child may try especially hard when she knows the social worker is watching. We may wrongly believe that such reactive effects are due to the independent variable.

The classic example of reactive effects was found in a series of studies carried out at the Hawthorne plant of the Western Electric Company in Chicago many years ago. Researchers were investigating the relationship between working conditions and productivity. When they increased the level of lighting in one section of the plant, productivity increased; a further increase in the lighting was followed by an additional increase in productivity. When the lighting was then decreased, however, production levels did not fall accordingly but continued to rise. The conclusion was that the workers were increasing their productivity not because of the lighting level but because of the attention they were receiving as participants in the study.

The term *Hawthorne effect* is still used to describe any situation in which the research participants' behaviors are influenced not by the independent variable but by the knowledge that they are taking part in a research project. (See Box 1.1 for additional details of the Hawthorne effect.) Another example of such a reactive effect is the placebo or sugar pill given to patients, which produces beneficial results because they believe it is medication.

Reactive effects can be controlled by ensuring that all participants in a research study, in both the experimental and control groups, appear to be treated equally. For example, if one group is to be shown an educational film, the other group should also be shown a film—some film carefully chosen to bear no relationship to the variable being investigated. If the study involves a change in the participants' routine, this in itself may be enough to change behavior, and care must be taken to continue the study until novelty has ceased to be a factor.

Interaction Effects

Interaction among the various threats to internal validity can have an effect of its own. Any of the factors already described as threats may interact with one another, but the most common interactive effect involves differential selection and maturation.

Let us say we are studying two groups of depressed clients. The intention was for these groups to be equivalent, in terms of both their motivation for treatment and their levels of depression. However, it turns out that Group A is more generally depressed than Group B. Whereas both groups may grow less motivated over time, it is likely that Group A, whose members were more depressed to begin with, will lose motivation more completely and more quickly than Group B. Inequivalent groups thus grow less equivalent over time as a result of the interaction between differential selection and maturation.

Relations Between Experimental and Control Groups

The final group of threats to internal validity has to do with the effects of the use of experimental and control groups that receive different interventions. These effects include diffusion of treatments, compensatory equalization, compensatory rivalry, and demoralization.

Diffusion or imitation of treatments may occur when the experimental and control groups talk to each other about the study. Suppose a study is designed that presents a new relaxation exercise to the experimental group and nothing at all to the control group. There is always the possibility that one of the participants in the experimental group will explain the exercise to a friend who happens to be in the control group. The friend explains it to another friend, and so on. This might be beneficial for the control group, but it invalidates the study's findings.

Compensatory equalization of treatment occurs when the person doing the study and/or the staff member administering the intervention to the experimental group feels sorry for people in the control group who are not receiving it and attempts to compensate them. For example, a social worker might take a control group member aside and covertly demonstrate the relaxation exercise. If a study has been ethically designed, there should be no need for guilt on the part of the social worker because some people are not being taught to relax. They can be taught to relax when the study is "officially" over.

Compensatory rivalry is an effect that occurs when the control group becomes motivated to compete with the experimental group. For example, a control group in a program to encourage parental involvement in school activities might get wind that something is up and make a determined effort to participate too, on the basis that "anything they can do, we can do better." There is no direct communication between groups, as in the diffusion of treatment effect—only rumors and suggestions of rumors. However, rumors are often enough to threaten the internal validity of a study.

In direct contrast with compensatory rivalry, demoralization refers to feelings of deprivation among the control group that may cause them to give up and drop out of the study, in which case this effect would be referred to as mortality. The people in the control group may also act up or get angry.

THREATS TO EXTERNAL VALIDITY

External validity is the degree to which the results of a research study are generalizable to a larger population or to settings outside the research situation or setting. If a research design is to have external validity, it must provide for selection of participants for the study that are representative of the population from which they were drawn.

Pretest-Treatment Interaction

The first threat to external validity, pretest-treatment interaction, is similar to the testing threat to internal validity. The nature of a pretest can alter the way participants respond to the experimental treatment, as well as to the posttest. Suppose, for example, that an educational program on racial tolerance is being evaluated. A pretest which measures the level of tolerance could well alert the participants to the fact that they are going to be educated into loving all their neighbors, but many people do not want to be "educated" into anything. They are satisfied with the way they feel and will resist the instruction. This will affect the level of racial tolerance registered on the posttest.

Selection-Treatment Interaction

The second threat to external validity is selection-treatment interaction. This threat commonly occurs when a research design cannot provide for random selection of participants from a population. Suppose we wanted to study the effectiveness of a family service agency staff, for example. If our research proposal was turned down by 50 agencies before it was accepted by the 51st, it is very likely that the accepting agency differs in certain important aspects from the other 50. It may accept the proposal because its social workers are more highly motivated, more secure, more satisfied with their jobs, or more interested in the practical application of the study than the average agency staff member.

As a result, we would be assessing the participants on the very factors for which they were unwittingly (and by default) selected—motivation, job satisfaction, and so on. The study may be internally valid, but, since it will not be possible to generalize the results to other family service agencies, it would have little external validity.

Specificity of Variables

The third threat to external validity, specificity of variables, has to do with the fact that a research project conducted with a specific group of people at a specific time and in a specific setting may not always be generalizable to other people at a different time and in a different setting. For example, it has been demonstrated that an instrument developed to measure the IQ levels of upper-socioeconomic level, Caucasian, suburban children does not provide an equally accurate measure of IQ when it is applied to lower-socioeconomic level children of racial minorities in the inner city.

Reactive Effects

The fourth threat to external validity is reactive effects which, as with internal validity, occur when the attitudes or behaviors of study participants are affected to some degree by the very act of taking a pretest. Thus, they are no longer exactly equivalent to the population from which they were randomly selected, and it may not be possible to generalize the results of the study to apply to that population. Because the pretest affects the study's participants, the results may be valid only for those who were pretested.

Multiple-Treatment Interference

The fifth threat to external validity, multiple-treatment interference, occurs if a participant is given two or more interventions in succession, so that the results of the first intervention may affect the results of the second one. A client attending treatment sessions, for example, may not seem to benefit from one therapeutic technique, so another is tried. In fact, however, the client may have benefited from the first technique but the benefit does not become apparent until the second technique has been tried. As a result, the effects of both techniques become commingled, or the results may be erroneously ascribed to the second technique alone.

Because of this threat, interventions should be given separately if possible. If the research design does not allow this, sufficient time should be allowed to elapse between the two interventions in an effort to minimize the possibility of multiple-treatment interference.

Researcher Bias

The final threat to external validity is researcher bias. Researchers, like people in general, tend to see what they want to see or expect to see. Unconsciously and without any thought of deceit, they may manipulate a study so that the actual results agree with the anticipated results. A practitioner may favor an intervention so strongly that the research study is structured to support it, or the results are interpreted favorably.

If we know which individuals are in the experimental group and which are in the control group, this knowledge alone might affect the study's results. Students whom an instructor believes to be bright, for example, often are given higher grades than their performance warrants, while students believed to be dull are given lower grades. The way to control for such researcher bias is to perform a double-blind experiment in which neither the participants nor the researcher knows who is in the experimental or control group or who is receiving a specific treatment intervention.

SUMMARY

A research study is said to be internally valid if any changes in the dependent variable, Y, result only from the introduction of an independent variable, X. In order to demonstrate internal validity, we must first document the time order of events. Next, we must identify and eliminate extraneous variables. Finally, we must control for the factors that threaten internal validity. In summary, threats to the internal validity of a research design address the assumption that changes in the dependent variable are solely because of the independent variable. "Ideal" experimental designs account for virtually all threats to internal validity—a rarity in social work research studies.

External validity is the degree to which the results of a research study are generalizable to a larger population or to settings other than the research setting. If a research study is to be externally valid, we must be able to demonstrate conclusively that the sample we selected was representative of the population from which it was drawn. If two or more groups are used in the study, we must be able to show that the two groups were equivalent at the beginning of the study. Most importantly, we must be able to demonstrate that nothing happened during the course of the study, except for the introduction of the independent variable, to change either the representativeness of the sample or the equivalence of the groups.

The degree of control we try to exert over threats to internal and external validity varies according to the research design. Threats to internal and external validity may be more or less problematic depending on what particular research design is selected. When we design a study, we must be aware of which threats will turn into real problems and what can be done to prevent or at least to minimize them. When doing an exploratory study, for example, we will not be much concerned about threats to external validity because an exploratory study is not expected to have any external validity anyway. Nor do we attempt to control very rigorously for threats to internal validity.

When we use a descriptive research design, we might be trying to determine whether two or more variables are associated. Often, descriptive designs are employed when we are unable, for practical reasons, to use the more rigorous explanatory designs. We do our best to control for threats to internal validity because, unless we can demonstrate internal validity, we cannot show that the variables are associated.

When using explanatory designs, we are attempting to show causation; that is, we are trying to show that changes in one variable cause changes in another. We try hard to control threats to internal validity because, if the study is not internally valid, we cannot demonstrate causation. We would also like the results of the study to be as generally applicable as possible and, to this end, we do our best to control for threats to external validity.

In the next chapter we will describe single-subject research designs at the exploratory, descriptive, and explanatory levels. The "ideal" experimental design is useful to keep in mind as a contrast to single-subject designs, along with knowing the threats to internal and external validity as presented in this chapter.

STUDY QUESTIONS

1. Discuss in detail the similarities and differences between the concepts of internal and external validity. Provide a social work example throughout your discussion.

2. List and discuss the threats to internal validity by using a common social work example of your choice.

3. List and discuss the threats to external validity by using a common social work example of your choice.

4. In the library, choose a social work research article. List and discuss the threats to internal and external validity that the study controlled for, and did not control for. Provide a rationale for your answers.

5. Design an "ideal" social work experiment that controls for all the threats to internal and external validity. You may select any topic that you desire.

6. Go to the library and find a published social work research article that controlled for as many threats to internal and external validity as possible. Go through the article and determine which internal and external validity factors the study controlled for, and which factors it did not control for. Hypothetically redesign the study in such a way where you could control for the factors that the original study did not. After doing this, would your hypothetical redesigned study have been feasible, given the contents of Chapters 2 through 5? Discuss in detail.

7. List other factors that you feel could be added as additional threats to *internal validity* besides the ones presented in this chapter. Provide a rationale for your response.

8. List other factors that you feel could be added as additional threats to *external validity* besides the ones presented in this chapter. Provide a rationale for your response.

9. Go to the library and identify two social work research articles that focused on the same topic area. Which study do you feel had the most *internal validity*. Why? Justify your response. Provide a rationale as to why it is more necessary to have high degrees of internal validity for research studies at descriptive or explanatory levels than at the exploratory level.

10. Go to the library and choose two social work research articles that focused on the same topic area. Which study do you feel had the most *external validity*? Why? Justify your response. Provide a rationale as to why it more necessary to have high degrees of external validity for research studies at the descriptive or explanatory levels than at the exploratory level.

REFERENCES AND FURTHER READINGS

Adams, G.R., & Schvaneveldt, J.D. (1991). *Understanding research methods* (2nd ed., pp. 101-118, 228-251). White Plains, NY: Longman.

Babbie, E.R. (1992). *The practice of social research* (6th ed., pp. 86-112). Pacific Grove, CA: Wadsworth.

Bailey, K.D. (1994). *Methods of social research* (4th ed., pp. 36-41, 275-292). New York: Free Press.

Campbell, D.T., & Stanley, J.C. (1963). *Experimental and quasi- experimental designs for research*. Skokie, IL: Rand McNally.

Frankfort-Nachmias, C., & Nachmias, D. (1992). *Research methods in the social sciences* (4th ed., pp. 97-99, 271-290). New York: St. Martin's Press.

Grinnell, R.M., Jr. (1993). Group research designs. In R.M. Grinnell, Jr. (Ed.), *Social work research and evaluation* (4th ed., pp. 118-153). Itasca, IL: F.E. Peacock.

Grinnell, R.M., Jr., & Stothers, M. (1988). Research designs. In R.M. Grinnell, Jr. (Ed.), *Social work research and evaluation* (3rd ed., pp. 199-239). Itasca, IL: F.E. Peacock.

Grinnell, R.M., Jr., & Williams, M. (1990). *Research in social work: A primer* (pp. 178-203). Itasca, IL: F.E. Peacock.

Judd, C.M., Smith E.R., & Kidder, I.H. (1991). *Research methods in social relations* (6th ed., pp. 27-36, 298-320). Fort Worth, TX: Harcourt Brace.

Leedy, P.D. (1993). *Practical research: Planning and design* (3rd ed., pp. 113-128, 137-147). New York: Macmillan.

Marlow, C. (1993). *Research methods for generalist social work practice* (pp. 66-68, 95-96, 137-138). Pacific Grove, CA: Wadsworth.

Monette, D.R., Sullivan, T.J., & DeJong, C.R. (1994). *Applied social research* (3rd ed., pp. 82-92). Fort Worth, TX: Harcourt Brace.

Neuman, W.L. (1994). *Social research methods* (2nd ed., pp. 55-78). Needham Heights, MA: Allyn & Bacon.

Royse, D.D. (1991). *Research methods in social work* (pp. 43-44, 79-81, 120-121, 217-232). Chicago: Nelson-Hall.

Rubin, A., & Babbie, E. (1993). *Research methods for social work* (2nd ed., pp. 29-30, 106-112, 357-365). Pacific Grove, CA: Wadsworth.

Toseland, R.W. (1985). Research methods. In R.M. Grinnell, Jr. (Ed.), *Social work research and evaluation* (2nd ed., pp. 115-130). Itasca, IL: F.E. Peacock.

Tripodi, T. (1974). *Uses and abuses of social research in social work.* New York: Columbia University Press.

Tripodi, T. (1981). The logic of research design. In R.M. Grinnell, Jr. (Ed.), *Social work research and evaluation* (pp. 198-225). Itasca, IL: F.E. Peacock.

Tripodi, T. (1985). Research designs. In R. M. Grinnell, Jr. (Ed.), *Social work research and evaluation* (2nd ed., pp. 231-259). Itasca, IL: F.E. Peacock.

Yegidis, B.L., & Weinbach, R.W. (1991). *Research methods for social workers* (pp. 73-90). White Plains, NY: Longman.

Chapter 10

Single-System Designs

IN THE PREVIOUS CHAPTERS we have covered the place of research in social work and presented the process of going from research problems to questions to hypotheses. In addition we now know how to operationalize variables within hypotheses and have learned what constitutes an "ideal" experiment, given the various threats to internal and external validity. Armed with this knowledge, we will now discuss the simplest of all types of research designs—the single-system research design.

On a very general level, single-system research designs are more "practice orientated" than "research orientated." That is, they are used more by social work practitioners than by social work researchers. Nevertheless, they can also be used in research situations when research designs that use two or more groups of research participants cannot be used (which is the topic of the next chapter).

PURPOSE OF SINGLE-SYSTEM DESIGNS

Research studies conducted to evaluate treatment interventions with social work clients are called single-system designs. They are also called *single-subject designs, single-case experimentations*, or *idiographic re-*

search. Single-system research designs are used to fulfil the major purpose of social work practice: to improve the situation of a client system—*an* individual client, *a* couple, *a* family, *a* group, *an* organization, or *a* community. Any of these client configurations can be studied with a single-system design. In short, they are used to study *one* individual or *one* group intensively, as opposed to studies that use two or more groups of research participants.

Single-system research design can provide information about how well a treatment intervention is working, so that alternative or complementary interventive strategies can be adopted if necessary. They can also indicate when a client's problem has been resolved. Single-system studies can be used to monitor client progress up to, and sometimes beyond, the point of termination.

They can be also used to evaluate the effectiveness of a social work program as a whole by aggregating or compiling the results obtained by numerous social workers serving their individual clients within the program. For example, a family therapy program might be evaluated by combining family outcomes on a number of families that have been seen by different workers.

REQUIREMENTS OF SINGLE-SYSTEM DESIGNS

In order to carry out a single-system research study, the client's problem must be identified, the desired objective to be achieved must be decided upon, the intervention that is most likely to eliminate the client's problem must be selected, the intervention must be implemented, and the client's progress must be continually monitored to see if the client's problem has been resolved, or at least reduced. If practitioners are careful to organize, measure, and record what they do, single-system studies will naturally take shape in the clients' files, and the results can be used to guide future interventive efforts.

Only three things are required when doing a single-system study. These are: (1) setting client objectives that are measurable, (2) selecting valid and reliable outcome measures, and (3) graphically displaying the results of the outcome measures.

Setting Measurable Objectives

One of the first tasks a worker does when initially seeing a client is to establish the purpose of why they are together. Why has the client approached the worker? Or, in many nonvoluntary situations, such as in probation and parole or child abuse situations, why has the worker approached the client? The two need to formulate objectives for their mutual working relationship. A specific, measurable, client desired outcome objective is known as a *client target problem*. Client target problems are feelings, knowledge levels, or behaviors that need to be changed.

Many times clients do not have just one target problem, they have many. They sometimes have a number of interrelated problems and, even if there is only one that is more important than the rest, they may not know what it is. Nevertheless, they may be quite clear about the desired outcome of their involvement with social work services. They may want to "fix" their lives so that, "Johnny listens when I ask him to do something," or "My partner pays more attention to me," or "I feel better about myself at work." Unfortunately, many clients express their desired target problems in vague, ambiguous terms, possibly because they do not know themselves exactly what they want to change; they only know that something should be different. If a worker can establish (with the guidance of the client) what should be changed, why it should be changed, how it should be changed, and to what degree it should be changed, the solution to the problem will not be far away.

For example, consider Heather, who wants her partner, Ben, to pay more attention to her. Heather may mean sexual attention, in which case the couple's sexual relations may be the target problem. On the other hand, Heather may mean that she and Ben do not socialize enough with friends, or that Ben brings work home from the office too often, or has hobbies she does not share, or any of a host of things.

Establishing clearly what the desired change would look like is the first step in developing the target problem. Without this, the worker and client could wander around forever through the problem maze, never knowing what, if anything, has been solved. Desired change cannot occur if no one knows what change is desired. It is, therefore, very important that the target problem to be solved be precisely stated as early as possible in the client-social worker relationship.

Continuing with the above example of Heather and Ben, and after a great deal of exploration, the worker agrees that Heather and Ben have many target problems to work on, such as improving their child discipline strategies, improving their budgeting skills, improving their communication skills, and many other issues that, when dealt with, can lead to a successful marriage. However, for now, they agree to work on one target problem of increasing the amount of time they spend together with friends. To do this, the worker, Heather, and Ben must conceptualize and operationalize the term "increasing the amount of time they spend together with friends." As we know from Chapters 5–7, a variable is conceptualized by defining it in a way that is relevant to the situation and operationalized in such a way that its indicators can be measured.

Heather may say that she wishes she and Ben could visit friends together more often. The target problem has now become a little more specific: It has narrowed from "increasing the amount of time they spend together with friends" to "Heather and Ben visiting friends more often." However, "visiting friends more often with Ben" is still an ambiguous term. It may mean once a month or every night, and the achievement of the target problem's solution cannot be known until the meaning of "more often" has been clarified.

If Heather agrees that she would be happy to visit friends with Ben once a week, the ambiguous objective may be restated as a specific, measurable objective—"to visit friends with Ben once a week." The social worker may discover later that "friends" is also an ambiguous term. Heather may have meant "her friends," while Ben may have meant "his friends," and the social worker may have imagined that "the friends" were mutual.

The disagreement about who is to be regarded as a friend may not become evident until the worker has monitored their progress for a month or so and found that no improvement was occurring. In some cases, poor progress may be due to the selection of an inappropriate interventive strategy. In other cases, it may mean that the target problem itself is not as specific, complete, and clear as it should be. Before deciding that the interventive strategy needs to be changed, it is always necessary to clarify with the client exactly what it is that specifically needs to be achieved.

Selecting Outcome Measures

A target problem cannot really be said to be measurable until it is decided how it will be operationalized, or measured. Can Heather and Ben, who wanted to visit friends more often, be trusted to report truthfully on whether the friends were visited? Suppose she says they were not visited and he says they were? Social workers must always be very conscious of what measurement methods are both available and feasible when formulating a target problem with a client. It may be quite possible for the social worker to telephone the friends and ask if they were visited; but, if the worker is not prepared to get involved with Heather's and Ben's friends, this measurement method will not be feasible. If this is the case, and if Heather and/or Ben cannot be trusted to report accurately and truthfully, there is little point in setting the target problem.

Heather's and Ben's target problem can be easily observed and measured. However, quite often, a client's target problem involves feelings, attitudes, knowledge levels, or events that are known only to the client and cannot be easily observed and/or measured.

Consider Bob, a client who comes to a social worker because he is depressed. The worker's efforts may be simply to lessen his target problem, depression, but how will the worker and/or Bob know when his depression has been alleviated or reduced? Perhaps he will say that he feels better, or his partner may say that Bob cries less, or the worker may note that he spends less time in therapy staring at his feet. All these are indicators that his depression is lessening, but they are not very valid and reliable indicators.

What is needed is a more "scientific method" of measuring depression. Fortunately, a number of paper-and-pencil standardized measuring instruments have been developed that can be filled out by the client in a relatively short period of time, can be easily scored, and can provide a fairly accurate picture of the client's condition. One such widely used instrument that measures depression is the General Contentment Scale (*GCS*) illustrated in Figure 6.1. Since higher scores indicate higher levels of depression, and lower scores indicate lower levels of depression, the target problem in Bob's case would be to reduce his score on the *GCS* to a level at which he can adequately function (which is usually a score of 30 or less).

People who are not depressed will still not score zero on the *GCS*. Everyone occasionally feels blue (Item 2) or downhearted (Item 10). There is a clinical cutting score that differentiates a clinically significant problem level from a nonclinically significant problem level, and it will often be this score that the client aims to achieve. If the target problem is, "to reduce Bob's score on the *GCS* to or below the clinical cutting score of 30," the worker will know not only what the target problem is, but precisely how Bob's success is to be measured.

Usually, client success, sometimes referred to as client outcome, can be measured in a variety of ways. For example, Bob's partner, Maria, may be asked to record the frequency of his crying spells, and the target problem here may be to reduce the frequency of these spells to once a week or less. Again, it would be important to further operationalize the term "crying spell" so that Maria knows exactly what it was she has to measure. Perhaps "crying spell" would be operationally defined as ten minutes or more of continuous crying, and a gap of at least ten minutes without crying would define the difference between one "spell" and another.

There are now two independent and complementary indicators of Bob's level of depression: the *GCS* as rated by Bob, and the number of his ten-minute crying spells per day as rated by Maria. If future scores on both indicators display improvement (that is, they both go down), the worker can be reasonably certain that Bob's depression is lessening and the intervention is effective.

If the two indicators do not agree, the worker will need to find out why. Perhaps Bob wishes to appear more depressed than he really is, and this is an area that needs to be explored. Or perhaps Maria is not sufficiently concerned to keep an accurate recording of the number of Bob's ten-minute crying spells per day; and it may be Maria's attitude that has caused Bob's crying in the first place. Accurate measurements made over time can do more than reveal the degree of a client's improvement. They can cast light on the problem itself and suggest new avenues to be explored, possibly resulting in the utilization of different interventive strategies.

Be that as it may, a client's target problem cannot be dealt with until it has been expressed in specific measurable indicators. These indicators cannot be said to be measurable until it has been decided how they will be measured. Specification of the target problem will, therefore, often include mention of an instrument that will be used to measure it. It will also include who is to do the measuring, and under what circumstances. For example, it may be decided that Bob will rate himself on the *GCS* daily after dinner, or once a week on Saturday morning, or Maria will make a daily record of all crying spells that occurred in the late afternoon after he returned home from work. The physical record itself is very important, both as an aid to memory and to track Bob's progress. In a single-system study, progress is always monitored by displaying the measurements made in the form of graphs.

Graphically Displaying Data

As we know from Chapter 6, the word *measurement* can be simply defined as the process of assigning a number or value to a variable. If the variable, or target problem, being considered is depression as rated by the *GCS*, and if Bob scores, say 72, 72 is the number assigned to Bob's initial level of depression. The worker will try to reduce his initial score of 72 to at least 30—the minimum desired score. The worker can then select and implement an intervention and ask Bob to complete the *GCS* again, say once a week, until the score of 30 has been reached. Bob's depression levels can be plotted (over a 12-week period) on a graph, such as the one shown in Figure 10.1.

In the graph, Bob's depression level for each week is plotted on the *y*-axis, while time, in weeks, is plotted on the *x*-axis. There is a reason for this. Obviously, the social worker is hoping that the selected intervention will result in lowering Bob's level of depression, over time, as measured by the *GCS*. In other words, the worker is hypothesizing that: If Intervention *A* is implemented, Bob's depression will decrease. In research terminology, the independent variable in this hypothesis is the intervention (*X*) and the dependent variable (*Y*) is Bob's depression level. The frequency of Bob's ten-minute crying spells per day, as recorded by Maria, could also be graphed.

EXPLORATORY SINGLE-SYSTEM DESIGNS

As discussed in previous chapters, exploratory, descriptive, and explanatory research studies fall on a knowledge-level continuum,

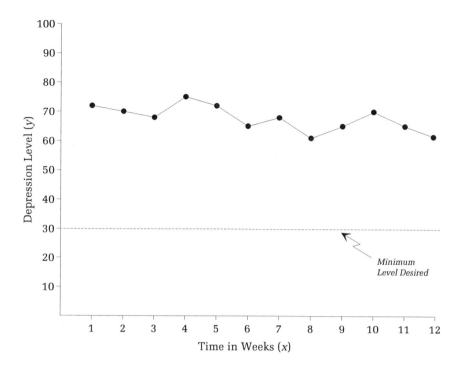

FIGURE 10.1 Bob's Depression Level Over Time

as presented in Figure 4.1. To review briefly, exploratory studies begin with little knowledge in the problem area and produce only uncertain knowledge. Descriptive studies provide further descriptive facts, while explanatory studies attempt to explain the facts already gathered and produce the most certain level of knowledge.

Single-system studies are categorized as exploratory, descriptive, or explanatory, depending on the level of certainty they provide regarding the effectiveness of the intervention in resolving the client's target problem. Inevitably, the least complex research designs, at the exploratory level, provide the least certainty about whether the intervention was effective in bringing about the desired change. We will briefly discuss three kinds of exploratory single-system designs: (1) The *B* design, (2) the *BC* design, and (3) the *BCD* design.

The *B* Design

The first type of exploratory single-system design is the *B* design, which is the simplest of all single-system designs. The italicized letter *B* refers to the fact that an intervention of some kind has been introduced. Let us take a simple example of how a *B* design works.

A couple, David and Donna, have had a long history of interrupting one another while the other is talking. They have tried to stop the pattern of this destructive behavior, to no avail. They have finally decided to do something about this and have sought out the services of a social worker. After some exploration, it becomes apparent that the couple need to concentrate on their interruptive behaviors. In short, the worker wishes to reduce the frequency with which David and Donna interrupt each other while conversing. This could be observed and measured by having them talk to each other while in weekly, one-hour sessions.

The worker teaches basic communication skills (the intervention) to the couple and has them practice these skills during each weekly session while other marital relationship issues are being addressed. Each week during therapy, while the couple is engaged in conversation, the worker makes a record of how many times each partner interrupts the other. Thus, in this situation, the worker is trying to reduce the number of interruptions—the target problem. For now, suppose that the data for David and Donna over a 12-week period look like those displayed in Figure 10.2.

Figure 10.2 shows that the number of times interruptions occurred

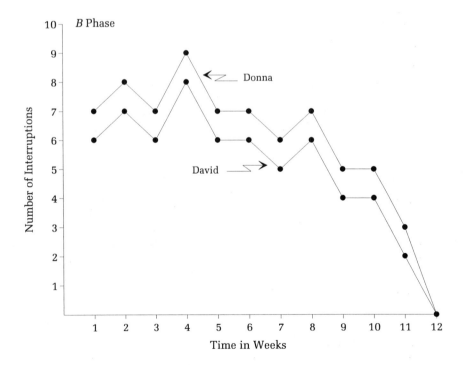

FIGURE 10.2   *B* Design: Frequency of Interruptions for a Couple During One Intervention Indicating an Improvement

decreased gradually over the 12-week period until it reached zero in the twelfth week—that is, until the goal of therapy had been achieved. Even so, the worker could continue to record the level of the target problem for a longer period of time to ensure that success was being maintained.

In this case, the worker hypothesized that if the intervention—teaching communication skills—was implemented, then the number of times the couple interrupted each other while conversing during therapy sessions would be reduced. Figure 10.2 shows that the target problem was achieved for both partners, but it does not show that the worker's hypothesis was in fact correct. Perhaps teaching communication skills had nothing to do with reducing the couple's interruptions. The interruptions may have been reduced because of something else the worker did (besides the communication skills training), or something the couple did, or something a friend did. There is even the possibility that their interruptions would have ceased if no one had done anything at all. Be that as it may, extraneous variables have not been controlled for. Thus, we cannot know how effective this particular intervention is in solving this particular target problem for this particular couple.

If we use the same interventive strategy with a second couple experiencing the same target problem and achieve the same results, it becomes more likely that the intervention produced the results. If the same results follow the same intervention with a third similar couple, it becomes more likely still. Thus, we can become more certain that an intervention causes a result the more times the intervention is successfully used with similar target problems.

However, if an intervention is used only once, as is the case with the exploratory *B* design, no evidence for causation can be inferred. All that can be gleaned from Figure 10.2 is that, for whatever reason, David's and Donna's target problem was reduced: or, if a graph such as Figure 10.3 is obtained instead, this indicates that the problem has not been resolved, or has been only partly resolved. If David and Donna continued to interrupt each other, week after week, a graph like the one shown in Figure 10.3 would be produced.

The data from graphs, such as the data presented in Figures 10.2 and 10.3, are extremely useful since a worker will be better able to judge whether the intervention should be continued, modified, or abandoned in favor of a different interventive strategy. In the simplest of terms, the *B* design only monitors the effectiveness of an intervention over time and indicates when the desired level of the target problem has been reached.

The *BC* and *BCD* Designs

The second and third types of exploratory single-system designs are the *BC* and *BCD* designs. In the *B* design previously described, the italicized letter *B* represents a single interventive strategy. Suppose now that a *B* intervention, such as communication skills training, is implemented with David and Donna, and a graph like the one shown in Figure 10.4 is obtained. The left side of the graph shows that the problem is not being resolved with the implementation of the *B* intervention, and the social worker may feel that it is time to change the intervention so a *C* intervention is tried starting the fifth week. Four weeks, for example, may have been as long as the worker was prepared to wait for the hoped-for change to occur for the *B* intervention to work.

As can be seen in Figure 10.4, the worker implemented a second different intervention, *C*, starting the fifth week and measured the target problem in the same way as before, by making weekly recordings of the number of times that each partner interrupts the other during the course of therapy sessions. These measurements are graphed as before, plotting the level of the client's target problem along the *y*-axis and the time in weeks along the *x*-axis. The data are shown in the *C* phase of Figure 10.4.

Figure 10.4 shows that no change occurred in the target problem after Intervention *B* was implemented, but the target problem was resolved following the implementation of Intervention *C*. As before,

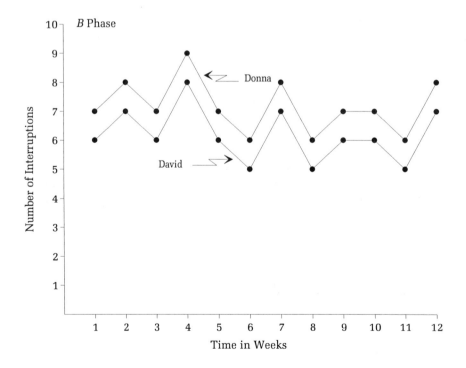

FIGURE 10.3　　*B* Design: Frequency of Interruptions for a Couple During One Intervention Indicating No Improvement

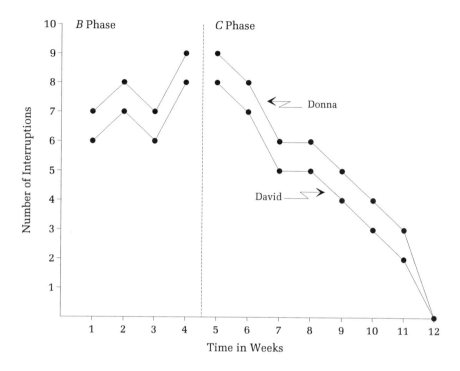

FIGURE 10.4   *BC* Design: Frequency of Interruptions for a Couple After Two Interventions Indicating an Improvement with the Second Intervention

extraneous variables have not been considered, and Figure 10.4 does not show that Intervention *C* caused the problem to be resolved: It shows only that success occurred during Intervention *C* but not during Intervention *B*.

In order to demonstrate causation, the worker would have to obtain successful results with Intervention *C* on a number of occasions with different couples experiencing the same target problem. Similarly, the inherent uselessness of Intervention *B* could be shown only if it was implemented unsuccessfully with other couples—an unlikely event since the most hopeful intervention surely would be implemented first.

If Intervention *C* does not work either, the worker will have to try yet another intervention (Intervention *D*). Combined graphs may be produced, as in Figure 10.5, illustrating the results of the entire *BCD* single-system design.

Since the *BC* and *BCD* designs involve successive, different interventions, they are sometimes known as successive interventions designs. It is conceivable that an *E* intervention might be necessary, forming a *BCDE* design, and even an *F*, forming a *BCDEF* design. Multiple-treat-

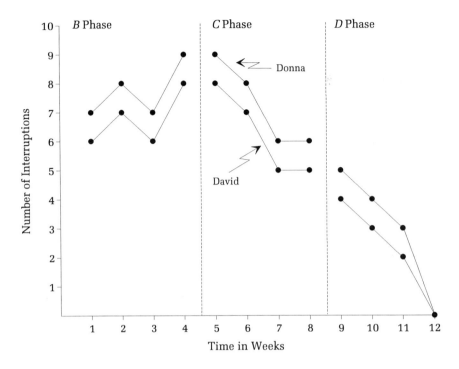

FIGURE 10.5 *BCD* Design: Frequency of Interruptions for a Couple After Three Interventions Indicating the Best Improvement with the Third Intervention

ment interference discussed in the previous chapter is a major threat to the external validity of successive intervention designs. Let us now turn our attention to descriptive single-system designs.

DESCRIPTIVE SINGLE-SYSTEM DESIGNS

One of the difficulties with the three exploratory-level designs previously discussed (*B*, *BC*, and *BCD* designs) is that they provide no information about the level of the client's target problem *before* the intervention was introduced. For example, Bob might show himself to be severely depressed according to his initial score of 72 (Figure 10.1) on the *GCS*. However, perhaps the cause of his depression is the recent death of his 20-year-old cat, Teddy; and the problem will resolve itself naturally as he recovers from Teddy's loss. Or perhaps he was more depressed on the day that he approached the worker than he usually is. Thus, it would have been useful if we had had an accurate measure of Bob's depression levels over time *before* he received social work services. Descriptive single-system designs provide such a procedure.

We will briefly discuss two types of descriptive single-system designs. They are: (1) the *AB* design, and (2) the *ABC* design.

The *AB* Design

An *AB* design is useful when a worker can afford to monitor a client's target problem for a short time *before* implementing an intervention. For example, suppose a social worker is seeing Juan, who experiences a great deal of anxiety in social situations. He is nervous when he speaks to his teacher or boss or when he meets people for the first time, and the prospect of speaking in public appalls him.

The worker could decide that progress for his target problem might be measured in two ways: first, Juan will complete the Interaction and Audience Anxiousness Scale (*IAAS*) that measures social anxiety. For the first four weeks, the worker will not intervene at all. The purpose of the worker's contact, in these weeks, will be merely to gather data on the initial level of his anxiety—that is, to gather baseline data.

The period in which initial data are being gathered is known as the *A* phase of the study. The italicized letter *A* symbolizes no interven-

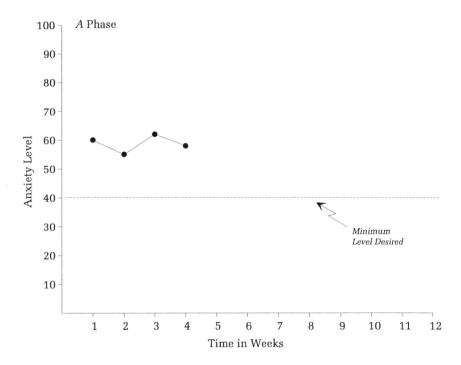

FIGURE 10.6   Magnitude of Juan's Anxiety Level Before an Intervention Indicating a Stable Baseline

tion—in the same way as the letters *B, C,* and *D* symbolize the first, second, and third interventive strategies, respectively. Suppose, now, that Juan scores 60 on the *IAAS* the first week he is assessed, 55 the second week, 62 the third, and 58 on the fourth. Juan's anxiety scores for this 4-week period before an intervention was introduced can be graphed as shown in Figure 10.6.

Taken together, the four scores in Figure 10.6 show that Juan's anxiety level is reasonably stable at about an average of 59. Since it has remained relatively stable over a 4-week period, the likelihood is that it will continue to remain at the same level if a social worker does not intervene: that is, Juan's problem will not solve itself. The worker would be even more justified to intervene immediately if Juan achieved anxiety scores as illustrated in Figure 10.7. Here, Juan's anxiety level is rising: his anxiety problem is growing worse.

Conversely, if he achieved the four scores shown in Figure 10.8, the worker might be reluctant to intervene, because Juan's anxiety level is decreasing anyway. If the worker did intervene, however, and his anxiety level continued to decrease, we would never know if the worker's intervention had a positive effect or if the same result would

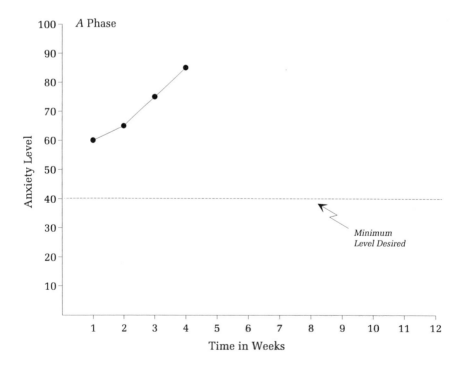

FIGURE 10.7   Magnitude of Juan's Anxiety Level Before an
Intervention Indicating a Deteriorating Baseline

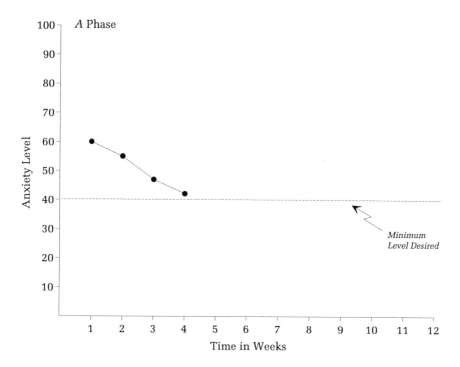

FIGURE 10.8   Magnitude of Juan's Anxiety Level Before an Intervention Indicating an Improving Baseline

have been achieved without it.

The four scores shown in Figure 10.9 vary to such an extent that it is not possible to tell how anxious Juan really is. Again, we would be reluctant to intervene because there would be no way of knowing whether Juan was making progress or not, and whether the intervention was helpful or not. In order to conduct an *AB* single-system research study—and in order to be helpful to a client—the level of the target problem must be stable (e.g., Figure 10.6), or getting worse (e.g., Figure 10.8) in the *A* phase.

Suppose that it has been established that Juan's target problem level is stable, as illustrated in Figure 10.6. An objective may then be set: to reduce Juan's social anxiety level to 40. Forty has been selected because people who suffer from social anxiety at a clinically significant level tend to score *above* 40 on the *IAAS*, while people whose social anxiety is not clinically significant score *below* 40. It will not really matter whether the objective is precisely met. If Juan becomes more confident in social situations, feels more ready to meet people, and only reaches a score of 45, this may be good enough to warrant termination of services.

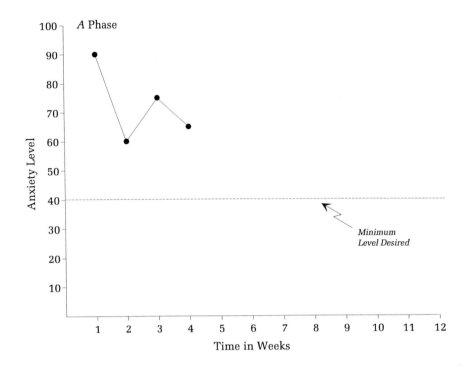

FIGURE 10.9   Magnitude of Juan's Anxiety Level Before an
Intervention Indicating a Fluctuating Baseline

Having produced a baseline graph and established a target problem,
the worker can now implement an intervention package that could
include such activities as role-playing through anxiety-producing
situations and coping strategies. Whatever the intervention package, it
is important that a record of its process is made so that another worker
will know, in the future, exactly what the specific intervention was.

Once the baseline, or *A* phase, has been established, the *B* phase will
proceed as in the three exploratory *B* designs previously discussed. Juan
will complete the *IAAS* weekly, or every two weeks, or however often is
appropriate, and the scores will be graphed. Figure 10.10 shows a
relatively stable *A* phase over the first four weeks (from Figure 10.6), and
a decreasing anxiety level over the next eight weeks, while the intervention is being implemented. The dashed vertical line on the graph
indicates the time at which the intervention was begun.

The worker could continue to monitor the level of Juan's target
problem after it has been achieved in order to ensure that progress is
being maintained. We cannot adequately judge the usefulness of an
intervention until it is known not only that it works, but that it continues
to work when it is no longer the focus of our attention. It is, therefore,
essential to make follow-up measurements whenever possible, perhaps

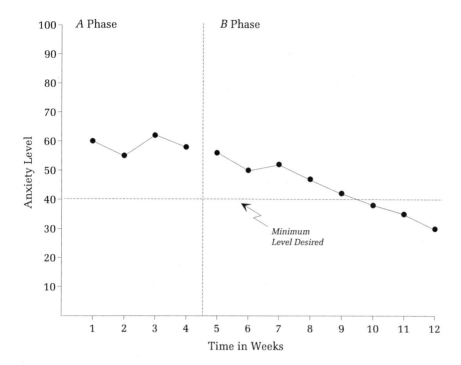

FIGURE 10.10   *AB* Design: Magnitude of Juan's Anxiety Level
Before and After an Intervention Indicating an
Improvement

a month, six months, and a year after the client's target problem appears
to have been resolved. The actual number and frequency of follow-up
measurements will depend on the type of problem and the client's
situation.

The *ABC* Design

The second type of descriptive single-system research design is the
ABC design. Figure 10.11 shows the same *A* phase as in Figure 10.10, but
now the *B* phase indicates that Juan's problem is not being satisfactorily
resolved. In this case, his worker will probably want to change the *B*
intervention, initiating a *C* intervention. Juan's problem level will be
continually measured over time and may progress to the level set in the
objective. On the other hand, if there is still no improvement, or an
insufficient improvement, a *D* intervention may need to be implemented.

As with the exploratory *BC* and *BCD* designs presented earlier,
descriptive *ABC* and *ABCD* single-system designs involve trying successive interventions until the target problem level is reached, or almost

reached. However, exploratory designs only enable workers to compare the progress made in each new phase with progress in the previous phase or phases. Look at Phase *B* in Figure 10.11. Juan's *B*-phase scores are slightly lower than his *A*-phase scores. Some improvement has occurred, although a worker may not have been able to judge that from the *B*-phase if baseline scores were not established. When the results are not clear-cut, it is the *A* phase that enables us to see whether there has been a little progress from the initial problem level, no progress at all, or perhaps even a regression.

When a new intervention is initiated in the *C* phase, the social worker is not really starting again from the beginning. The worker is starting from where the problem level was at the end of the *B* phase. If the *C* intervention is successful in resolving the problem, it is impossible to tell, without further studies, whether the *C* intervention would have worked alone or whether it was the combination of *B* and *C* that did the trick. If a *D* intervention is employed as well, the various effects of *B*, *C*, and *D* grow even more intertwined, so that we cannot know which intervention had what effect—even supposing that a given intervention

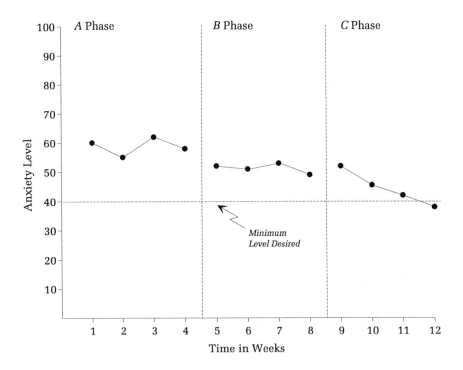

FIGURE 10.11 *ABC* Design: Magnitude of Juan's Anxiety Level Before and After Two Interventions Indicating an Improvement with the *C* Intervention

had any effect whatsoever. We will now turn our attention to explanatory single-system designs.

EXPLANATORY SINGLE-SYSTEM DESIGNS

Explanatory single-system designs attempt to come to grips with the problem of cause and effect. If a worker wants to know whether a particular intervention is effective in a particular problem area, the following question needs to be answered: Did intervention X cause result Y? At an explanatory level, the worker needs to be sure that nothing other than the intervention caused the result.

As we know from the previous chapter, a research study in which changes in the dependent variable result only from changes in the independent variable is said to be internally valid. Explanatory single-system research designs attempt to control for the threats to internal validity.

In order to conduct an internally valid study, three factors need to be taken into account. First, we must show that the independent variable occurred before the dependent variable. Second, the inevitable cohort of extraneous variables must be identified and dealt with. Third, a worker will need to consider other general factors that may pose a threat to internal validity. For example, an improvement in a client's level of self-esteem may occur not only from the interventive efforts. The improvement may be due to changes in another aspect of the client's life, such as getting a new job, or an intervention by another practitioner such as being placed on medication. Alternatively, things may improve spontaneously.

Explanatory single-system research designs attempt to control for such other occurrences by showing that there were two or more times in which improvement was noted in the client after a given intervention. If such is the case, then the likelihood of the improvement being related to other rival hypotheses is decreased. We will briefly discuss three types of explanatory single-system research designs. They are: (1) the *ABAB* design, (2) the *BAB* design, and (3) the *BCBC* design.

The *ABAB* Design

As the name might imply, an *ABAB* single-system research design is simply two descriptive *AB* designs strung together. This design is most appropriate with interventions that produce temporary or easily removable effects, or when an intervention is withdrawn but measurements on the client's target problem continue to be made.

Referring back to Juan, whose target problem is social anxiety, Figure 10.10 illustrates a descriptive *AB* design as previously described. It shows a stable *A* or baseline phase, followed by a successful *B* phase, where his social anxiety level is gradually reduced to below 40 during the 10th week. However, It cannot be certain that the intervention caused the reduction in anxiety until the same intervention has been tried again and has achieved the same result. The more times the same intervention is followed by the same result, the more certain it will become that the intervention caused the result.

Suppose, now, that Juan successfully reached his objective score of 40 during the first *B* phase (6th week) as illustrated in Figure 10.12. After services are withdrawn, Juan then experiences some social reversals as his anxiety mounts once more as indicated in the second *A* Phase in Figure 10.12. The worker provides services for the second time and has Juan complete the same *IAAS* during the second *B* phase.

The worker goes through the same process as was done the first time, establishing a baseline score, or *A* phase, in the first few weeks before the introduction of an intervention. The same intervention is implemented, and measurements of Juan's progress are obtained through the *B* phase, producing almost the same result.

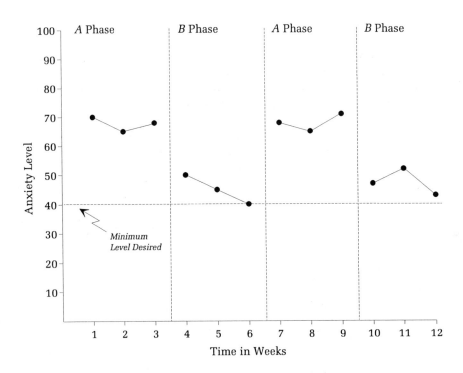

FIGURE 10.12   *ABAB* Design: Magnitude of Juan's Anxiety Level Before and After an Intervention Indicating High Deterioration in the Second *A* Phase

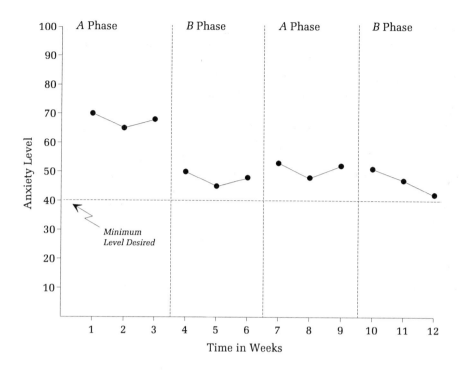

FIGURE 10.13   *ABAB* Design: Magnitude of Juan's Anxiety Level Before and After an Intervention Indicating Low Deterioration in the Second *A* Phase

We can now be more certain that the intervention caused the result since the same intervention was followed by the same result on two separate occasions. In this example, Juan's social anxiety level returned to the original baseline level—the level established in the first *A* phase. From a research perspective, this is an ideal state of affairs, since the first *AB* study can now be duplicated almost exactly. However, from a practice perspective, it is worrisome as we would like to think that a client will continue to benefit from an intervention after it has been withdrawn.

In fact, many clients do continue to benefit. Juan may have learned and remembered techniques for reducing his anxiety, and it would be unusual for his problem to return to its exact original level. Figure 10.13 illustrates a scenario in which Juan's anxiety problem did not return to its original level.

In a case such as that shown in Figure 10.13, it is still quite possible to conduct an *ABAB* study. The baseline scores in the second *A* phase are relatively stable, even though they show an improvement over the first *A* phase; and the second *B* phase shows once again that the intervention has been followed by a reduction in Juan's social anxiety level.

Sometimes it is important to continue to measure the target problem even after it appears to have been resolved and the intervention has been withdrawn. Those workers who continue to measure a client's target problem, perhaps while working on a different issue, are essentially constructing another baseline. This can be used as an additional *A* phase if the client suffers a regression and needs the intervention to be repeated.

An *ABAB* design in which the target problem, once resolved, reverts to its original level, is known as a reversal design. Such a design may be implemented accidentally. We never intend that the client's target problem should reoccur. If an *ABAB* design is to be conducted purposefully, in order to attain more certainty about the effectiveness of an intervention, then another way to proceed is to use a multiple-baseline design.

Multiple-Baseline Designs. In multiple-baseline designs, the *AB* phase is duplicated not with the same client and the same target problem but with two or more different clients (e.g., Figure 10.14), across two or more different settings (e.g., Figure 10.15), or across two or more different problems (e.g., Figure 10.16).

Two or More Clients. Suppose a worker has not just one client with a social anxiety problem but two or more. He or she could establish a baseline with each client, implement an identical intervention with each one, and compare several *AB* designs with one another. If the *B* phases show similar results, the worker has grounds to speculate that the intervention caused the result.

As always, we must take care that the effect ascribed to the intervention did not result instead from extraneous variables. For example, if the worker's socially anxious clients all happened to be residents of the same nursing home, some event in the nursing home could have contributed to the reduction in their anxiety: perhaps a newly instituted communal activity. This possibility can be controlled for—that is, we can ensure that extraneous variables have not occurred—by introducing the same intervention with each client at different times. Figure 10.14 illustrates an example of a multiple-baseline design across three clients who are being seen by a social worker for anxiety problems.

Had an extraneous variable been responsible for the reduced anxiety demonstrated by Breanne, the other two clients, Warren and Alison, would also have demonstrated reduced anxiety, even though the worker was not intervening on their behalf. The fact that the baseline scores of the second two clients remained stable until the introduction of the intervention is a good indication that no extraneous variables were present, and that the intervention is a probable cause of the result.

While a multiple-baseline design requires more effort than a simple

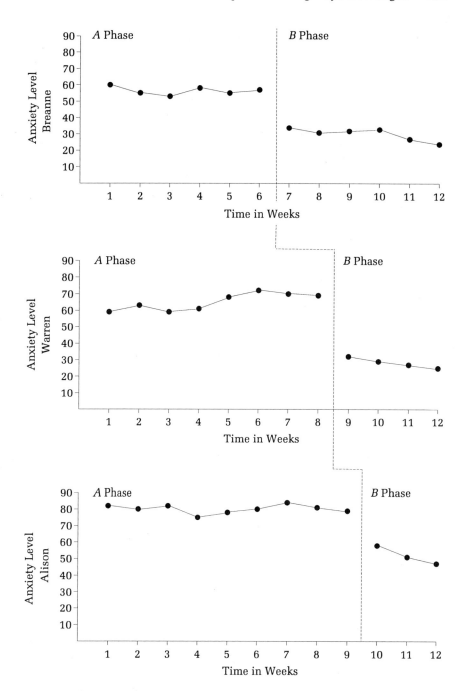

FIGURE 10.14 Multiple-Baseline Design Across Clients: Magnitude of Anxiety Levels for Three Clients Indicating an Improvement

AB design, it is often clinically feasible. A multiple-baseline study across clients can sometimes be carried out by several workers at the same time.

Two or More Settings. Another way to conduct a multiple-baseline study is to use not separate clients, but two or more separate settings. Suppose that an objective is to reduce the number of a child's temper tantrums. Three parallel single-system research studies could be conducted: one at home, one at school, and one at the daycare center where the child goes after school. At home, a parent might count the number of temper tantrums per day, both before and during the intervention. A teacher might do the same thing at school, as would a staff member at the daycare center. Again, extraneous variables can be controlled for by beginning the *B* phase at different times, as illustrated in Figure 10.15.

Two or More Problems. A third way to conduct a multiple-baseline study is to use the same intervention to tackle different target problems. Suppose that Joan is having trouble with her daughter, Anita. In addition, Joan is having trouble with her in-laws and with her boss at work. After exploration, a social worker may believe that all these troubles stem from her lack of assertiveness. Thus, Joan's intervention would be assertiveness training.

Progress with Anita might be measured by the number of times each day she is flagrantly disobedient. Progress can be measured with Joan's in-laws by the number of times she is able to utter a contrary opinion, and so on. Since the number of occasions on which Joan has an opportunity to be assertive will vary, these figures might best be expressed in percentiles. Figure 10.16 illustrates an example of a multiple-baseline design that was used to assess the effectiveness of Joan's assertiveness training in three problem areas.

Whether it is a reversal design or a multiple-baseline design, an *ABAB* explanatory design involves establishing a baseline level for the client's target problem. This will not be possible if the need for intervention is acute, and sometimes the very thought of an *A*-type design will have to be abandoned. However, it is sometimes possible to construct a retrospective baseline—that is, to determine with a reasonable degree of accuracy what the level of the target problem was *before* an intervention is implemented.

The best retrospective baselines are those that do not depend on the client's memory. If the target problem occurs rarely, memories may be accurate. For example, Tai, a teenager, and his family may remember quite well how many times he ran away from home during the past month. They may not remember nearly so well if the family members were asked how often he behaved defiantly. Depending on the target problem, it may be possible to construct a baseline from archival data:

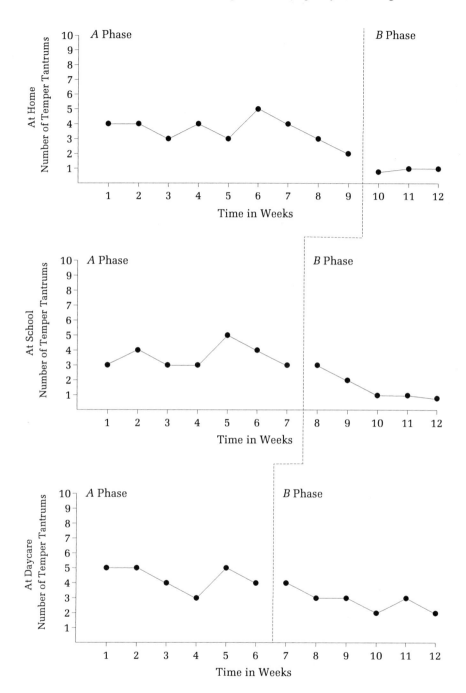

FIGURE 10.15   Multiple-Baseline Design Across Settings: Number
of Temper Tantrums for One Client in Three
Settings Indicating an Improvement

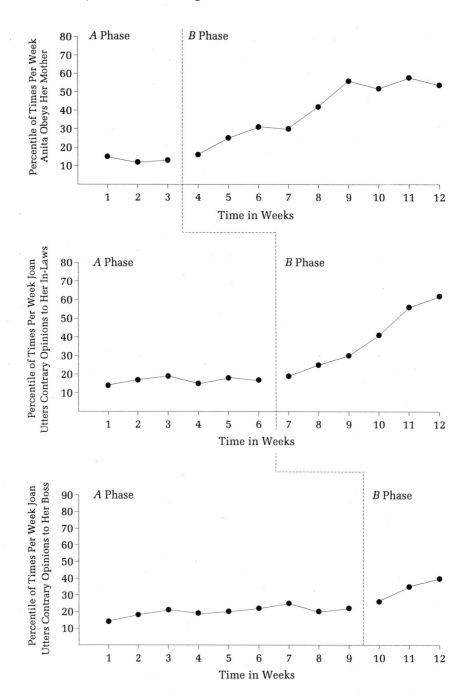

FIGURE 10.16   Multiple-Baseline Design Across Client Target Problems: Magnitude of Three Client Target Problem Areas for One Client Indicating an Improvement

that is, from written records, such as school attendance sheets probation orders, employment interview forms, and so forth.

Although establishing a baseline usually involves making at least three measurements before implementing an intervention, it is also acceptable to establish a baseline of zero, or no occurrences of a desired event. For example, a target problem might focus upon the client's reluctance to enter a drug treatment program. The baseline measurement would then be that the client did not go (zero occurrences) and the desired change would be that the client did go (one occurrence). A social worker who has successfully used the same tactics to persuade a number of clients to enter a drug treatment program has conducted a multiple-baseline design across clients.

As previously discussed, a usable baseline should show either that the client's problem level is stable (e.g., Figure 10.6) or that it is growing worse (e.g., Figure 10.7). However, sometimes an *A*-type design can be used even though the baseline indicates a slight improvement in the target problem (e.g., Figure 10.8). The justification must be that the intervention is expected to lead to an improvement that will exceed the anticipated improvement if the baseline trend continues.

For example, perhaps a child's temper tantrums are decreasing by one or two a week, but the total number per week is still 18 to 20. If a worker thought the tantrums could be reduced to four or five a week, or they could be stopped altogether, the worker would be justified in implementing an intervention even though the client's target problem was improving slowly by itself.

In a similar way, a worker may be able to implement an *A*-type design if the client's baseline is unstable, provided that the intervention is expected to exceed the largest of the baseline fluctuations. Perhaps the child's temper tantrums are fluctuating between 12 and 20 per week in the baseline period and it is hoped to bring them down to less than 10 per week.

Nevertheless, there are some occasions when a baseline cannot be established or is not usable, such as when a client's behaviors involve self-injurious ones. Also, sometimes the establishment of a baseline is totally inappropriate. For example, suppose a boy is referred to a school social worker because he has been caught starting fires at school. Could you imaging what would be going through the principal's head if the worker told the principal that baseline data were needed before an intervention could be implemented? On these occasions, a descriptive *B*-type design can be implemented without collecting baseline data.

The *BAB* Design

As the name suggests, a *BAB* design is an *ABAB* design without the first *A* phase. Many times a social worker may decide that immediate intervention is needed and does not have time to collect baseline data. The client's progress can be monitored, as is done in a *B* design, and the intervention can be withdrawn later when the problem appears to be resolved. However, previous experience has indicated that sometimes even the best-resolved client problems tend to reoccur, and the worker therefore, continues to measure the target problem level, constructing an *A* phase almost incidentally. When the client's target problem does reoccur, the worker still has a good record of what happened to the problem level after the intervention was withdrawn. Figure 10.17 illustrates an example of a *BAB* design.

Since there is no initial baseline data, we cannot know whether the resolution of the client's target problem on the first occasion had anything to do with the intervention. The problem may have resolved itself, or some external event may have resolved it. Nor can we know the degree to which the problem level changed during the intervention, since there was no baseline data with which to compare the final result. An indication of the amount of change can be obtained by comparing the first and last measurements in the *B* phase, but the first measurement

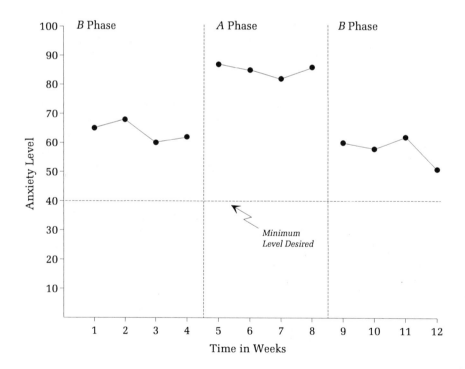

FIGURE 10.17   *BAB* Design: Magnitude of Juan's Anxiety Level During and After an Intervention Indicating High Deterioration in the *A* Phase

may have been an unreliable measure of the client's target problem level. The client may have felt more anxious that day, or less anxious, than usual; and a baseline is necessary to compensate for such fluctuations.

Since the effectiveness of the intervention on the first occasion is unknown, there can be no way of knowing whether the intervention was just as effective the second time it was implemented, or less or more effective. All we know is that the problem level improved twice, following the same intervention; and this is probably enough to warrant using the intervention again with another client.

The *BCBC* Design

In the same way that an *ABAB* design comprises two *AB* designs, a *BCBC* design is simply two *BC* designs strung together. In order to conduct a *BC* design, we can implement an intervention without collecting baseline data, and subsequently introduce a second intervention, both of which may be potentially useful. Although the social worker does not have baseline data, and thus has no record of how serious the problem was initially, the worker is able to use this design to compare the efficacy of the two or more different interventions.

ADVANTAGES AND DISADVANTAGES

This section will explore some of the more common advantages and disadvantages in using single-system research designs.

Advantages

Single-system research studies can benefit clients in a number of ways, both directly and indirectly. A social worker is obliged to think through the client's target problem more carefully than might otherwise have been done, since the client's problem must be operationally defined in a way that will allow it to be measured. Desired change must be specified in the form of a client target problem so that we know when the objective has been achieved. In other words, a worker must know precisely what the client's problem is and what it is that the client wants to change.

A single-system research design also requires that a careful, visual record be kept of whatever change occurs in the client's target problem. When graphs are produced, everyone concerned can see what changes have really occurred and what changes they only think are occurring. Possibly, the study will not be very successful. There might be fluctuations in the baseline data, for example, that make it impossible to carry out an intended *AB* study. However, these very fluctuations may throw light upon the problem. For example, a client named Darcy may discover that she is more depressed on days when she visits her sister in the nursing home. Her worker may then be able to trace Darcy's depression to an unadmitted fear of dependency and death.

As findings from single-system research studies are duplicated, they offer increasing guidance as to what specific interventions work with what specific kinds of clients in what specific circumstances. They can also generate more precise hypotheses for testing in the increasingly complex group research designs discussed in Chapter 11. However, the most important advantage of single-system studies is that they can be undertaken by line-level social workers seeing clients on a day-to-day basis. They are consistent with case needs in everyday practice situations, and they are neither expensive to implement nor time-consuming.

Single-system designs have additional advantages. First, they do not limit a worker to any particular theoretical or practice approach. The worker can intervene in any way desired, as long as he or she knows exactly what was done, and in what sequence. Second, the graphed results build up a repertoire of successful intervention strategies. If client records are adequate, a worker can look back at a specific target problem he or she may have encountered a year ago. This process would help remind the worker about what worked and what did not, and how former clients progressed.

Disadvantages

The first and most obvious limitation of a single-system research study is that it may not work. The client may have a problem that cannot be changed in the 4-to-12-week period that is normal for an *AB* study. Or the selected intervention, and the next one, and the one after that may be unsuccessful in bringing about the desired change. Of course, a study can continue for longer than twelve weeks—it can continue for as long as necessary—but often clients, and social workers too, tire of making measurements after the first three months, and the study will die a natural death if it is not brought to a planned conclusion.

Second, simply because an intervention worked with one client, does not necessarily mean that it will be as effective with a similar client. The issue of generalizability to other cases, or the external validity, was described in the previous chapter. Suffice it to say that in single-system designs we sacrifice concerns about generalizability and focus on how well an intervention works for one client system. Generalizability is essentially impossible to establish in single-system studies; we would have to be able to demonstrate that the clients to whom the intervention is given are representative of a larger group of clients to whom the intervention might be applied.

Then, there may be problems with operational definitions and with measurements. A mother who is asked to keep count of her daughter's temper tantrums may exaggerate in order to impress the worker with the severity of her daughter's problem. Or she may forget to count and invent a figure in order to save herself embarrassment. Or she may merely be unsure of just what constitutes "a temper tantrum." Does shouted defiance count, or improper language, or a covert kick at her little brother, or must it be a prolonged assault on furniture or persons? However minutely we try to define these, there is often a period of confusion at the beginning of the study, when the hoped-for baseline data never actually seem to be collected.

The usual problems with measurement also apply. Measuring instruments may not be reliable or valid, measurements may not be taken regularly, or the act of measuring may influence the target problem being measured.

Finally, single-system designs work best for interventions that are specific to certain problem areas, rather than to general methods of problem solving. Thus, for example, teaching behavioral skills to become more assertive, or relaxation-training to help overcome phobias fit with single-system designs nicely, since the intervention can be easily withdrawn by not providing the intervention in a particular session. If a social worker is using generic counseling methods, though, these may not be as easily withdrawn without a concern for the client.

SUMMARY

Single-system studies are undertaken for the purpose of monitoring client progress up to, and sometimes beyond, the point of termination. Information gained in this way helps to judge whether the intervention should be changed, modified, or terminated, and whether it is good enough to use with another client. The three requirements for a single-system study are: setting measurable objectives, selecting outcome measures, and graphically displaying data.

An objective is a specific, measurable, desired outcome and is referred to as a client target problem. Before it can be said to be measurable, each concept in it must be conceptualized and operationalized—that is completely and specifically defined—and the measuring instrument to be used must be specified.

In a single-system study, change in the target problem is always monitored by displaying the measurements made in the form of graphs such as the 17 figures displayed in this chapter. Single-system studies can be categorized as exploratory, descriptive, or explanatory, depending on the level of certainty they provide regarding the effectiveness of the intervention in resolving the target problem. The least complex research designs, at the exploratory level, provide the least certainty about whether the intervention was effective in bringing about the desired change. Exploratory single-system research designs include *B*, *BC*, and *BCD* designs, where the italicized letters *B*, *C*, and *D* represent the first, second, and third interventive strategies, respectively.

Descriptive single-system designs include *AB* and *ABC* designs, where the italicized letter *A* represents a period of no intervention, during which baseline data are collected. Baseline data provide data about the initial problem level, allowing us to judge whether an intervention is necessary, or might be harmful, and whether a gentle or vigorous intervention is most appropriate. Measurement of the initial problem level over time also lets us judge the effectiveness of the intervention since we can see the degree of change that has occurred.

Exploratory and descriptive designs provide no evidence for causation if they are used only once. Conversely, explanatory single-system designs attempt to come to grips with the problem of cause and effect. They do so by ensuring that the intervention preceded the result, and by controlling for extraneous variables. The fact that interventions are provided, withdrawn, and provided once again, deals with many of the potential threats to internal validity that were discussed in detail in the previous chapter.

Explanatory single-system designs include *ABAB, BAB,* and *BCBC* designs. An *ABAB* design in which the target problem, once resolved, reverts back to its original level is known as a reversal design. A multiple-baseline design is one in which the *AB* phase is duplicated not with the same client and the same problem but with two or more different clients, two or more different settings, or across two or more different problems.

In the following chapter we will discuss group research designs. These types of designs complement single-system research designs in that they sometimes use two or more groups of research participants, where single-system designs use only one group.

STUDY QUESTIONS

1. Discuss in your own words the purpose of single-system research designs. Use a social work example throughout your discussion.

2. List and discuss in detail the three requirements that single-system designs must have in order for them to be useful to social work practitioners and researchers. Use a social work example throughout your discussion.

3. List and discuss in detail the *exploratory* single-system research designs. Provide a social work example of each.

4. List and discuss in detail the *descriptive* single-system research designs. Provide a social work example of each.

5. List and discuss in detail the *explanatory* single-system research designs. Provide a social work example of each.

6. What do descriptive single-system research designs have that exploratory ones do not? Provide a social work example in your discussion.

7. What do explanatory single-system research designs have that descriptive ones do not? Provide a social work example in your discussion.

8. List and discuss in detail the advantages and disadvantages of single-system research designs. Provide a social work example throughout your discussion.

9. When is it inappropriate to implement an *A*-phase when trying to achieve a single-system research design? Provide a social work example throughout your discussion.

10. Go to the library and identify an article that used an exploratory single-system research design. What do you feel the article contributed to the knowledge base of social work? Why? Justify your response. Answer the above questions with both an article that used a descriptive design and one that used an explanatory design.

REFERENCES AND FURTHER READINGS

Barlow, D.H., Hayes, S.C., & Nelson, R.O. (1984). *The scientist practitioner: Research and accountability in clinical and educational settings.* Elmsford, NY: Pergamon.

Bloom, M., Fischer, J., & Orme, J. (1994). *Evaluating practice: Guidelines for the accountable professional* (2nd ed.). Englewood Cliffs, NJ: Prentice-Hall.

Bostwick, G.J., & Kyte, N.S. (1993). Measurement in research. In R.M. Grinnell, Jr. (Ed.), *Social work research and evaluation* (4th ed., pp. 174-197). Itasca, IL: F.E. Peacock.

Fischer, J., & Corcoran, K. (1994). *Measures for clinical practice: A sourcebook* (2nd ed., 2 vols.). New York: Free Press.

Gabor, P.A., & Grinnell, R.M., Jr. (1994). *Evaluation and quality improvement in the human services* (pp. 123-147). Needham Heights, MA: Allyn & Bacon.

Hersen, M., & Barlow, D.H. (1984). *Single-case experimental designs: Strategies for studying behavior change* (2nd ed.). Elmsford, NY: Pergamon.

Hudson, W.W. (1981). Development and use of indexes and scales. In R.M. Grinnell, Jr. (Ed.), *Social work research and evaluation* (pp. 130-155). Itasca, IL: F.E. Peacock.

Hudson, W.W. (1982). *The clinical measurement package: A field manual.* Pacific Grove, CA: Wadsworth.

Hudson, W.W., & Thyer, B.A. (1987). Research measures and indices in direct practice. In A. Minahan (Ed.), *Encyclopedia of social work* (pp. 487-498). Washington, DC: National Association of Social Workers.

Jordan, C., Franklin, C., & Corcoran, K.J. (1993). Standardized measuring instruments. In R.M. Grinnell, Jr. (Ed.), *Social work research and evaluation* (4th ed., pp. 198-220). Itasca, IL: F.E. Peacock.

Marlow, C. (1993). *Research methods for generalist social work practice* (pp. 29, 151-173). Pacific Grove, CA: Wadsworth.

Monette, D.R., Sullivan, T.J., & DeJong, C.R. (1994). *Applied social research* (3rd ed., pp. 282-311). Fort Worth, TX: Harcourt Brace.

Nelson, J.C. (1988). Single-subject research. In R.M. Grinnell, Jr. (Ed.), *Social work research and evaluation* (3rd ed., pp. 362-399). Itasca, IL: F.E. Peacock.

Nurius, P.S., & Hudson, W.W. (1993). *Human services: Practice, evaluation, and computers.* Pacific Grove, CA: Brooks/Cole.

Polster, R.A., & Lynch, M.A. (1981). Single-subject designs. In R.M. Grinnell, Jr. (Ed.), *Social work research and evaluation* (pp. 373-418). Itasca, IL: F.E. Peacock.

Polster, R.A., & Lynch, M.A. (1985). Single-subject designs. In R.M. Grinnell, Jr. (Ed.), *Social work research and evaluation* (2nd ed., pp. 381-431). Itasca, IL: F.E. Peacock.

Royse, D.D. (1991). *Research methods in social work* (pp. 53-77). Chicago: Nelson-Hall.

Rubin, A., & Babbie, E. (1993). *Research methods for social work* (2nd ed., pp. 292-328). Pacific Grove, CA: Wadsworth.

Thyer, B. (1993). Single-system research designs. In R.M. Grinnell, Jr. (Ed.), *Social work research and evaluation* (4th ed., pp. 94-117). Itasca, IL: Peacock.

Yegidis, B.L., & Weinbach, R.W. (1991). *Research methods for social workers* (pp. 126-142). White Plains, NY: Longman.

Chapter 11

Group Designs

XAMPLES OF RESEARCH DESIGNS were introduced in the last chapter with single-system designs because they represent a class of designs that is comparatively consistent and uncomplicated. More often than not, single-system designs all have the same purpose: to evaluate the effects of social work interventions. They usually have the same independent variable–the intervention–and the same dependent variable–the clients' outcome. The study is done at the individual level, with a single person, group, or system.

However, single-system research designs do not necessarily have to have an independent variable. They can be used to track the progress of some variable over time such as the number of AIDS patients admitted to a local hospital per year over a five-year period, for example. In this situation, there is no independent variable; the only variable being monitored over time is one dependent variable–number of AIDS patients admitted to a local hospital per year over a five year period.

Understanding single-system designs as presented in the last chapter lays a good foundation for understanding more complex group research designs. But only some of the group research designs discussed in this chapter are complex; like single-system research designs, group research designs also cover the entire range of knowledge levels, from exploratory, to descriptive, to explanatory. Where a research design (either single-system or group) fits on this continuum depends on both the amount of prior knowledge on a topic area and the certainty with which the results can be interpreted.

Exploratory group research designs, also called preexperimental or nonexperimental, only explore the research question or problem area. These designs do not produce statistically sound data or conclusive results, nor do they intend to. Their purpose is to describe and build a foundation of general ideas and tentative theories that can be explored later with more precise and hence more complex research designs and the corresponding data-gathering techniques.

In the middle range are the descriptive designs, sometimes referred to as quasi-experimental ("quasi" means having some resemblance). A quasi experiment resembles an explanatory group research design in some aspects, but lacks at least one of the necessary requirements, usually random selection from a population or random assignment of research participants to two or more groups.

At the highest level are the explanatory designs, also called experimental designs or "ideal" experiments as presented in Chapter 8. These designs have the largest number of requirements, all of which will be examined later in this chapter. They are best used in confirmatory research studies where the area under study is well developed, theories abound, and testable hypotheses can be formulated on the basis of previous work or existing theories. These designs seek to establish causal relationships between the dependent and independent variables.

TABLE 11.1   Knowledge Levels and Corresponding Research Designs

Knowledge Levels	Research Designs
1. Exploratory	*a*: One-group posttest-only design
	b: Multigroup posttest-only design
	c: Longitudinal case study design
	d: Longitudinal survey design
2. Descriptive	*a*: Randomized one-group posttest-only design
	b: Randomized cross-sectional and longitudinal survey design
	c: One-group pretest-posttest design
	d: Comparison group posttest-only design
	e: Comparison group pretest-posttest design
	f: Interrupted time-series design
3. Explanatory	*a*: Classical experimental design
	b: Solomon four-group design
	c: Randomized posttest-only control group design

While, in a particular case, a group research design may need to be complex to accomplish the purpose of the study, a design that is unnecessarily complex costs more, takes more time, and probably will not serve its purpose nearly as well as a simpler one. In choosing a research design (whether single-system or group), therefore, the principle of parsimony must be applied: The simplest and most economical route to the objective is the best choice. The three knowledge levels and the group research designs that are usually associated with each are listed in Table 11.1.

EXPLORATORY DESIGNS

At the lowest level of the continuum of knowledge that can be derived from research studies are exploratory group research designs. An exploratory study explores a research question about which little is already known, in order to uncover generalizations and develop hypotheses that can be investigated and tested later with more precise and, hence, more complex designs and data-gathering techniques.

The four examples of exploratory designs given in this section do not use pretests; they measure the dependent variable only after the independent variable has been introduced. Therefore, they cannot be used to identify if changes took place in study participants; they simply describe the state of the participants after they had received the independent variable. However, as will be shown, there does not necessarily have to be an independent variable in a study—the researcher may just want to measure some variable in a particular population such as the number of people who receive AFDC benefits over a ten-year period. In this situation, there is no independent variable.

One-Group Posttest-Only Design

The one-group posttest-only design (Design 1*a*) is sometimes called the one-shot case study or cross-sectional case study design. It is the simplest of all the group research designs.

Suppose in a particular community, Rome, Wisconsin, there are numerous parents who are physically abusive toward their children. The city decides to hire a school social worker, Antonia, to implement a program that is supposed to reduce the number of parents who physically abuse their children. She conceptualizes a 12-week child abuse prevention program (the intervention) and offers it to parents who have children in her school who wish to participate on a voluntary basis. A simple research study is then conducted to answer the question, "Did the parents who completed the program stop physically abusing their children?" The answer to this question will determine the success of the intervention.

There are many different ways in which this program can be evaluated. However, for now, and to make matters as simple as possible, we are going to evaluate it by simply counting how many parents stopped physically abusing their children after they attended the program.

At the simplest level, the program could be evaluated with a one-group posttest-only design. The basic elements of this design are illustrated in Figure 11.1. This design can also be written as follows:

$$X \quad O_1$$

Where:

X = Independent variable (Child Abuse Prevention Program, the intervention)

O_1 = First and only measurement of the dependent variable (number of parents who stopped physically abusing their children, the program's outcome, or program objective)

All that this design provides is a measure (O_1) of what happens when one group of people is subjected to one treatment or experience (X). The program's participants were not randomly selected from any particular population, and, thus, the results of the findings cannot be generalized to any other group or population.

It is safe to assume that all the members within the program had physically abused their children before they enrolled, since people who do not have this problem would not enroll in such a program. But, even if the value of O_1 indicates that some of the parents did stop being violent with their children after the program, it cannot be determined whether they quit because of the intervention (the program) or because of some other rival hypothesis.

Perhaps a law was passed that made it mandatory for the police to arrest anyone who behaves violently toward his or her child, or perhaps the local television station started to report such incidents on the nightly news, complete with pictures of the abusive parent. These other extraneous variables may have been more important in persuading the parents to cease their abusive behavior toward their children than their volun-

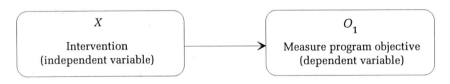

X	O_1
Intervention (independent variable)	Measure program objective (dependent variable)

FIGURE 11.1   One-Group Posttest-Only Design

tary participation in the program. In sum, this design does not control for many of the threats to either internal or external validity that were discussed in Chapter 8. In terms of internal validity, the threats that are applicable and that are not controlled for in this design are history, maturation, differential selection, and mortality.

Cross-Sectional Survey Design. Let us take another example of a one-group posttest-only design that *does not* have an independent variable, unlike the child abuse prevention program mentioned above. In survey research, this kind of a group research design is called a cross-sectional survey design.

In a cross-sectional survey, the researcher surveys *only once* a cross-section of some particular population. In addition to Antonia's child abuse prevention program geared for parents, she may also want to start another program geared for children—a child abuse educational program taught to children in the school. However, before Antonia starts the program geared for the children, she wants to know what parents think about the idea. She may send out questionnaires to all the parents or she may decide to personally telephone every second parent, or every fifth or tenth, depending on how much time and money she has. The results of her survey constitute a single measurement, or observation, of the parents' opinions of her second proposed program (the one for the children) and may be written as:

$$O_1$$

The symbol O_1 represents the entire cross-sectional survey design since such a design involves making only a single observation. Note that there is no X, as there is really no independent variable. Antonia only wants to ascertain the parents' attitudes toward her proposed program—nothing more, nothing less.

Multigroup Posttest-Only Design

The multigroup posttest-only design (Design 1*b*) is an elaboration of the one-group posttest-only design (Design 1*a*) in which more than one group is used. To check a bit further into the effectiveness of Antonia's program for parents who have been physically abusive toward their children, for example, she might decide to locate several more groups of parents who had completed the program and see how many of them had stopped abusing their children—and so on, with any number of groups.

This design can be written in symbols as follows:

Experimental Group 1: $X \quad O_1$
Experimental Group 2: $X \quad O_1$

Experimental Group 3: X O_1
Experimental Group 4: X O_1

Where:

X = Independent variable (Child Abuse Prevention Program, the intervention)

O_1 = First and only measurement of the dependent variable (number of parents who stopped physically abusing their children, the program's outcome, or program objective)

With the multigroup design it cannot be assumed that all four Xs (the independent variables) are equivalent because the four programs might not be exactly the same; one group might have had a different facilitator, the program might have been presented differently, or the material could have varied in important respects. Nothing is known about whether any of the participants would have stopped being violent anyway, even without the program. It certainly cannot be assumed that any of the groups were representative of the larger population. Thus, as in the case of the one group posttest-only design, the same threats to the internal and the external validity of the study might influence the results of the multigroup posttest design.

Longitudinal Case Study Design

The longitudinal case study design (Design 1c) is exactly like the one-group posttest-only design (Design 1a), only it provides for more measurements of the dependent variable. This design can be written in symbols as follows:

$$X \quad O_1 \quad O_2 \quad O_3 \ldots$$

Where:

X = Independent variable (Child Abuse Prevention Program, the intervention)

O_1 = First measurement of the dependent variable (number of parents who stopped physically abusing their children, the program's outcome, or program objective)

O_2 = Second measurement of the dependent variable (number of parents who stopped physically abusing their children, the program's outcome, or program objective)

O_3 = Third measurement of the dependent variable (number of parents who stopped physically abusing their children, the program's outcome, or program objective)

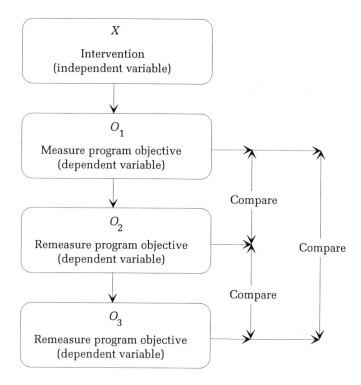

FIGURE 11.2   Longitudinal Case Study Design

The basic elements of the longitudinal case study design are illustrated in Figure 11.2 above. The same design is called a panel, cohort, developmental, or dynamic case study design.

Suppose that, in our example, Antonia is interested in the long-term effects of the child abuse prevention program. Perhaps the program was effective in helping some people to stop physically abusing their children, but will they continue to refrain from abusing their children?

One way to find out is to measure the number of parents who physically abuse their children at intervals, say at the end of the program, the first three months after the program, then the next three months after that, and every three months for the next two years. If the program is expressed in symbols, the symbols would represent the following elements:

X = Independent variable (Child Abuse Prevention Program, the intervention)

O_1 = First measurement of the dependent variable (number of parents who stopped physically abusing their children, the program's outcome, or program objective)

O_2 = Second measurement of the dependent variable (number of parents who stopped physically abusing their children, the program's outcome, or program objective)

O_3 = Third measurement of the dependent variable (number of parents who stopped physically abusing their children, the program's outcome, or program objective)

Design 1c can be used to monitor the effectiveness of treatment interventions over time and can be applied not just to groups but also to single client systems as described in the last chapter. However, all of the same threats to the internal and external validity that were described in relation to the previous two exploratory designs also apply to this design.

Longitudinal Survey Design

Unlike cross-sectional surveys where the variable of interest (usually the dependent variable) is measured only once, longitudinal surveys (Design 1d) provide data at various points so that changes can be monitored over time. Longitudinal survey designs can be written as:

$$O_1 \quad O_2 \quad O_3$$

Where:

O_1 = First measurement of some variable
O_2 = Second measurement of some variable
O_3 = Third measurement of some variable

Longitudinal survey designs usually have no independent variables and can broken down into three types: (1) trend studies, (2) cohort studies, and (3) panel studies.

Trend Studies. A trend study is used to find out how a population changes over time. For example, Antonia, the school social worker mentioned previously, may want to know if parents who have young children enroled in her school are becoming more receptive to the idea of the school teaching their children child abuse prevention education in the second grade. She may survey all the parents of Grade 2 children this year, all the parents of the new complement of Grade 2 children next year, and so on until she thinks she has sufficient data.

Each year the parents surveyed will be different but they will all be parents of Grade 2 children. In this way, Antonia will be able to determine whether parents are becoming more receptive to the idea of introducing child abuse prevention material to their children as early as

Grade 2. In other words, she will be able to measure any attitudinal trend that is, or is not, occurring.

The research design can still be written:

$$O_1 \quad O_2 \quad O_3$$

Where:

O_1 = First measurement of some variable for a sample
O_2 = Second measurement of some variable for a different sample
O_3 = Third measurement of some variable for yet another different sample

Cohort Studies. Cohort studies are often used over time to follow a group of people who have shared a similar experience—for example, AIDS survivors or sexual abuse survivors, or parents of grade school children. Perhaps Antonia is interested in knowing whether parents' attitudes toward the school offering abuse prevention education to second grade students change as their children grow older. She may survey a sample of the Grade 2 parents who attend a Parent Night this year, and survey a different sample of parents who attend a similar meeting from the same parent population next year, when the children are in Grade 3. The following year, when the children are in Grade 4, she will take another different sample of those parents who attend Parent Night. Although different parents are being surveyed every year, they all belong to the same population of parents whose children are progressing through the grades together. The selection of the samples was not random, though, because parents who take the time to attend Parent Night may be different from those who stay at home.

The research design may be written:

$$O_1 \quad O_2 \quad O_3$$

Where:

O_1 = First measurement of some variable for a sample drawn from some population
O_2 = Second measurement of some variable for a different sample drawn from the same population one year later
O_3 = Third measurement of some variable for a still different sample, drawn from the same population after two years

Panel Studies. In a panel study, the *same individuals* are followed over a period of time. Antonia might select one particular sample of parents, for example, and measure their attitudes toward child abuse prevention education in successive years.

Again, the design can be written:

$$O_1 \quad O_2 \quad O_3$$

Where:

O_1 = First measurement of some variable for a sample of individuals

O_2 = Second measurement of some variable for the same sample of
individuals one year later

O_3 = Third measurement of some variable for the same sample of
individuals after two years

A trend study is interested in broad trends over time. A cohort study provides data about people who have shared similar experiences. In neither case do we know anything about *individual* contributions to the changes that are being measured. A panel study provides data that the researcher can use to look at change over time as experienced by particular individuals.

DESCRIPTIVE DESIGNS

At the midpoint of the knowledge continuum are descriptive designs, which have some but not all of the requirements of an "ideal" experiment as presented in Chapter 8. They usually require specification of the time order of variables, manipulation of the independent variable, and establishment of the relationship between the independent and dependent variables. They may also control for rival hypotheses and use a second group as a comparison (not a control). The requirement that descriptive designs lack most frequently is random selection of participants from a population and random assignment to two or more groups.

Social work researchers are seldom in a position to randomly assign study participants to either an experimental or control group. Sometimes the groups to be studied are already in existence; sometimes ethical issues are involved. For example, it would be unethical to assign clients who need immediate help to two random groups, only one of which is to receive the intervention. Since a lack of random assignment will affect the internal and external validities of the study, the descriptive research design must try to compensate for this. The six examples of descriptive research designs presented in this section do this in various ways.

Randomized One-Group Posttest-Only Design

The distinguishing feature of the randomized one-group posttest-only design (Design 2*a*) is that members of the group are deliberately and randomly selected for it. Otherwise, this design is identical to the exploratory one-group posttest-only design (Design 1*a*).

The randomized one-group posttest-only design is illustrated in Figure 11.3. In symbols, it is written as follows:

$$R \quad X \quad O_1$$

Where:

R = Random selection from a population
X = Independent variable
O_1 = First and only measurement of the dependent variable

In the example of the child abuse prevention program, the difference in this design is that the group does not accidentally assemble itself by including anyone who happened to be interested in volunteering for the program. Instead, group members are randomly selected from a population, say, of all the 400 parents who were reported to child welfare authorities for having physically abused a child and who wish to receive voluntary treatment in Rome, Wisconsin in 1996. These 400 parents

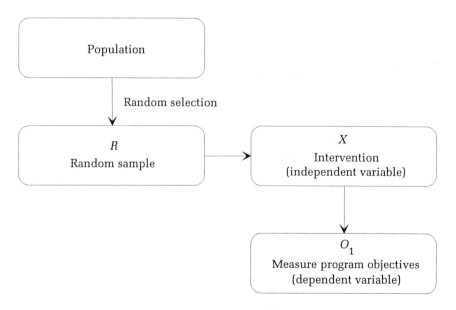

FIGURE 11.3 Randomized One-Group Posttest-Only Design

comprise the population of all the physically abusive parents who wish to receive treatment in Rome, Wisconsin. They also comprise the sampling frame for the study that will be discussed in the following chapter.

The sampling frame of 400 people is used to select a simple random sample of 40 physically abusive parents who voluntarily wish to receive treatment. The program (X) is administered to these 40 people, and the number of parents who stopped being abusive toward their children after the program is determined (O_1). If this design is written for this particular example, the symbols represent:

> R = Random selection of 40 people from the population of physically abusive parents who voluntarily wish to receive treatment in Rome, Wisconsin
> X = Child Abuse Prevention Program
> O_1 = Number of parents in the program who stopped being physically abusive to their children

Say that the program fails to have the desired effect, and 39 of the 40 people continue to physically harm their children after participating in the program. Because the program was ineffective for the sample and the sample was randomly selected, it can be concluded that it would be ineffective for the physically abusive parent population of Rome, Wisconsin–the other 360 who did not go through the program. In other words, because a representative random sample was selected, it is possible to generalize the program's results to the population from which the sample was drawn.

Since no change in the dependent variable occurred, it is not sensible to consider the control of rival hypotheses. Antonia need not wonder what might have caused the change–X, her program, or an alternative explanation. However, if the program had been successful, it would not be possible to ascribe success solely to it, because Antonia would have no idea what other extraneous variables might have contributed to it. The same four threats to the internal validity that affected the nonrandomized one-group posttest-only design could also influence the results of this design.

Randomized Cross-Sectional and Longitudinal Survey Design

As we discussed earlier, a cross-sectional survey obtains data only once from a sample of a particular population. If the sample is a random sample–that is, if it represents the population from which it was drawn–then the data obtained from the sample can be generalized to the entire population. A cross-sectional survey design using a random sample can be written:

$$R \quad O_1$$

Where:

R = Random sample drawn from a population
O_1 = First and only measurement of the dependent variable

The randomized cross-sectional survey design is illustrated in Figure 11.4.

In a similar manner, cohort, trend, or panel longitudinal survey studies can be written as:

$$R_1O_1 \quad R_2O_2 \quad R_3O_3$$

Where:

R_1O_1 = First measurement of some variable for a random sample
R_2O_2 = Second measurement of some variable for a random sample one year later
R_3O_3 = Third measurement of some variable for a random sample after two years

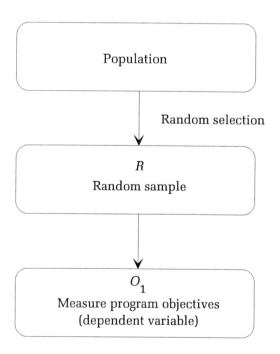

FIGURE 11.4   Randomized Cross-Sectional Survey Design

The randomized longitudinal survey design is illustrated as in Figure 11.5.

Explanatory surveys look for associations between variables. Often, the suspected reason for the relationship is that one variable caused the other. In Antonia's case, she has two studies going on: the child abuse prevention program for parents who have physically abused their children, and her survey of parental attitudes toward the school that is teaching second-grade children child abuse prevention strategies. The success of the child abuse prevention program (her program) may have caused parents to adopt more positive attitudes toward the school in teaching their children child abuse prevention (her survey). In this situation, the two variables, the program and survey, become commingled.

Demonstrating causality is a frustrating business at the best of times because it is so difficult to show that nothing apart from the independent

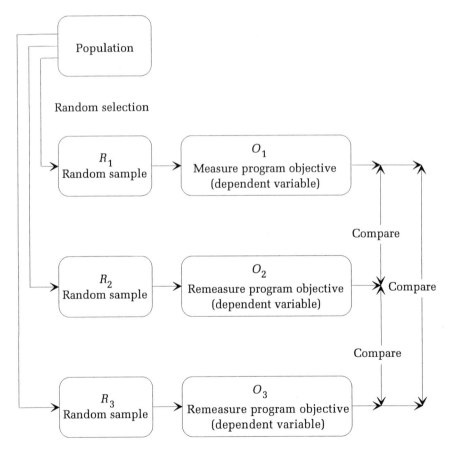

FIGURE 11.5   Randomized Longitudinal Survey Design

variable could have caused the observed change in the dependent variable. Even supposing that this problem is solved, it is impossible to demonstrate causality unless data are obtained from random samples and are generalizable to entire populations.

One-Group Pretest-Posttest Design

The one-group pretest-posttest design (Design 2c) is also referred to as a before-after design because it includes a pretest of the dependent variable, which can be used as a basis of comparison with the posttest results. This design is illustrated in Figure 11.6 and written as follows:

$$O_1 \quad X \quad O_2$$

Where:

O_1 = First measurement of the dependent variable
X = Independent variable, the intervention
O_2 = Second measurement of the dependent variable

The one-group pretest-posttest design, in which a pretest precedes the introduction of the independent variable and a posttest follows it, can be used to determine precisely how the independent variable affects a particular group. The design is used often in social work decision

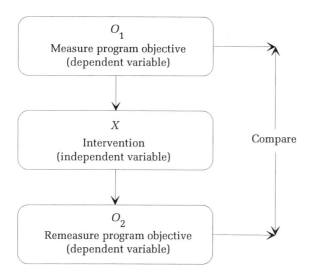

FIGURE 11.6   One-Group Pretest-Posttest Design

making—far too often, in fact, because it does not control for many rival hypotheses. The difference between O_1 and O_2, on which these decisions are based, therefore, could be due to many other factors rather than the independent variable.

Let us take another indicator of how Antonia's child abuse prevention program could be evaluated. Besides counting the number of parents who stopped physically abusing their children as the only indicator of the program's success, she could have a second outcome indicator such as reducing the parents' risk for abusive and neglecting parenting behaviors. This dependent variable could be easily measured by the Adult-Adolescent Parenting Inventory (*AAPI*). It consists of 32 items and takes about 20 minutes to complete. The first 14 items are illustrated in Figure 11.7. The *AAPI* measures four variables about parents: their inappropriate parental expectations of the child, their lack of empathy toward the child's needs, their parental value of physical punishment, and their parent-child role reversal. It is written at the fifth grade reading level and can be administered orally to nonreaders.

Let us say that Antonia had the parents complete the *AAPI before* the child abuse prevention program (O_1) and *after* it (O_2). In this example, history would be a rival hypothesis or threat to internal validity because all kinds of things could have happened between O_1 and O_2 to affect the participants' behaviors and feelings, such as the television station deciding to publicize the names of parents who are abusive to their children. Testing also could be a problem. Just the experience of taking the pretest could motivate some participants to stop being abusive toward their children. Maturation—in this example, the children becoming more mature with age so that they became less difficult to discipline —would be a further threat. Instrumentation could also influence the results of the study and, finally, interactions among threats might occur.

On the positive side, this design controls for the threat of differential selection, since the participants are the same for both pretest and posttest. Second, mortality would not affect the outcome, because it is the differential drop-out between groups that causes this threat and, in this example, there is only one group.

Comparison Group Posttest-Only Design

The comparison group posttest-only design (Design 2*d*) improves on the exploratory one-group and multigroup posttest-only designs by introducing a comparison group that does not receive the independent variable, but is subject to the same posttest as those who do (the experimental group). A group used for purposes of comparison is usually referred to as a comparison group in an exploratory or descriptive design and as a control group in an explanatory design. While a control group is always randomly assigned, a comparison group is not.

Adult-Adolescent Parenting Inventory

	Strongly Agree	Agree	Uncertain	Disagree	Strongly Disagree
1. Young children should be expected to comfort their mother when she is feeling blue.	SA	A	U	D	SD
2. Parents should teach their children right from wrong by sometimes using physical punishment.	SA	A	U	D	SD
3. Children should be the main source of comfort and care for their parents.	SA	A	U	D	SD
4. Young children should be expected to hug their mother when she is sad.	SA	A	U	D	SD
5. Parents will spoil their children by picking them up and comforting them when they cry.	SA	A	U	D	SD
6. Children should be expected to verbally express themselves before the age of one year.	SA	A	U	D	SD
7. A good child will comfort both of his/her parents after the parents have argued.	SA	A	U	D	SD
8. Children learn good behavior through the use of physical punishment.	SA	A	U	D	SD
9. Children develop good, strong charcters through very strict discipline.	SA	A	U	D	SD
10. Parents should expect their children who are under three years to begin taking care of themselves.	SA	A	U	D	SD
11. Young children should be aware of ways to comfort their parents after a hard day's work.	SA	A	U	D	SD
12. Parents should slap their child when s/he has done something wrong.	SA	A	U	D	SD
13. Children should always be spanked when they misbehave.	SA	A	U	D	SD
14. Young children should be responsible for much of the happiness of their parents.	SA	A	U	D	SD

Please go to next page.

FIGURE 11.7 Adult-Adolescent Parenting Inventory

The basic elements in this design are illustrated in Figure 11.8. It is written as follows:

$$\text{Experimental Group:} \quad X \quad O_1$$
$$\text{Comparison Group:} \qquad \quad O_1$$

Where:

X = Independent variable, the intervention
O_1 = First and only measurement of the dependent variable

In Antonia's child abuse prevention program, if the January, April, and August sections are scheduled but the August sessions are cancelled for some reason, those who would have been participants in that section could be used as a comparison group. If the values of O_1 on the *AAPI* were similar for the experimental and comparison groups, it could be concluded that the program was of little use, since those who had experienced it (those receiving X) were not much better or worse off than those who had not.

A problem with drawing this conclusion, however, is that there is no evidence that the groups were equivalent to begin with. Selection, mortality, and the interaction of selection and other threats to internal validity are, thus, the major difficulties with this design. The comparison group does, however, control for such threats as history, testing, instrumentation, and statistical regression.

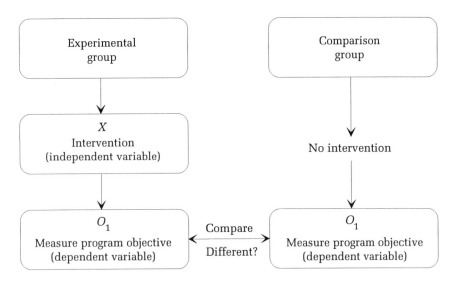

FIGURE 11.8   Comparison Group Posttest-Only Design

Comparison Group Pretest-Posttest Design

The comparison group pretest-posttest design (Design 2e) elaborates on the one-group pretest-posttest design (Design 2c) by adding a comparison group. This second group receives both the pretest (O_1) and the posttest (O_2) at the same time as the experimental group, but it does not receive the independent variable. The elements of this design are shown in Figure 11.9. In symbols, it is written as follows:

$$\text{Experimental Group:} \quad O_1 \quad X \quad O_2$$
$$\text{Comparison Group:} \quad O_1 \qquad O_2$$

Where:

O_1 = First measurement of the dependent variable, the parents' scores on the *AAPI*

X = Independent variable, the intervention

O_2 = Second measurement of the dependent variable, the parents' scores on the *AAPI*

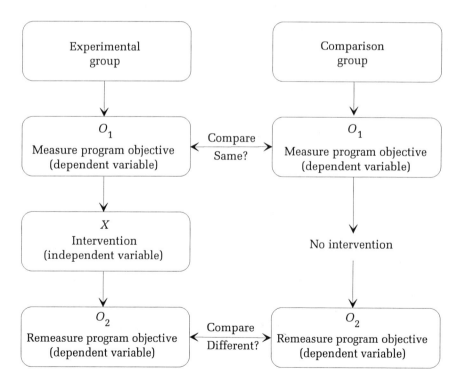

FIGURE 11.9   Comparison Group Pretest-Posttest Design

The experimental and comparison groups formed under this design will probably not be equivalent, because members are not randomly assigned to them. The pretest scores on the *AAPI*, however, will indicate the extent of their differences. If the differences are not statistically significant, but are still large enough to affect the posttest, the statistical technique of analysis of covariance can be used to compensate for this. As long as the groups are equivalent at pretest, then, this design controls for nearly all of the threats to internal validity. But, because random selection and assignment were not used, the external validity threats remain.

Interrupted Time-Series Design

In the interrupted time-series design (Design 2*f*), a series of pretests and posttests are conducted on a group of participants over time, both before and after the independent variable is introduced. The basic elements of this design are illustrated in Figure 11.10.

An interrupted time-series design might be written in symbols as follows:

$$O_1 \quad O_2 \quad O_3 \quad X \quad O_4 \quad O_5 \quad O_6$$

Where:

Os = Measurements of the dependent variable
X = Independent variable

This design takes care of the major weakness in the descriptive one-group pretest-posttest design (Design 2*c*), which does not control for rival hypotheses. Suppose, for example, that a new policy is to be introduced into an agency whereby all promotions and raises are to be tied to the number of educational credits acquired by social workers. Since there is a strong feeling among some workers that years of experience ought to count for more than educational credits, the agency's management decides to examine the effect of the new policy on morale.

Because agency morale is affected by many things and varies normally from month to month, it is necessary to ensure that these normal fluctuations are not confused with the results of the new policy. Therefore, a baseline is first established for morale by conducting a number of pretests over, say, a six-month period before the policy is introduced. Then, a similar number of posttests is conducted over the six months following the introduction of the policy. This design would be written as follows:

$$O_1 \quad O_2 \quad O_3 \quad O_4 \quad O_5 \quad O_6 \quad X \quad O_7 \quad O_8 \quad O_9 \quad O_{10} \quad O_{11} \quad O_{12}$$

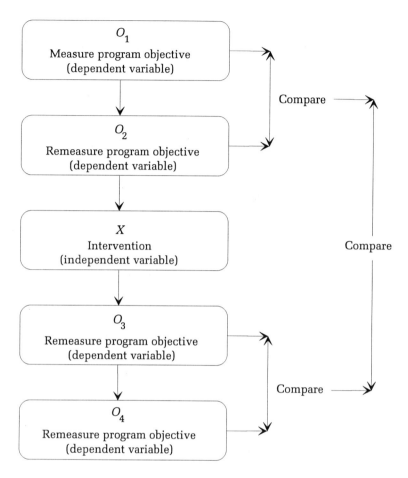

FIGURE 11.10   Interrupted Time-Series Design

The same type of time-series design can be used to evaluate the result of a treatment intervention with a client or client system, as in the single-system designs described in the previous chapter. Again, without randomization, threats to external validity still could affect the results, but most of the threats to internal validity are addressed.

EXPLANATORY DESIGNS

Explanatory group research designs approach the "ideal" experiment most closely. They are at the highest level of the knowledge continuum, have the most rigid requirements, and are most able to produce results that can be generalized to other people and situations. Explanatory designs, therefore, are most able to provide valid and reliable research results that can serve as additions to a social worker's theoretical knowledge base.

The purpose of an explanatory design is to establish a causal connection between the independent and dependent variable. The value of the dependent variable could always result from chance rather than from the influence of the independent variable, but there are statistical techniques for calculating the probability that this will occur.

Classical Experimental Design

The classical experimental design (Design 3*a*) is the basis for all the experimental designs. It involves an experimental group and a control group, both created by random sampling and random assignment methods. As Figure 11.11 shows, both groups take a pretest (O_1) at the same time, after which the independent variable (X) is given only to the experimental group, and then both groups take the posttest (O_2). This design is written as follows:

$$\begin{array}{lcccc}
\text{Experimental Group:} & R & O_1 & X & O_2 \\
\text{Control Group:} & R & O_1 & & O_2
\end{array}$$

Where:

R = Random selection from a population and random assignment to group
O_1 = First measurement of the dependent variable
X = Independent variable, the intervention
O_2 = Second measurement of the dependent variable

Because the experimental and control groups have been randomly assigned, they are equivalent with respect to all important variables. This group equivalence in the design helps control for rival hypotheses, because both groups would be affected by them in the same way. Many of the threats to internal validity are controlled for in this design.

Solomon Four-Group Design

The Solomon four-group research design (Design 3*b*) involves four rather than two randomly assigned groups as in Design 3*a*. There are two experimental groups and two control groups, but the pretest is taken by only one of each of these groups. Experimental Group 1 takes a pretest, receives the independent variable, and then takes a posttest. Experimental Group 2 also receives the independent variable but takes only the posttest. The same is true for the two control groups; Control Group 1 takes both the pretest and posttest, and Control Group 2 takes only the

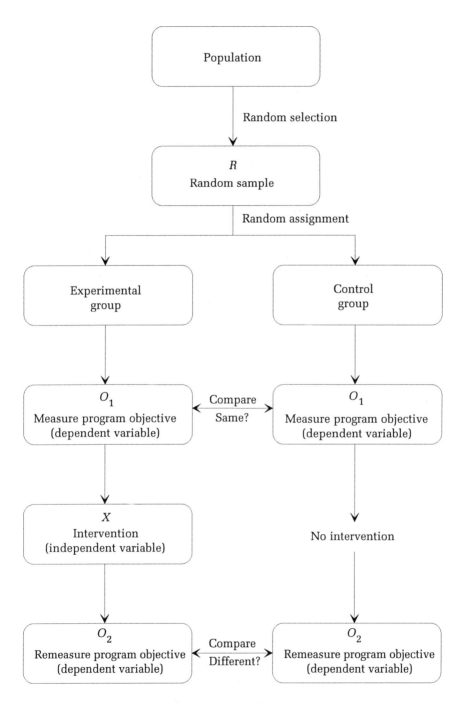

FIGURE 11.11   Classical Experimental Design

posttest. This design is written in symbols as follows:

$$
\begin{array}{lcccc}
\text{Experimental Group 1:} & R & O_1 & X & O_2 \\
\text{Control Group 1:} & R & O_1 & & O_2 \\
\text{Experimental Group 2:} & R & & X & O_2 \\
\text{Control Group 2:} & R & & & O_2 \\
\end{array}
$$

Where:

R = Random assignment to group
O_1 = First measurement of the dependent variable
X = Independent variable, the intervention
O_2 = Second measurement of the dependent variable

The advantage of the Solomon four-group research design is that it allows for the control of testing effects, since one of the experimental groups and one of the control groups do not take the pretest. All of the threats to internal validity are addressed when this design is used. However, it has the disadvantage that twice as many study participants are required, and it is considerably more work to implement than the classical experimental design.

Randomized Posttest-Only Control Group Design

The randomized posttest-only control group research design (Design 3c) is identical to the descriptive comparison group posttest-only design (Design 2d), except that participants are randomly assigned to two groups. This design, therefore, has a control group rather than a comparison group.

The randomized posttest-only control group research design usually involves only two groups, one experimental and one control. There are no pretests. The experimental group receives the independent variable and takes the posttest; the control group only takes the posttest. The basic elements of this design are illustrated in Figure 11.12. This design can be written as follows:

$$
\begin{array}{lccc}
\text{Experimental Group:} & R & X & O_1 \\
\text{Control Group:} & R & & O_1 \\
\end{array}
$$

Where:

R = Random selection from a population and random assignment to group
X = Independent variable, the intervention
O_1 = First and only measurement of the dependent variable

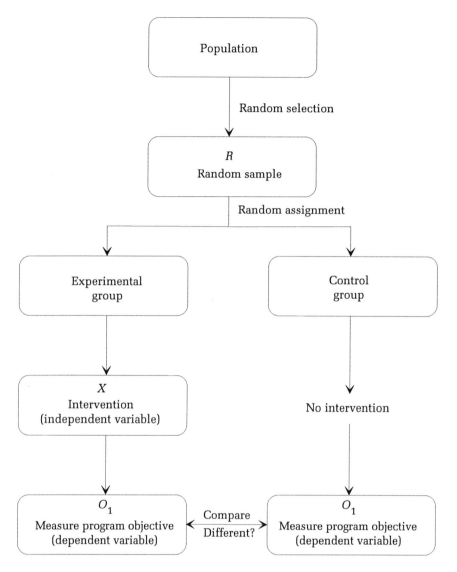

FIGURE 11.12   Randomized Posttest-Only Control Group Design

Suppose a researcher wants to test the effects of two different treatment interventions, X_1 and X_2. In this case, Design 3c could be elaborated upon to form three randomly assigned groups, two experimental groups (one for each intervention) and one control group. This design would be written as follows:

$$
\begin{array}{lccc}
\text{Experimental Group 1:} & R & X_1 & O_1 \\
\text{Experimental Group 2:} & R & X_2 & O_1 \\
\text{Control Group:} & R & & O_1
\end{array}
$$

Where:

R = Random selection from a population and random assignment to group
X_1 = Different independent variable than X_2
X_2 = Different independent variable than X_1
O_1 = First and only measurement of the dependent variable

In addition to measuring change in a group or groups, a pretest also helps to ensure equivalence between the control and experimental groups. As you know, this design does not have a pretest. However, the groups have been randomly assigned, as indicated by R, and this, in itself, is theoretically enough to ensure equivalence without the need for a confirmatory pretest. This design is useful in situations where it is not possible to conduct a pretest or where a pretest would be expected to strongly influence the results of the posttest due to the effects of testing. This design also controls for many of the threats to internal validity.

SUMMARY

Group research designs are conducted with groups of cases rather than on a case-by-case basis. They cover the entire range of research questions and provide designs that can be used to gain knowledge on the exploratory, descriptive, and explanatory levels.

Exploratory designs are used when little is known about the field of study and data are gathered in an effort to find out "what's out there." These ideas are then used to generate hypotheses that can be verified using more rigorous research designs. Descriptive designs are one step closer to determining causality. Of the components necessary for an "ideal" experiment, descriptive designs usually lack either random assignment or control over rival hypotheses, and sometimes both. Explanatory designs are useful when considerable preexisting knowledge is available about the research question under study and a testable hypothesis can be formulated on the basis of previous work. They have more internal and external validity than exploratory and descriptive designs, so they can help establish a causal connection between two variables.

No one research design is inherently inferior or superior to the others. Each has advantages and disadvantages in terms of time, cost, and the data that can be obtained. Social work researchers who are familiar with all three categories of group research designs will be equipped to select the one that is most appropriate to a particular research question.

STUDY QUESTIONS

1. In your own words, discuss the similarities and differences between single-system designs as presented in Chapter 10 and group research designs as presented in this chapter. Use a social work example throughout your discussion.

2. In your own words, discuss the similarities and differences between *exploratory* single-system designs as presented in Chapter 10 and *exploratory* group research designs as presented in this chapter. Use a social work example throughout your discussion.

3. In your own words, discuss the similarities and differences between *descriptive* single-system designs as presented in the previous chapter and *descriptive* group research designs as presented in this chapter. Use a social work example throughout your discussion.

4. In your own words, discuss the similarities and differences between *explanatory* single-system designs as presented in the previous chapter and *explanatory* group research designs as presented in this chapter. Use a social work example throughout your discussion.

5. Discuss the differences among trend studies, cohort studies, and panel studies. Use a social work example throughout your discussion.

6. Review Chapter 8. List all the group research designs and indicate the threats to internal and external validity that each design controls for. Provide a rationale for each one of your responses. Provide a social work example to illustrate each one of your points.

7. Go to the library and find a social work article that reports on a research study that used an *exploratory* research design. How could have this study been done using a "higher level" group research design?

8. Go to the library and find a social work article that reports on a research study that used a *descriptive* research design. How could have this study been done using a "higher level" group research design?

9. Design a perfect group research study, at the explanatory level, that takes into account all the threats to internal and external validity. What ethical issues do you see if your study was in fact implemented?

10. Out of all the group research designs presented in this chapter, which one do you think is used most often in social work research? Why? Justify your answer. Which one do you think is least utilized? Why? Justify your answer.

REFERENCES AND FURTHER READINGS

Adams, G.R., & Schvaneveldt, J.D. (1991). *Understanding research methods* (2nd ed., pp. 101-118, 228-251). White Plains, NY: Longman.

Babbie, E.R. (1992). *The practice of social research* (6th ed., pp. 86-112). Pacific Grove, CA: Wadsworth.

Bailey, K.D. (1994). *Methods of social research* (4th ed., pp. 36-41, 275-292). New York: Free Press.

Campbell, D.T., & Stanley, J.C. (1963). *Experimental and quasi-experimental designs for research.* Skokie, IL: Rand McNally.

Frankfort-Nachmias, C., & Nachmias, D. (1992). *Research methods in the social sciences* (4th ed., pp. 97-99, 271-290). New York: St. Martin's Press.

Grinnell, R.M., Jr. (1993). Group research designs. In R.M. Grinnell, Jr. (Ed.), *Social work research and evaluation* (4th ed., pp. 118-153). Itasca, IL: F.E. Peacock.

Grinnell, R.M., Jr., & Stothers, M. (1988). Research designs. In R.M. Grinnell, Jr. (Ed.), *Social work research and evaluation* (3rd ed., pp. 199-239). Itasca, IL: F.E. Peacock.

Grinnell, R.M., Jr., & Williams, M. (1990). *Research in social work: A primer* (pp. 138-176). Itasca, IL: F.E. Peacock.

Judd, C.M., Smith E.R., & Kidder, I.H. (1991). *Research methods in social relations* (6th ed., pp. 27-36, 298-320). Fort Worth, TX: Harcourt Brace.

Leedy, P.D. (1993). *Practical research: Planning and design* (3rd ed., pp. 113-128, 137-147). New York: Macmillan.

Marlow, C. (1993). *Research methods for generalist social work practice* (pp. 66-68, 95-96, 137-138). Pacific Grove, CA: Wadsworth.

Monette, D.R., Sullivan, T.J., & DeJong, C.R. (1994). *Applied social research* (3rd ed., pp. 82-92). Fort Worth, TX: Harcourt Brace.

Neuman, W.L. (1994). *Social research methods* (2nd ed., pp. 55-78). Needham Heights, MA: Allyn & Bacon.

Royse, D.D. (1991). *Research methods in social work* (pp. 43-44, 79-81, 120-121, 217-232). Chicago: Nelson-Hall.

Rubin, A., & Babbie, E. (1993). *Research methods for social work* (2nd ed., pp. 29-30, 106-112, 357-365). Pacific Grove, CA: Wadsworth.

Tripodi, T. (1981). The logic of research design. In R.M. Grinnell, Jr. (Ed.), *Social work research and evaluation* (pp. 198-225). Itasca, IL: F.E. Peacock.

Tripodi, T. (1985). Research designs. In R.M. Grinnell, Jr. (Ed.), *Social work research and evaluation* (2nd ed., pp. 231-259). Itasca, IL: F.E. Peacock.

Yegidis, B.L., & Weinbach, R.W. (1991). *Research methods for social workers* (pp. 73-90). White Plains, NY: Longman.

Chapter 12

Sampling

C LOSELY ASSOCIATED with the formulation of group research designs as presented in Chapter 11 is the specification of the sampling plan, or the methods that will be used to ensure that the individuals selected for the study's sample actually represent the population from which they were drawn. These participants then provide the necessary data for answering the study's research question or testing the study's hypothesis.

Ideally, data should be obtained from or about each and every person (or event or object) in a given population. In practice, however, it is rarely possible to obtain data from each individual; such a process would be too time-consuming and costly. Therefore, a common practice is to gather data from selected people from a population and to use these individuals to represent the population from which they were drawn. If the selection is carried out in accordance with the requirements of sampling theory, the data obtained from the selected people should quite accurately pertain to the population from which they were drawn.

PROBABILITY SAMPLING PROCEDURES

Random sampling, also known as probability sampling, is a procedure in which all the people (or units) in the population have the same known probability of being selected for the sample. Probability is the same thing as chance—for example, the chance of winning a lottery. If every person in the population is to have the same chance of being selected, it is obviously necessary to have a list of all the people in the population. Such a list is known as a *sampling frame*.

There are four types of probability sampling procedures: (1) simple random sampling, (2) systematic random sampling, (3) stratified random sampling, and (4) cluster random sampling.

Simple Random Sampling

Let us continue with the example that we used in the previous chapter of Antonia, a school social worker at Wilson Elementary School in Rome, Wisconsin. She wants to teach second-grade students how to protect themselves from being physically abused. Thus, she wants to institute a program that will teach these children how to defend themselves from being abused. Before Antonia institutes the program, however, she wants to make sure the parents approve of their children learning such material.

Let us say that Antonia wants to conduct a simple study with single mothers who have at least one child attending her school. She wants to ascertain the mothers' opinions of her idea—that is, teaching their children about the prevention of child abuse. In order to gather data—via the parents' opinions, that is—to help her decide if the content should be taught to second-grade children, Antonia wants to send out survey questionnaires to 100 single mothers who have one or more children at Wilson.

Before Antonia's survey can be sent out, she needs to do several things. First, she needs to construct a sampling frame of all single mothers who have children in the school. Suppose that there are 1,000 names in the sampling frame, representing 1,000 single mothers. Second, Antonia assigns a number to each one. The first single mother on the list is assigned 0001, the second 0002, and so on. Then Antonia takes a book of random numbers, opens the book and picks a digit at random. The first half of a page in such a book is shown in Table 12.1.

Suppose the digit Antonia happens to pick is 1, in the second number in the eighth row in the fourth column from the left. (That whole number is 81864). The three digits immediately to the right of 1 are 8, 6, and 4; thus, Antonia has chanced on the number 1864. She picks four digits in total because the highest number in the sampling frame, 1000, has four digits. The number 1864 is greater than 1000 so Antonia ignores it. Going down the column, 9547 is also more than 1000 so Antonia ignores it also. The next one, 0215, is less than 1000, so Antonia selects single mother number 0215 to take part in the study. After 0722 and 0455, there are no numbers less than 1000 in the fourth column (using

TABLE 12.1   Partial Table of Random Numbers

45823	68184	44863	98829	56521	74091	09650	
67254	60805	90103	61257	10162	45575	22159	
12685	04687	39883	11410	77807	62677	75969	
26495	22349	59342	51877	20947	06649	65092	
24588	21677	57694	92446	76819	05564	32148	
05934	67766	15685	90940	68806	96220	59042	
26078	11818	90159	14001	50967	61153	08832	(8)1864
20965	85682	40814	81864	37856	72596	10727	↑
30983	76835	09299	09547	50497	66522	01298	
55397	50861	16920	90215	70961	61849	66381	
46830	97572	70083	30722	73760	67983	57953	
58732	91838	95826	26713	70317	38187	04484	
06975	77484	95791	75856	08121	10513	63264	
15348	92636	30403	65385	30577	11889	80350	
60345	07306	16036	39854	39967	43613	56677	
59045	34622	21652	04720	30227	57056	92546	
44988	88071	06990	70455	68242	01372	34339	
35045	38738	11476	78561	81350	03077	57500	

the last four digits) so Antonia turns to the numbers in the fifth column (last four digits). Here, she selects eight more single mothers, numbers 0162, 0947, 0967, 0497, 0961, 0317, 0577 and 0227. She continues to select her research participants in this way until she has her sample of 100.

Systematic Random Sampling

The second probability sampling procedure is systematic random sampling. Here, the size of the population is divided by the desired sample size to give a sampling interval, k.

$$k = \frac{\text{Size of Population}}{\text{Desired Sample Size}}$$

Put more simply, if Antonia wants half the population to be in the sample, she selects every other single mother. If she wants a third of the population, she selects every third, a quarter every fourth, a fifth, every fifth, and so on. Since she has a total population of 1000 and she wants a sample of 100, in this instance she will select every tenth single mother on her list.

The problem with this method is that every single mother does not have the same chance of being selected for the study. If every tenth one is selected, starting with the first, single mothers with numbers 2 through 9, 11 through 19, and so on, have no chance of being chosen. In the case of Antonia's study, this may not matter, but suppose she was surveying residents in a rooming house to see how happy they were with their living arrangements. If she decided to survey the occupants of every sixth room and the rooms happen to be arranged six to a floor, there is a danger that all the rooms selected will have something in common. Perhaps they are all at the end farthest from the communal bathroom, and, therefore, the occupants of these rooms are less satisfied with their living arrangements than are the occupants of the other rooms.

This kind of bias can occur whenever the sampling frame is arranged in any particular order, and we must take care that the order will make no difference to the sample selected. Antonia's single mothers, for example, may be listed in alphabetical order; but, for Antonia's purposes, this will not matter.

Stratified Random Sampling

The third type of random sampling procedure is stratified random sampling. Suppose Antonia believes that the age of the children will influence the single mothers' attitudes toward child abuse prevention education. She may look at her population and count the numbers of single mothers with children in four age groups: 5-7, 8-10, 11-13, and 14-16. In her single-mother population of 1000, she finds 300 with children aged 5-7, 350 with children aged 8-10, 250 with children aged 11-13, and 100 with children aged 14-16. She might sample this population proportionally, selecting one-tenth of each category to make up her sample. That is, she would randomly select 30 from the 5-7 category, 35 from the 8-10 category, 25 from the 11-13 category and 10 from the 14-16 category, for a total sample of 100, as illustrated in Table 12.2.

TABLE 12.2   Stratified Random Sampling Example

Category	Number	1/10 Proportionate Sample	Number and (Disproportionate Sampling Fractions) for a Sample of 25 Per Category
Parents with children aged 5–7	300	30	25 (1/12)
Parents with children aged 8–10	350	35	25 (1/14)
Parents with children aged 11–13	250	25	25 (1/10)
Parents with children aged 14–16	100	10	25 (1/4)
Totals	1,000	100	100

However, Antonia may also believe that single mothers of older children will provide valuable information about the effects of child abuse prevention educational programs taught to second-grade children, since the older children may have experienced the content already. She may, therefore, want more than the 10 single mothers of 14-16 year olds that she would get with proportional sampling, and she may prefer to sample disproportionately instead. When Antonia samples disproportionately, she does not worry about selecting one-tenth, or any other fraction, from each category. Instead, she selects 25 single mothers from each category regardless of the total number in the category. As Table 12.2 shows, the sampling fraction for the various categories is now 1/12, 1/14, 1/10, and 1/4 respectively.

Cluster Random Sampling

The final type of random sampling is cluster sampling. This procedure is useful when it is not possible to construct a sampling frame. For example, we may wish to survey people who are homeless, street gang members, or even all the people in a city—groups for whom it is unlikely that there will be an accurate list. Or, suppose Antonia wants to survey all the people in her city about child abuse prevention educational programs to be taught to second-grade children in all schools in the city. She does not have a list of all the people, but she does have a list of all the communities in the city and she can use this list as an alternative sampling frame.

Antonia could randomly select a community or cluster and survey everyone living there. She would then know for sure what this community thinks about her idea since she talked to every member of it. However, there is the possibility that people in the community she selected may tend to be young couples with children who have different opinions than people in a second community who tend to be mostly senior citizens. Perhaps Antonia ought to survey the second community as well. Then, there is a third community, inhabited largely by penniless artists, writers, and students who might have yet a different opinion. Each community is reasonably homogeneous: That is, the people in the community are very like each other. But the communities themselves are totally unlike; that is, they are heterogeneous with respect to each other.

Antonia may not have time to survey everyone in all three clusters, but she might survey, say, ten streets in each of the clusters, selected at random; or perhaps she could survey not every house on her chosen streets but only some houses, also selected at random. The difficulty here is that, since Antonia is not surveying everyone in the community, she might happen to select people who do not give a true picture of that community. Box 12.1 presents a diagram of how a multistage cluster sampling works for a large-scale project.

NONPROBABILITY SAMPLING PROCEDURES

In nonprobability sampling, not all the people in the population have the same probability of being included in the sample and, for each one of them, the probability of inclusion is unknown. This form of sampling is often used in exploratory research studies where the purpose of the study is only to collect as much data as possible about a particular issue. There are four types of nonprobability sampling procedures: (1) convenience sampling, (2) purposive sampling, (3) quota sampling, and (4) snowball sampling.

Box 12.1

Sampling Design for a Nationwide Survey

Survey organizations such as the Survey Research Center (SRC) at the University of Michigan use multistage cluster sampling to conduct nationwide surveys. The steps involved in selecting the SRC's national sample in the 1970s are roughly diagrammed in the accompanying figure. The steps are numbered and labeled according to the type of unit selected.

Step 1. The United States is divided into *primary areas* consisting of counties, groups of counties, or metropolitan areas. These areas are stratified by region and a proportionate stratified sample of seventy-four areas is selected.

Step 2. The seventy-four areas are divided into *locations* such as towns, cities, and residual areas. After these have been identified and stratified by population size, a proportionate stratified sample of locations is drawn within each area.

Step 3. All sample locations are divided into *chunks*. A chunk is a geographic area with identifiable boundaries such as city streets, roads, streams, and county lines. After division into chunks, a random sample of chunks is drawn.

Step 4. Interviewers scout each sample chunk and record addresses and estimates of the number of housing units at each address. They then divide the chunks into smaller units called *segments*, and a random sample of segments is selected.

Step 5. Within each sample segment either all or a sample of the housing units, usually about four, are chosen for a given study. Finally, for every housing unit in the sample, interviewers randomly choose one respondent from among those eligible, which ordinarily consists of all U.S. citizens 18 years of age or older.

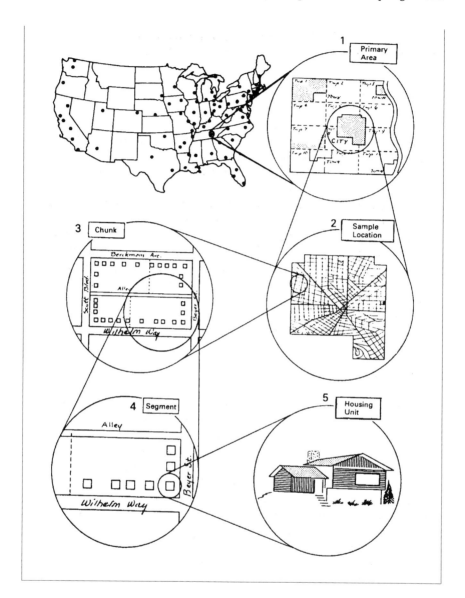

Convenience Sampling

Convenience sampling is the simplest of the four nonprobability sampling procedures and is sometimes called accidental or availability sampling. As its name suggests, it involves selecting for the sample the first people or units who happen to be convenient or available. Antonia might survey all the single mothers who happen to call at the school office in a certain week. Obviously, the single mothers who happen to call at the school's office are not in the least representative of all the single mothers who have at least one child at the school.

Purposive Sampling

Purposive sampling is used when it is necessary to choose a particular sample of some kind. For example, if Antonia wants information on other child abuse prevention educational programs taught to second grade children, she may decide to survey people who have made a special study of such programs. If she is pretesting a questionnaire that must be comprehensible to less well-educated single mothers while not appearing simplistic to the better educated, she may select a small sample of single mothers comprising the extremes in educational level.

In the same way, if she knows from previous studies that single mothers with younger children tend to be more concerned about child abuse prevention education being taught in schools than single mothers with older children, she might restrict her sample to single mothers of younger children. None of these samples are random. They are selected with a particular purpose in mind.

Quota Sampling

In quota sampling, the researcher decides, on the basis of theory, that a certain number of people with particular characteristics should be included in the sample. For example, Antonia may want to compare single mothers whose children have been exposed to child abuse prevention educational programs with single mothers whose children, taught in the same schools, have not been exposed. Further, she may want to compare single mothers of children aged 5-9 with single mothers of children aged 10-14. This gives her four categories, *A, B, C,* and *D,* as illustrated in Table 12.3.

Antonia may decide to survey 20 single mothers from each category, or, if she wants more single mothers with older children, she may decide on 25 from each of categories *C* and *D* and only 15 from each of catego-

TABLE 12.3   Quota Sampling Matrix of Children's Ages by Children's Exposure to Child Abuse Prevention Educational Programs

	Children's Exposure to Programs	
Children's Ages	Yes	No
5 – 9 Years	Category *A*	Category *B*
10 – 14 Years	Category *C*	Category *D*

ries *A* and *B*. Whatever quotas she decides on, she has to find enough single mothers to fill them who satisfy the two conditions with respect to their children's ages and their children's exposure to the child abuse prevention educational programs.

Snowball Sampling

The final type of nonprobability sampling, snowball sampling, is a matter of finding one person with the desired characteristics and using this person to locate others with similar characteristics. For example, if Antonia wants to study the effects of a child abuse prevention educational program for those people who have gone through such a program, she could contact just one such child. This child, in turn, may provide names of other children who were taught the content and so on, until Antonia has a sample of the desired size. Box 12.2 presents an interesting discussion of sex bias and sampling procedures.

Box 12.2

Sex Bias and Sampling

In recent years feminists have been sensitizing social researchers to the relationship of women's issues to research. For example, Chapter 5 presented a discussion dealing with the treatment of gender in operationalizing variables, excerpted from a pamphlet prepared by members of Committees on the Status of Women in Sociology. All aspects of the research process can be affected by sex bias, and sampling is one area where such bias can be particularly problematic. Even probability sampling can be affected by sex bias, for example, when we inappropriately decide to exclude a particular gender from our sampling frame.

Perhaps the most commonly encountered sex bias problem in sampling is the unwarranted generalization of research findings to the population as a whole when one gender is not adequately represented in the research sample. (The same type of problem, by the way, is encountered when certain minority groups are inadequately represented in the sample but generalizations are made to the entire population.)

Campbell (1983) reviewed the occurrence of sex biases in the sex-role research literature and identified a number of illustrations of this problem. For example, she cited studies on achievement motivation and on management and careers whose samples included only white, middle-class male subjects but whose conclusions did not specify that their generalizations were limited to individuals with those attributes. She was particularly critical of life-cycle research, as follows:

> Nowhere is the effect of bias on sampling more evident than in the popular and growing field of the life cycle or stages. Beginning with Erikson's...work on the "Eight Stages of Man" to Levingson's *Seasons of a Man's Life*...the study of life cycles has focused on male subjects. When women are examined, it is in terms of how they fit or don't fit the male model. Without empirical verification, women are said to go through the same cycles as men...or are said to go through cycles that are antithetical to men's...Based on a survey of the literature on life cycles, Sangiuliano...concluded that "Mostly we (researchers) persist in seeing her (woman) in the reflected light of men"... (p. 206)

The inadequate representation of a particular gender in a sample can be much subtler than just excluding them entirely or including an insufficient proportion of them. It could also occur due to biased data-collection procedures, even when the number of individuals of a particular sex is not the issue. For example, Campbell notes that the Gallup poll interviews male subjects beginning at 6:00 P.M., while conducting most interviews with females between 4:00 and 6:00 P.M. Thus, Campbell argues that most professional women would not be home before 6:00 P.M. and are not adequately represented in the sample. If she is correct, then even if the overall proportion of women in the Gallup poll seems to be sufficient, the views expressed by the women in the sample are not adequately representative of the views of the population of women.

As another example, if we wanted to generalize about gender-related differences in job satisfaction, we would not want to select our sample only from those work settings where professional or managerial positions go predominately to men and where semi-professional clerical jobs go predominately to women.

There may be instances, however, when the exclusion of a particular gender from a study's sample is warranted or inescapable—instances where only one gender is relevant and where generalizations will be restricted to that gender. Thus, only one gender would be included in the sample of a survey of client satisfaction in a program whose clientele all happen to be of the same gender. For example, perhaps it is a group support program for battered women or for rape victims.

But we must be on guard not to let any sex-role biases improperly influence us to deem a particular gender irrelevant for a given study. For example, we should not be predisposed to restrict our samples to men when we study things like aggression, management, unemployment, or criminal behavior and to women when we study things like parenting, nurturing, or housekeeping.

SAMPLE SIZE

Before a sample can be selected, it is obviously necessary to decide how large the sample needs to be. The correct sample size for any particular study depends on how confident we need to be about the results. If Antonia wants to be completely confident about single mothers' opinions on child abuse prevention education being taught to second grade children, she needs to survey every single mother: That is, she must not draw a sample at all. Generally speaking, the more single mothers she surveys, the more confident she can be that the results of the survey reflect the opinions of the single-mother population.

The sample size also depends on how homogeneous, or how alike, the population is. If Antonia's population of single mothers were all identical robots, she would need only to survey one to be completely confident of the opinions of the rest. If they were all middle-aged, middle-income Caucasian Catholics, she would need to survey fewer than if they comprised a wide range of ethnic and religious groups of varying ages and incomes.

Sample size must also be considered in relation to the number of categories required. If Antonia wants to look at single mothers of 5-9 year old children and single mothers of 10-14 year old children, she will need two single mothers—one from each category—even if all the single mothers are identical robots. The more dissimilar the single mothers are, the more she will need to survey in each of the categories she wants to consider. In addition, if there are very few single mothers in one category, she may need to survey all the single mothers in that category, or at least a large proportion of them, while surveying smaller proportions of single mothers in the other categories.

Generally speaking, the larger the sample the better, taking into account restrictions of time and cost. With respect to the minimum sample size required, experts differ. Some say that a sample of 30 is large enough to perform basic statistical procedures, while others advise a minimum sample size of 100. There are formulas available for calculating sample size but they are complicated and difficult to use. Usually, a sample size of one-tenth of the population is considered sufficient to provide reasonable control over sampling error. The same one-tenth convention also applies to categories of the population: One-tenth of each category can be included in the sample.

ERRORS

Errors in research findings may result either from the sampling procedure, in which case they are called sampling errors, or from other errors arising in the study, called nonsampling errors.

Sampling Errors

Sampling errors have to do with the fact that a representative sample—a sample that exactly represents the population from which it was drawn—almost never exists in reality. When Antonia surveys a random sample of single mothers, she will not obtain exactly the same results from the sample as she would have obtained had she surveyed the entire single-mother population. The difference between the results she did obtain and the results she would have obtained comprises the sampling error.

In order to better understand the concept of representativeness, suppose that two variables are particularly important in determining whether single mothers will approve of child abuse prevention education taught to second-grade children in schools: the mother's degree of belief that her own child is at risk of abuse (Figure 12.1); and the mother's degree of fear that child abuse prevention education may somehow psychologically harm her child (Figure 12.2).

Suppose further that these two variables can be measured, both for a random sample of 100 single mothers and for the entire single-mother population of 1000. All the single mothers in the school may be asked to rate the degree to which they feel their own children are at risk of abuse, on a scale of 1 to 10, from "no risk at all" to "very high risk." A graph may then be drawn of the number of single mothers on the vertical axis against rating of risk on the horizontal axis, as illustrated in Figure 12.1.

As Figure 12.1a shows, a few single mothers in the population feel that their children are at high risk (rating the risk as 10 on the scale), a few feel that there is very little risk (a rating of 1), and most single mothers believe that there is moderate risk. If a random sample of single mothers is then selected from the single-mother population and the same procedure is carried out, almost identical results may be obtained, as shown in Figure 12.1b. The degree of similarity between graphs 12.1a

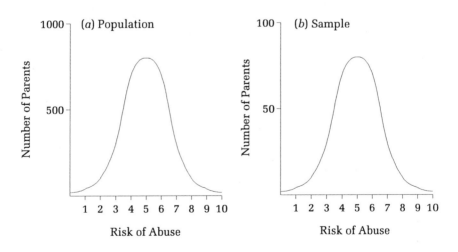

FIGURE 12.1   Rating of Risk Distributions from a Population and a Random Sample

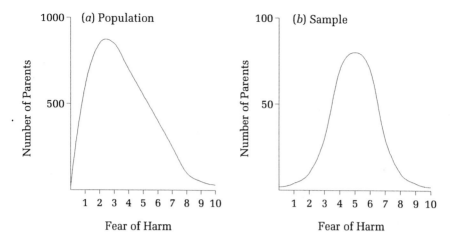

FIGURE 12.2   Rating of Fear of Harm Distributions from a
Population and a Random Sample

and 12.1*b* is the degree to which the sample is representative of the
population, with respect to the belief that their children are at risk.

Now suppose that the single-mother population and the sample are
separately asked to rate the degree to which they fear that child abuse
prevention education may somehow harm their children. The results for
the population and the sample are shown in Figure 12.2.

As Figure 12.2*a* shows, the majority of the population have very
little fear that their children will be harmed by child abuse prevention
being taught in schools. A few have extreme fear, a few have moderate
fear, and a few have no fear at all. Conversely, the majority of the sample
display moderate fear that their children will be harmed; the hump of
the graph, which is skewed to the left in Figure 12.2*a* is essentially
centered in Figure 12.2*b*. If these graphs were placed one on top of
another, they would not coincide. Thus, the sample does not very
adequately represent the single-mother population, with respect to fear
that their children will be harmed.

In sum, while no sample will perfectly represent the population from
which it was drawn, it is quite probable that a randomly drawn sample
will represent the population adequately with respect to one variable. It
is less probable that the sample will represent the population adequately
with respect to two variables, and, the more variables there are, the less
probable adequate representation becomes. A member of congress, for
example, may represent his or her constituents' views on state-funded
abortions exactly, but it is unlikely that their views on Medicare will
also be reflected, as well as their views on capital punishment and their
views on national health care.

Nonsampling Errors

Nonsampling errors include all the errors arising in a study that have nothing to do with sample selection. Unlike sampling errors, they cannot be mathematically calculated. Indeed, a primary danger is that we may not know they exist. For example, a research participant may circle "strongly agree" on a measuring instrument when he or she meant to circle "strongly disagree." We may misinterpret the writing on a questionnaire or enter the wrong number into the computer, or even interview the wrong person because there are two streets with the same name.

The total error in a research study is the sampling error plus the nonsampling error. Clearly, it is of little use to go to great lengths to draw a representative sample without taking meticulous care with every other task.

SUMMARY

The totality of people or objects with which a study is concerned is called a population. The process of selecting people from the population to take part in a research study is known as sampling, and the people or other units that are selected comprise a sample.

A sample of people to be surveyed may be selected from the total population using probability or nonprobability sampling methods. Probability sampling, also known as random sampling, is a procedure in which all the people or units in the population have the same known probability of being selected for the sample. This procedure requires a list of all the people in the population, called a sampling frame.

A probability sample can be selected from a sampling frame using one of four main procedures: simple random sampling, systematic random sampling, stratified random sampling, and cluster random sampling. Simple random sampling involves the use of a book of random numbers. Systematic random sampling uses a sampling interval, which is the ratio of the size of the population to the desired sample size. Stratified random sampling is a method in which we divide the population into strata or categories and select a random sample from each category, either proportionately or disproportionately. Cluster sampling is useful when it is not possible to construct a sampling frame of all the members of the population, and a list of clusters—for example, communities in a city—is used as an alternative sampling frame.

In nonprobability sampling, not all the people in the population have the same probability of being included in the sample and, for each one of them, the probability of inclusion is unknown. There are four types of nonprobability sampling procedures: convenience sampling, purposive sampling, quota sampling, and snowball sampling.

Before a sample can be selected, it is obviously necessary to decide how large the sample needs to be. The correct sample size for any particular study depends on how confident we need to be about the results. Generally speaking, the larger the sample, the more confident we can be that the results of the survey reflect the opinions of the population as a whole.

However, the correct sample size also depends on how homogeneous the population is and on the number of categories required. A sample size of one-tenth of the population is generally considered to give sufficient control over sampling errors.

Errors in a study's results may result either from the sampling procedure, in which case they are called sampling errors, or from other errors arising in the study, called nonsampling errors. Sampling errors have to do with the fact that a representative sample—a sample that exactly represents the population from which it was drawn—almost never exists in reality. The difference between the results obtained from the sample and the results that would have been obtained from the total population comprises the sampling error.

Nonsampling errors include all the errors arising in a study that have nothing to do with sample selection—for example, mistakes and omissions on the part of the research participants and the researcher. The total error in a research study is the sampling error plus the nonsampling error.

STUDY QUESTIONS

1. In your own words, list and discuss the four types of probability sampling procedures. Discuss the advantages and disadvantages of each. Provide a social work example of how each one can be used in a research study.

2. In your own words, list and discuss the four types of nonprobability sampling procedures. Discuss the advantages and disadvantages of each. Provide a social work example of how each one can be used in a research study.

3. Discuss the major differences between probability and nonprobability sampling procedures. When is one method better than the other? Provide a social work example throughout your discussion.

4. Discuss how a researcher can use a table of random numbers to select a probability sample.

5. Discuss the two types of errors that can occur when selecting a sample and recording the participants responses. Provide a social work example throughout your discussion.

6. Go to the library and select a social work research article. What kind of sample was used in the study? Justify your response. How could the

researcher have selected a more representative sample? Provide a rationale for your response.

7. Discuss how a cluster sample would be useful for you to obtain if your research question was, ""How many people in your local community want to obtain a BSW?"

8. Let us say the social work student body is being asked how they liked their research classes. What type of sample would you use to select the students' views? Provide a rationale for your response.

9. What type of sample would you use if you want to gather the opinions of past students who specialized in community organization within your program who are now practicing social work in your local community?

10. Review Chapter 11. What kinds of samples do you feel would be most appropriate for exploratory designs? Descriptive designs? Explanatory designs? Justify your response and use a social work example throughout your discussion.

REFERENCES AND FURTHER READINGS

Campbell, P.B. (1983). The impact of societal biases on research methods. In B.L. Richardson & J. Wirtenberg (Eds.), *Sex role research* (pp. 197-213). New York: Praeger Publishers.

Frankfort-Nachmias, C., & Nachmias, D. (1992). *Research methods in the social sciences* (4th ed., pp. 169-193). New York: St. Martin's Press.

Gabor, P.A. (1993). Sampling. In R.M. Grinnell, Jr. (Ed.), *Social work research and evaluation* (4th ed., pp. 154-170). Itasca, IL: F.E. Peacock.

Gabor, P.A., & Grinnell, R.M., Jr. (1994). *Evaluation and quality improvement in the human services* (pp. 190-207). Needham Heights, MA: Allyn & Bacon.

Grinnell, R.M., Jr., & Williams, M. (1990). *Research in social work: A primer* (pp. 116-136). Itasca, IL: F.E. Peacock.

Leedy, P.D. (1993). *Practical research: Planning and design* (3rd ed., pp. 197-213). New York: Macmillan.

Marlow, C. (1993). *Research methods for generalist social work practice* (pp. 103-123). Pacific Grove, CA: Wadsworth.

Monette, D.R., Sullivan, T.J., & DeJong, C.R. (1994). *Applied social research* (3rd ed., pp. 119-152). Fort Worth, TX: Harcourt Brace.

Royse, D.D. (1991). *Research methods in social work* (pp. 113-122). Chicago: Nelson-Hall.

Rubin, A., & Babbie, E. (1993). *Research methods for social work* (2nd ed., pp. 217-260). Pacific Grove, CA: Wadsworth.

Seaberg, J.R. (1981). Sampling procedures and techniques. In R.M. Grinnell, Jr. (Ed.), *Social work research and evaluation* (pp. 71-92). Itasca, IL: F.E. Peacock.

Seaberg, J.R. (1985). Sampling. In R.M. Grinnell, Jr. (Ed.), *Social work research and evaluation* (2nd ed., pp. 133-148). Itasca, IL: F.E. Peacock.

Seaberg, J.R. (1988). Utilizing sampling procedures. In R.M. Grinnell, Jr. (Ed.), *Social work research and evaluation* (3rd ed., pp. 240-257). Itasca, IL: F.E. Peacock.

Part IV

Collecting Data

IN THE FOUR CHAPTERS OF PART IV, we introduce readers to basic data collection procedures, statistical analyses, and report writing—the final stages in the research process. More specifically, Chapter 13 provides a brief discussion of how surveys are used to collect data, while the following chapter illustrates other nonsurvey data collection options. Chapter 15 presents simple uncomplicated ways in which data can be analyzed, and the last chapter discusses how to prepare a final research report based on the study's research proposal.

Chapter 13

Surveys

I
N THE LAST TWO CHAPTERS, we presented group designs and sampling
procedures, respectively. This chapter will consider research designs
and sampling in the context of collecting data from a large population in a relatively short amount of time. Surveys can be used to collect
data from the residents of a nursing home, from social workers who have
placed children into foster care in the past year in a particular region, or
from all the citizens of a city or county.

Data may be collected from these various populations by means of
surveys—mailed questionnaires, or personal or telephone interviews
conducted with a selected sample of respondents. The process of formulating and implementing a survey research design is known as survey
research. The generic steps of a survey research study are presented in
Figure 13.1.

PURPOSE OF SURVEY RESEARCH

The purpose of conducting survey research is to gather data about a
situation that *already exists*. The "already exists" aspect is important
since some other designs involve manipulation of the independent variable in order to measure associated changes in the dependent variable

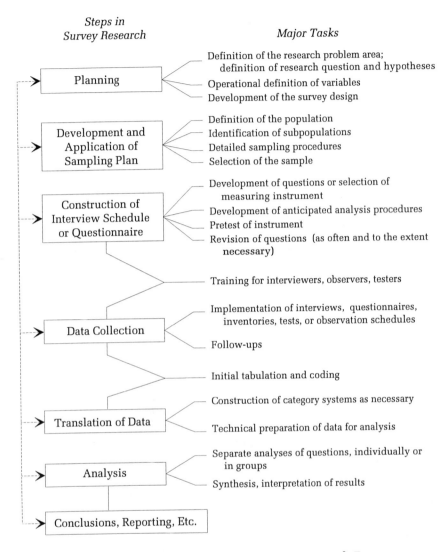

Steps in
Survey Research

Major Tasks

Planning
— Definition of the research problem area; definition of research question and hypotheses
— Operational definition of variables
— Development of the survey design

Development and Application of Sampling Plan
— Definition of the population
— Identification of subpopulations
— Detailed sampling procedures
— Selection of the sample

Construction of Interview Schedule or Questionnaire
— Development of questions or selection of measuring instrument
— Development of anticipated analysis procedures
— Pretest of instrument
— Revision of questions (as often and to the extent necessary)

— Training for interviewers, observers, testers

Data Collection
— Implementation of interviews, questionnaires, inventories, tests, or observation schedules
— Follow-ups

— Initial tabulation and coding

Translation of Data
— Construction of category systems as necessary
— Technical preparation of data for analysis

Analysis
— Separate analyses of questions, individually or in groups
— Synthesis, interpretation of results

Conclusions, Reporting, Etc.

FIGURE 13.1   Steps and Tasks in the Survey Research Process

(e.g., Design 4*a*, as presented in Chapter 11). In contrast, researchers conducting a survey do not manipulate anything. For example a survey could merely measure individuals' attitudes toward current welfare legislation as they already exist, with no attempt to change those beliefs.

Survey research can be used to measure not only existing attitudes but also behaviors, knowledge levels, and feelings. For example, we may want to know what proportion of senior citizens are abused by their children, or what people think about a particular social service, or what feelings foster children have toward their biological parents.

DESIGNS

A survey design can be formulated at the exploratory, descriptive, or explanatory level. An exploratory survey will be appropriate when very little is known about the research question being considered.

A descriptive survey will be useful when it is necessary to accurately describe a certain population: for example, to discover whether senior citizens who are abused by their children have any particular characteristics in common. We may not, however, be able to randomly select their informants, thus limiting the predictive power of the study's results.

An explanatory survey randomly selects individuals from a population, and, consequently, views their opinions and attitudes as representative of those of the entire population from which the sample was drawn. Thus, the responses of a small group are used to predict the responses of the larger group, because one does not have the time and resources to contact every individual in the population. Politicians, for example, make extensive use of polls that collect data on intended voting patterns from a small, but representative, sample of people, and use these data to predict whether they are likely to be reelected.

Exploratory Surveys

In our fast-changing society, we are often presented with problem areas about which we know very little. AIDS has come to the public attention relatively recently, so have elder abuse, religious abuse, child sexual abuse, and the aging of people who are psychiatrically challenged. People experiencing problems in these areas cannot be adequately served unless we can gain an initial understanding of the circumstances in which the problems tend to occur. What services are most needed by AIDS victims? What factors precipitate elder abuse? What kinds of problems do the aging people who are psychiatrically challenged face?

It is clear that the most sensible way to obtain these kinds of data is to ask someone who is likely to know. Elder abuse might be explored by posing questions, or items, to elders who have been abused, their families, and those involved in their care, through either personal or telephone interviews, or mailed questionnaires. The primary difficulty in doing this is knowing what items to ask.

Often, an exploratory survey is conducted for the sole purpose of discovering what issues should be addressed in an interview schedule (e.g., Figure 13.8) or standardized measuring instrument (e.g., Figures 6.1 & 11.7), and what specific items should be asked. We can select a small number of knowledgeable people such as senior citizens and their families, social workers, physicians, and residential care workers. We can determine important issues with their help, and then construct a tentative list of items.

Once the items have been formulated, they can be tested for phrasing and relevance on a small sample of the population for whom they are intended. If 300 senior citizens are to be surveyed, for example, a draft questionnaire may be presented to 10 or 15 senior citizens, not to collect information about abuse, but for the sole purpose of testing and revising the items contained within the questionnaire. Sometimes, this process is referred to as a pretest and is used to enhance the content and face validities of the instrument.

In a similar manner, other questionnaires may be pretested on small samples of social workers, family members, physicians, and residential care workers, respectively. Once the questionnaires have been found to be relevant and practical, they can be presented to larger samples of social workers, family members, and so on, to gather the data required for a descriptive study.

Descriptive Surveys

The purpose of a descriptive survey is to obtain data about a particular social problem. For example, a rehabilitation services agency might want to know how many elderly people who are physically disabled live in the community, how old they are, what gender they are, where they live, what sort of disability they have, and so forth. The study may show that a higher proportion of women than men live in nursing homes, that the very old of either gender are a small minority, and that levels of disability are more severe in males. The study will not explain the findings; it will merely document the facts as they exist.

As we have seen from Chapter 12, the totality of people or objects with which a study is concerned is known as a population. If the study has to do with all the senior citizens living in a particular city, the population is all the senior citizens living in that city. If the study is restricted to senior citizens living in a nursing home, then the population is all the senior citizens living in the nursing home. We cannot conduct a study within the confines of a nursing home and apply the results to senior citizens living elsewhere in the city, even to those in other nursing homes.

If the population is large, it will probably not be possible to survey every member, and certain members will have to be selected instead. As we know from the previous chapter, the process of selecting people to take part in a research study is known as sampling, and the people—or other units, such as case files—that are selected comprise a sample.

As presented in Chapter 11, a sample may be surveyed only once or on a number of occasions over time. A research design that requires the survey instrument or questionnaire to be presented only once is known as a cross-sectional survey design. A design in which the instrument is presented more than once on successive occasions is called a longitudinal survey design.

Explanatory Surveys

Explanatory surveys provide increased confidence that the obtained results can be generalized to the population from which the sample was drawn. In the last chapter, Antonia wants to know how parents feel about child abuse prevention education being taught to their children. Antonia may decide that it is too time-consuming to send questionnaires to a randomly selected group of parents. Instead, she will stand at the door on parent-teacher interview days and talk to all the parents who come through. The problem with this is that parents who come to interviews may hold different opinions on a number of issues from parents who do not. In other words, parents who are interested enough to attend parent-teacher interviews may not be representative of the parent body as a whole. She would not be using an explanatory research design as she did not utilize random sampling.

DATA COLLECTION METHODS

In survey research, data are usually collected by administering questionnaires or conducting interviews. Questionnaires may be sent through the mail or personally administered to an individual or group (e.g., Figure 7.3); interviews may be conducted in person or by telephone, from a written list of items known as an *interview schedule* (e.g., Figure 13.8). Both questionnaires and interviews have their advantages and disadvantages in terms of time, cost, flexibility, and the quantity and quality of the data obtained.

Questionnaires

There are two main ways in which questionnaires can be administered. The respondent can administer it to himself or herself, in which case it is called a *self-administered questionnaire*; or the researcher can administer it to a group of respondents together, in which cased it is called a *group-administered questionnaire*.

Self-Administered Questionnaires. An example of a self-administered questionnaire is a mailed questionnaire sent out in the hope that the recipient will fill it out and return it. All too often, this is a forlorn hope. A response rate of fifty percent for mailed questionnaires is considered adequate; sixty percent is good; seventy percent or more is excellent. There are just too many people who forget about the questionnaire or cannot be bothered to complete it, or who peer at the forms in bewilderment, stuff them in a drawer, and finally throw them out.

The difficulty here is that there may be some essential difference between the people who respond and the people who do not. Perhaps the people who respond are prepared to take the time because they hold

---

[University Letterhead]

Dear _____:

    As part of my doctoral program in Social Welfare at the University of Washington, I am seeking information about the attitudes and perceptions of mental health agency staff regarding program evaluation and accountability of mental health professionals.

    As an employee of one of the mental health agencies in this state, you are being asked to complete two questionnaires regarding the subjects mentioned above. The first questionnaire is attached. The second questionnaire will follow in approximately four months. Each questionnaire will take about 20-30 minutes to complete. Should you complete the first questionnaire, I ask that this be an expression of your intent to complete the second questionnaire although participation in both cases is entirely voluntary. You are free to withdraw your consent to participate or discontinue participation at any time.

    All questionnaires will be kept in a locked file and I am the only person who will have access to this file. All questionnaires will be destroyed 6 months following completion of the study.

    I hope you will be willing to help in this project but wish to assure you that your participation is entirely voluntary. You are welcome to ask questions regarding the study and your participation in it. I will be visiting your agency when I distribute the questionnaires or you may contact me at the University. I wish to remind you that your comments will remain strictly confidential. Thank you for your assistance and co-operation.

_____ Investigator   _____ Date
    Joan Avery

    I voluntarily agree to complete this questionnaire and have the opportunity to ask questions.

_____ Respondent   _____ Date

FIGURE 13.2   Example of a Simple Cover Letter

	YES	NO
1. Does the letter communicate the appeal to respondents?	_____	_____
2. Does it include a reasonable explanation of the study by anticipating and countering respondents' questions?	_____	_____
3. Does it set forth the benefits of the study?	_____	_____
4. Does it describe the importance of the respondent to the study and indicate that no one else can be substituted?	_____	_____
5. Does it exceed the maximum of one page?	_____	_____
6. Does it appear under an appropriate letterhead?	_____	_____
7. Do the individualized name and address and the date appear on the letter?	_____	_____
8. Is the investigator's individually applied signature included?	_____	_____
9. Does the letter include a confidentiality statement and explanation of the coding procedures?	_____	_____
10. Does the attachment to the cover letter include a stamped, self-addressed questionnaire reply envelope?	_____	_____
11. Does the letter indicate how results will be shared with respondents?	_____	_____
12. Are there instructions for indicating that a copy of the results is wanted (e.g., placing name and address on back of return envelope)?	_____	_____
13. Is the letter reproduced on a word processor?	_____	_____

FIGURE 13.3   Checklist for Developing a Cover Letter

strong opinions on the issue being addressed, while nonrespondents are generally apathetic. If this is the case, the data gathered will reflect not the opinions of all the people surveyed but only the opinions of those who took the trouble to respond. If all the people surveyed comprise a random sample of a larger population, the actual data gathered will not be data from a random sample. Instead, the data will have been obtained from only part of the sample, which differs in unknown ways from the other part.

As discussed in Chapter 12, data that are not obtained from a random sample cannot be generalized to the total population. Researchers who get a low response rate to a mailed questionnaire will still not have the needed information about the population, although they may have a great deal of information about the people who responded.

There are a number of things that can be done to increase the response rate. First, the questionnaire can be made to look important, so that it is less likely to be mistaken for junk mail. It is always helpful to write a cover letter, preferably under the letterhead of the organization sponsoring the survey and signed by someone with an official title. The cover letter should state what the survey is for and why it is important that the particular recipient should participate. Anonymity or confidentiality should be promised, and thanks for cooperation rendered in advance. An example of a survey cover letter coauthored by Michael J. Austin and Jill Crowell is presented in Figure 13.2. A short checklist that they used in the development of their cover letter is presented in Figure 13.3. Donald A. Dillman has outlined mailing procedures (Figure 13.4) and follow-up procedures (Figure 13.5) that should encourage a higher response rate when conducting a mailed survey.

Some recipients, particularly those from minority groups, may feel that they have been overstudied already and that their time is being

	YES	NO
1. Is the envelope an unusual size, shape, or color to attract attention, along with embellishments such as "Immediate reply requested"?	___	___
2. Has the size of the questionnaire and envelope been determined in relationship to using first-class postage and minimizing the appearance of bulky contents?	___	___
3. Has a mailing list been developed which includes the number of the questionnaire beside the name of the respondent?	___	___
4. Are the envelope contents folded together when inserted so that respondents will find all relevant materials on opening the envelope?	___	___
5. Is the mailing planned for early in the week in anticipation of time needed to forward mail to new addresses?	___	___
6. Will the mailing avoid a holiday period when respondents are likely to be away from home, and will it avoid December and the crush of holiday mail?	___	___

FIGURE 13.4   Checklist for Survey Mailing Procedures

	YES	NO
1. Is there a preprinted follow-up postcard for mailing one week after mailing of cover letter?	____	____
2. Does the postcard include the respondent's name and address and the investigator's signature?	____	____
3. Does it thank the respondent if the questionnaire has already been returned?	____	____
4. Is a second follow-up letter ready for sending three weeks after mailing of the cover letter, with a replacement questionnaire and return envelope?	____	____
5. Is a third follow-up letter ready for certified mailing to remaining nonrespondents seven weeks after original mailing, with a replacement questionnaire and return envelope?	____	____

FIGURE 13.5   Checklist for Survey Follow-up Procedures

wasted by yet another study that will be of no direct benefit to them. Something more than a letter is called for under these circumstances. The researchers may have to meet with members of the group to explain why the study is important and in what ways the results will further the interests of the group.

Assuming that recipients are sufficiently impressed by the cover letter to glance at the questionnaire, the questionnaire itself must be relevant, nonoffensive, nonthreatening, and preferably short. Obviously, every effort will be made to avoid giving offense, but offense is often a matter of nuance and perception, varying from culture to culture.

A pretest, in which the items themselves are reviewed by people of similar background to that of the intended respondents, should help to eliminate words and phrasing that may be perceived as offensive. A pretest may also serve to ensure that the items are understood. Respondents who do not understand a particular item will not provide an answer, or—worse still—will provide an answer to what they thought the item was. In some cases, they may attempt to provide socially desirable answers in order to impress the official organization that sent out the survey. The fact that they have been promised confidentiality may make no difference; they may believe that the researchers, and possibly the whole of officialdom, are judging them personally on the basis of their responses.

It follows, therefore, that items of a sensitive nature or items that might be perceived to be threatening should be kept to a minimum. In addition, it is often helpful to state at the beginning of the questionnaire that this is not a test and there are no right or wrong answers.

Types of Questions. In general, items asked in a mailed questionnaire, and in a research interview as well, can be classified as *closed-ended* or *open-ended* items. Closed-ended questions—for example, "Do you agree with child abuse education being taught in schools?"—limit the respondent to expressing a "yes" or "no," selecting a level of agreement, or choosing one of a number of response categories. Sometimes, this is the best way to get an answer on sensitive issues.

People who are reluctant to write a sentence expressing an opinion may be quite willing to express the same opinion by circling a number or putting a check mark on a line. However, the very ease of circling a number may tempt some people to express an opinion on a subject they know nothing about. If it is necessary to assess the extent of the respondent's knowledge or understanding, an open-ended question may be more appropriate.

Open-ended questions—"What do you think about offering a child abuse prevention educational program in schools?"—are designed to encourage free responses without the limitation of preset categories. This is particularly useful when the researchers do not know enough about the subject area to know what categories would be appropriate. Parents may think of aspects of such a program that would not occur to the researchers.

An open-ended question allows respondents to express themselves both at greater depth and more precisely. A disadvantage is that open-ended items take longer to answer and sometimes intimidate people who have little skill at writing. Most questionnaires include both closed-ended and open-ended items, and it is understood that open-ended items are more time-consuming for the respondent than closed-ended items.

At the exploratory level, open-ended items will be asked frequently since the researchers will not yet have enough information on the topic to allow them to formulate precise and structured items. At the descriptive level, there will be fewer open-ended items and, at the explanatory level, fewer still. In general, the explanatory end of the knowledge-level continuum requires highly structured questions that allow the data to be coded for computer analysis, whereas, at the exploratory end, all that is required is as much data as possible.

Group-Administered Questionnaires. The second way a questionnaire can be administered to research participants is through group administration. One of the major disadvantages of self-administered, mailed questionnaires previously presented is the low response rate. Administering the questionnaire personally to a group (or groups) of

	YES	NO
1. Does the face sheet of the questionnaire include general information about the purpose of the study?	____	____
2. Is there an indication of how much time it should take to complete the questionnaire?	____	____
3. Is a separate consent form attached to the questionnaire for the respondent to sign?	____	____
4. Does the face sheet include all necessary instructions for completing all items (e.g., "Don't skip around." "Answer all items to the best of your ability.")?	____	____

FIGURE 13.6   Checklist for Introducing Group-Administered Questionnaires

respondents may result in a higher response rate. For example, if Antonia's study on child abuse prevention being taught to second graders involves a number of schools, she may hold a meeting for parents in each school, spend a few moments discussing why she wants to collect the data that she does, and then ask the parents to fill out the questionnaire. She will be there to answer the parents' questions and to clarify items on the questionnaire, and the personal touch may engender more enthusiasm for her study on the parents' part. Figure 13.6 presents a checklist for introducing a questionnaire to a group of people, and Figure 13.7 presents a checklist for its administration (Clemens, 1971).

Interviews

The second way of collecting data for surveys is through interviews. There are two main types of interviews that can be used: personal interviews and telephone interviews.

Personal Interviews. Interviewing people in person yields a higher response rate than mailing questionnaires, since a person at the door is less easily ignored than a form in the mailbox. The responses given may also be more spontaneous and more informative. What people say "off the top of their heads" is free of the self-censorship often encountered in written responses, and there is no opportunity to erase an answer and replace it with a more "appropriate" and perhaps less valid response.

In addition, skilled interviewers are sensitive to body language. A hesitation, an interruption of eye contact, or an unexplained frown can

	YES	NO
1. Are there enough questionnaires?	___	___
2. Have plans been developed for persons unable to attend the questionnaire completion session to complete and return the instrument at another time?	___	___
3. Have all staff been notified in writing and verbally at a staff meeting about the date and time of the group administration?	___	___
4. Has the physical environment been checked in advance to make sure there will be sufficient space and adequate lighting for writing?	___	___
5. Have efforts been made to anticipate and eliminate possible sources of noise or distraction during the questionnaire completion session?	___	___
6. Are there plans to read aloud the instructions on the face sheet at the questionnaire completion session?	___	___
7. Will specific instructions be given on how to mark the questionnaire or answer sheet?	___	___
8. Is sufficient time allowed for questions from respondents before beginning to complete the questionnaire?	___	___
9. Will clarification announcements based on respondents' questions about an item on the questionnaire be made slowly, in a clear voice that is loud enough for all to hear?	___	___
10. Are all questionnaires to be collected immediately after completion and checked for completed identification information and consent form signature?	___	___
11. Have all respondents been informed of a sign-up roster to receive copies of the results of the study?	___	___
12. Will each respondent be personally thanked when the questionnaire is returned?	___	___
13. Are follow-up letters to be sent to agency administrators and key staff members who facilitate the implementation of the group-administered questionnaire?	___	___

FIGURE 13.7   Checklist for Administration of Group-Administered Questionnaires

lead the interviewer to probe for explanations, which may provide an unexpected wealth of extra information.

The opportunity to probe for additional data is particularly important at the exploratory level, where the rule is generally the more data, the better. At the explanatory level only very specific data are required, but the presence of a trained interviewer is useful here, too, since more detailed and complex items can be asked in person than are possible in a mailed questionnaire. The interviewer can ensure that each item is asked and that the answer is actually given by the respondent. There will be no opportunity for others in the house to lean over the respondent's shoulder and influence the nature of the responses.

Usually, the interviewer will pose the items exactly as they appear on the interview schedule, in the same words and in the same order. Wording can be very important. For example, the item, "Wouldn't you agree that it's all right to spank children sometimes?" invites the answer "yes." Researchers who want the respondent's unbiased opinion about corporal punishment, or any other sensitive issue, will be careful to phrase the item in a nonleading manner and to place it in the interview schedule so that it can be approached with maximum delicacy. An example of an interview schedule that was used in a research study on foster care placement is contained in Figure 13.8. Notice how the data obtained in the figure could not have been as easily obtained through a self-administered questionnaire (Jenkins & Norman, 1972).

Interviews have some very definite advantages over mailed questionnaires, primarily related to a higher response rate, spontaneity, flexibility, serendipity (the ability to uncover accidental additional information), and control over the environment (the ability to ensure that all items are answered by the respondent and no one else).

However, an interview also has some limitations when compared to a mailed questionnaire. Perhaps the most obvious disadvantage is its high cost and the considerable amount of time involved. Postage for mailed questionnaires is far less expensive than hiring, training, and supervising interviewers and paying their travel costs. Further, some interview situations may require that the interviewer just take notes and write them up later: an added expense in terms of time, and a possible source of error if the interviewer is not able to transcribe exactly what the respondent said. An interviewer may also influence an answer by tone of voice, by emphasizing a word or phrase, by showing comfort or discomfort with a particular item, or even merely by appearance. The interviewer's own age, gender, physical appearance, and language or accent, can all affect the nature of the responses.

If respondents are widely spread geographically or live in hard-to-reach places, the mail may reach them more easily than the interviewer. Even if the interviewer does reach them, the timing may not be convenient. Also, respondents may provide poor answers because, for example, the interviewer arrived when the baby's diaper needed changing, the

A. Main Question: Respondent's Statement of Problem

1. First of all, would you tell me in your own words what brought about the placement of _____ away from home in foster care?

    (Probe if not spontaneously answered.)

    1a. Who first had the idea to place _____?

        (1) Did anyone oppose it or disagree with it?

            If yes:

                a. Who?
                b. Why?

    1b. Were any attempts made to make other arrangements for _____ other than placement?

        If yes:

            a. What?
            b. Who did this?
            c. Why didn't it work out?

    1c. Was there anyone whom you usually depend on who couldn't or didn't help out?

        If yes:

            a. Who? (relationship)
            b. Why did the individual not help out?

    1d. Did all your children who were in your home go into placement at that time?

        If no:

            a. Which children were not placed at that time (name, age, gender, father)?
            b. Why weren't they placed?

    1e. Who was caring for _____ just before he/she was placed?

        If other than natural mother:

            a. For how long had he or she been caring for _____?

            b. Why was he or she caring for the child (rather than the child's mother)?

FIGURE 13.8   Opening Portion of an Interview Schedule on Foster Care Placement

dog was barking, or dinner was burning.

In addition, some respondents may not wish to be reached personally. They may not want the interviewer to visit their homes, spouses, friends, and children: they may be afraid that the neighbors are watching, or they may not believe that what they say will be held in strict confidence. A questionnaire that comes in the mail and goes out the same way may be perceived as anonymous and safer. In addition, it can be completed at the respondent's convenience, possibly in dribs and drabs.

The Interviewer-Interviewee Relationship. An important difference between a mailed questionnaire and a research interview is that a questionnaire does not involve a relationship between the researcher and the respondent, and an interview does. It may be a brief, ephemeral sort of relationship but it is a relationship nonetheless, and we have seen, already, that an interviewer can influence the respondent's answers by showing comfort or discomfort, by tone of voice, or even merely by appearance.

In certain limited respects, the relationship between a research interviewer and a respondent is the same as the relationship between a social worker and a client. In both situations, the social worker or interviewer tries to create a climate in which the respondent feels able to give complete and honest information. In both situations, the person's dignity and sense of worth must be upheld; confidentiality must be protected; and the person's self-determination, including the right to refuse to answer any item, must be respected.

There are also significant differences between a research interview and a practice interview. The most important difference is that the purpose of practice interviews is to help clients help themselves—a practice interview is *for* the client. Conversely, the purpose of research interviews is to gather the data needed to answer the research question—a research interview is *for* the researcher. This is not to say, of course, that the information provided will not benefit the respondent indirectly later on—we hope it will—but our immediate intent in the research interview is not to directly benefit the respondent; it is only to gather the kind of information that will be useful for the research study.

This may sound selfish and hard-hearted, but it is in fact very difficult for research interviewers, who are often trained social workers, to listen to a respondent's troubles without feeling a desire to help. These good intentions, if not kept firmly in check, may result in a pseudotherapeutic interview that does nothing at all for the research study and may be actually damaging to the respondent. The interviewer is *not* the respondent's social worker. He or she may be unfamiliar with the respondent's history and personal situation, and is under a professional obligation, in any case, not to interfere with some other worker's client (if this is the case).

It is vitally important, therefore, that the respondent know from the beginning who the interviewer is, why he or she is there, and what the interview will be about. Once this is established, it will be easier for the interviewer to take control of the interview, asking the items contained within the interview schedule in the right words, in the right order, and in a manner relevant to the study (e.g., Figure 13.8). A research interview is always controlled by the interviewer and is often narrowly focused on specific topics. Conversely, in a practice interview, it may be advisable to let the client lead the discussion into whatever areas seem relevant.

In sum, warmth, empathy, and genuineness have a place in the research interview just as they do in the practice interview, but it is a more limited place. The research interview is a more objective, ephemeral contact, controlled by the interviewer for the purpose of obtaining data relevant to the research study. The same thing applies to a telephone interview, which will be discussed next.

Telephone Interviews. The second type of interview is the telephone interview. A phone call is more convenient than a personal interview in that several telephone interviews can be conducted in the time it takes to make one house call. However, the kind of relationship established over the phone is usually different from the kind established in person. To begin with, the respondent might not agree to the interview, finding it less traumatic to hang up the phone than to reject a person knocking at the door.

The fact that the interviewer cannot see the respondent means that the advantage of observing body language will be lost. Since the respondent also cannot see the interviewer, warmth, genuineness, encouragement, and interest will all have to be conveyed by choice of words and voice tone. If this is not adequately achieved, the respondent may answer the items but is unlikely to volunteer added information. On the other hand, some people find it easier to discuss sensitive issues with someone whom they do not know, cannot see, and are never likely to meet, than with someone sitting opposite them in their living room.

Research studies have attempted to compare data obtained by telephone interviews with data obtained by face-to-face contact, but opinions still differ as to the relative effectiveness of the two techniques. Some researchers hold that there is little difference in either the quality or quantity of data obtained. Others maintain that telephone interviews usually yield about one-third to one-quarter of the amount of data obtained from face-to-face interviews.

Steven L. McMurtry (1993) presents a brief comparison between face-to-face interviews, mail surveys, and telephone surveys, in Figure 13.9.

ADVANTAGES AND DISADVANTAGES

Like other data collection methods, surveys have advantages and limitations. They are particularly useful for describing the characteristics of large populations. A carefully selected probability sample in conjunction with a well-designed questionnaire makes it possible to gather, in a reasonable time, at a reasonable cost, a large amount of data that can

Technique	Advantages	Disadvantages
Face-to-face Interview	○ Highest response rate ○ People tend to provide more thoughtful answers ○ Allows for longer, more open-ended responses ○ Allows recording of nonverbal information ○ Can reach disabled or illiterate respondents ○ Interviewer can clarify questions for respondent ○ Respondents more willing to answer sensitive questions	○ Highest cost ○ Highest chance for introduction of experimenter bias ○ Respondent may react to personality of interviewer rather than content of the interview ○ Interviewer may misrecord response
Mail Survey	○ Lowest cost ○ Subjects can read and respond to questions at their own pace ○ Visual arrangement of items on written instrument can facilitate comprehension ○ Provides greatest sense of anonymity/ confidentiality ○ Lowest chance of introduction of experimenter bias	○ Lowest response rate ○ Feasible only with subjects having relatively good reading skills ○ No opportunity to clarify confusing items ○ Difficult to get in-depth or open-ended responses ○ Cannot insure that intended respondents are the actual respondents
Telephone Survey	○ Relatively low cost ○ Can be completed quickly ○ Interviewer can clarify questions for respondent ○ Can reach respondents with poor reading/writing skills ○ Allows direct computer data entry	○ Not useful for low-income respondents who do not have a telephone ○ High initial vocal interaction, misses non-verbal responses ○ Requires simple questions, unless a copy of the survey instrument is mailed in advance

FIGURE 13.9   Advantages and Disadvantages to Principal Approaches to Data Collection in Survey Research

be analyzed in fairly complex ways. Surveys determine unemployment rates, voting intentions, and the like with almost uncanny accuracy; and no other data collection method has this general capability.

Surveys are flexible in the sense that many items may be asked on a given topic. In this way, a number of variables can be considered, and data analysis may uncover a complexity of relationships. The standardization of items on a questionnaire can also be a strength since every respondent is asked exactly the same item in exactly the same way, and the same interpretation is always given to a particular response.

However, standardization can also be a disadvantage. Items designed to be minimally relevant to everyone are likely to be especially relevant to no one. This is a major reason why surveys so often seem to be superficial in their treatment of complex topics. As with everything else designed for a mass audience, square pegs must be forced into round holes, with the result that the unique contributions of the "square" respondents will often be lost to the study. This problem can be offset by the use of open-ended items and sophisticated data analyses, but it is inherent to survey research.

Similarly, survey questionnaires can only elicit the specific attitudes, feelings, cognitions, or behaviors of the respondents with respect to a particular subject area. They cannot capture the context in which these attitudes or feelings occurred—the flavor and texture of the respondent's life situation. Such contextual data may occasionally be available to interviewers but can only be gathered to any real extent by an observer, or a participant observer.

Finally, surveys are subject to the uncertainties of all self-reported data. There is no guarantee that the respondent is telling the truth; and even respondents who intend to tell the truth may provide inaccurate or distorted data because they want to impress, or they cannot really remember, or for any number of other reasons. The questionnaire itself may sometimes be the instrument of this distortion. People who have given no thought to the issue of child abuse may suddenly form an opinion when confronted with an item, and the opinion they form may well be influenced by the particular wording of that item.

In sum, surveys tends to be strong on reliability but weak on validity. Standard items asked and interpreted in a standard manner go a long way toward reducing unreliability, on the parts of both the respondent and the researcher. On the other hand, the same standardization means that the answers will be less complete, less a reflection of the respondent's real opinion on the issue, and thus less valid.

SUMMARY

The purpose of conducting survey research is to gather data about a situation that already exists. Survey research designs can be used to measure not only existing attitudes but also behaviors, cognitions, and feelings. Like other research designs, a survey design can be formulated on an exploratory, descriptive, or explanatory level.

STUDY QUESTIONS

1. Describe in your own words the purpose of survey research. Why are surveys useful? Describe the steps that a survey research study would take in reference to finding out how satisfied social workers are with their social work education.

2. Describe in detail the three types of designs that surveys can take. Provide a social work example of each one. List the types of data that can be gathered in each survey design.

3. Describe in detail the two main data collection methods that can be used in survey research. Provide a social work example of each using one common research problem. In other words, how could your survey be conducted using questionnaires or interviews? How could have it been conducted using both? Discuss the advantages and disadvantages of using the two primary data collection methods.

4. Discuss in detail the two types of questionnaires that can be used in survey research. In which situations is one better than the other? Provide a rationale for your response. Use a social work example to illustrate your points.

5. What are the two types of questions that can be included in a questionnaire or interview schedule? Provide a social work example of each.

6. When is an open-ended item better to use than a closed-ended item? Provide a rationale for your response.

7. Discuss the commonalities and differences between personal interviews and telephone interviews used in survey research. In which situation is one better than the other?

8. Go to the library and identify a social work research article that used a mailed survey questionnaire to gather the data for the study. How could the study have used personal interviews rather than survey questionnaires to provide data to answer the research question? Provide a rationale for your response. What type of data would the interviews provide that the mailed questionnaire did not? Justify your answer.

9. For the study in Question 8, provide an in-depth critique using the contents of this chapter as a guide. Also, discuss areas of sampling, research design, operationalization of variables, generalizability, limitation, usefulness of findings, etc.

10. How would you have done the study in Question 8 differently, via a different survey method, given the same research question? Discuss in detail and be very specific. Keep in mind the context of the study (Chapter 2).

REFERENCES AND FURTHER READINGS

Austin, M.J., & Crowell, J. (1981). Survey research. In R.M. Grinnell, Jr. (Ed.), *Social work research and evaluation* (pp. 226-254). Itasca, IL: F.E. Peacock.

Austin, M.J., & Crowell, J. (1985). Survey research. In R.M. Grinnell, Jr. (Ed.), *Social work research and evaluation* (2nd ed., pp. 275-305). Itasca, IL: F.E. Peacock.

Babbie, E.R. (1992). *The practice of social research* (6th ed., pp. 260-283). Pacific Grove, CA: Wadsworth.

Bailey, K.D. (1994). *Methods of social research* (4th ed., pp. 147-215). New York: Free Press.

Clemens, W.V. (1971). Test administration. In R.L. Thorndike (Ed.). *Educational measurement* (2nd ed., pp. 108-119). Washington, DC: American Council on Education.

Dillman, D.A. (1978). *Mail and telephone surveys: The total design method.* New York: Wiley.

Frankfort-Nachmias, C., & Nachmias, D. (1992). *Research methods in the social sciences* (4th ed., pp. 215-237). New York: St. Martin's Press.

Gochros, H.L. (1981). Research interviewing. In R.M. Grinnell, Jr. (Ed.), *Social work research and evaluation* (pp. 255-290). Itasca, IL: F.E. Peacock.

Gochros, H.L. (1985). Research interviewing. In R.M. Grinnell, Jr. (Ed.), *Social work research and evaluation* (2nd ed., pp. 306-342). Itasca, IL: F.E. Peacock.

Gochros, H.L. (1988). Research interviewing. In R.M. Grinnell, Jr. (Ed.), *Social work research and evaluation* (3rd ed., pp. 267-299). Itasca, IL: F.E. Peacock.

Grinnell, R.M., Jr., & Williams, M. (1990). *Research in social work: A primer* (pp. 204-231). Itasca, IL: F.E. Peacock.

Jenkins, S., & Norman, E. (1972). *Filial deprivation and foster care.* New York: Columbia University Press.

Judd, C.M., Smith E.R., & Kidder, I.H. (1991). *Research methods in social relations* (6th ed., pp. 100-127, 213-227). Fort Worth, TX: Harcourt Brace.

Leedy, P.D. (1993). *Practical research: Planning and design* (3rd ed., pp. 185-195, 213-216). New York: Macmillan.

McMurtry, S.L. (1993). Survey research. In R.M. Grinnell, Jr. (Ed.), *Social work research and evaluation* (4th ed., pp. 262-289). Itasca, IL: F.E. Peacock.

Marlow, C. (1993). *Research methods for generalist social work practice* (pp. 65-77). Pacific Grove, CA: Wadsworth.

Mindel, C.H., & McDonald, L. (1988). Survey research. In R.M. Grinnell, Jr. (Ed.), *Social work research and evaluation* (3rd ed., pp. 300-322). Itasca, IL: F.E. Peacock.

Monette, D.R., Sullivan, T.J., & DeJong, C.R. (1994). *Applied social research* (3rd ed., pp. 153-186). Fort Worth, TX: Harcourt Brace.

Neuman, W.L. (1994). *Social research methods* (2nd ed., pp. 221-258). Needham Heights, MA: Allyn & Bacon.

Royse, D.D. (1991). *Research methods in social work* (pp. 101-128). Chicago: Nelson-Hall.

Rubin, A., & Babbie, E. (1993). *Research methods for social work* (2nd ed., pp. 332-356). Pacific Grove, CA: Wadsworth.

Yegidis, B.L., & Weinbach, R.W. (1991). *Research methods for social workers* (pp. 193-207). White Plains, NY: Longman.

Chapter 14

Nonsurveys

I N THE LAST CHAPTER we discussed how data can be collected by means of surveys (administering questionnaires or conducting interviews). As mentioned, surveys are the data collection method most utilized by social workers in research studies. Nevertheless, surveys have their limitations. For example, people responding to interview schedules or questionnaires are necessarily providing their own perceptions of the issue under investigation; that is, they are providing *self-reported data*. Self-reported data have an inherent disadvantage in that their reliability depends entirely on the characteristics and motivations of the people providing them.

Let us take an example of a limitation that is inherent in surveys. A mother completing a mailed survey questionnaire used to determine her satisfaction with an after-school play program may agree that her child receives a nutritious snack. In fact, she may have no idea whether her child receives a snack at all, let alone what kind, but she may not want to say so for fear that she will be considered a neglectful mother. The only way to determine whether the program actually provides nutritious snacks is to watch them being given out; and, even then, there is the possibility that they are only being given out because the researcher happens to be watching.

Nevertheless, observations by others (*objective* observation, that is) generally provide more reliable data than survey self-report data. This chapter will discuss four different nonsurvey, non-self-report data collection methods that can also be used in social work research studies: (1) structured observation, (2) participant observation, (3) secondary analysis, and (4) content analysis. On a general level, these four data collection methods utilize a form of observation (by others).

In general, observational data lie on a continuum, from *structured observations* at one end to *unstructured observations* at the other. Unstructured observations are nonsystematic and consist of qualitative or narrative accounts provided by one or more observers, without the use of structured numerical categories to describe variables. Social work practitioners make unstructured observations all the time when working with clients, and these data can be very useful in generating further clinical or research questions to be tested. In other words, unstructured observational data are useful at the exploratory end of the knowledge continuum.

Conversely, the explanatory research study requires structured data that are precise, standardized, and largely unaffected by the biases of the observer. Let us now turn to one of the most objective nonsurvey data collection methods, structured observations.

STRUCTURED OBSERVATION

As previously mentioned, collecting data by asking people questions about their thoughts, feelings, or behaviors sometimes may not yield valid results. Research participants may give distorted answers for any number of reasons. They may remember incorrectly, or they may want to please the researcher or obtain a good report, or they may even have convinced themselves that they are behaving in a certain way when their actual behaviors are very different. For example, a mother may believe that she praises her child often when in fact the child is hardly praised at all.

One way of coping with erroneous perceptions is to encourage research participants to monitor their own behaviors: that is, to observe themselves. A mother might be asked to count the number of times each day she praises her child and, if she counts honestly, she may then realize that she gives less praise than she thought she did. Once she is aware of her behavior, she may change her behavior and, in this case, changing the behavior may well be the purpose of the social work intervention.

One important advantage of having the mother do the counting is that data collection takes place in the natural environment. Situations are not artificially contrived, as they might be in the laboratory or in the social worker's office or in a playgroup where the researcher is watching and taking notes. Of course, the situation is not entirely natural since the mother is looking for good behaviors to praise and keeping count of them, but it is sometimes the best that can be done if data need to be collected about events in ordinary life over a fairly lengthy period.

An alternative strategy might be to involve the mother's partner. Because he is a familiar figure, the mother and child may interact more naturally in front of him, perhaps more naturally than they would if the mother were also burdened with the counting. He will be able to give his whole attention to counting, he may be more objective than the mother since it is not his behavior that is being observed, and the data he obtains may therefore give a more reliable picture of how often the child is praised by the mother in the normal, everyday routine. In addition, the mother is less likely to change her behavior during data collection since she is not counting and will probably be less aware of the results.

An objective, valid, reliable, and accurate description of a behavior, as it *presently exists* in the natural environment, is invaluable to social work practitioners and researchers alike. As discussed in Chapter 10, on single-system designs, a practitioner cannot know whether an intervention to change a particular target problem is effective unless baseline data have been collected. In other words, a research participant can best be helped to solve a problem (assuming that an intervention to help the person solve the problem will be implemented) if there is some way to measure the person's initial problem level.

Similarly, practitioners can best be helped to improve their treatment techniques if their present techniques can be observed and measured. For example, a director of a social service agency might wish to identify the interventive techniques commonly used by the social workers within the agency. This could be done by having trained observers watch videotapes of treatment interviews and/or listen to audiotapes. The type and frequency of the various techniques employed could be easily calculated.

Researchers also often need data on actual behaviors in the natural environment. For example, nothing can be known about aggressive behavior, or any other type of behavior for that matter, until it has been observed and measured as it naturally occurs. The purpose here is not to change the behavior—it is only to study it. Thus, a method of observation must be found that will not affect the behavior that is being measured. The only real way to achieve this is to observe unseen, without telling the people concerned that they are being watched. As presented in Chapter 2, such a procedure is never ethical: research participants can be involved in a study only if they have given their informed written consent. After they have done this, they can be watched by people who are called observers. Remember, the purpose of the observers is to collect valid, reliable, and objective data.

Role of the Observers

This section presents the factors affecting the selection, the training, and the evaluation of observers. Observers generally fall into three categories. First, there are outside observers, often professionally trained, who are hired for the specific purpose of recording data. Second, there are indigenous observers, who are naturally a part of the research participant's environment; and, third, there are self-observers, the research participants themselves.

When trying to decide from which category observers should be selected, four factors must be taken into account: cost; time, including both the observer's time and the timeframe of the research or practice situation; the type of data required; and clinical considerations, such as intrusion into the research participant's life, or the wisdom of having one family member record the behavior of another.

Outside Observers. Observers brought in for the purpose of recording data must be paid at professional rates and may not always be available. Since they are unfamiliar to others in the natural environment, they will intrude into the research participant's life in a way that indigenous observers would not. In some cases, their very presence may be enough to alter the very behavior they are observing, thus producing erroneous results. On the other hand, they are more objective than indigenous observers because they have no vested interest in the events they are observing.

The training and experience of outside observers make them more reliable and, in addition, enables them to use sophisticated data recording procedures to obtain data on complex variables. Outside observers are selected when the complexity of the data required for a research study warrants their cost. In addition, they can be used when it is considered that an intrusion into the research participant's life will not invalidate the study's results. They can also be used when one-way mirrors are employed.

Indigenous Observers. Indigenous observers are people who are normally a part of the research participant's environment. They may be family members or friends or staff members in an institution, such as a residential home, hospital, school or agency. Such people have their own jobs to do, and major considerations in employing them as observers will be their availability and the amount of time required to collect the data. A nursing home social worker, for example, may not have the time to count the frequency of a resident's crying spells, and the worker may be off duty in the evenings when the crying spells occur most often.

As stated in Chapter 3, one of the criteria for selecting a research question is researchability; and a question is only researchable if the necessary data can be collected. We may occasionally find ourselves in a position where data collection by an outside observer is too costly, data collection by the research participant is too unreliable, and data collection by an indigenous observer is too time-consuming or intrusive. If this is the case, the research question as it stands is not researchable, and a different data collection method will be needed—perhaps a slightly different formulation of the research question, requiring a different data collection method.

The problems of time and cost do not loom quite so large when the indigenous observer is a family member. Even so, the observer may not be home in the mornings, for example, when the target problem, the variable being observed, may be at its worst, and it is not so easy for one family member to observe another unobtrusively as it would be for a staff member in a larger, institutional setting. A research participant who is aware of being watched might alter the target problem, even subconsciously. In addition, the selection of one family member over another to fill the role of observer may give rise to all sorts of jealousies and tensions and may be clinically unwise.

Since indigenous observers cannot be expected to have experience in data collection, they will need to be carefully trained. Even with training, they will probably only be able to cope with simple recording procedures and discrete, straightforward target problems. Unless two indigenous observers are simultaneously making recordings, the reliability of the observations cannot be determined.

If two observers are involved, interobserver reliability is likely to be lower, anyway, than it would be with outside observers, and disagreements over data may have the additional unintended effect of promoting conflict within the staff or family. The type and reliability of data obtained from indigenous observers are therefore often limited.

Self-Observers. The third category from which observers can be selected are the owners of the target problems, the research participants themselves. Self-reports are often the only possible method of data collection when the target problem is a feeling or state known only to the research participant, or when the setting in which the problem occurs precludes the presence of an observer.

The main limitation of self-reports is reliability. Even when the research participant wants the recording to be unbiased and accurate, it is very difficult to prevent the act of recording from interfering with the problem being recorded. Some recording methods cannot be used to self-record because it is not possible to simultaneously experience the problem and do the recording.

Sometimes, self-reports can be verified by other observers. Research participants who report feelings of depression, for example, may suffer from crying spells or unusual sleeping patterns that can be observed by others. As far as possible, the researcher should not rely on one data collection method but should collect the same or complementary data in two or preferably three different ways.

So far, in this chapter, we have been discussing precise, standardized, and largely objective observations—that is, structured observations. At the other end of the observational continuum lie unstructured observations, usually narrative or qualitative descriptions of events. However, even unstructured observations can be less scientific or more scientific, ranging from a completely random scribble every now and then to a systematic, regular record, planned to serve a definite purpose, with validity and reliability controlled.

PARTICIPANT OBSERVATION

The second nonsurvey data collection method is participant observation, which, as the name suggests, is conducted by someone who is also a participant in the events being observed. As we have said, it is not easy to observe, participate, and record data simultaneously. It is usually a matter of participating some of the time and observing at other times; and the question is how much time is to be spent in doing each.

If participation and observation are visualized as a continuum, with "complete participant" at one end and "complete observer" at the other, two other points along the continuum can be identified as "observer-participant" and "participant-observer." This continuum is illustrated in Figure 14.1.

Roles of the Observers

The points on the continuum displayed in Figure 14.1 can be thought of as roles that researchers might play.

Complete Participant. In the first role as complete participant (to the far left of the continuum), the researcher interacts as naturally as possible with everyone around, and no one knows that he or she is not a bonafide member of the community, school, or other organization. This role is most useful in exploratory studies where we are not entirely sure of what we hope to observe. It has the advantage that we may be made

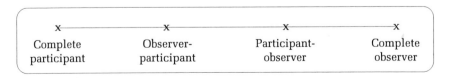

FIGURE 14.1   Continuum of Participant Observation

privy to information that would be denied to an outsider.

However, there are definite disadvantages. First, such a role is ethically untenable since the people being observed are involuntary participants in a study they know nothing about. If confidential disclosures are included in a formal report without the consent of the informants, the ethical position becomes even worse. Second, if we pretend to be members of the group for long enough, we may *become* members: that is, we may overidentify with group concerns and lose the ability to make "objective" observations. Third, the observations we do make will have to be recorded secretly, with all the difficulties associated with any illicit activity.

Observer-Participant. The second role, that of observer-participant, is far less stressful and more ethically correct. In this role, we participate as fully as possible, but we are no longer bonafide members of the group, and the people being observed know and understand what we are doing. We have the opportunity to conduct interviews and record our observations openly at the same time as events of interest occur.

The disadvantages, of course, are that we may no longer be privy to in-group confidences, and the people around us may change their behavior because they now know that they are being observed. However, a strange face in an environment becomes a familiar face relatively quickly, and it will often not be long before changed behaviors revert back to ordinary, everyday behaviors. It is not uncommon for researchers to spend some time in an environment before beginning to record data in order to enable others to perceive them as familiar, nonthreatening, nonjudgmental, and nonintrusive. The participant-observer role is most useful in an exploratory or descriptive level research study.

Participant-Observer. The third role, that of participant-observer, is more formal than the other two. Participation is limited, and most of our time is spent making and recording observations. Our observations are usually structured, in the sense that we know what kinds of behaviors we are looking for and we have operationally defined them so that we can distinguish them from other behaviors. We may also record our observations on a chart or some formal recording sheet rather than just on a piece of paper; and sometimes we may observe in company with another observer so that interobserver reliability can be determined. Obviously, this kind of role is more suited to a descriptive study.

Complete Observer. In the fourth role, that of complete observer, we have no personal interaction at all with the individuals being observed, as all of our time is spent observing and recording our observations. Here, of course, we are probably conducting a descriptive or explanatory study.

SECONDARY ANALYSIS

The third nonsurvey data collection method is secondary analysis, the process of analyzing already-existing data. Data collection through structured observations and participant observations, or by means of surveys (Chapter 13), can be time-consuming and expensive. Busy practitioners and administrators often do not have the time or money to collect data; and they may not be able to wait to make decisions until the relevant data have been collected, analyzed, and compiled into a final report. This will be particularly the case if the needed data must be collected over a lengthy period of time.

For example, the problem may be that there is a high turnover among a volunteer Aunts-at-Large program befriending motherless children, with a consequent negative impact upon the children involved and upon the public image of the program. Agency administrators would like to know what variables contribute to premature termination so that they can screen their volunteers and perhaps match Aunts with children more effectively.

Unfortunately, the research studies needed to answer this question will involve examining the characteristics of volunteers who terminate early compared with those who do not, and also looking at the characteristics of the children and the dynamics of the match. The researchers will not be able to begin to analyze the data until a reasonable number of volunteers have terminated, and the final report will not be produced for some time after that. In short, the information necessary to guide decision making will not be available in time to prevent further trauma to volunteers and children, as well as further damage to the program's image.

All this supposes that new data have to be collected. However, sufficient information might possibly be provided by analyzing *existing data*. The agency will certainly have some data about its volunteers, both those who have terminated and those who have not, and it will also have data about the families being served. Information on screening and matching procedures should be available, together with such things as notes from screening interviews, progress reports by volunteers, evaluation reports on volunteers, termination records where applicable (at least giving reasons for leaving), and perhaps even "satisfaction" questionnaires completed periodically by children and their families.

The researchers may not have all the data they would like, but they should have enough to provide a good indication of what is wrong and what can be done to correct it. If there is not enough money to hire outside researchers, agency staff themselves may be able to analyze their own data and come up with their own conclusions.

Public agencies such as the Census Bureau make data available, and so do many state and local agencies. With the advent of computers, management information systems (MIS) are increasingly being used to store, process, retrieve, and analyze data on various aspects of social work service, client outcomes, practitioner activities, costs, and so forth. Secondary analysis is becoming a common data collection method among social work researchers.

As is the case with surveys and observational data, secondary analysis can be used at each of the three levels on the knowledge continuum: exploratory, descriptive, and explanatory. At an exploratory level, if we are not quite sure what we hope to find, we can examine all the possibilities of a situation until we find some variables that might possibly be associated with one another. For example, perhaps Aunts who have no families of their own tend to stay on longer than Aunts who do have families, or vice versa. Perhaps younger children do better with older, mother-figure volunteers, where older children are better matched with "sisters." Perhaps volunteers who produce glowing, no-cloud-in-the-sky progress reports are those who tend to terminate abruptly, whereas those who use their reports to express their doubts are the ones who carry on.

Computers can test large numbers of variables to find out whether and to what degree they are related. The danger here is that a large enough data base massaged for long enough will invariably produce a few relationships that are not true relationships at all but are due to chance. At the exploratory level, this is an irritation rather than a problem, since any relationship found is still only a tentative idea, which will have to be written in the form of a hypothesis and tested later using a more rigorous research method. Exploratory studies use *inductive logic* to build theories and generate hypotheses. That is, they use empirical data to suggest relationships between and among variables, which, in turn, suggest theories, from which hypotheses may be derived.

The next step on the knowledge continuum is the descriptive study. The administrators of the agency might suspect, as a result of the exploratory work, that volunteers are not sufficiently trained in what to expect from the children and terminate prematurely because the children are unable, at least initially, to form the kind of close, warm relationships that the volunteers want. A secondary analysis of the agency's data on training may reveal that training hours have been cut, and the reduced training program does not address the issue of expectations.

If other, similar agencies are prepared to release their data, secondary analysis might provide a comparison of their respective training schedules and turnover rates. The study will not attempt to explain why training has been cut, why expectations are not addressed, what the effects might be on volunteers and children, or why one agency possibly differs from another. All that is accomplished is a description of the existing situation.

The final step on the knowledge continuum is the explanatory study.

Here, an attempt is made to answer the "why" questions by formulating and testing a hypothesis or set of hypotheses, which are derived from theory through *deductive* logic. For example, agency administrators may theorize, on the basis of exploratory and descriptive work, that one of the reasons volunteers join the agency is to have their own needs met. If those needs are not met either through the Aunt-child relationship or through bonding between volunteers, premature termination will occur. A one-tailed hypothesis deduced from this theory may be that "agencies in which volunteers meet regularly to support each other will experience a lower volunteer termination rate than agencies in which no such meetings occur."

This hypothesis can be tested by means of secondary analysis if other agencies can provide data about volunteer support mechanisms and termination rates. Difficulties will be encountered if some of the needed data are unavailable or there are some data missing from the data sets provided by the other agencies: if, for example, one agency has no information about volunteer support and another has lost its termination figures for the latter half of 1995 because a new computer system was being installed. Missing data are always problematic, but at least the agency administrators will know they have a problem.

More subtle and often unrecognized problems can arise when the data that are provided are unreliable or invalid. Many people—and social workers are no exception—tend to assume that data gathered by others are necessarily correct, especially if the numbers come from an official or prestigious source. This may not always be the case, and the researcher has the responsibility to check the validity and reliability of any data used in a secondary analysis.

CONTENT ANALYSIS

Craig Winston LeCroy and Gary Solomon (1993) have provided an excellent discussion of the fourth nonsurvey data collection method, content analyses. This section has been slightly modified from their work.

Content analyses are similar to secondary analyses, discussed above, in that both use available data sources. In content analysis, however, the data are generated by quantifying units of analysis in the content of recorded communications so they can be counted. Thus, while the sources are available and direct methods of data collection such as observations, surveys, and questionnaires need not be used, new data are generated by the process of content analysis.

Because content analyses allow social work researchers to investigate research questions without needing to collect original data, researchers can formulate questions about anything that has taken place and been recorded. The research question may involve content describing some historical situation or something that occurred a moment ago. In either case, the content is defined, coded, and tallied to generate new data that may be analyzed immediately or at some future date.

If a research question can be stated in terms that meet the criteria of specificity, relevancy, researchability, feasibility, and ethical acceptability (see Chapter 2), and if recorded communications on the question exist, a content analysis could well be the best method of collecting data to investigate it. And content analyses are well suited to the study of communications because they address the questions of who says what to whom, why, how, and with what effect. The "what" of a research study, or the defining aspect, is found in the content of the text to be researched.

Characteristics of Content Analyses

In content analysis, communications are examined in a systematic, objective, and quantitative manner. To be systematic, a content analysis must follow specified procedures. For example, a researcher who wants to compare the lyrics in the songs of three different rock groups must systematically use the same procedures in examining the content for each group. If the same procedures are not used, the results will not be considered reliable and valid. It could be argued that the difference in the way the criteria were applied to the groups is a source of bias or error in the results, which occurs when researchers structure their data collection procedures to confirm their own predictions or support their theoretical positions.

Objectivity is another characteristic of content analysis that helps ensure validity and avoid bias. This characteristic is concerned with making the criteria or rules used to categorize the contents of the text impartial and objective. Clearly defining the criteria to be applied and making explicit the rules to be used in classifying the content of a communication help control any special interest or ideology that might influence the research study.

In the study of rock lyrics, for example, the rules to be used in categorizing the lyrics must be specified. Otherwise a conclusion that rock lyrics consist of sexual and violent content, or a conclusion that they are harmless, could be considered invalid. While people interested in the results of the research study might not agree with the categories that were devised, the standards for deciding how to categorize the data and code them for recording would be clear, so others could evaluate how the conclusions had been reached. Objective procedures also allow other researchers to replicate the study; even if they have different biases, if they follow the same rules for categorizing the content, the results should be the same.

Content analysis focuses on the operational definition or quantification of the dependent variable (and sometimes the independent variable) in a research question or hypothesis. Before the content of any communication can be analyzed it must be possible to quantify it in some manner. For example, in a research study to examine the way women are portrayed in children's books, the number of times women are portrayed as mothers and as workers outside the home could be counted. The unit of analysis is women. Each time a unit occurs in a particular category (mother or worker), it is "counted" and recorded in that category.

A common use of content analysis is recording the frequency with which certain symbols or themes appear in a communication. For example, Dodd, Foerch, and Anderson (1988) did a content analysis of women and racial and ethnic minorities as subjects of newsmagazine covers, an indication of their coverage in the content of a particular issue. The covers of *Time* and *Newsweek* from 1953 through 1987 were studied, and each appearance of a woman or minority member was counted. The researchers then could determine whether these variables were represented in relation to their proportions in the U.S. population and whether there had been changes in the subjects of the covers and cover stories over time.

When quantification is used in this manner, the results are usually presented in terms of proportions or percentages. For example, a content analysis of a diary may reveal that the term *love* made up 5 percent of the total words used or that it appeared on 61 percent of the pages. Also, an analysis could show an increase in use of the term between certain dates.

However, quantification is not always that easy. Often researchers attempt to examine not just the frequency of a variable but also its intensity, or its latent content. For example, to compare how liberal two congressional candidates are, a content analysis of their speeches could be done. In addition to counting the number of "liberal" statements each one made, according to some specified criteria, there might be an attempt to evaluate how liberal each statement is. The task of devising adequate categories then would become much more complicated. Perhaps each statement could be rated as extremely liberal, moderately liberal, or minimally liberal. Because the concept of liberalism is becoming increasingly difficult to define in terms of political parties or ideologies, there would be limits to the possible options in using such a content analysis.

CHOOSING A DATA COLLECTION METHOD

In this chapter, we have presented different ways to collect non-survey, non-self-report data, through four nonsurvey methods: structured observation, participant observation, secondary analysis, and content analysis. (We presented data collected through surveys in the previous chapter.) There are many different ways in which data can be collected, and the method finally chosen will depend on three interlinking factors: the kind of data needed; the resources available, including money, time, personnel, and access to possible data sources; and the nature of the research participants.

The kind of data needed will obviously depend on the nature of the research question. If we need to tap the opinions or measure the attitudes of a large number of people, we have little choice but to mount a survey. We may send out questionnaires or conduct personal or telephone interviews, depending on time and cost considerations and the characteristics of the research respondents. Perhaps the people we wish to survey are unlikely to have a telephone and are even less likely to return a questionnaire. We will then have no recourse but to go to their doors and knock, and the time involved in doing this will mean that fewer people can be surveyed.

There is always the issue of balance. We will try to measure the variables of interest as directly as possible within the limitations of available resources. If the variable is a behavior that can be observed, for example, it can be observed using the most appropriate of the observation methods discussed in this chapter. If it is a feeling, attitude, or state known only to the respondent, a standardized measurement can be used as presented in Chapter 7, or we will ask the respondent to complete a self-rating scale, or we will find some indicator of the state—crying spells in the case of depression, for example—that we or others can observe.

Preferably, we should use as many different methods of measuring the same variable as possible. It goes without saying that we will check to ensure that the measuring instruments we use are valid and reliable; but no instrument is entirely valid and reliable. Similar results from different measuring instruments will allow us to be more certain that we are obtaining an accurate measure of the right variable.

SUMMARY

This chapter presented four different nonsurvey, non-self-report data collection methods that can be used in social work research studies: structured observation, participant observation, secondary analysis, and content analysis. Each has its advantages and disadvantages.

In sum, selecting a data collection method is a matter of deciding what has to be measured and choosing the most direct and appropriate method of making the measurement, giving due consideration to the available resources and the characteristics of the research participants. Sometimes, the most direct method will not be practically possible. We may not be able to act as participant-observers in street gangs or watch young offenders to see how often they reoffend. We may not even have the time to collect new data at all. Then, it is a matter of deciding what other way there is of making the measurement; perhaps through secondary analysis of existing data. Whenever possible, we will use more than one data collection method, employing instruments which we know to be valid and reliable.

Now that we know the various methods that can be used to collect data, for any given research study, our next task is to analyze them—the topic of Chapter 15.

STUDY QUESTIONS

1. In your own words, describe the main similarities and differences between survey data collection methods (last chapter) and nonsurvey data collection methods (this chapter). Present a common social work example throughout your discussion.

2. What do nonsurvey, non-self-report data collection methods control for that self-report surveys do not control for? Provide a social work example in your discussion.

3. What are structured observations? List and discuss how they can be used in social work research studies. What are their advantages? What are their disadvantages? Provide a social work research situation where you would use this type of nonsurvey data collection method.

4. List and discuss the three roles that observers can take while doing structured observations. Provide a social work example throughout your discussion. List the advantages and disadvantages of each one.

5. What is participant observation? List and discuss how it can be used in social work research studies. What are its advantages? What are its disadvantages? Provide a social work research situation where you would use this type of nonsurvey data collection method. What are the main differences between structured observation and participant observations?

6. List and discuss the three roles that observers can take while doing structured observations. Provide a social work example throughout your discussion. List the advantages and disadvantages of each one.

7. What is secondary analysis? List and discuss how it can be used in social work research studies. What are its advantages? What are its disadvantages? Provide a social work research situation where you would use this type of nonsurvey data collection method for each of the three knowledge levels.

8. What is content analysis? List and discuss how it can be used in social work research studies. What are its advantages? What are its disadvantages? Provide a social work research situation where you would use this type of nonsurvey data collection method for each of the three knowledge levels.

9. Discuss how a data collection method is chosen for any given research study. What are the various factors that must be taken into account before selecting a data collection method?

10. Go to the library and find a social work research article that used a survey as the data collection method (last chapter). Describe how the study could have used another nonsurvey data collection method (this chapter) to answer the same research question. What different kinds of data would have the other data collection method provided that the one used did not?

REFERENCES AND FURTHER READINGS

Adams, G.R., & Schvaneveldt, J.D. (1991). *Understanding research methods* (2nd ed., pp. 285-308). White Plains, NY: Longman.

Babbie, E.R. (1992). *The practice of social research* (6th ed., pp. 311-344). Pacific Grove, CA: Wadsworth.

Bailey, K.D. (1994). *Methods of social research* (4th ed., pp. 293-320). New York: Free Press.

Dodd, D.K., Foerch, B.J., & Anderson, H.T. (1988). Content analysis of women and racial minorities as news magazine cover persons. *Journal of Social Behavior and Personality, 3,* 231-236.

Epstein, I. (1985). Quantitative and qualitative methods. In R.M. Grinnell, Jr. (Ed.), *Social work research and evaluation* (2nd ed., pp. 263-274). Itasca, IL: F.E. Peacock.

Epstein, I. (1988). Quantitative and qualitative methods. In R.M. Grinnell, Jr. (Ed.), *Social work research and evaluation* (3rd ed., pp. 185-198). Itasca, IL: F.E. Peacock.

Frankfort-Nachmias, C., & Nachmias, D. (1992). *Research methods in the social sciences* (4th ed., pp. 291-318). New York: St. Martin's Press.

Hoshino, G., & Lynch, M.M. (1981). Secondary analysis of existing data. In R.M. Grinnell, Jr. (Ed.), *Social work research and evaluation* (pp. 333-347). Itasca, IL: F.E. Peacock.

Hoshino, G., & Lynch, M.M. (1985). Secondary analyses. In R.M. Grinnell, Jr. (Ed.), *Social work research and evaluation* (2nd ed., pp. 370-380). Itasca, IL: F.E. Peacock.

Judd, C.M., Smith E.R., & Kidder, I.H. (1991). *Research methods in social relations* (6th ed., pp. 287-296, 425-449). Fort Worth, TX: Harcourt Brace.

LeCroy, C.W., & Solomon, G. (1993). Content analysis. In R.M. Grinnell, Jr. (Ed.), *Social work research and evaluation* (4th ed., pp. 304-316). Itasca, IL: F.E. Peacock.

Leedy, P.D. (1993). *Practical research: Planning and design* (3rd ed., pp. 223-239). New York: Macmillan.

Marlow, C. (1993). *Research methods for generalist social work practice* (pp. 81-83, 237). Pacific Grove, CA: Wadsworth.

Monette, D.R., Sullivan, T.J., & DeJong, C.R. (1994). *Applied social research* (3rd ed., pp. 187-212). Fort Worth, TX: Harcourt Brace.

Neuman, W.L. (1994). *Social research methods* (2nd ed., pp. 81, 261-278). Needham Heights, MA: Allyn & Bacon.

Ramos, R. (1981). Participant observation. In R.M. Grinnell, Jr. (Ed.), *Social work research and evaluation* (pp. 348-360). Itasca, IL: F.E. Peacock.

Ramos, R. (1985). Participant observation. In R.M. Grinnell, Jr. (Ed.), *Social work research and evaluation* (2nd ed., pp. 343-356). Itasca, IL: F.E. Peacock.

Royse, D.D. (1991). *Research methods in social work* (pp. 149-172). Chicago: Nelson-Hall.

Rubin, A. (1988). Secondary analyses. In R.M. Grinnell, Jr. (Ed.), *Social work research and evaluation* (3rd ed., pp. 323-341). Itasca, IL: F.E. Peacock.

Rubin, A. (1993). Secondary analyses. In R.M. Grinnell, Jr. (Ed.), *Social work research and evaluation* (4th ed., pp. 290-303). Itasca, IL: F.E. Peacock.

Rubin, A., & Babbie, E. (1993). *Research methods for social work* (2nd ed., pp. 404-431, 449-501). Pacific Grove, CA: Wadsworth.

Taylor, J.B. (1993). The naturalistic research approach. In R.M. Grinnell, Jr. (Ed.), *Social work research and evaluation* (4th ed., pp. 53-78). Itasca, IL: F.E. Peacock.

Toseland, R.W. (1993). Choosing a data collection method. In R.M. Grinnell, Jr. (Ed.), *Social work research and evaluation* (4th ed., pp. 317-328). Itasca, IL: F.E. Peacock.

Watts, T.D. (1981). Ethnomethodology. In R.M. Grinnell, Jr. (Ed.), *Social work research and evaluation* (pp. 361-372). Itasca, IL: F.E. Peacock.

Watts, T.D. (1985). Ethnomethodology. In R.M. Grinnell, Jr. (Ed.), *Social work research and evaluation* (2nd ed., pp. 357-369). Itasca, IL: F.E. Peacock.

Yegidis, B.L., & Weinbach, R.W. (1991). *Research methods for social workers* (pp. 102-111). White Plains, NY: Longman.

Chapter 15

Data Analysis

A
FTER THE DATA ARE COLLECTED, they need to be analyzed—the topic of this chapter. To be honest, a thorough understanding of statistical methods is far beyond the scope of this single chapter.
Such comprehension necessitates more in-depth study, through taking
one or more statistics courses. Instead, this chapter describes a select
group of basic statistical analytical methods that are used frequently in
many social work research studies. Our emphasis will not be on providing and calculating formulas, but will be on helping you to understand the underlying rationale for their use.

We will describe two groups of statistical procedures. The first group
is called *descriptive statistics*, which simply describe and summarize
one variable for a sample or population. They provide information about
only the group included in the study. The second group of procedures
is called *inferential statistics*, which determine if we can generalize
information learned about a sample to the population from which it was
drawn. In other words, knowing what we know about a particular
sample, can we infer that the rest of the population is similar to the
sample that we have studied? Before we can answer this question,
however, we need to know the level of measurement for each variable
being analyzed. Let us now turn to a brief discussion of the four different
levels of measurement that a variable can take.

LEVELS OF MEASUREMENT

The specific statistic(s) used to analyze the data collected is dependent on the type of data that are gathered. The characteristics or qualities that describe a variable are known as its *attributes*. For example, the variable *gender* has only two characteristics or attributes—*male* and *female*—since gender in humans is limited to male and female, and there are no other possible categories or ways of describing gender. The variable *ethnicity* has a number of possible categories: *African American, Native American, Asian, Hispanic American,* and *Caucasian* are just five examples of the many attributes of the variable ethnicity. A point to note here is that the attributes of gender differ in kind from one another—male is different from female—and, in the same way, the attributes of ethnicity are also different from one another.

Now consider the variable *income*. Income can only be described in terms of amounts of money: $15,000 per year, $288.46 per week, and so forth. In whatever terms a person's income is actually described, it still comes down to a number. Since every number has its own category, as we mentioned before, the variable income can generate as many categories as there are numbers, up to the number covering the research participant who earns the most. These numbers are all attributes of income and they are all different, but they are not different in *kind*, as male and female are, or Native American and Hispanic; they are only different in *quantity*.

In other words, the attributes of income differ in that they represent more or less of the same thing, whereas the attributes of gender differ in that they represent different kinds of things. Income will, therefore, be measured in a different way from gender. When we come to measure income, we will be looking for categories that are lower or higher than each other; when we come to measure gender, we will be looking for categories that are different in kind from each other.

Mathematically, there is not much we can do with categories that are different in kind. We cannot subtract Hispanics from Caucasians, for example, whereas we can quite easily subtract one person's annual income from another and come up with a meaningful difference. As far as mathematical computations are concerned, we are obliged to work at a lower level of complexity when we measure variables like ethnicity than when we measure variables like income. Depending on the nature of their attributes, all variables can be measured at one (or more) of four measurement levels: (1) nominal, (2) ordinal, (3) interval, or (4) ratio.

Nominal Measurement

Nominal measurement is the lowest level of measurement and is used to measure variables whose attributes are different in kind. As we have seen, gender is one variable measured at a nominal level, and ethnicity is another. *Place of birth* is a third, since "born in California," for example, is different from "born in Chicago," and we cannot add "born in California" to "born in Chicago," or subtract them or divide them, or do anything statistically interesting with them at all.

Ordinal Measurement

Ordinal measurement is a higher level of measurement than nominal and is used to measure those variables whose attributes can be rank ordered: for example, socioeconomic status, sexism, racism, client satisfaction, and the like. If we intend to measure *client satisfaction*, we must first develop a list of all the possible attributes of client satisfaction: that is, we must think of all the possible categories into which answers about client satisfaction might be placed. Some clients will be *very satisfied*—one category, at the high end of the satisfaction continuum; some will be *not at all satisfied*—a second category, at the low end of the continuum; and others will be *generally satisfied*, *moderately satisfied*, or *somewhat satisfied*—three more categories, at differing points on the continuum, as illustrated in Figure 15.1.

Figure 15.1 is a five-point scale, anchored at all five points with a brief description of the degree of satisfaction represented by the point. Of course, we may choose to express the anchors in different words, substituting *extremely satisfied* for *very satisfied*, or *fairly satisfied* for *generally satisfied*. We may select a three-point scale instead, limiting the choices to *very satisfied*, *moderately satisfied,* and *not at all satisfied*; or we may even use a ten-point scale if we believe that our respondents will be able to rate their satisfaction with that degree of accuracy.

Whichever particular method we select, some sort of scale is the only measurement option available because there is no other way to categorize client satisfaction except in terms of more satisfaction or less satisfaction. As we did with nominal measurement, we might assign numbers to each of the points on the scale. If we used the five-point scale in Figure 15.1, we might assign a 5 to *very satisfied*, a 4 to *generally satisfied*, a 3 to *moderately satisfied*, a 2 to *somewhat satisfied*, and a 1 to *not at all satisfied*.

Here, the numbers do have some mathematical meaning. Five (*very satisfied*) is in fact better than 4 (*generally satisfied*), 4 is better than 3,

Very satisfied	Generally satisfied	Moderately satisfied	Somewhat satisfied	Not at all satisfied

FIGURE 15.1   5-Point Scale to Measure Client Satisfaction

3 is better than 2, and 2 is better than 1. However, the numbers say nothing about *how much better* any category is than any other. We cannot assume, for example, that the difference in satisfaction between *very* and *generally* is the same as the difference between *generally* and *moderately*: we cannot assume that the intervals between the anchored points on the scale are all the same length. Most definitely, we cannot assume that a client who rates a service at 4 (*generally satisfied*) is twice as satisfied as a client who rates the service at 2 (*somewhat satisfied*).

In fact, we cannot attempt any mathematical manipulation at all. We cannot add the numbers 1, 2, 3, 4, and 5, nor can we subtract, multiply, or divide them. As its name might suggest, all we can know from ordinal measurement is the order of the categories.

Interval Measurement

Some variables, such as client satisfaction, have attributes that can be rank ordered—from *very satisfied* to *not at all satisfied*, as we have just discussed. However, as we also saw, these attributes cannot be assumed to be the same distance apart if they are placed on a scale; and, in any case, the distance they are apart has no real meaning. No one can measure the distance between *very satisfied* and *moderately satisfied*; we only know that the one is better than the other.

Conversely, for some variables, the distance, or interval, separating their attributes *does* have meaning, and these variables can be measured at the interval level. An example in physical science would be the Fahrenheit or Celsius temperature scales. The difference between 80 degrees and 90 degrees is the same as the difference between 40 and 50 degrees. However, 80 degrees is not twice as hot as 40 degrees; nor does zero degrees mean no heat at all.

In the social sciences, interval measures are most commonly used in connection with standardized measuring instruments. When we look at a standardized intelligence test, for example, we can say that the difference between IQ scores of 100 and 110 is the same as the difference between IQ scores of 95 and 105, based on the scores obtained by the many thousands of people who have taken the test over the years. As with the temperature scales mentioned above, a person with an IQ score of 120 is not twice as intelligent as a person with a score of 60: nor does a score of 0 mean no intelligence at all.

Ratio Measurement

The highest level of measurement, ratio measurement, is used to measure variables whose attributes are based on a true zero point. It may not be possible to have zero intelligence, but it is certainly possible to have zero children or zero money. Whenever a question about a particular variable might elicit the answer "none" or "never," that variable can be measured at the ratio level. For example, the question, "How many times have you seen your social worker?" might be answered, "Never." Other variables commonly measured at the ratio level include length of residence in a given place, age, number of times married, number of organizations belonged to, number of antisocial behaviors, number of case reviews, number of training sessions, number of supervisory meetings, and so forth.

With a ratio level of measurement we can meaningfully interpret the comparison between two scores. A person who is 40 years of age, for example, is twice as old as a person who is 20 and half as old as a person who is 80. Children aged 2 and 5, respectively, are the same distance apart as children aged 6 and 9. Data resulting from ratio measurement can be added, subtracted, multiplied, and divided. Averages can be calculated and other statistical analyses can be performed.

It is useful to note that, while some variables *can* be measured at a higher level, they may not need to be. For example, income can be measured at a ratio level because it is possible to have a zero income but, for the purposes of a particular study, we may not need to know the actual incomes of our respondents, only the range within which their incomes fall. A respondent who is asked how much he or she earns may be reluctant to give a figure ("mind your own business" is a perfectly legitimate response) but may not object to checking one of a number of income categories, choosing, for example, between:

1. less than $5,000 per year
2. $5,001 to $15,000 per year
3. $15,001 to $25,000 per year
4. $25,001 to $35,000 per year
5. more than $35,000 per year

Categorizing income in this way reduces the measurement from the ratio to the ordinal level. It will now be possible to know only that a respondent checking Category 1 earns less than a respondent checking Category 2, and so on. While we will not know *how much* less or more one respondent earns than another and we will not be able to perform statistical tasks such as calculating average incomes, we will be able to say, for example, that 50 percent of our sample falls into Category 1, 30 percent into Category 2, 15 percent into Category 3, and 5 percent into Category 4. If we are conducting a study to see how many people fall in each income range, this may be all we need to know.

In the same way, we might not want to know the actual ages of our sample, only the range in which they fall. For some studies, it might be enough to measure age at a nominal level—to inquire, for example, whether respondents were born during the depression, or whether they were born before or after 1990. In short, when studying variables that can be measured at any level, the measurement level chosen depends on what kind of data are needed, and this in turn is determined by why the data are needed, which in turn is determined by the research question.

COMPUTER APPLICATIONS

The use of computers has revolutionized the analysis of empirical data. Where previous generations of researchers had to rely on hand-cranked adding machines to calculate every small step in the data analysis, today we can enter raw scores into a personal computer, and, with few complications, direct the computer program to execute just about any statistical test imaginable. Seconds later, the results are available. While the process is truly miraculous, the risk is that, even though we have conducted the correct statistical analysis, we may not understand what the results mean, a factor that will almost certainly affect how the data are interpreted.

We can code information from all four levels of measurement into a computer for data analysis. The coding of nominal data is perhaps the most complex, because we have to create categories that correspond with certain possible responses for a variable. For example, one type of nominal level data that is often gathered from research participants is *place of birth*. If, for the purposes of our study, we are interested in whether our research participants were born in either the United States or Canada, we would assign only three categories to *place of birth*: *United States, Canada* and *other*. The *other* category appears routinely at the end of lists of categories and acts as a catch-all, to cover any category that may have been omitted.

When entering nominal level data into a computer, because we do not want to enter *Canada* every time the response on the questionnaire is Canada, we may assign it the code number 1, so that all we have to enter is 1. Similarly, the United States may be assigned the number 2, and "other" may be assigned the number 3. These numbers have no mathematical meaning: We are not saying that Canada is better than the United States because it comes first, or that the United States is twice as good as Canada because the number assigned to it is twice as high. We are merely using numbers as a shorthand device to record *qualitative* differences: differences in *kind*, not in amount.

Most coding for ordinal, interval, and ratio level data is simply a matter of entering the final score, or number, from the measuring instrument that was used to measure the variable directly into the computer. For example, if a person scored a 45 on the *GCS* (Figure 6.1), the number 45 would be entered into the computer.

Although almost all data entered into computers is in the form of numbers, we need to know at what level of measurement each exists, so that we can choose the appropriate statistic(s) to describe and compare the variables. Now that we know how to measure variables at four different measurement levels, let us turn to the first group of statistics that can be helpful for the analyses of data—descriptive statistics.

DESCRIPTIVE STATISTICS

Descriptive statistics are commonly used in most research studies. They describe and summarize a variable(s) of interest and portray how that particular variable is distributed in the sample, or population. Before looking at descriptive statistics, however, let us examine a social work research example that will be used throughout this chapter.

Thea Black is a social worker who works in a treatment foster care program. The program focuses on children who have behavioral problems who will be placed with "treatment" foster care parents. These parents are supposed to have parenting skills that will help them provide the children with the special needs they require. Thus, Thea's program also teaches parenting skills to these treatment foster care parents. She assumes that newly recruited foster parents are not likely to know much about parenting children who have behavioral problems. Therefore, she believes that they would benefit from a training program that teaches these skills to help them to deal effectively with the special needs of these children who will soon be living with them.

Thea hopes that her parenting skills training program would increase the knowledge about parental management skills for the parents who attended. She assumes that, with such training, the foster parents would be in a better position to support and provide clear limits for their foster children.

After offering the training program for several months, Thea became curious about whether the foster care providers who attended the program were, indeed, lacking in knowledge of parental management skills that she believed they were lacking in the first place. She was fortunate to find a valid and reliable standardized measuring instrument that measures the knowledge of such parenting skills, the Parenting Skills Scale (*PSS*). Thea decided to find out for herself how much the newly recruited parents knew about parenting skills—clearly a descriptive research question. At the beginning of one of her training sessions (before they were exposed to the skills training program), she handed out the *PSS*, asking the 20 individuals in attendance to complete it and also to include information about their gender, years of education, and whether they had ever participated in a parenting skills training program before. All of these three variables could be potentially extraneous ones that might influence the level of knowledge of parenting skills of the 20 participants.

For each foster care parent, Thea calculated the *PSS* score, called a *raw score* because it has not been sorted or analyzed in any way. The total score possible on the *PSS* is 100, with higher scores indicating greater knowledge of parenting skills. The scores for the *PSS* scale, as well as the other information collected from the 20 parents, are listed in Table 15.1.

At this point, Thea stopped to consider how she could best utilize the data that she had collected. She had data at three different levels of measurement. At the nominal level, Thea had collected data on gender (3rd column), and whether the parents had any previous parenting skills training (4th column). Each of these variables can be categorized into two responses. Gender is either male or female, whereas previous training is either present or absent.

The scores on the *PSS* (2nd Column) are ordinal because, although the data are sequenced from highest to lowest, the differences between units cannot be placed on an equally spaced continuum. Nevertheless, many measures in the social sciences are treated as if they are at an interval level, even though equal distances between scale points cannot be proved. This assumption is important because it allows for the use of inferential statistics on such data. Finally, the information on years of formal education (5th column) that was collected by Thea is clearly at

TABLE 15.1   Data Collected for Four Variables
from Foster Care Providers

Participant #	PSS Score	Gender	Previous Training	Years of Education
1	95	male	no	12
2	93	female	yes	15
3	93	male	no	8
4	93	female	no	12
5	90	male	yes	12
6	90	female	no	12
7	84	male	no	14
8	84	female	no	18
9	82	male	no	10
10	82	female	no	12
11	80	male	no	12
12	80	female	no	11
13	79	male	no	12
14	79	female	yes	12
15	79	female	no	16
16	79	male	no	12
17	79	female	no	11
18	72	female	no	14
19	71	male	no	15
20	55	female	yes	12

the ratio level of measurement, because there are equally distributed points and the scale has an absolute zero.

In sum, it seemed to Thea that the data could be used in at least two ways. First, the information collected about each variable could be described to provide a picture of the characteristics of the group of foster care parents. This would call for descriptive statistics. Secondly, she might look for relationships between some of the variables about which she had collected data, procedures that would utilize inferential statistics. For now let us begin by looking at how the first type of descriptive statistic can be utilized with Thea's data set.

Frequency Distributions

One of the simplest procedures that Thea can employ is to develop a frequency distribution of her data. Constructing a frequency distribution involves counting the occurrences of each value, or category, of the variable and ordering them in some fashion. This *absolute* or *simple frequency distribution* allows us to see quickly how certain values of a variable are distributed in the sample or population studied.

The *mode*, or the most commonly occurring score, can be easily spotted in a simple frequency distribution (see Table 15.2). In this example, the mode is 79, a score obtained by five parents on the *PSS* scale. The highest and the lowest score are also quickly identifiable. The top score was 95, while the foster care parent who performed the least well on the *PSS* scored 55.

There are several other ways to present frequency data. A commonly used method that can be easily integrated into a simple frequency distribution table is the *cumulative frequency distribution*, shown in

TABLE 15.2 Simple Frequency Distribution of Parental Skill Scores

Score	Absolute Frequency
95	1
93	3
90	2
84	2
82	2
80	2
79	5
72	1
71	1
55	1

TABLE 15.3   Cumulative Frequency and Percentage
Distributions of Parental Skill Scores

Score	Absolute Frequency	Cumulative Frequency	Percentage Distribution
95	1	1	5
93	3	4	15
90	2	6	10
84	2	8	10
82	2	10	10
80	2	12	10
79	5	17	25
72	1	18	5
71	1	19	5
55	1	20	5
	20		100

Table 15.3.

In Thea's data set, the highest *PSS* score, 95, was obtained by only
one individual. The group of individuals who scored 93 or above on the
PSS measure includes four foster care parents. If we want to know how
many scored 80 or above, if we look at the number across from 80 in the
cumulative frequency column, we can quickly see that 12 of the parents
scored 80 or better.

Other tables utilize percentages rather than frequencies, sometimes
referred to as *percentage distributions*, shown in the right-hand column
in Table 15.3. Each of these numbers represents the percentage of
participants who obtained each *PSS* value. For example, five individuals
scored 79 on the *PSS*. Since there was a total of 20 foster care parents, 5
out of the 20, or one-quarter of the total, obtained a score of 79. This
corresponds to 25% of the participants.

Finally, *grouped frequency distributions* are used to simplify a table
by grouping the variable into equal-sized ranges, as is shown in Table
15.4. Both absolute and cumulative frequencies and percentages can also

TABLE 15.4   Grouped Frequency Distribution
of Parental Skill Scores

Score	Absolute Frequency	Cumulative Frequency	Absolute Percentage
90 – 100	6	6	30
80 – 89	6	12	30
70 – 79	7	19	35
60 – 69	0	19	0
50 – 59	1	20	5

be displayed using this format. Each is calculated in the same way that was previously described for nongrouped data, and the interpretation is identical.

For example, looking at the absolute frequency column, we can quickly identify the fact that seven of the foster care parents scored in the 70-79 range on the *PSS*. By looking at the cumulative frequency column, we can see that 12 of 20 parents scored 80 or better on the *PSS*. Further, from the absolute percentage column, it is clear that 30% of the foster parents scored in the 80-89 range on the knowledge of parenting skills scale. Only one parent, or 5% of the group, had significant problems with the *PSS*, scoring in the 50-59 range.

Note that each of the other variables in Thea's data set could also be displayed in frequency distributions. Displaying years of education in a frequency distribution, for example, would provide a snapshot of how this variable is distributed in Thea's sample of foster care parents. With two category nominal variables, such as gender (male, female) and previous parent skills training (yes, no), however, cumulative frequencies become less meaningful and the data are better described as percentages. For example, Thea noted that 55% of the foster care parents who attended the training workshop were women (obviously the other 45% were men) and that 20% of the parents had already received some form of parenting skills training (while a further 80% had not been trained).

Measures of Central Tendency

We can also display the values obtained on the *PSS* in the form of a graph. A *frequency polygon* is one of the simplest ways of charting frequencies. The graph in Figure 15.2 displays the information that we had previously put in Table 15.2. The *PSS* score is plotted in terms of how many of the foster care parents obtained each score.

As can be seen from Figure 15.2, most of the scores fall between 79 and 93. The one extremely low score of 55 is also quickly noticeable in such a graph, because it is so far removed from the rest of the values.

A frequency polygon allows us to make a quick analysis of how closely the distribution fits the shape of a normal curve. A *normal curve*, also known as a *bell-shaped distribution* or a *normal distribution*, is a frequency polygon in which the greatest number of responses fall in the middle of the distribution and fewer scores appear at the extremes of either very high or very low scores (see Figure 15.3).

Many variables in the social sciences are assumed to be distributed in the shape of a normal curve. For example, low intelligence is thought to be relatively rare as compared to the number of individuals with average intelligence. On the other end of the continuum, extremely gifted individuals are also relatively uncommon.

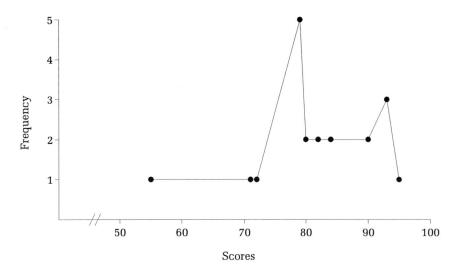

FIGURE 15.2   Frequency Polygon of Parental Skill Scores
                   (from Table 15.2)

Of course, not all variables are distributed in the shape of a normal curve. Some are such that a large number of people do very well (as Thea found in her sample of foster care parents and their parenting skill levels). Other variables, such as juggling ability, for example, would be charted showing a fairly substantial number of people performing poorly. Frequency distributions of still other variables would show that

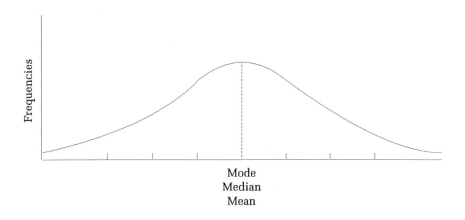

FIGURE 15.3   The Normal Distribution

some people do well, and some people do poorly, but not many fall in between. What is important to remember about distributions is that, although all different sorts are possible, most statistical procedures assume that there is a normal distribution of the variable in question in the population.

When looking at how variables are distributed in samples and populations it is common to use measures of *central tendency*, such as the mode, median, and mean, which help us to identify where the typical or the average score can be found. These measures are utilized so often because, not only do they provide a useful summary of the data, they also provide a common denominator for comparing groups to each other.

Mode. As mentioned earlier, the mode is the score, or value, that occurs the most often—the value with the highest frequency. In Thea's data set of parental skills scores the mode is 79, with five foster care parents obtaining this value. The mode is particularly useful for nominal level data. However, knowing what score occurred the most often provides little information about the other scores and how they are distributed in the sample or population. Because the mode is the least precise of all the measures of central tendency, the median and the mean are better descriptors of ordinal level data and above.

Median. The median is the score that divides a distribution into equal parts or portions. In order to do this, one must rank order the scores, so at least an ordinal level of measurement is required. In Thea's sample of 20 *PSS* scores, the median would be the score above which the top ten scores lie and below which the bottom ten fall. As can be seen in Table 15.2, the top ten scores finish at 82, and the bottom ten scores start at 80. In this example, the median is 81, since it falls between 82 and 80.

Mean. The mean is the most sophisticated measure of central tendency and is useful for interval or ratio levels of measurement. It is also one of the most commonly utilized statistics. A mean is calculated by summing the individual values and dividing by the total number of values. The mean of Thea's sample is $95 + 93 + 93 + 93 + 90 + 90 + ... 72 + 71 + 55/20 = 81.95$. In this example, the obtained mean of 82 (we rounded off for the sake of clarity) is larger than the mode of 79 or the median of 81. The mean is one of the previously mentioned statistical procedures that assumes that a variable will be distributed normally throughout a population. If this is not an accurate assumption, then the median might be a better descriptor. The mean is also best used with relatively large sample sizes where extreme scores (such as the lowest score of 55 in Thea's sample) have less influence.

Measures of Variability

While measures of central tendency provide valuable information about a set of scores, we are also interested in knowing how the scores scatter themselves around the center. A mean does not give a sense of how widely distributed the scores may be: This is provided by measures of variability such as the range and the standard deviation.

Range. The range is simply the distance between the minimum and the maximum score. The larger the range, the greater the amount of variation of scores in the distribution. The range is calculated by subtracting the lowest score from the highest. In Thea's sample, the range is 40 (95 – 55).

The range assumes equal intervals and so should be used only with interval or ratio level data. It is, like the mean, sensitive to deviant values, because it depends on only the two extreme scores. For example, we could have a group of four scores ranging from 10 to 20: 10, 14, 19, and 20. The range of this sample would be 10 (20 – 10). If one additional score that was substantially different from the first set of four scores was included, this would change the range dramatically. In this example, if a fifth score of 45 was added, the range of the sample would become 35 (45 – 10), a number that would suggest quite a different picture of the variability of the scores.

Standard Deviation. The standard deviation is the most well-used indicator of dispersion. It provides a picture of how the scores distribute themselves around the mean. Used in combination with the mean, the standard deviation provides a great deal of information about the sample or population, without our ever needing to see the raw scores. In a normal distribution of scores, described previously, there are six standard deviations: three below the mean and three above, as is shown in Figure 15.4.

In this perfect model we always know that 34.13% of the scores of the sample will fall within one standard deviation above the mean, and another 34.13% will fall within one standard deviation below the mean. Thus, a total of 68.26%, or about two-thirds of the scores, will be between +1 standard deviation and –1 standard deviation from the mean. This leaves almost one-third of the scores to fall farther away from the mean, with 15.87% (50% – 34.13%) above +1 standard deviation, and 15.87% (50% – 34.13%) below –1 standard deviation. In total, when looking at the proportion of scores that fall between +2 and –2 standard deviations, 95.44% of scores can be expected to be found within these parameters. Furthermore, 99.74% of the scores will fall between +3 standard deviations and –3 standard deviations about the mean. Thus, finding scores that fall beyond 3 standard deviations above and below the mean should be a rare occurrence.

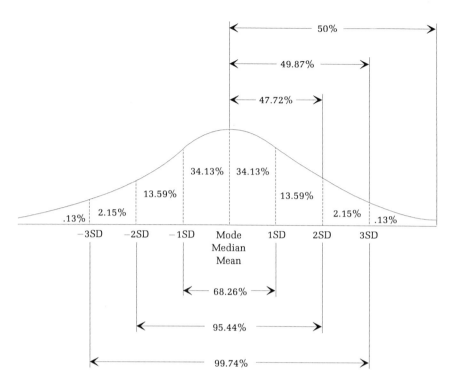

FIGURE 15.4   Proportions of the Normal Curve

The standard deviation has the advantage, like the mean, of taking all values into consideration in its computation. Also similar to the mean, it is utilized with interval or ratio levels of measurement and assumes a normal distribution of scores.

Several different samples of scores could have the same mean, but the variation around the mean, as provided by the standard deviation, could be quite different, as is shown in Figure 15.5a. Two different distributions could have unequal means and equal standard deviations, as in Figure 15.5b, or unequal means and unequal standard deviations, as in Figure 15.5c.

The standard deviation of the scores of Thea's foster care parents was calculated to be 10. Again, assuming that the variable of knowledge about parenting skills is normally distributed in the population of foster care parents, the results of the *PSS* scores from the sample of parents about whom we are making inferences can be shown in a distribution such as the one presented in Figure 15.6.

As can be seen in Figure 15.6, the score that would include 2 standard deviations, 102, is beyond the total possible score of 100 on the test. This is because the distribution of the scores in Thea's sample of parents does not entirely fit a normal distribution. The one extremely

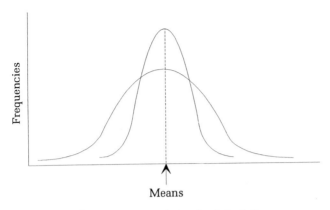

(*a*)   Equal means, unequal standard deviations

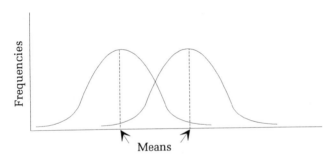

(*b*)   Unequal means, equal standard deviations

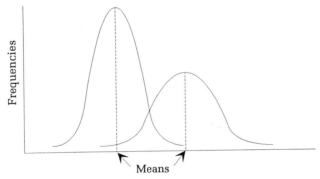

(*c*)   Unequal means, unequal standard deviations

FIGURE 15.5   Variations in Normal Distributions

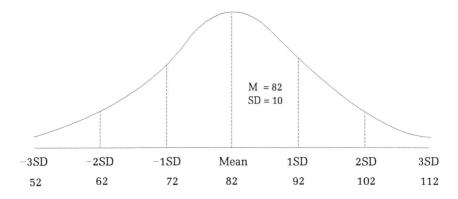

M = 82
SD = 10

−3SD	−2SD	−1SD	Mean	1SD	2SD	3SD
52	62	72	82	92	102	112

FIGURE 15.6   Distribution of Parental Skill Scores

low score of 55 (see Table 15.1) obtained by one foster care parent would have affected the mean, as well as the standard deviation.

INFERENTIAL STATISTICS

The goal of inferential statistical tests is to rule out chance as the explanation for finding either associations between variables or differences between variables in our samples. Since we are rarely able to study an entire population, we are almost always dealing with samples drawn from that population. The danger is that we might make conclusions about a particular population based on a sample that is uncharacteristic of the population it is supposed to represent. For example, perhaps the group of foster parents in Thea's training session happened to have an unusually high level of knowledge of parenting skills.

If Thea assumed that all the rest of the foster parents that she might train in the future were as knowledgeable, she would be overestimating their knowledge, a factor that could have a negative impact on the way she conducts her training program.

To counteract the possibility that the sample is uncharacteristic of the general population, statistical tests take a conservative position as to whether or not we can conclude that there are relationships between the variables within our sample. The guidelines to indicate the likelihood that we have, indeed, found a relationship or difference that fits the population of interest are called *probability levels*.

The convention in most social science research is that variables are significantly associated or groups are significantly different if we are relatively certain that in 19 samples out of 20 (or 95 times out of 100) from a particular population, we would find the same relationship. This corresponds to a probability level of .05, written as ($p < .05$).

Probability levels are usually provided along with the results of the statistical test to demonstrate how confident we are that the results actually indicate statistically significant differences. If a probability level is greater than .05 (e.g., .06, .10), this indicates that we did not find a statistically significant difference.

Statistics That Determine Associations

There are many statistics that can determine if there is an association between two variables. We will briefly discuss two: chi-square and correlation.

Chi-Square. The *chi-square test* requires measurements of variables at only the nominal or ordinal level. Thus, it is very useful since much data in social work are gathered at these two levels of measurement. In general, the chi-square test looks at whether specific values of one variable tend to be associated with specific values of another. In short, we use it to determine if two variables are related. However, it cannot be used to determine if one variable *caused* another.

In thinking about the foster care parents that were in her training program, Thea was aware that women are more typically responsible for caring for their own children than men. Even if they are not mothers themselves, they are often in professions such as teaching and social work where they are caretakers. Thus, she wondered whether there might be a relationship between having had previous training in parenting skills and gender, such that women were less likely to have taken such training since they already felt confident in their knowledge of parenting skills. As such, her one-tailed hypothesis was that fewer women than men would have previously taken parenting skills training courses. Thea could examine this possibility with her 20 foster care parents using a chi-square test.

In terms of gender, Thea had data from the nine (45%) men and 11 (55%) women. Of the total group, four (20%) had previous training in foster care training, while 16 (80%) had not. As shown in Table 15.5, the first task was for Thea to count the number of men and women who had previous training and the number of men and women who did not have

TABLE 15.5   Frequencies (and Percentages) of Gender by Previous Training (from Table 15.1)

Gender	Previous Training		Totals
	Yes	No	
Male	1 (11)	8 (89)	9
Female	3 (27)	8 (73)	11
Totals	4 (20)	16 (80)	20

TABLE 15.6 Chi-Square Table for Gender by
Previous Training (from Table 15.5)

Gender	Previous Training	No Previous Training
Male	O = 1 E = 1.8	O = 8 E = 7.2
Female	O = 3 E = 2.2	O = 8 E = 8.8

χ^2 = .8, df = 1, p > .05
O = observed frequencies (from Table 15.5)
E = expected frequencies

previous training. She put these data in one of the four categories in Table 15.5. The actual numbers are called *observed frequencies*. It is helpful to transform these raw data into percentages, making comparisons between categories much easier.

We can, however, still not tell simply by looking at the observed frequencies whether there is a statistically significant relationship between gender (male or female) and previous training (yes or no). To do this, the next step is to look at how much the observed frequencies differ from what we would expect to see if, in fact, if there was no relationship. These are called *expected frequencies*. Without going through all the calculations, the chi-square table would now look like Table 15.6 for Thea's data set.

Since the probability level of the obtained chi-square value in Table 15.6 is greater than .05, Thea did not find any statistical relationship between gender and previous training in parenting skills. Thus, statistically speaking, men were no more likely than women to have received previous training in parenting skills; her research hypothesis was not supported by the data.

Correlation. Tests of correlation investigate the strength of the relationship between two variables. As with the chi-square test, correlation cannot be used to imply causation, only association. Correlation is applicable to data at the interval and ratio levels of measurement. Correlational values are always decimalized numbers, never exceeding ±1.00.

The size of the obtained correlation value indicates the strength of the association, or relationship, between the two variables. The closer a correlation is to zero, the less likely it is that a relationship exists between the two variables. The plus and minus signs indicate the direction of the relationship. Both high positive (close to +1.00) or high negative numbers (close to −1.00) signify strong relationships.

In positive correlations, though, the scores vary similarly, either increasing or decreasing. Thus, as parenting skills increase, so does self-esteem, for example. A negative correlation, in contrast, simply means that as one variable increases the other decreases. An example would be that, as parenting skills increase, the stresses experienced by foster parents decrease.

Thea may wonder whether there is a relationship between the foster parents' years of education and scores on the *PSS* knowledge test. She might reason that the more years of education completed, the more likely the parents would have greater knowledge about parenting skills. To investigate the one-tailed hypothesis that years of education is positively related to knowledge of parenting skills, Thea can correlate the *PSS* scores with each person's number of years of formal education using one of the most common correlational tests, known as Pearson's *r*.

The obtained correlation between *PSS* score and years of education in this example is $r = -.10$ ($p > .05$). It was in the opposite direction of what she predicted. This negative correlation is close to zero, and its probability level is greater than .05. Thus, in Thea's sample, the parents' *PSS* scores are not related to their educational levels. If the resulting correlation coefficient (*r*) had been positive and statistically significant ($p < .05$), it would have indicated that as the knowledge levels of the parents increased so would their years of formal education. If the correlation coefficient had been statistically significant but negative, this would be interpreted as showing that as years of formal education increased, knowledge scores decreased.

If a correlational analysis is misinterpreted, it is likely to be the case that the researcher implied causation rather than simply identifying an association between the two variables. If Thea were to have found a statistically significant positive correlation between knowledge and education levels and had explained this to mean than the high knowledge scores were a result of higher education levels, she would have interpreted the statistic incorrectly.

Statistics That Determine Differences

Two commonly used statistical procedures, *t*-tests and analysis of variance (ANOVA), examine the means and variances of two or more separate groups of scores to determine if they are statistically different from one another. *T*-tests are used with only two groups of scores, whereas ANOVA is used when there are more than two groups. Both statistical methods are characterized by having a dependent variable at the interval or ratio level of measurement, and an independent, or grouping, variable at either the nominal or ordinal level of measurement.

Several assumptions underlie the use of both *t*-tests and ANOVA. First, it is assumed that the dependent variable is normally distributed in the population from which the samples were drawn. Second, it is assumed that the variance of the scores of the dependent variable in the different groups is roughly the same. This assumption is called *homogeneity of variance*. Third, it is assumed that the samples are randomly drawn from the population—a rarity in social work research situations.

Nevertheless, as mentioned in Chapter 11 on group research designs, it is a common occurrence in social work that we can neither randomly select nor randomly assign individuals to either the experimental or the control group. In many cases this is because we are dealing with already-intact groups, such as Thea's foster care parents.

However, breaking the assumption of randomization presents a serious drawback to the interpretation of the research findings that must be noted in the limitations and the interpretations section of the final research report (next chapter). One possible difficulty that might result from nonrandomization is that the sample may be uncharacteristic of the larger population in some manner. It is important, therefore, that the results not be used inferentially; that is, the findings must not be generalized to the general population. The design of the research study is, thus, reduced to an exploratory or descriptive level, being relevant to only those individuals included in the sample.

Dependent T-Tests. Dependent *t*-tests are used to compare two groups of scores from the same individuals. The most frequent example in social work research is looking at how a group of individuals change from before they receive a social work intervention (pre) to afterwards (post). For example, Thea decided that, while knowing the knowledge levels of the foster care parents before receiving training was interesting, it did not give her any idea whether her program helped the parents to improve their skill levels. In other words her research question became: "After being involved in the program, did parents know more about parenting skills than before they started?" Her hypothesis was that knowledge of parenting skills would improve after participation in her training program.

Thea managed to contact all of the foster care parents in the original group (Group A) one week after they had graduated from the program and asked them to fill out the *PSS* knowledge questionnaire once again. Since it was the same group of people who were responding twice to the same questionnaire, the dependent *t*-test was appropriate. The research design is as follows:

$$O_1 \quad X \quad O_2$$

Where:

O_1 = First administration of the *PSS*, the dependent variable

X = The skills training program, the independent variable
O_2 = Second administration of the *PSS*, the dependent variable

Using the same set of scores collected by Thea previously as the pre-test, the mean *PSS* was 82, with a standard deviation of 10. The mean score of the foster care parents after they completed the program was calculated as 86, with a standard deviation of 8.

A *t*-value of 3.9 was obtained, significant at the .05 level, indicating that the levels of parenting skills significantly increased after the foster care parents participated in the skill training program.

The results suggest that the average parenting skills of this particular group of foster care parents significantly improved (from 82 to 86) after they had participated in Thea's program.

Independent T-Tests. Independent *t*-tests are used for two groups of scores that have no relationship to each other. For example, if Thea had *PSS* scores from one group of foster care parents and then collected more *PSS* scores from a second group of foster care parents, these two groups would be considered independent, and the independent *t*-test would be the appropriate statistical analysis to determine if there was a statistically significant difference between the means of the two groups' *PSS* scores. This design could be written as:

Mean of Group A: O_1
Mean of Group B: O_1

Where:

O_1 = Mean score on the *PSS* before they went through the skills training program

Thea decided to compare the average *PSS* score for the first group of foster care parents (Group A) to the average *PSS* score of parents in her next training program (Group B). This would allow her to see if the first group (Group A) had been unusually talented, or conversely, were less well-versed in parenting skills than the second group (Group B). Her hypothesis was that there would be no differences in the levels of knowledge of parenting skills between the two groups.

Since Thea had *PSS* scores from two different groups of participants (Groups A & B), the correct statistical test to identify if there are any statistical differences between the means of the two groups is the independent *t*-test. Let us use the same set of numbers that we previously used in the example of the dependent *t*-test in this analysis, this time considering the posttest *PSS* scores as the scores of the second group of foster care parents. As can be seen from Figure 15.7, the mean *PSS* of Group A was 82 and the standard deviation was 10. Group B

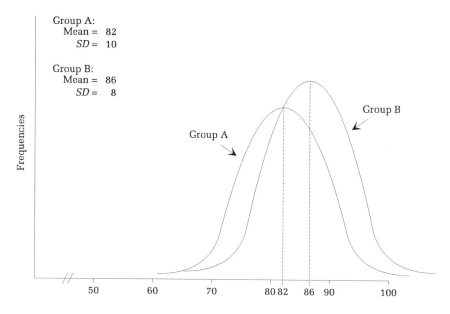

FIGURE 15.7   Frequency Distributions of *PSS* Scores From Two
Groups of Foster Care Providers

scored an average of 86 on the *PSS*, with a standard deviation of 8. Although the means of the two groups are four points apart, the standard deviations in the distribution of each are fairly large, so that there is considerable overlap between the two groups. This would suggest that statistically significant differences will not be found.

The obtained *t*-value to establish whether this four-point difference (86 – 82) between the means for two groups was statistically significant was calculated to be *t* = 1.6 with a *p* > .05. The two groups were, thus, not statistically different from one another and Thea's hypothesis was supported. Note, however, that Thea's foster care parents were not randomly assigned to each group, thus breaking one of the assumptions of the *t*-test. As discussed earlier, this is a serious limitation to the interpretation of the study's results. We must be especially careful not to generalize the findings beyond the groups included in the study.

Note that in the previous example, when using the same set of numbers but a dependent *t*-test, we found a statistically significant difference. This is because the dependent *t*-test analysis is more robust than the independent *t*-test, since having the same participant fill out the questionnaire twice, under two different conditions, controls for many extraneous variables, such as individual differences, that could negatively influence an analysis of independent samples.

One-Way Analysis of Variance. A one-way ANOVA is the extension of an independent *t*-test that uses three or more groups. Each set of scores is from a different group of participants. For example, Thea might use the scores on the *PSS* test from the first group of foster care parents from whom she collected information before they participated in her program, but she might also collect data from a second and a third group of parents before they received the training. The test for significance of an ANOVA is called an *F*-test. One could actually use an ANOVA procedure on only two groups and the result would be identical to the *t*-test. However, unlike the *t*-test, obtaining a significant *F*-value in a one-way ANOVA does not complete the analysis. Because ANOVA looks at differences between three or more groups, a significant *F*-value only tells us that there is a statistically significant difference among the groups: It does not tell us between which ones.

To identify this, we need to do a *post-hoc* test. A variety are available, such as Duncan's multiple range, Tukey's Honestly Significant Difference test, and Newman-Keuls, and are provided automatically by most computer statistical programs. But one caution applies: A post-hoc test should be used *only after finding a significant F*-value, because some of the post-hoc tests are more sensitive than the *F* test and so might find significance when the *F*-test does not. Generally, we should use the most conservative test first, in this case the *F*-test.

In the example of Thea's program, let us say that she collected data on a total of three different groups of foster care parents. The research design could be written as follows:

$$\text{Group A:} \quad O_1$$
$$\text{Group B:} \quad O_1$$
$$\text{Group C:} \quad O_1$$

There is no *X* in the design, since the measures were taken before the training (the *X*) was provided. The first group of foster care parents scored an average of 82 on the *PSS* (standard deviation 10). The second group scored an average of 86 (standard deviation 8), while the mean score of the third group was 88 with a standard deviation of 7.

The obtained *F*-value for the one way ANOVA is 2.63, with a $p > .05$. Thus, we must conclude that there are no statistically significant differences between the means of the groups (i.e., 82, 86, 88). Since the *F*-value was not significant, we would not conduct any post-hoc tests. This finding would be interesting to Thea, since it suggests that all three groups of foster care parents started out with approximately the same knowledge levels, on the average, before receiving training.

SUMMARY

In this chapter, we have provided a beginning look at the rationale behind some of the most commonly used statistical procedures, both those that describe samples and those that analyze data from a sample in order to make inferences about the larger population.

The level of measurement of the data is key to the kind of statistical procedures that can be utilized. Descriptive statistics are utilized with data from all levels of measurement. The mode is the most appropriate measure of central tendency for measurements of this level. It is only when we have data from interval and ratio levels that we can utilize inferential statistics—those that extend the statistical conclusions made about a sample by applying them to the larger population.

Descriptive measures of central tendency, such as the mode, median, and mean of a sample or population, all provide different kinds of information, each of which are applicable only to some levels of measurement. In addition to knowing the middle or average of a distribution of scores as provided by measures of central tendency, it is useful to know the value of the standard deviation that shows us how far away from the mean the scores are distributed. It is assumed that many variables studied in social work can be found in a normal distribution in the total population. Consequently many descriptive and inferential statistics assume such a distribution for their tests to be valid.

Chi-square and correlation are both statistical tests that determine whether variables are associated, although they do not show causation. In contrast, *t*-tests and analysis of variance (ANOVA) are statistical procedures for determining whether the mean and variance in one group (often a treatment group) is significantly different from those in another (often a comparison or control group).

While there are many other statistical procedures, the ones presented in this chapter are utilized frequently. A beginning understanding of the logic and rationale for each test will be useful when reading the social work research literature. Now that our data have been analyzed, the next thing to do in a research study is to write up the final report telling others what we found—the topic of the following chapter.

STUDY QUESTIONS

1. Describe in detail each level of measurement. Use a social work example in your discussion. Discuss how the variable, educational level, could be classified as all four.

2. Describe the purpose of descriptive statistics. How can they be used in social work research situations? Provide a social work example in your discussion.

3. Describe the purpose of inferential statistics. How can they be used in social

work research situations? Provide a social work example in your discussion.

4. Discuss how computers can help aid in the data analysis phase of the research process.

5. What are the benefits to the reader when statistics are reported in a journal article? Be specific and concrete in your response.

6. Go to the library and select a social work research article. What statistics did the author use? Describe how he or she could have used other statistics to make the report more meaningful to the reader.

7. List and fully describe the three measures of central tendency and the two measures of variability. Provide a social work example throughout your discussion.

8. List and fully describe the two statistics that can help us to determine if there is an association between two variables. When is one used over the other? Why?

9. List and fully describe the three statistics that can help us to determine if there are any statistically significant differences between the means of two or more groups. Use a social work example throughout your discussion.

10. Describe the main differences between *t*-tests and ANOVA. When is one used over the other?

REFERENCES AND FURTHER READINGS

Adams, G.R., & Schvaneveldt, J.D. (1991). *Understanding research methods* (2nd ed., pp. 331-365). White Plains, NY: Longman.

Anderson, D.R., Sweeney, D.J., & Williams T.A. (1986). *Statistics: Concepts and applications*. St. Paul, MN: West.

Andrews, F.M., Klem, L., Davidson, T.N., O'Malley, P.M., & Rodgers, W.L. (1995). *A guide for selecting statistical techniques for analyzing social science data* (3rd ed.). Ann Arbor, MI: Institute for Social Research, The University of Michigan.

Babbie, E.R. (1992). *The practice of social research* (6th ed., pp. 338-397, 429-433, 397-406, 433-459). Pacific Grove, CA: Wadsworth.

Bailey, K.D. (1994). *Methods of social research* (4th ed., pp. 377-414). New York: Free Press.

Brown, R.W. (1992). *Graph it! How to make, read, and interpret graphs*. Englewood Cliffs, NJ: Prentice-Hall.

Craft, J.L. (1990). *Statistics and data analysis for social workers* (2nd ed.). Itasca, IL: F.E. Peacock.

Darlington, R.B., & Carlson, P.M. (1987). *Behavioral statistics: Logic and methods*. New York: Free Press.

Foddy, W.H. (1988). *Elementary applied statistics for the social sciences*. New York: Harper & Row.

Frankfort-Nachmias, C., & Nachmias, D. (1992). *Research methods in the social sciences* (4th ed., pp. 339-425, 447-468). New York: St. Martin's Press.

Freund, J.E. (1988). *Modern elementary statistics* (7th ed.). Englewood Cliffs, NJ: Prentice-Hall.

Howell, D.C. (1987). *Statistical methods for psychology* (2nd ed.). Boston:

Duxbury Press.

Judd, C.M., Smith E.R., & Kidder, I.H. (1991). *Research methods in social relations* (6th ed., pp. 351-424). Fort Worth, TX: Harcourt Brace.

Khazanie, R. (1986). *Elementary statistics: In a world of applications* (2nd ed.). Glenview, IL: Scott, Foresman.

Kiess, H.O. (1989). *Statistical concepts for the behavioral sciences.* Needham Heights, MA: Allyn & Bacon.

Krishef, C.H. (1987). *Fundamental statistics for human services and social work.* Boston: Duxbury Press.

Leedy, P.D. (1993). *Practical research: Planning and design* (3rd ed, pp. 42-45, 243-273, 278-294). New York: Macmillan.

Loether, H.J., & McTavish, D.G. (1988). *Descriptive and inferential statistics: An introduction* (3rd ed.). Needham Heights, MA: Allyn & Bacon.

Marlow, C. (1993). *Research methods for generalist social work practice* (pp. 189-210, 213-229). Pacific Grove, CA: Wadsworth.

Miller, E.L. (1986). *Basic statistics: A conceptual approach for beginners.* Muncie, IN: Accelerated Development.

Monette, D.R., Sullivan, T.J., & DeJong, C.R. (1994). *Applied social research* (3rd ed., pp. 364-394). Fort Worth, TX: Harcourt Brace.

Neuman, W.L. (1994). *Social research methods* (2nd ed., pp. 282-313). Needham Heights, MA: Allyn & Bacon.

Reid, S. (1987). *Working with statistics.* Cambridge, MA: Polity Press.

Royse, D.D. (1991). *Research methods in social work* (pp. 173-191). Chicago: Nelson-Hall.

Rubin, A., & Babbie, E. (1993). *Research methods for social work* (2nd ed., pp. 449-533). Pacific Grove, CA: Wadsworth.

Shavelson, R.J. (1988). *Statistical reasoning for the behavioral sciences* (2nd ed.). Needham Heights, MA: Allyn & Bacon.

Stahl, S.M., & Hennes, J.D. (1980). *Reading and understanding applied statistics* (2nd ed.). St. Louis, MO: Mosby.

Weinbach, R.W., & Grinnell, R.M., Jr. (1995). *Statistics for social workers* (3rd ed.). White Plains, NY: Longman.

Wilcox, R.R. (1987). *New statistical procedures for the social sciences: Modern solutions to basic problems.* Hillsdale, NJ: Lawrence Erlbaum Associates.

Wright, S.E. (1986). *Social science statistics.* Needham Heights, MA: Allyn & Bacon.

Chapter 16

Writing Proposals and Reports

W E HAVE COVERED all the necessary steps to conduct a research study, up to and including the analysis of data. The only step remaining in the research process is to inform others about the study's findings. When the data analysis is completed, a report is written showing other social work professionals what has been discovered.

In this chapter, we discuss both how to write a research proposal, which is done *before* the study begins, and how to write a research report, which is done *after* the study is completed. They will be presented together because a research proposal describes what is *proposed* to be done, while a research report describes what *has been* done. As will be emphasized throughout the chapter, there is so much overlap between the two that a majority of the material written for a research proposal can be used in writing the final research report.

This chapter will incorporate most of the contents of the preceding ones, so it is really a summary of the entire research process (and this book) up to report writing. We will use an example of Lula Wilson, a social work practitioner and researcher who wants to do a research study on children who come to her women's emergency shelter with their mothers. She has been working at the shelter for the past two years. The shelter is located in a large urban city.

WRITING PROPOSALS

When writing a research proposal, we must always keep in mind the purposes for its development. These are, primarily, to get permission to do the study and, second, perhaps to obtain some funds with which to do it.

There is a third purpose—to persuade the people who will review the proposal that its author, Lula, is competent to carry out the intended study. Finally, the fourth purpose of a proposal is to force Lula to write down exactly what is going to be studied, why it is going to studied, and how it is going to studied. In doing this, she may think of aspects of the study that had not occurred before. For example, she may look at the first draft of her proposal and realize that some essential detail was forgotten—for instance, that the research participants (in her case, children) who are going to fill out self-report standardized measuring instruments must be able to read.

The intended readers of the proposal determine how it will be written. It is important to remember that the reviewers will probably have many proposals to evaluate at once. Some proposals will need to be turned down because there will not be sufficient funds, space, or staff time, to accept all of them. Thus, proposal reviewers are faced with some difficult decisions on which to accept and which ones to reject. People who review research proposals often do so on a voluntary basis.

With the above in mind, the proposal should be written so that it is easy to read, easy to follow, easy to understand, clearly organized, and brief. It must not ramble or go off into anecdotes about how Lula became interested in the subject in the first place. Rather, Lula's proposal must describe her proposed research study simply, clearly, and concisely.

Now that we know the underlying rationale for the proposal, the next step is to consider what content it should include. This depends to some extent on who will be reviewing it. If the proposal is submitted to an academic committee, for example, it will often include more of a literature review and more details of the study's research design than if it were submitted to a funding organization. Some funding bodies specify exactly what they want included and in what order; others leave it to the author's discretion.

The simplest and most logical way to write the proposal is in the same order that a research study is conducted. For example, when a research study is done, a general topic area is decided upon as presented in Chapter 3. This is followed by a literature review in an attempt to narrow the broad research area into more specific research questions or hypotheses as presented in Chapters 4 and 5. We will now go back and look at how each step of a research study leads to the writing of a parallel section in a research proposal. Let us turn to the first task of proposal writing, specifying the research topic.

Part 1: Research Topic

The first step in beginning a research study is to decide what the study will be about. The first procedure in writing a proposal, therefore, is to describe, in general terms, what it is that is going to be studied. Lula may write, for example, that her proposed study's general problem area is the:

General Problem Area:
problems experienced by children who witness the husband physically abusing the wife (wife abuse).

The first task is to convince the proposal reviewers that the general problem area is a good one to study. This task is accomplished by outlining the significance of Lula's proposed study in three specific social work areas: its practical significance, its theoretical significance, and its social policy significance.

Depending on to whom the proposal is submitted, Lula may go into detail about these three areas or describe them briefly. It may be known, for example, that the funding organization that will review the proposal is mostly interested in improving the effectiveness of individual social workers in their day-to-day practice activities. If this is the case, the reviewers will more likely be interested in the practical significance of Lula's proposed study than its theoretical and/or policy significance.

Therefore, Lula's proposal would neither go into detail about how her study might generate new social work theory, nor elaborate on the changes in social policy that might follow directly from the study's results. Since Lula is going to submit the proposal to the women's emergency shelter where she works, she would be smart in obtaining informal input from the agency's executive director at this stage in writing the proposal. Informal advice at an early stage is astronomically important to proposal writers.

In sum, Part 1 of the proposal describes *what* is going to be studied and *why* it should be studied. One should thoroughly reread Chapters 1-3 in this book before writing Part 1 of a research proposal.

Part 2: Literature Review

The second part of a proposal contains the literature review. This is not simply a list of all the books and journal articles that vaguely touch on the general problem area mentioned in Part 1. When a research study is done, it is basically trying to add another piece to a jigsaw puzzle already begun by other researchers. The purpose of a literature review, then, is to show how *Lula's* study fits into the whole.

The trouble is that it might be a very big whole. There may be literally hundreds of articles and books filled with previous research studies on the study's general topic area. If Lula tries to list every one of these, the reviewers of the proposal, probably her colleagues who work with her at the shelter, will lose both interest and patience somewhere in the middle of Part 2. The literature review has to be selective—listing enough material to show that Lula is thoroughly familiar with her topic area, but not enough to induce stupor in the reviewer. This is a delicate and sensitive balance. She should include findings from recent research studies along with any classical ones.

On the other side of the coin, another possibility is that previous research studies on Lula's general topic area may be limited. In this case, all available material is included. However, her proposal can also branch out into material that is partially related or describes a parallel topic area. Lula might find a research article, for example, that claims that children whose parents are contemplating divorce have low social interaction skills. This does not bear directly on the matter of problems children have who witnessed wife abuse (the general problem area mentioned above). However, since marital separation can be a result of wife abuse, it might be indirectly relevant.

A literature review serves a number of purposes. First, it shows the reviewers that Lula understands the most current and central issues related to the general topic area that she proposes to study. Second, it points out in what ways her proposed study is the same as, or different from, other similar studies. Third, it describes how the results of her proposed study will contribute to solving the puzzle. Fourth, it introduces and conceptually defines all the variables that will be examined throughout the study.

At this stage, Lula does not operationally define her study's variables—that is, in such a way that allows their measurement. They are only abstractly defined. For example, if Lula is going to study the social interaction skills of children who witness wife abuse, her proposal so far introduces only the concepts of children, wife abuse, children witnessing wife abuse, and children's social interaction skills. They will be operationally defined in Part 5. Elaine Bouey and Gayla Rogers (1993) and Gayla Rogers and Elaine Bouey (1993) have written two book chapters on how to do literature reviews that are recommended reading before writing Part 2 of a research proposal.

Part 3: Conceptual Framework

A conceptual framework takes the variables that have been mentioned in Part 2, illustrates their possible relationship to one another, and discusses why the relationship exists the way it is proposed and not in some other, equally possible way. The author's suppositions might be based on past professional experience. For example, Lula has observed numerous children who accompanied their mothers to women's emergency shelters. She has made subjective observations of these children over the past two years and finally wishes to test out two hunches objectively. First, Lula believes, that children who have witnessed wife abuse *seem to* have lower social interaction skills than children who have not witnessed wife abuse. Second, Lula believes that of the children who have been a witness to wife abuse, boys *seem to* have lower social interaction skills than girls. However, these two hunches are based on only two-year subjective observations, which need to be objectively tested—the purpose of her research study.

As we know from Chapters 4 and 5, ideally, Lula's hunches should be integrated with existing theory or findings derived from previous research studies. In any case, Lula should discuss these assumptions and the reasons for believing them as the basis for the variables that are included in her proposed study.

In sum, Lula wants to see if children who have witnessed wife abuse have lower social interaction skills than do children who have not witnessed it. And of the children who have witnessed wife abuse, she wants to determine whether boys have lower social interaction skills than girls. It must be remembered that the two areas her study proposes to explore have been delineated out of her past experiences and have not been formulated on existing theory or previous research findings.

Part 4: Questions and Hypotheses

As discussed in Chapter 4, when an exploratory or descriptive study is done on a topic that little is known about, only general research questions are asked. Many general research questions relating to Lula's general problem area can be asked. One of the many could be:

General Research Question:
Is there a relationship between children witnessing wife abuse and their social interaction skills?

On the other hand, when a descriptive or explanatory study is done on a topic where a lot of previous research studies have been previously done, a specific hypothesis can be formulated. A specific hypothesis derived from the above general research question might be:

Specific Research Hypothesis:
Children who have witnessed wife abuse will have lower social interaction skills than children who have not witnessed such abuse.

Part 5: Operational Definitions

As mentioned, variables are abstractly and conceptually defined in the conceptual framework part of the proposal (Part 3). Part 5 provides operational definitions of them; that is, they must be defined in ways in which they can become measurable.

Let us take Lula's simple research hypothesis previously mentioned. In this hypothesis there are four main variables that must be operationalized before Lula's study can begin: children, wife abuse, children witnessing wife abuse, and children's social interaction skills. Each must be described in such a way that there is no ambiguity as to what they mean.

For example, what constitutes a child? How old must the child be? Does the child have to be in a certain age range, for example between the ages of 5-10? Does the child have to be a biological product of either the mother or the father? Can the child be a stepchild? Can the child be adopted? Does the child have to live full-time at home?

Since Lula's study is at the descriptive level, she may wish to define a child operationally in such a way that permits the largest number of children to be included in the study. She would, however, go to the literature and find out how other researchers have operationally defined "children," and she would use this operational definition if it made sense to her.

However, in a simple study such as this one, a child could be operationally defined as "any person who is considered to be a child as determined by the mother." This is a very vague operational definition, at best, but it is more practical than constructing one such as, "a person between the ages of 5-17 who has resided full-time with the biological mother for the last 12-month period."

If such a complex operational definition was utilized, Lula would have to provide answers to questions as: Why the ages of 5-17, why not 4-18? What is the specific reason for this age range? Why must the child live at home full-time, why not part-time? Why must the mother be the biological mother, why not a nonbiological mother? What about biological fathers? Why must the child have had to live at home for the past 12 months, why not two years, four years? In short, Lula's operational definition of a child must make sense and be based on a rational or theoretical basis. For now, Lula is going to make matters simple: A child in her study will be operationally defined as any child whose mother validates their relationship. This simple operational definition makes the most practical sense to Lula.

Let us now turn to Lula's second variable—wife abuse. What is it? Does one partner have to shove, push, or threaten the other? How would a child, as operationally defined above, know when it occurs? Does a husband yelling at his wife imply wife abuse? If so, does it have to last a long time? If it does, what is a long time? Is Lula interested in the frequency, duration, or magnitude of yelling—or all three? A specific operational definition of wife abuse has to be established in order for the study to be of any value.

Like most variables, there are as many operational definitions of wife abuse as there are people willing to define it. For now, Lula is going to continue to make her descriptive study simple by operationally defining wife abuse as, "women who say they have been physically abused by their partners." Lula can simply ask each woman who enters the shelter if she believes she has been physically abused by her partner. The data provided by the women will be "yes" or "no." Lula could have looked at the frequency, duration, or magnitude of such abuse, but for this study, the variable is a dichotomous one: Either wife abuse occurred, or it did not occur—as reported by the women. Questions regarding its frequency (how many times it occurred), its duration (how long each episode lasted), and its magnitude (the intensity of each episode) are not asked.

The third variable in Lula's hypothesis is the child (or children) who witness wife abuse. Now that operational definitions of a "child" and "wife abuse" have been formulated, how will she know that a child has witnessed such an abuse? Each child could be asked directly, or a standardized checklist of possible verbal and physical abuses that a child might have witnessed can be given to the child, who is then asked how many times such abuse has been observed.

Obviously, the child would have to know what constitutes wife abuse to recognize it. In addition, the child would have to be old enough to respond to such requests, and the operational definition that is used for wife abuse must be consistent with the age of the child. For example, the child must be able to communicate to someone that wife abuse has in fact occurred—not to mention the question of whether the child could recognize it in the first place.

In Lula's continuing struggle to keep her study as simple as possible, she operationally defines "a child witnessing wife abuse" by asking the mothers who come to the women's emergency shelter if their child(ren) witnessed the physical abuse. She is only interested in the women who come to the shelter as a result of being physically abused by their partners. Women who come to the shelter for other reasons are not included in her study. It must be kept in mind that Lula's study is focusing only upon physical abuse and not emotional or mental abuse.

So far, Lula's study is rather simple in terms of operational definitions. Up to this point she is studying mothers who bring their child(ren) with them to one women's emergency shelter. She simply asks the mother if the person(s) with her is her child(ren), which operationally defines "child." The mother is asked if she believes her partner physically abused her, which defines "wife abuse." The mother is also asked if the child(ren) who is accompanying her to the shelter saw the physical abuse occur, which operationally defines "children witnessing wife abuse."

Let us now turn to Lula's fourth and final variable in her hypothesis—the children's social interaction skills. How will they be measured? What constitutes the social skills of a child? They could be measured in a variety of ways through direct observations of parents, social work practitioners, social work researchers, social work practicum students, teachers, neighbors, and even members from the children's peer group. They could also be measured by a standardized measuring instrument such as the ones discussed in Chapter 7. Lula decides to use one of the many standardized measuring instruments that measure social interaction skills of children, named the Social Interaction Skills of Children Assessment Instrument (*SISOCAI*).

All in all, Part 5 of a proposal provides operational definitions of all important variables that were abstractly defined in Part 3. It should be noted that the four variables that have been operationally defined should be defined from the available literature, if appropriate. (This procedure makes a study's results generalizable from one research situation to another.) However, there may be times when this is not possible. The proposal must specify what data gathering instruments are going to be used, including their validity and reliability, as presented in Chapters 6 and 7.

In summary, let us review how Lula intends to operationally define her four key variables: child, wife abuse, child witnessing wife abuse, and children's social interaction skills:

1. *Child.* Any person who the mother claims is her child.
2. *Wife Abuse.* Asking the mother if her partner physically abused her.
3. *Child Witnessing Wife Abuse.* Asking the mother if the child(ren) who accompanied her to the shelter witnessed the abuse.
4. *Children's Social Interaction Skills.* The *SISOCAI* score for each child in the study.

The above four operational definitions are rather rudimentary, at best. There are many more sophisticated ways of operationally defining them. However, alternative definitions will not be explored, because Lula wants to keep her research proposal as uncomplicated as possible as she knows that the shelter does not want a study that would intrude too heavily into its day-to-day operations. On a very general level, the more complex the operational definitions of variables used in a research study, the more the study will intrude on the research participants' lives—in addition to the agency's day-to-day operations.

Joel Fischer (1993) has provided a few criteria that need to be examined when evaluating Parts 1-5 of a research proposal. These criteria, with some modifications, are presented below:

1. Adequacy of the proposal's literature review
2. Clarity of the problem area and research question under investigation
3. Clarity of the statement of the research hypothesis (if applicable)
4. Clarity of the specification of the independent variable, at an abstract and conceptual level (if applicable)
5. Clarity of the specification of the dependent variable, at an abstract and conceptual level
6. Reasonableness of the described relationship between the independent and dependent variables (if applicable)
7. Specification of other rival hypotheses
8. Clarity of the researcher's orientation
9. Clarity of the study's purpose
10. Clarity of the study's auspices
11. Reasonableness of the author's assumptions

The eleven criteria above should be gone over very carefully, and authors of proposals should try to respond to them all before going on to Part 6, the study's research design.

Part 6: Research Design

This part of a research proposal presents the study's research design. Suppose Lula formulated two related research hypotheses from her general problem area mentioned above:

Research Hypothesis 1:
Children who have witnessed wife abuse will have lower social interaction skills than children who have not witnessed such abuse.

Research Hypothesis 2:
Of those children who have witnessed wife abuse, boys will have lower social interaction skills than girls.

In relation to Research Hypothesis 1, Lula's study would use the children who accompanied their mothers to the women's emergency shelter. These children would then be broken down into two groups, (1) those children who witnessed wife abuse, and (2) those children who did not witness it (as determined by the mother).

A very simple two group research design could be used to test Research Hypothesis 1, such as:

Children who Have Witnessed Wife Abuse: O_1
Children who Have Not Witnessed Wife Abuse: O_1

Where:

O_1 = Measurement of the child's social interaction skills (*SIS-OCAI*)

The average social interaction skill score, via the *SISOCAI*, between the two groups can then be compared.

In relation to Research Hypothesis 2, within the group of children who have witnessed wife abuse, the children's social interaction skills, via the *SISOCAI*, between the boys and girls can be compared. This simple procedure would test Research Hypothesis 2. A simple two group research design could be used to test Research Hypothesis 2, such as:

Boys: O_1
Girls: O_1

Where:

O_1 = Measurement of the child's social interaction skills (*SIS-OCAI*)

In Lula's study, there are two separate miniresearch studies running at the same time—Research Hypotheses 1 and 2. All Lula wants to do is to see if there is an association between the social interaction skills of children who have and have not witnessed wife abuse (Research Hypothesis 1). In addition, for those children who have witnessed wife abuse, she wants to see if boys have lower social interaction skills than girls (Research Hypothesis 2).

In Part 6 of a research proposal, information should be included about what data will be collected, how these data will be collected, and who will be the research participants.

Next, Lula must now describe the data to be collected. She will have her research assistant complete the *SISOCAI* for each child during a half-hour interview. Finally, the conditions under which the data will be gathered are discussed; that is, the research assistant will complete the *SISOCAI* for each selected child one day after the mother entered the shelter.

Of necessity, recording all of this will involve some repetition. For example, Part 5, when discussing operational definitions, discussed what data would be collected, and how. Part 7, the next part, will discuss the study's sample and population (i.e., who will be studied) in much more detail. It is repeated in Part 6, both to give an overview of the whole research process, and to form links between Parts 5 and 7 so that the entire proposal flows smoothly. Chapters 8-11 in this book provide a good background for the writing of Part 6 of a research proposal.

Part 7: Population and Sample

This part of the proposal presents a detailed description of who will be studied. Lula's research study will use the children who accompanied their mothers to one women's emergency shelter who wish to voluntarily participate, and whose mothers agree that they can be included in the study. The children will then each go into one of two distinct groups: those who have witnessed wife abuse, and those who have not (according to the mothers, that is). Lula's study could have used a comparison group of children from the same local community who have never witnessed wife abuse and have never been to a women's emergency shelter. However, Lula chose to use only those children who accompanied their mothers to the shelter where she works.

There is no question of random selection from some population, and it is not possible to generalize the study's findings to any general population of children who have and have not witnessed wife abuse. The results of Lula's study will apply only to the children who participated in it. Chapter 12 in this book should be reread before writing Part 8 of a research proposal.

Part 8: Data Collection

This part of a research proposal presents a detailed account of how the data are going to be collected—that is, the specific data collection method(s) that will be used to collect the data. As we know, data can be collected using interviews (individual or group), surveys (mail or telephone), direct observations, participant observations, secondary analyses, and content analyses. Lula is going to collect data on the dependent variable by having her research assistant complete the *SISOCAI* for each identified child during a one-half hour interview one day after the mother enters the shelter with her child(ren). Those mothers who do not bring their children with them will not be included in Lula's study.

In addition to the children, their mothers are also going to be interviewed to some small degree. Each mother will be asked by Lula if she believes her partner physically assaulted her. These responses will then be used to operationally define "wife abuse." Each mother will also provide data on whether or not her child(ren) who accompanied her to the shelter saw the abuse occur. The mothers' responses will then operationally define whether or not the child(ren) witnessed wife abuse.

Finally, this section should discuss ethical issues involved in data collection, such as the ones presented in Chapter 2. Chapters 13 and 14 in this book present various data collection methods that can be used in research studies. These chapters should be reread thoroughly before writing Part 8 of a research proposal.

Part 9: Data Analysis

This part of a research proposal describes the way the data will be analyzed, including the statistical procedures to be used, if any. Having clearly specified the research design in Part 6, this part specifies exactly what statistical test(s) will be used to answer the research questions or hypotheses. Most of the more common statistical procedures were presented in the previous chapter.

The *SISOCAI* produces interval-level data and a child's social interaction skill score on this particular instrument can range from 0-100, where higher scores mean higher (better) social skills than lower scores. Since there are two groups of children that are being used to test both research hypotheses, and the dependent variable (*SISOCAI*) is at the interval-level of measurement, an independent *t*-test would be used to test both research hypotheses. In addition to the previous chapter, Robert W. Weinbach and Richard M. Grinnell's book (1995) should be read before completing Part 9 of a research proposal.

Part 10: Limitations

There are limitations in every research study, often due to problems that cannot be eliminated entirely—even though steps can be taken to reduce them. Lula's study is certainly no exception. Limitations inherent in a study might relate to the validity and reliability of the measuring instruments, or to the generalizability of the study's results. Sometimes the data that were needed could not be collected, for some reason. In addition, this part should mention all extraneous variables that have not been controlled for.

For example, Lula may not have been able to control for all the factors that affect the children's social interaction skills. Although she believes that having witnessed wife abuse leads to lower social skills for boys as compared to girls, it may not be possible to collect reliable and valid data about whether the children saw or did not see an abuse occur. In Lula's study, she is going to simply ask the mothers, so in this case, she has to take the mothers' word for it.

She could ask the children, however. This would produce another set of limitations in and of itself. For example, it would be difficult for Lula to ascertain whether a child did or did not see a form of wife abuse as perceived by the child. It may be hard for a child to tell what type of abuse occurred. Also the frequency, duration, and magnitude of a particular form of wife abuse may be hard for the child to recall. All of these limitations, and a host of others, must be delineated in this part of the proposal. In addition, asking a child if he or she saw the abuse occur might prove to be a traumatic experience for the child.

Some limitations will not be discovered until the study is well underway. However, many problems can be anticipated and these should be included in the proposal, together with the specific steps that are intended to minimize them.

Part 11: Administration

The final part of a research proposal contains the organization and resources necessary to carry out the study. First, Lula has to find a base of operations (e.g., a desk and telephone). She has to think about who is going to take on the overall administrative responsibility for the study. What staff will be involved? How many individuals will be needed? What should their qualifications be? What will be their responsibilities? To whom are they responsible? What is the chain of command? Finally, Lula has to think about things such as a computer, stationery, telephone, travel, and parking expenses.

When all of the details have been put together, an organizational chart can be produced that shows what will be done, by whom, where, and in what order. The next step is to develop a time frame. By what date should each anticipated step be completed? Optimism about completion dates should be avoided, particularly when it comes to allowing time to analyze the data and writing the final report (to be discussed shortly). Both of these activities always take far longer than anticipated, and it is important that they be properly done—which takes more time than originally planned.

When the organizational chart and time frame have been established, the final step is to prepare a budget. Lula has to figure out how much each aspect of the study—such as office space, the research assistant's time, staff time, and participants' time, if any—will cost.

We have now examined eleven parts that should be included when writing a research proposal. Not all proposals are organized in precisely this way; sometimes different headings are used or information is put in a different part of the proposal. For example, in some proposals, previous studies are discussed in the conceptual framework section rather than in the literature review. Much depends on for whom the proposal is being written and on the author's personal writing style.

Much of the content that has been used to write the eleven parts of a research proposal can be used to write the final research report. Let us now turn to that discussion.

WRITING REPORTS

A research report is a way of describing the completed study to other people. The findings can be reported by way of an oral presentation, a book, or a published paper. The report may be addressed solely to colleagues at work or to a worldwide audience. It may be written simply, so that everyone can understand it, or it may be so highly technical that it can only be understood by a few.

The most common way of sharing a study's findings with other professionals is to publish a report in a professional journal. Most journal reports run about twenty-five double-spaced, typewritten pages, including figures, tables, and references.

As we know, research proposals are written with the proposal reviewers in mind. Similarly, a research report is written with its readers in mind. However, some of the readers who read research reports will want to know the technical details of how the study's results were achieved, others will only want to know how the study's results are relevant to social work practice, without the inclusion of the technical details.

There are a number of ways to deal with this situation. First, a technical report can be written for those who can understand it, without worrying too much about those who cannot. In addition, a second report can be written that skims over the technical aspects of the study and concentrates mostly on the practical application of the study's findings. Thus, two versions of the same study can be written; a technical one, and a nontechnical one.

The thought of writing two reports where one would suffice will not appeal to very many of us, however. Usually, we try to compensate for this by including those technical aspects of the study which are necessary to an understanding of the study's findings. This is essential, because readers will not be able to evaluate the study's findings without knowing how they were arrived at.

However, life can be made easier for nontechnical audiences by including some explanation of the technical aspects and, in addition, paying close attention to the practical application of the study's results. In this way, we will probably succeed in addressing the needs of both audiences—those who want all the technical details and those who want none.

A research report can be organized in many different ways depending on the intended audience and the author's personal style. Often, however, the same common-sense sequence is followed that was laid out in Figure 1.1, when the basic problem-solving method was discussed. In order to solve a problem, the problem must be specified, ways of solving it must be explored, a solution to solve the problem must be tried, and an evaluation must take place to see if the solution worked.

In general, this is the way to solve practice and research problems. It is also the order in which a research report is written. First, a research problem is defined. Then, the method used to solve it is discussed. Next, the findings are presented. Finally, the significance of the findings to the social work profession are discussed.

Part 1: Problem

Probably the best way to begin a research report is to explain simply what the research problem is. Lula might say, for example, that the study's purpose was to ascertain if children who have witnessed wife abuse have lower social interaction skills than children who have not witnessed such abuse. In addition, the study wanted to find out, of those children who have witnessed wife abuse, if boys have lower social interaction skills than girls.

But why would anyone want to know about that? How would the knowledge derived from Lula's study help social workers? Thinking back to Part 1 of her proposal, this question was asked and answered once before. In the first part of her proposal, when the research topic was set out, the significance of the study was discussed in the areas of practice, theory, social policy. This material can be used, suitably paraphrased, in Part 1 of the final report.

One thing that should be remembered, though, is that a research report written for a journal is not, relatively speaking, very long. A lot of information must be included in less than twenty-five pages, and the author cannot afford to use too much space explaining to readers why this particular study was chosen. Sometimes, the significance of the study will be apparent and there is no room to belabor what is already obvious.

In Part 2 of the proposal, a literature review, was done in which Lula's proposed study was compared to other similar studies, highlighting similarities and differences. Also, key variables were conceptually defined. In her final report, she can use both the literature review and her conceptually defined variables that she presented in her proposal. The literature review might have to be cut back if space is at a premium, but the abstract and conceptual definitions of all key variables must be included.

In Part 3 of her proposal, she presented a conceptual framework. This can be used in Part 1 of the final report, where Lula must state the relationships between the variables she is studying.

In Part 4 of the research proposal, a research question or hypothesis to be answered or tested was stated. In the final report, we started out with that, so now we have come full circle. By using the first four parts of the proposal for the first part of the research report, we have managed to considerably cut down writing time. In fact, Part 1 of a research report is nothing more than a cut-and-paste job of the first four parts of the research proposal. Actually, if the first four parts of the research proposal were done correctly, there should be very little original writing within Part 1 of a research report.

One of the most important things to remember when writing Part 1 of a research report is that the study's findings have to have some form of utilization potential for social workers, or the report would not be worth writing in the first place. More specifically, the report must have some practical, theoretical, or policy significance. Part 1 of a research report tells why the study's findings would be useful to the social work profession. This is mentioned briefly but is picked up later in Part 4.

Part 2: Method

Part 2 of a research report contains the method(s) used to answer the research problem. This section usually includes descriptions of the study's research design, a description of the research participants who participated in the study (study's sample), and a detailed description of the data gathering procedures (who, what, when, how), and presents the operational definition of all variables.

Once again, sections of the original research proposal can be used. For example, in Part 5 of the proposal, key variables were operationally defined; that is, they were defined in a way that would allow them to be measured. When and how the measurements would occur were also presented. This material can be used again in the final report.

Part 6 of the proposal described the study's research design. This section of the proposal was used—about half way through—to link the parts of the study together into a whole. Since a research design encompasses the entire research process from conceptualizing the problem to disseminating the findings, Lula could take this opportunity to give a brief picture of the entire process. This part presents who would be studied (the research participants, or sample), what data would be gathered, how the data would be gathered, when the data would be gathered, and what would be done with the data once obtained (analysis).

In the final report, there is not a lot of space to provide this information in detail. Instead, a clear description of how the data were obtained from the measuring instruments must be presented. For example, Lula could state in this part of the report, that "a research assistant rated each child on the *SISOCAI* during a one-half hour interview one day after the mother entered the shelter."

Joel Fischer (1993) has provided a few criteria that need to be examined when evaluating the method section of a research report. These criteria, with some modifications, are presented below:

1. Clarity of the specification of the kinds of changes desired (if applicable)
2. Appropriateness of the outcome measures in relation to the purpose of the study (if applicable)
3. Degree of validity of the outcome measures (if applicable)
4. Degree of reliability of the outcome measures (if applicable)
5. Degree of use of a variety of outcome measures such as subjective and objective measures (if applicable)
6. Clarity about how the data were collected

7. Clarity about who collected the data
8. Degree of error in the collection of data
9. Clarity of the description of the research design
10. Adequacy of the research design (in terms of purpose)
11. Clarity and adequacy of time between pretest and posttest (if applicable)
12. Appropriateness in the use of a control group(s) (if applicable)
13. Appropriateness in the use of random assignment procedures (if applicable)
14. Appropriateness in the use of matching procedures (if applicable)
15. Degree of experimental and control group equivalency at pretest (if applicable)
16. Degree of control for effects of history (if applicable)
17. Degree of control for effects of maturation (if applicable)
18. Degree of control for effects of testing (if applicable)
19. Degree of control for effects of instrumentation (if applicable)
20. Degree of control for statistical regression (if applicable)
21. Degree of control for differential selection of clients (if applicable)
22. Degree of control for differential mortality (if applicable)
23. Degree of control for temporal bias (if applicable)
24. Degree of control for integrity of the intervention (if applicable)
25. Ability to distinguish causal variable(s) (if applicable)
26. Degree of control for interaction effects (if applicable)
27. Overall degree of success in maximizing internal validity (16-26)
28. Adequacy of sample size
29. Degree of accuracy in defining the population
30. Degree of adequacy in the representativeness of the sample drawn from the population (if applicable)
31. Degree of control for reactive effects of testing—interaction with independent variable (if applicable)
32. Degree of control for interaction between selection and experimental variable (if applicable)
33. Degree of control for special effects of experimental arrangements (if applicable)
34. Degree of control for multiple-treatment interference (if applicable)
35. Overall degree of success in maximizing external validity

Many of the above criteria are not applicable to Lula's study. However, they can be used in evaluating other, more complex, studies.

Part 3: Findings

Part 3 of a report presents the study's findings. Unfortunately, Lula's original proposal will not be of much help here because she did not know what she would find when it was written—only what she hoped to find.

One way to begin Part 3 of a report is to prepare whatever figures, tables, or other data displays that are going to used. For now, let us take

TABLE 16.1 Means and Standard Deviations of Social
Interaction Skills of Children Who Did and Did
Not Witness Wife Abuse

Witness Spouse Abuse?	Mean	Standard Deviation	*N*
Yes	45	11	40
No	75	9	40
Averages	60	10	

Lula's Research Hypothesis 1 as an example of how to write up a study's findings. Suppose that there were 80 children who accompanied their mothers to the shelter. All of the mothers claimed they were physically abused by their partners. Lula's research assistant rated the 80 children's social skills, via the *SISOCAI*, one day after they accompanied their mothers to the shelter. Thus, there are 80 *SISOCAI* scores. What is she going to do with all that data?

The goal of tables and figures is to organize the data in such a way that the reader takes them in at a glance and says, "Ah! Well, it's obvious that the children who witnessed wife abuse had lower *SISOCAI* scores than the children who did not see such abuse."

As can be seen from Table 16.1, the average *SISOCAI* score for all of the 80 children is 60. These 80 children would then be broken down into two subgroups: those who witnessed wife abuse, and those who did not—according to their mothers, that is. For the sake of simplicity let us say there were 40 children in each subgroup. In the first subgroup, the average *SISOCAI* score for the 40 children is 45; in the second subgroup, the average *SISOCAI* score for the 40 children is 75.

Table 16.1 allows the reader to quickly compare the average *SISOCAI* score for each subgroup. The reader can see, at a glance, that there is a 30-point difference between the two average *SISOCAI* scores (75 − 45 = 30). The children who witnessed wife abuse scored 30 points lower, on the average, on the *SISOCAI* than those children who did not witnesses wife abuse. Thus, by glancing at Table 16.1, Lula's Research Hypothesis 1 is supported in that children who witness wife abuse had lower social interaction skills than children who did not witness it.

However, it is still not known from Table 16.1 whether the 30-point difference between the two average *SISOCAI* scores is large enough to be statistically significant. The appropriate statistical procedure for this design is the independent *t*-test, as described in the previous chapter. The results of the *t*-test could also be included under Table 16.1, or they could be described in the findings section as follows:

> The result of an independent *t*-test between the *SISOCAI* scores of children who witnessed wife abuse as compared to those children who did not witness it was statistically significant ($t = 3.56$, $df = 78$, $p < .05$). Thus,

children who witnessed wife abuse had statistically significantly lower social interaction skills, on the average, than children who did not witness such abuse.

Table 16.2 presents the study's findings for Lula's second research hypothesis. This table uses the data from the 40 children who witnessed wife abuse (from Table 16.1). As can be seen from Tables 16.1 and 16.2, the average social skill score for the 40 children who witnessed wife abuse is 45. Table 16.2 further breaks down these 40 children into two subgroups: boys and girls. Out of the 40 children who witnessed wife abuse, 20 were boys and 20 were girls. As can be seen from Table 16.2, boys had an average social skill score of 35 as compared with the average score for girls of 55. Thus, the boys scored, on the average, 20 points lower than the girls. So far, Lula's second research hypothesis is supported.

However, it is still not known from Table 16.2 whether the 20-point difference between the two average *SISOCAI* scores is large enough to be statistically significant. The appropriate statistical procedure for this design is the independent *t*-test, as described in the previous chapter. The results of the *t*-test could also be included under Table 16.2, or they could be described in the findings section as follows:

> The result of an independent *t*-test between the *SISOCAI* scores for boys and girls who witnessed wife abuse was statistically significant ($t = 2.56$, $df = 38$, $p < .05$). Thus, boys had statistically significant lower social interaction skills, on the average, than girls.

Once a table (or figure) is constructed, the next thing that has to be done is to describe in words what it means. Data displays should be self-explanatory if done correctly. It is a waste of precious space to repeat in the text something that is perfectly apparent from a table or figure.

At this point, Lula has to decide whether she is going to go into a lengthy discussion of her findings in this part of the report or whether she is going to reserve the discussion for the next part. Which option is chosen often depends on what there is to discuss. Sometimes it is more

TABLE 16.2   Means and Standard Deviations of Social Interaction Skills of Boys and Girls Who Witnessed Wife Abuse (from Table 16.1)

Gender	Mean	Standard Deviation	N
Boys	35	12	20
Girls	55	10	20
Averages	45	11	

sensible to combine the findings with the discussion, pointing out the significance of what has been found as she goes along.

Joel Fischer (1993) has provided a few criteria that need to be examined when evaluating the findings section of a research report. These criteria, with some modifications, are presented below:

1. Adequacy of the manipulation of the independent variable (if applicable)
2. Appropriateness in the use of follow-up measures (if applicable)
3. Adequacy of data to provide evidence for testing of the hypotheses (if applicable)
4. Clarity in reporting the statistics (if applicable)
5. Appropriateness in the use of statistical controls (if applicable)
6. Appropriateness of statistics utilized (if applicable)
    a. Statistics appropriate to level of measurement
    b. Use of between-groups procedures
    c. Multivariate statistics used appropriately
    d. Post hoc tests used appropriately
    e. Overall appropriateness of statistics

Many of the above criteria are not applicable to Lula's study. However, they can be used in evaluating other, more complex, studies.

Part 4: Discussion

The final part of a research report presents a discussion of the study's findings. Care should be taken not to merely repeat the study's findings that were already presented in Part 3. It can be tempting to repeat one finding in order to remind the reader about it preliminary to a discussion, and then another finding, and then a third... and, before we know it, we have written the whole of the findings section all over again and called it a discussion. What is needed here is control and judgment—a delicate balance between not reminding the reader at all and saying everything twice.

On the other hand, Lula might be tempted to ignore her findings altogether, particularly if she did not find what she expected. If the findings did not support her hypothesis, she may have a strong urge to express her viewpoint anyway, using persuasive prose to make up for the lack of quantitative objective evidence. This temptation must be resisted at all costs. The term "discussion" relates to what she found, not to what she thinks she ought to have found, or to what she might have found under slightly different circumstances.

Perhaps she did manage to find a relationship between the variables in both of her hypotheses. However, to her dismay, the relationship was the opposite of what she predicted. For example, suppose her data indicated that children who did not witness wife abuse had lower social interaction skills than children who witnessed it (this is the opposite of what she predicted). This unexpected result must be discussed, shedding whatever light on the surprising finding. Any relationship between two variables is worthy of discussion, particularly if they seem atypical or if they are not quite what was anticipated.

A common limitation in social work research has to do with not being able to randomly sample research participants from a population. Whenever we cannot randomly select or assign research participants to two or more groups, the sample cannot be considered to be truly representative of the population in question, and we cannot generalize the study's results back to the population of children who witnessed or did not witness wife abuse in the community. The simplest way to deal with this limitation is to state it directly.

Another major limitation in this study is that we will never know the social skills of children who did not accompany their mothers to the shelter. The social skills of children who stay home may somehow be quite different from those children who accompanied their mothers. In fact, there are a host of other limitations in this simple study, including the simple fact that, in reference to Research Hypothesis 2, boys who did not see wife abuse may also have lower social interaction skills than girls—this was never tested in Lula's study. Nevertheless, we should also bear in mind the fact that few social work studies are based on truly representative random samples. In Lula's study, however, she still managed to collect some interesting data.

Joel Fischer (1993) has provided a few criteria that need to be examined when evaluating the utilization potential of a study's findings. These criteria, with some modifications, are presented below:

1. Degree of relevance to social work practice
2. Overall soundness of the study (internal validity)
3. Degree of generalizability of the study's findings to other populations and settings (external validity)
4. Degree to which the independent variables are accessible to control by the social workers (if applicable)
5. Extent to which a meaningful difference would occur if the independent variable were utilized in actual social work practice situations (if applicable)
6. Degree of economic feasibility of the independent variable if utilized in actual social work practice settings (if applicable)
7. Degree of ethical suitability of the manipulation of the independent variable
8. Extent to which the research question or hypothesis has been addressed (if applicable)

Many of the above criteria are not applicable to Lula's study. However, they can be used in evaluating other, more complex, studies. All social work researchers would like to be able to generalize their findings beyond the specific research setting and sample. From a research perspective (not a practice perspective), Lula is not really interested in the specific children in this particular study. She is more interested in children who witness wife abuse in general. Technically, the results of her study cannot be generalized to other populations of children who witness wife abuse, but she can suggest that she might find similar results with other children who accompany their mothers to similar women's shelters. She can imply and can recommend further research studies into the topic area.

Sometimes we can find support for our suggestions in the results of previous studies that were not conclusive either, but that also managed to produce recommendations. It might even be a good idea to extract these studies from the literature review section in Part 1 of the report and resurrect them in the discussion section.

On occasion, the results of a study will not agree with the results of previous studies. In this case, we should give whatever explanations seem reasonable for the disagreement and make some suggestions whereby the discrepancy can be resolved. Perhaps another research study should be undertaken that would examine the same or different variables. Perhaps, next time, a different research design should be used or the research hypothesis should be reformulated. Perhaps other operational definitions could be used. Suggestions for future studies should always be specific, not just a vague statement to the effect that more research studies need to be done in this area.

In some cases, recommendations can be made for changes in social work programs, interventions, or policies based on the results of a study. These recommendations are usually contained in reports addressed to people who have the power to make the suggested changes. When changes are suggested, the author has to display some knowledge about the policy or program and the possible consequences of implementing the suggested changes.

Finally, a report is concluded with a summary of the study's findings. This is particularly important in longer reports or when a study's findings and discussion sections are lengthy or complex. Sometimes, indeed, people reading a long report read only the summary and a few sections of the study that interests them.

Joel Fischer (1993) has provided a few criteria that need to be examined when evaluating the discussion section of a research report. His criteria, with some modifications, are presented below:

1. Degree to which the data support the research hypothesis (if applicable)
2. Extent to which the researcher's conclusions are consistent with the data gathered
3. Degree of uniformity between tables and text
4. Degree of researcher bias
5. Clarity as to cause of changes in the dependent variable (if applicable)

6. Degree to which potential rival hypotheses were dealt with in the discussion
7. Reasonableness of opinions about the study's implications
8. Adequacy in relating the study's findings to previous studies through the literature
9. Adequacy of conclusions for generalizing beyond the study's data
10. Appropriateness in the handling of unexpected consequences

SUMMARY

The purpose of writing a research proposal is fourfold. A research proposal is necessary, first, to obtain permission to carry out the study and, second, to secure the funds with which to do it. Third, the researcher needs to convince the proposal reviewers that he or she is competent enough to do the study. Fourth, we need to think over precisely what we want to study, why we want to study it, what methods we should use, and what difficulties we are likely to encounter.

A research proposal should be well organized and easy to read so that reviewers have a clear picture of each step of the study. The information included in most proposals can be set out under eleven general headings, or parts: research topic, literature review, conceptual framework, questions and hypotheses, operational definitions, research design, population and sample, data collection, data analysis, limitations, and administration.

Using a majority of the material from the research proposal, a research report is written that can be broken down into four general headings, or parts: problem, method, findings, and discussion. The four parts of a research report parallel the eleven parts of the research proposal. This is not surprising, since both the report and the proposal are describing the same study.

In summary, the first part of the research report—problem—includes the first four parts of the proposal: research topic, literature review, conceptual framework, and questions and hypotheses. Similarly, the second part of the research report—method—includes the next four parts of the proposal: operational definitions, research design, population and sample, and data collection. Part 3, in a research report—findings—discusses the methods used to analyze the data; that is, data analysis, Part 9 in the proposal. And in the final part of the research report—discussion—includes the limitations discussed in Part 10 of the proposal, along with the ones that cropped up when the study was actually being implemented.

STUDY QUESTIONS

1. Discuss the purpose of a research proposal. Present the benefits of writing one before a research study is actually conducted. Present a social work

example throughout your discussion.

2. Thoroughly describe in your own words the eleven parts of a research proposal. Present a social work example throughout your discussion.

3. Discuss the purpose of research reports. Why are they necessary for the social work profession?

4. Thoroughly describe in your own words the four parts of a research report. Present a social work example throughout your discussion.

5. Go to the library and select a social work article. Did the article follow the same sequence of parts as presented in this chapter? How could the contents of the article have been reformulated to fit the four parts as described in this chapter? Discuss in detail.

6. What other limitations, besides the ones mentioned in this chapter, should Lula include in her final research report? Discuss each one in detail. For example, what about the social interaction skills of children who not only witnessed wife abuse but were also physically abused by their fathers?

7. Go to the library and select a social work research article. Write a hypothetical research proposal for the study using the contents of this chapter as a guide.

8. Write an explanatory-level research proposal that Lula could have written with her same general problem area: problems experienced by children who witness one parent physically abusing the other.

9. Write a hypothetical research report based on the research proposal that you wrote for Question 8.

10. Write a final research report that Lula could submit to a professional social work journal using the findings of her study.

REFERENCES AND FURTHER READINGS

Bouey, E., & Rogers, G. (1993). Retrieving information. In R.M. Grinnell, Jr. (Ed.), *Social work research and evaluation* (4th ed., pp. 388-401). Itasca, IL: F.E. Peacock.

Fischer, J. (1981). A framework for evaluating empirical research reports. In R.M. Grinnell, Jr. (Ed.), *Social work research and evaluation* (pp. 569-589). Itasca, IL: F.E. Peacock.

Fischer, J. (1985). Evaluating research reports. In R.M. Grinnell, Jr. (Ed.), *Social work research and evaluation* (2nd ed., pp. 476-482). Itasca, IL: F.E. Peacock.

Fischer, J. (1993). Evaluating positivistic research reports. In R.M. Grinnell, Jr. (Ed.), *Social work research and evaluation* (4th ed., pp. 347-366). Itasca, IL: F.E. Peacock.

Krathwohl, D.R. (1965). *How to prepare a research proposal*. Syracuse, NY: Syracuse University Press.

Moss, K.E. (1985). Research proposals. In R.M. Grinnell, Jr. (Ed.), *Social work research and evaluation* (2nd ed., pp. 445-458). Itasca, IL: F.E. Peacock.

Moss, K.E. (1988). Writing research proposals. In R.M. Grinnell, Jr. (Ed.), *Social work research and evaluation* (3rd ed., pp. 429-445). Itasca, IL: F.E. Peacock.

Reid, W.J. (1981). Research reports and publication procedures. In R.M. Grinnell, Jr. (Ed.), *Social work research and evaluation* (pp. 553-568). Itasca, IL: F.E. Peacock.

Reid, W.J. (1985). Writing research reports. In R.M. Grinnell, Jr. (Ed.), *Social work research and evaluation* (2nd ed., pp. 459-475). Itasca, IL: F.E. Peacock.

Reid, W.J. (1988). Writing research reports. In R.M. Grinnell, Jr. (Ed.), *Social work research and evaluation* (3rd ed., pp. 446-464). Itasca, IL: F.E. Peacock.

Reid, W.J. (1993). Writing research reports. In R.M. Grinnell, Jr. (Ed.), *Social work research and evaluation* (4th ed., pp. 332-346). Itasca, IL: F.E. Peacock.

Rogers, G., & Bouey, E. (1993). Reviewing the literature. In R.M. Grinnell, Jr. (Ed.), *Social work research and evaluation* (4th ed., pp. 388-401). Itasca, IL: F.E. Peacock.

Weinbach, R.W., & Grinnell, R.M., Jr. (1995) *Statistics for social workers* (3rd ed.). White Plains, NY: Longman.

Glossary

A phase: In single-system designs, a phase in which the baseline measurement of the target problem is established before the intervention is implemented.

Alternate-forms method: A method for establishing reliability of a measuring instrument by administering, in succession, equivalent forms of the same instrument to the same group of individuals.

Applied research: A search for practical results that can be utilized to solve problems or in practice applications.

B phase: In single-system designs, the intervention phase, which may include simultaneous measurement.

Baseline: A period of time, usually three or four data collection periods, in which the level of the client's target problem is measured while no intervention is carried out; designated as the *A* phase in single-system designs.

Bias: Not neutral; an inclination to some form of prejudice or preconceived position.

Classical experimental design: An explanatory research design with randomly selected and randomly assigned experimental and control groups in which the dependent variable is measured before and after treatment (the independent variable) for both groups, but only the experimental group receives treatment.

Client system: An individual client, a couple, a family, a group, an organization, or a community that can be studied with a single-system design.

Closed-ended questions: Items in a measuring instrument that require respondents to select one of several response categories provided; also known as fixed-alternative question.

Cluster sampling: A multistage probability sampling procedure in which the population is divided into groups or clusters and the clusters, rather than the individuals, are selected for inclusion in the sample.

Coding: (1) In data analysis, translating data from respondents onto a form that can be read by a computer; (2) In naturalistic research, marking the text with codes for content categories.

Cohort studies: Longitudinal surveys that use successive random samples to monitor how the characteristics of specific groups of people who share certain characteristics or experiences (cohorts) change over time.

Collaterals: Professionals or staff members who serve as indigenous observers in data collection.

Comparative rating scale: A rating scale in which respondents are asked to compare an individual person, concept, or situation to others.

Comparison group: A nonexperimental group to which participants have not been randomly assigned for purposes of comparison with the experimental group. *See* Control group.

Comparison group posttest-only design: A descriptive research design with experimental and comparison groups in which the dependent variable is measured once for both groups, and only the experimental group receives treatment (the independent variable).

Comparison group pretest-posttest design: A descriptive research design with two groups, experimental and comparison, in which the dependent variable is measured before and after treatment for both groups, but only the experimental group receives treatment.

Compensation: Attempts by experimenters to compensate for lack of treatment for control group members by administering it to them; a threat to internal validity.

Compensatory rivalry: Motivation of control group members to compete with experimental group members; a threat to internal validity.

Concept: An understanding, idea, or mental image; a way of viewing and categorizing objects, processes, relations, and events.

Conceptual framework: A frame of reference that serves to guide a research study and is developed from theories, findings from a variety of other studies, and the author's personal experiences and values.

Concurrent validity: A form of criterion validity that is concerned with the ability of a measuring instrument to predict accurately an individual's status by comparing concurrent ratings or scores on several instruments.

Constant: A concept that does not vary and does not change; a characteristic that has the same value for all individuals or events in a research study.

Constant error: Systematic error in measurement; error due to factors that consistently or systematically affect the variable being measured and that are concerned with the relative stability of qualities of respondents to a measuring instrument.

Content analysis: A data-collection method in which communications are analyzed in a systematic, objective, and quantitative manner to produce new data.

Content validity: The extent to which the content of a measuring instrument reflects the concept that is being measured and in fact measures that concept and not another.

Contributing partner: A social work role in which the worker joins forces with others who perform different roles in the research process.

Control group: A group of randomly selected and randomly assigned participants in a study who do not receive the experimental treatment and are used for comparison purposes. *See* Comparison group.

Convenience sampling: A nonprobability sampling procedure that relies on the closest and most available subjects to constitute a sample.

Cover letter: A letter to potential research participants that is written under the official letterhead of the sponsoring organization and describes the study and its purpose.

Cross-sectional design: A survey research design in which data are collected to indicate characteristics of a sample or population at a particular moment in time.

Data: In research, measurements systematically collected in strict compliance with a research design.

Data collection method: Procedures specifying techniques to be employed, measuring instruments to be utilized, and activities to be conducted in implementing a research study.

Deduction: A conclusion about specific cases based on the assumption that they share a characteristic with an entire class of similar cases.

Deductive reasoning: Forming a theory, making a deduction from the theory, and testing this deduction, or hypothesis, against reality; in research, applied to theory in order to arrive at hypotheses that can be empirically tested.

Demoralization: Feelings of deprivation among control group members which may cause them to drop out of a study; a threat to internal validity.

Dependent variable: A variable that is dependent on or caused by another variable; an outcome variable, which is not manipulated directly but is measured to determine if the independent variable has had an effect.

Descriptive research: Research undertaken to increase precision in the definition of knowledge in a problem area where less is known than at the explanatory level; situated at the middle of the knowledge continuum.

Differential scales: A questionnaire-type scale in which respondents are asked to consider questions representing different positions along a continuum and select those with which they agree.

Differential selection: A potential lack of equivalency among the pre-formed groups; a threat to internal validity.

Diffusion of treatments: Problems that may occur when the experimental and control group members talk to each other about a study; a threat to internal validity.

Direct observation: A method of data collection in which the focus is entirely on physical behavior and the observer remains apart from the group or persons being observed.

Duration recording: A method of data collection that includes directly observing the target problem and recording the length of time each occurrence lasts within a specified observation period.

Error of central tendency: A measurement error due to the tendency of observers to rate respondents in the middle, rather than consistently too high or too low.

Ethics in research: The requirement that data be collected and analyzed with careful attention to accuracy of measurement, fidelity to logic, and respect for the feelings and rights of respondents.

Evaluative designs: Single-system research designs that merely examine the question, "Did the client system improve during the course of social work intervention?"

Experimental designs: (1) Explanatory research designs or "ideal" experiments; (2) Single-system research designs that examine the question, "Did the client system improve because of social work intervention?"

Experimental group: In an experimental research design, the group of participants exposed to the manipulation of the independent variable.

Explanatory research: Research undertaken to infer cause-effect and directional relationships in an area where a substantial body of research findings is already in place; situated at the top end of the knowledge continuum. *See* "Ideal" experiment.

Exploratory research: Research undertaken to gather data or facts in an area of inquiry where very little is already known; situated at the lowest end of the knowledge continuum. *See* Nonexperimental design.

External validity: The extent to which the findings of a research study can be generalized to a larger population than the sample of research participants or to individuals or settings outside the research situation.

Face validity: The degree to which a measurement has self-evident meaning and measures what it appears to measure.

Frequency recording: A method of data collection by direct observations in which each occurrence of the target problem during a specified observation period is recorded.

Generalizing results: Extending or applying the findings of a research study to individuals or situations not directly tested.

Goal Attainment Scales: Using a modified measurement scale to evaluate client or program outcomes by collecting opinions on specific areas of individual change from clients, judges, or social workers.

Graphic rating scale: A rating scale that describes an attribute on a continuum from one extreme to the other, with points of the continuum ordered in equal intervals and then assigned numbers.

Group research designs: Designs conducted with groups of cases for the purpose of answering research questions or testing hypotheses.

Halo effect: A measurement error due to the tendency of observers to be influenced by a single favorable trait or to let their general impressions affect their ratings of a single trait or characteristic.

Hawthorne effect: Effects on participants' behaviors or attitudes attributable to their knowledge that they are taking part in a research project; a reactive effect.

Heterogeneity of respondents: The extent to which the study's participants, respondents, or clients differ from one another.

History in research design: The possibility that events not accounted for in the design may alter the second and subsequent measurements of the dependent variable; a threat to internal validity.

Homogeneity of respondents: The extent to which study participants, respondents, or clients are similar to one another.

Hypothesis: A theory-based prediction of the expected results in a research study; a tentative explanation of a relationship or a supposition that a relationship may exist.

Hypothetico-deductive method: A hypothesis-testing approach in which researchers derive hypotheses on the basis of deductions from theory; often equated with positivistic approach to research.

"Ideal" experiment: An experimental design that approaches certainty about causality most closely and which includes manipulation of the independent variable, control of rival hypotheses, and random sampling and random assignment procedures.

Idiographic research: Research focused on a unique or individual issue or situation.

Independent variable: A variable that is not dependent on another variable but is said to cause or determine changes in the dependent variable; an antecedent variable that is directly manipulated in order to assess its effect on the dependent variable.

Indigenous observers: People who are naturally a part of the research participants' environment and who perform the data collection function; includes relevant others (family members, peers, etc.) and collaterals (caseworkers, staff members, etc.).

Inductive reasoning: Building on specific observation of events, things, or processes to make inferences or more general statements; in research, applied to data collection and research results to make generalizations and see if they fit the theory.

Informed consent: Signed statements obtained from participants in a research study prior to initiation of the project to inform them what their participation entails and that they are free to decline participation.

Institutional review boards (IRBs): The boards set up by institutions that engage in frequent research studies with individuals to review and monitor the studies conducted under their auspices in order to protect research participants and to ensure that ethical issues in research studies are recognized and responded to in the research design and procedures.

Instrumentation: Weaknesses of a measuring instrument, such as invalidity, unreliability, improper administrations, or mechanical breakdowns; a threat to internal validity.

Interaction effects: Effects produced by the combination of two or more threats to internal validity.

Internal consistency: The extent to which the scores on two comparable halves of a measuring instrument are similar; inter-item consistency.

Internal validity: The extent to which it can be demonstrated that the independent variable in an experiment is the only cause of change in the dependent variable; soundness of the experimental procedures and measuring instruments.

Interobserver reliability: The stability or consistency of observations made by two or more observers at one point in time.

Interrater reliability: The degree to which two or more independent observers, coders, or judges produce consistent results.

Interrupted time-series design: An explanatory research design in which there is only one group, and the dependent variable is measured repeatedly before and after treatment.

Interval level of measurement: The level that has an arbitrarily chosen zero point and classifies variables by rank ordering them on an equally spaced continuum.

Interval recording: A method of data collection that involves continuous, direct observation of an individual during specified observation periods divided into intervals of equal time.

Interview schedule: A measuring instrument used to collect data in face-to-face and telephone interviews.

Intraobserver reliability: The stability of observations made by a single observer at several points in time.

Item reliability: Consistency of a respondent's answers to different questions on a measuring instrument.

Itemized rating scales: A measuring instrument that presents a series of statements on which respondents or observers are to rank different positions on the attribute being named.

Knowledge level continuum: The range of knowledge levels, from exploratory to descriptive to explanatory, at which research studies can be conducted, as well as the levels that might be attained by studies.

Longitudinal case study: An exploratory research design in which there is only one group and the dependent variable is measured more then once.

Longitudinal design: A survey research design in which the measuring instrument is administered to a sample of respondents repeatedly over time; used to detect dynamic processes such as opinion change.

Magnitude recording: A direct-observation method of soliciting and recording data on amount, level, or degree of the target problem during each occurrence.

Matching: Technique of assigning study participants to groups so that the experimental and control groups are approximately equivalent in pretest scores or other characteristics, or so that all differences except the experimental condition are eliminated.

Maturation: Unplanned change in research participants due to mental, physical, or other processes operating over time; a threat to internal validity.

Mean: Average score or position on a group of scores or outcome measures.

Measurement: The assignment of labels or numerals to the properties or attributes of observations, events, or objects according to a rule or system.

Measurement error: Any variation in measurement that cannot be attributed to the variable being measured; variability in responses produced by individual differences and other extraneous variables.

Measuring instrument: Instruments such as questionnaires or rating scales used to measure the variables in a research study.

Mortality: Loss of research participants through normal attrition over time in an experimental design that requires retesting; a threat to internal validity.

Multigroup posttest-only design: An exploratory research design in which there is more than one group and the dependent variable is measured only once for each group.

Multiple-baseline designs: Single-subject designs that enable researchers to draw causal inferences regarding the relationship between a specific treatment intervention and its effect on a client's target problem; help control for extraneous variables by having more than one baseline period and intervention phase.

Multiple-treatment interference: Effects of the results of the first treatment on the results of the second and subsequent treatments; a threat to external validity.

Multistage probability sampling: Probability sampling procedures used when a comprehensive list of the population does not exist and it is not possible to construct one.

Nominal level of measurement: The level that classifies variables by assigning names or categories that are mutually exclusive and exhaustive.

Nonexperimental design: A research design at the exploratory, or lowest, level of the knowledge continuum; also called preexperimental.

Nonprobability sampling: Sampling procedures in which all of the persons, events, or objects in the sampling frame have an unknown, and usually different, probability of being included in the sample.

Nonsampling errors: Errors in study results that are not due to the sampling procedures.

Norm: In measurement, an average or set group standard of achievement that can be used to interpret individual scores; normative data describing statistical properties of a measuring instrument such as means and standard deviations.

Normal curve: A symmetrical curve that graphically represents a standard distribution of scores or mean frequencies.

Obtrusive methods: Direct data collection procedures that can influence the variables under study or the responses of participants; methods that produce reactive effects.

One-group posttest-only design: An exploratory research design in which the dependent variable is measured only once.

One-group pretest-posttest design: A descriptive research design in which the dependent variable is measured before and after treatment.

Open-ended questions: Unstructured questions in which the response categories are not specified or detailed.

Operational definition: Explicit specification of a concept in such a way that its measurement is possible. *See* Quantification.

Ordinal level of measurement: The level that classifies variables by rank ordering them from high to low or from most to least.

Outcome: The effect of manipulation of the independent variable on the dependent variable; the end product of a treatment intervention.

Outcome measure: The criterion or basis for measuring effects of the independent variable or change in the dependent variable; a measuring instrument.

Outside observers: Trained observers who are not part of the research participants' environment and who are brought in to record data.

p-value: The level of probability for a test of statistical significance; a measure of the relationship between the independent and dependent variables.

Panel studies: Longitudinal studies that follow the same individuals (the panel) over time, by surveying them on successive occasions.

Participant observation: Participation by the observer or researcher in the life of those being observed.

Population: An entire set, or universe, of people, objects, or events of concern to a research study, from which a sample is selected.

Posttest: Measurement of the dependent variable after the introduction of the independent variable.

Predictive validity: A form of criterion validity that is concerned with the ability of a measuring instrument to predict future performance or status on the basis of present performance or status.

Pretest: (1) Measurement of the dependent variable prior to the introduction of the independent variable; (2) Administration of a measuring instrument to a group who will not be included in the study to determine difficulties respondents may have in answering questions and the general impression given by the instrument; also called a pilot study.

Pretest-treatment interaction: Effects of the pretest on the responses of study participants to introduction of the independent variable or the experimental treatment; a threat to external validity.

Probability sampling: Sampling procedures in which every member of the designated population has a known probability of being selected for the sample.

Problem area: In social work research, an expressed difficulty pertaining in a general way to a situation in client systems or society, about which something researchable is unknown.

Problem-solving process: A generic method with specified phases for solving problems; also described as scientific method.

Pure research: A search for theoretical results that can be utilized to develop theory and expand the social work knowledge bases.

Purposive sampling: A nonprobability sampling procedure in which individuals with particular characteristics are purposefully selected for inclusion in the sample; also known as judgmental or theoretical sampling.

Quantification: In measurement, the reduction of data to numerical form in order to analyze it by way of mathematical or statistical techniques.

Quantitative data: Data that measure quantity or amount in variables or constants.

Quasi-experiment: A research design at the descriptive level of the knowledge continuum that resembles an "ideal" experiment, but does not allow for random selection or assignment of study participants to groups and often does not control for rival hypotheses.

Questionnaire-type scale: A type of measuring instrument using multiple responses that are combined to form a single overall score for a respondent.

Quota sampling: A nonprobability sampling procedure in which the relevant characteristics of the sample are identified, the proportion of these characteristics in the population is determined, and participants are selected from each category until the predetermined proportion (quota) has been achieved.

r-value: the correlation coefficient, a measure of association between variables; also called Pearson's *r* or product-moment correlation.

Random assignment: The process of assigning individuals to experimental or control groups so that the groups are equivalent; also referred to as randomization.

Random error: Variable error in measurement; error due to unknown or uncontrolled factors that affect the variable being measured and the process of measurement in an inconsistent fashion.

Random numbers table: A computer-generated or published table of numbers in which each number has an equal chance of appearing in each position in the table.

Random sampling: An unbiased selection process conducted so that all members of the population have an equal chance of being selected to participate in a research study.

Randomized cross-sectional survey design: A descriptive research design in which there is only one group, the dependent variable is measured only once, the participants are randomly selected from the population, and there is no independent variable.

Randomized longitudinal survey design: A descriptive research design in which there is only one group, the dependent variable is measured more than once, and participants are randomly selected from the population before each treatment.

Randomized one-group posttest-only design: A descriptive research design in which there is only one group, the dependent variable is measured only once, and participants are randomly selected from the population.

Randomized posttest-only control group design: An explanatory research design in which there are two or three randomly selected and randomly assigned groups, the control group does not receive treatment, and the experimental groups receive different treatments.

Rank-order scale: A comparative rating scale in which the rater is asked to rank specific individuals in relation to one another on some characteristic.

Rating scale: A type of measurement instrument in which responses are rated on a continuum or in an ordered set of categories, with numerical values assigned to each point or category.

Ratio level of measurement: The level that has a nonarbitrary, fixed zero point and classifies variables by rank-ordering them on an equally spaced continuum.

Raw scores: Scores derived from administration of a measuring instrument to research participants or groups.

Reactive effect: (1) An effect on outcome measures due to the awareness of study participants that they are being observed or interviewed; a threat to external and internal validity; (2) Alteration of the variables being measured or the respondents' performance on the measuring instrument due to administration of the instrument.

Reliability: (1) The degree of accuracy, precision, or consistency in results of a measuring instrument, including the ability to produce the same results when the same variable is measured more than once or repeated applications of the same test on the same individual produce the same measurement; (2) The degree to which individual differences on scores or in data are due either to true differences or to errors in measurement.

Reliability coefficient: A statistical representation of the relationship or correlation between two sets of scores.

Replication: Repetition of the same research procedures by a second researcher for the purpose of determining if earlier results can be duplicated.

Research consumer: A social work role reflecting the ethical obligation to base interventions on the most up-to-date research knowledge available.

Research design: A plan of procedures for collecting and analyzing data to investigate a research question or test a hypothesis; major classifications are single-system and group designs.

Research hypothesis: A statement about the research question that predicts the existence of a particular relationship between the independent and dependent variables.

Research question: A particular topic, issue, or problem of concern or interest to the researcher which is specified from the problem area.

Researchability: The extent to which problems are researchable or can be resolved through consideration of evidence or measurement data.

Researcher bias: The tendency of researchers to find results they expect to find; a threat to external validity.

Response categories: Possible responses that are assigned to each question in a standardized instrument, with the low value generally indicating a low level of the variable being measured and a larger value indicating a higher level.

Response rate: The total number of responses obtained on a measuring instrument divided by the total number of responses requested, usually expressed in the form of a percentage.

Response set: Personal style; the tendency of respondents to respond to a measuring instrument in a particular way, regardless of the question asked, or the tendency of observers or interviewers to react in certain ways; a source of constant error.

Rival hypothesis: A hypothesis that is a plausible alternative to the research hypothesis and might explain the results as well or better; a hypothesis involving extraneous variables other than the independent variable in the research hypothesis; also referred to as an alternative hypothesis.

Robust results (generalization): Results that are capable of standing up to further research; constitute the aims of science.

Rules of correspondence: A characteristic of measurement that stipulates that numerals or symbols are assigned to properties of objects according to specified rules.

Sample: A subset of a population of individuals, objects, or events chosen to participate in or be considered in a study; unbiased sample selection makes it possible to draw inferences about the entire population of people, objects, or events.

Sampling error: (1) The degree of difference that can be expected between the sample and the population from which it was drawn; (2) A mistake in study results that is due to sampling procedure.

Sampling frame: A listing of units (people, objects, or events) in a population from which a sample is selected.

Sampling plan: A method of selecting members of a population for inclusion in a research study; using procedures that make it possible to draw inferences about the population from the sample statistics.

Sampling theory: The logic of methods of ensuring that a sample and a population are similar in all relevant characteristics.

Science: Knowledge that has been obtained and tested through use of the scientific method.

Scientific community: A group that shares the same general norms for both research activity and acceptance of scientific findings and explanations.

Scientific method: The principles and procedures used in the systematic pursuit of knowledge, involving as necessary steps the recognition and formulation of a problem, the collection of data through observation and, if possible, experiment, the formulation of hypotheses, and the testing of the hypotheses formulated; also referred to as problem solving.

Secondary analysis: A data utilization method in which available data that predate the formulation of a research study are used to answer the research question or test the hypothesis.

Selection-treatment interaction: The relationship between manner of selecting research participants and their response to treatment; a threat to external validity.

Self-anchored scales: A rating scale in which respondents rate themselves on a continuum of values, according to their own referents for each point.

Semantic differential scales: A modified measurement scale in which respondents rate their perceptions of the concept under study along three dimensions—evaluation, potency, and activity.

Simple random sampling: A one-stage probability sampling procedure in which members of a population are selected one at a time, without chance of being selected again, until the desired sample size is obtained.

Single-system research designs: Designs in which data are collected about a single client system—an individual, group, or community—in order to evaluate the outcome of an intervention for the client system.

Situation-specific variable: A variable that may be observable only in certain environments and under certain circumstances, or with particular people.

Snowball sampling: A nonprobability sampling procedure in which the researcher can use persons selected for inclusion in the sample to identify and include additional individuals from the population.

Social desirability: (1) A response set in which respondents tend to answer questions in a way that they perceive as giving favorable impressions of themselves; (2) The inclination of data providers to report data that present a socially desirable impression of themselves or their reference groups. Also referred to as impression management.

Social work research: Scientific inquiry in which acceptable methodology is used to solve research problems and create new, generally applicable knowledge in the field of social work.

Solomon four-group design: An explanatory research design with four randomly assigned groups, two experimental and two control; the dependent variable is measured before and after treatment for one experimental and one control group, but only after treatment for the other two groups, and only experimental groups receive the treatment.

Specificity of variables: A characteristic of variables in research conducted with a certain sample at a certain time and in a certain setting that may not be generalizable to others, a different time, or a different setting; a threat to external validity.

Split-half method: A method for establishing the reliability of a measuring instrument by dividing it into comparable halves and comparing the similarity between the scores.

Standard deviation: A measure that denotes the average deviation of scores about the mean and thus reflects the amount of variability in the data.

Standardized measuring instruments: Instruments, usually professionally developed, that provide for uniform administration and scoring and generate normative data against which later results can be evaluated.

Statistic: A single number that can be used to summarize, analyze, or evaluate a group of observations; the product of a statistical test.

Statistical regression: The tendency for extremely high or low scores to regress, or shift, toward the average (mean) score on subsequent tests; a threat to internal validity.

Statistical significance: Significance of a relationship between variables in a statistical sense; statistically significant results are at a level of probability (usually .05) determined by a statistical test.

Statistics: the branch of mathematics concerned with the collection and analysis of data using statistical techniques.

Stratified random sampling: A one-stage probability sampling procedure in which the population is divided into two or more strata to be sampled separately, using simple random or systematic random sampling techniques.

Structured observations: A method of data collection in which people are observed in their natural environments using specified methods and measurement procedures.

Summated scale: A questionnaire-type scale in which respondents are asked to indicate the degree of their agreement or disagreement with each question.

Survey research: A research process in which data are collected with a survey type of measuring instrument to obtain opinions or answers from a population or sample of respondents in order to describe or study them as a group.

Systematic random sampling: A one-stage probability sampling procedure in which every person at a designated interval in the population list is selected to be included in the sample for a study.

Target problem: (1) In single-system designs, the problems social workers seek to solve for their clients; (2) A measurable behavior, feeling, or cognition that is either a problem in itself or symptomatic of some other problem.

Temporal stability: Consistency of responses to a measuring instrument over time; reliability of an instrument across forms and across administrations.

Testing effect: The effect that taking a pretest might have on posttest scores; a threat to internal validity.

Test-retest reliability: Reliability of a measuring instrument established through repeated administration to the same group of individuals.

Theory: A reasoned set of propositions, derived from and supported by established evidence, that serves to explain a group of phenomena; a conjectural explanation that may or may not be supported by research data.

Time-series design: *See* Interrupted time-series design.

Treatment group: *See* Experimental group.

Trend studies: Longitudinal studies that utilize data from surveys carried out at periodic intervals on samples drawn from a particular population.

Unit of analysis: A concrete research case (person, object, or event) or the sample or population relevant to the research question.

Unobtrusive methods: Data collection procedures that do not influence the variable under study or the responses of participants; methods that avoid reactive effects.

Validity: (1) The extent to which a measuring instrument measures the variable it is supposed to measure and measures it accurately; (2) The degree to which an instrument is able to do what it is intended to do, in terms of both experimental procedures and measuring instruments (internal validity) and generalizability of results (external validity); (3) The degree to which scores on a measuring instrument correlate with measures of performance on some other criterion.

Variable: A concept with characteristics that can take on different values.

Working hypothesis: An assertion about a relationship between variables that may not be true but is plausible and worth examining; also referred to as a tentative or guiding hypothesis.

Index

THE BOOK'S MANUFACTURE

Research in Social Work: An Introduction,
Second Edition, was typeset by
Andrukow Compositors,
Calgary, Alberta, Canada.
The typeface is Melior for text and display.
Internal design, page layouts, tables, and figures
were done by Andrukow Compositors,
Calgary, Alberta, Canada.
Printing and binding were done by
Arcata Graphics, Kingsport, Tennessee.